Who Are the People of God?

Who Are the People of God?

Early Christian Models of Community

Howard Clark Kee

Yale University Press   New Haven and London

Published with assistance from the Mary Cady Tew Memorial Fund.

Designed by Rebecca Gibb.
Set in Weiss and Syntax types by Marathon Typography Service, Inc., Durham, North Carolina.
Printed in the United States of America by Edwards Brothers, Ann Arbor, Michigan.

Library of Congress Cataloging-in-Publication Data
Kee, Howard Clark.
    Who are the people of God? : early Christian models of community / Howard Clark Kee.
        p.   cm.
    Includes bibliographical refrences and index.
    ISBN 0-300-05952-3 (cloth: alk. paper)
            0-300-07063-2 (pbk.: alk. paper)
    1. People of God—History of doctrines—Early church, ca. 30–600.   2. Church—History of doctrines—Early church, ca. 30–600.   3. Christianity—Origin.   I. Title.
BV598.K425   1994
270.1—dc20   94-13883
                                                                              CIP

The paper in this book meets the guidelines for permanence and durability of the Committee on Production Guidelines for Book Longevity of the Council on Library Resources.

10   9   8   7   6   5   4   3   2

Contents

Preface   vii

Introduction
Ancient History and Contemporary Historiography   1

Chapter One
Models of Community in the Literature of Postexilic Judaism   17

Chapter Two
The Community of the Wise   55

Chapter Three
The Law-abiding Community   88

Chapter Four
The Community Where God Dwells among His People   121

Chapter Five
The Community of Mystical Participation   145

Chapter Six
The Ethnically and Culturally Inclusive Community   179

Chapter Seven
The Community Models Develop in the Post–New Testament Period   208

Critical Note
Priority in the Gospel Tradition   229

Notes   235

Index   271

Preface

This book represents the cumulative and synthesized results of years of scholarly research, including investigation along historical, archaeological, linguistic, sociological, literary, exegetical, and theological lines. It runs counter to some contemporary attempts to discover (invent?) a simple conceptual core out of which Christianity developed. In this work, the effort is to combine theory and practice to demonstrate an approach and a method by which the rich diversity of Second Temple Judaism and nascent Christianity can be brought into focus. Special thanks for challenge and encouragement from colleagues and students at Boston University, in the seminars of the Society of Biblical Literature and the Studiorum Novi Testamenti Societas, and in the Philadelphia Seminar on Christian Origins, to which I have returned since formal retirement.

Introduction

Ancient History and Contemporary Historiography

The discovery of the Dead Sea Scrolls in 1947 and of a Gnostic library two years earlier in Egypt has provided biblical scholars with information and insights that have resulted in a fresh historical reconstruction of Judaism and nascent Christianity in the period from 200 B.C.E. to 200 C.E. This challenge has been heightened by archaeological finds in Israel and the wider Mediterranean world that provide new evidence about the development of Judaism in this era. Concurrent with these new finds have appeared fresh analyses of such well-known Jewish documents as the Mishnah and Talmud, as well as the so-called Apocrypha and Pseudepigrapha, which have resulted in radical reappraisal of the development of Judaism from post-exilic times into the Roman era.

In spite of the admirable surge of interest in these new or newly understood materials, many historians in this field have failed to take into account the fresh insights from sociologists, anthropologists, and philosophers about the social nature of knowledge and personal identity, and their vital implications for historical study. The analytical methods derived from the work of sociologists of knowledge emphatically call into question the theories of historical development and the categories into which nineteenth- and many twentieth-century historians of Christian origins have classified the evidence. These historiographical missteps include the invention of artificial categories (such as the simplistic distinction between Palestinian Judaism and Hellenistic Judaism[1]), the projection of later developments into earlier times, and the rendering of supposedly historical judgments on the basis of modern philosophical preferences.[2] Obvious instances include the adoption of Hegel's notion of the progress of human thought through tension between thesis and antithesis, as evident in Baur's simple distinction between Palestinian and Hellenistic Judaism. In this century, similar historical judg-

1

ments based on philosophical preferences appeared in Adolf von Harnack's reduction of the essence of Christianity (and thus the basic teaching of Jesus) in terms of a simplistic moral idealism to the fatherhood of God, the brotherhood of man, and the infinite worth of the human soul; and in Rudolf Bultmann's identification of the primal Christian message with the existentialist notion of the call to decision, for which the death and resurrection of Jesus are vivid symbols, not significant historical events.

I shall have occasion to draw repeatedly on the insights of Jacob Neusner, whose extensive and perceptive writings have demonstrated in detail that Judaism at the turn of the eras was not at a normative stage, but in a multifaceted formative process that was to move toward conceptual and institutional conformity in the second to the sixth century C.E., producing the Mishnah and Talmud.[3] Rather than surveying unsatisfactory categories and methods that continue to be used by contemporary historians and theologians in relation to the origins of Christianity in the matrix of postbiblical Judaism, it is essential to sketch the origins and strategy of a historically responsible and fruitful method that has emerged in recent decades, which is an outgrowth of insights offered by sociologists engaged in analysis of what constitutes human knowledge.

The Import of Sociology of Knowledge for Historiography

In the latter decades of the twentieth century, developments in the social sciences and philosophy have had implications that call for reappraisal and reconstitution of the tasks of historical, literary, and theological analysis of human culture, including the biblical world. Certain sociologists, in addition to assessing concrete social phenomena and trends in the social structures of human life, have given attention to the social nature of linguistic communication and even of knowledge itself. This has given rise to the concept and procedures of what is called sociology of knowledge. Concurrent with this epistemological development has been the recognition among philosophers as well as sociologists that historical inquiry must take into account as fully as possible, not merely so-called facts as isolated phenomena, but the symbol systems in terms of which life is lived in any culture and which provide meaning and value for the members of the society under investigation. How these methods arose and what they import for historical study are sketched below.

Crucial insights contributing to these major epistemological shifts in the social sciences and in historiography were the linguistic philosophy of Ludwig Wittgenstein,[4] the fundamental insights of Thomas S. Kuhn regarding scientific methods,[5] and the emergence of sociology of knowledge.[6] All of these intellectual insights show that human language and the concepts communicated by it are not merely arbitrary or neutral elements, but that language itself as well as what it communicates is the product of a sociocultural group that shares a world of perceptions, convictions, understandings, and modes of expression. To understand what is being communicated, therefore, the interpreter must seek to enter into the shared world of assumptions and conventions in which the communicator lives and from which the message is sent out to others. What anyone thinks he or she knows is not simply a matter of universally self-evident, "objective" facts, but is pervasively conditioned by the sociocultural setting of the knower.

Language as a Communal "Game"

In his *Philosophical Investigations I*, Ludwig Wittgenstein represents language as a form of life, which operates within a community as an agreed-upon set of rules or assumptions and which he therefore calls a "language game."[7] The examples that he adduces include giving and obeying orders, constructing an object from a description, reporting an event, forming and testing a hypothesis, presenting the results of an experiment, making up and telling stories, jokes, songs, and plays, solving arithmetic problems, and asking, thanking, greeting, cursing, and praying. In a collection of aphorisms published under the title On Certainty, Wittgenstein describes knowledge as a language game, based on assumptions and inherited traditions, with its convictions anchored in all the questions one raises as well as the answers that are offered.[8] Together these constitute the rules of the game.

The implications of Wittgenstein's view of language for biblical interpretation have been spelled out by Anthony Thiselton. He identifies as the social basis for language in the biblical writings the opening up of a perspective that allows the interpreter to notice what has always been there to be seen; the shift from concern with generalities of formal logic to the particularities of specific language situations, which may result in a change in understanding of concepts; the recognition that language games are grounded in accepted rules governing human life and activities, which are always subject to historical change; and the realization that there is no point in seeking for a logical a priori behind the specific social context of training and upbringing that characterizes specific communities. The language of religious experience is part of a shared public tradition and gains intelligibility because it is anchored in a history shared by a community. What one believes and what one expects have meaning only in relation to the shared experience of others.[9]

The import of Wittgenstein's philosophy of language for the social sciences as well as for historiography has been traced by David Bloor: "The established meaning of a word does not determine its future applications. The development of a language game is not determined by its past verbal form. Meaning is created by acts of use. . . . Use determines meaning." In contrast to the notion that words have timeless transcendent meanings, Bloor coins the term "finitism," which he defines as awareness that meaning extends as far as, but not beyond, the finite range of circumstances in which a word is actually used—although allowance is made for new uses and meanings of words that may emerge in the future. What keeps Wittgenstein's view of language from being too flexible is his recognition that language users are trained in a body of conventionalized practices, according to which locally accepted standards of relevance must be used if communication is to take place. The implications of these insights are equally important for the historian's analysis of evidence and for self-criticism, since both the historian and the evidence must be recognized as operating within linguistic conventions whose meaning is relative to the social setting rather than to timeless conceptual models.[10]

The decisions that the interpreter makes about classification of the evidence are dependent on the overall perspective and activity of the community from which the data derive rather than on inherent truths or even experimental demonstrability. What is called for is description rather than evaluation. But shifts take place in the language games—both in the development of a tradition and in interpretive modes. Bloor observes, "When we detect a change in a language game we must look for a shift in goals and purposes of its players which is sufficiently widespread and sufficiently uniform to yield that change." Faced with competing usages, we must look for rival groups and track down the causes of rivalry; if we see the language games merging with one another, we must look for and try to explain the continuities and alliances between their players. When concepts are used within "the bounded territory of a specialist discipline," the enterprise must be guided by a set of local conventions. "There is no meaning without language games, and no language games without forms of life." Even mathematical procedures, which many of our contemporaries regard as the essence of objectivity, derive their compelling force, not from some transcendent status, but from being accepted and used by a specific group of people. As Bloor notes, "The depth and degree of opposition between different methodologies says more about their proponents than about the inherent relation of ideas that are involved." He offers the basic observation that "if meaning equals use, then it equals the whole use and nothing but the use." And he pleads, "If we are going to describe, then let us really look and see."[11] Wittgenstein's insights into language lead away from the abstract, the classificatory, and the transcendent modes of analysis and call for analyzing in social context the evidence as well as the members of the scholarly community who have been scrutinizing it. Both the language of the tradition and that of the analysts must be seen in terms of their respective social contexts.

The philosophical import of these inights into more appropriate and revealing modes of linguistic analysis is articulated by Susanne Langer in *Philosophy in a New Key*. Noting that the earlier dominance of empiricism has been effectively challenged through the growing awareness that our sense data are primarily symbols, she writes: "The edifice of human knowledge stands before us, not as a vast collection of sense reports, but as a structure of *facts that are symbols* and *laws that are meanings*. The discredited notion of the finality of sense data has given way to the widening recognition that symbolism is the cue for a new epoch of epistemology." In every age and culture, language has developed through the gradual accumulation and elaboration of verbal symbols, with the result that speech is the symbolic transformation of experience. But in addition to speech, there is another kind of symbolic process that is neither practically nor verbally communicative, but is effective and communal in its impact: ritual.[12] The fact that belief, myth, and ritual in societies other than our own may appear to us as irrational or monstrous led Grace De Laguna to the conclusion that their purpose is to establish and maintain the social solidarity of the group.[13] Langer states this differently when she notes that ritual reinforces solidarity, rather than creating it. Both the verbal modes of symbolization (from myth to critical analysis) and the nonverbal modes (ritual, dreams, visions, art) are manifestations of the symbol making and symbol using that are essential throughout human society.

Unlike fairy tales told for entertainment, myth as a mode of social orientation is evident when not only the social forces (persons, customs, laws, traditions) but also the cosmic forces that provide the larger context for human existence are taken into account. This kind of transformation of symbols employs not fiction but "the supreme concepts of life" that the symbols represent, by which men and women "orient themselves religiously in the cosmos."[14] It is not surprising that this insight of Langer was adopted by the anthropologist Clifford Geertz in his land-mark work *The Interpretation of Cultures*.[15] Before turning to an examination of this and related insights in the social sciences, we must look at the similar basic shift that has occurred in the natural sciences.

Paradigms in the Natural Sciences

Science, Thomas S. Kuhn asserts, always juxtaposes a particular set of experiences with a particular paradigm, so that no pure language of observation has ever been devised: "No language . . . restricted to reporting a world fully-known in advance can produce mere neutral and objective reports of 'the given.'" The choice of the interpretive paradigm in itself determines large areas of experience. Kuhn illustrates his points by showing that, after the development of atomic theory, "chemists came to live in a world where reactions behaved quite differently from the way they had before." Thus, since even the percentage compositions of well-known compounds were different, "the data themselves had changed," and the scientists, subsequent to the change of paradigm, were working "in a different world." In another example, after Kuhn shows how Isaac Newton's new laws of motion and dynamics transformed Galileo's line of inquiry about the heavenly bodies in the cosmos, he notes that it is changes of this sort "in the formulation of questions and answers" that, far more than empirical discoveries, "account . . . for major scientific transitions."[16] Through recognition of this basic epistemological factor, the social sciences lead us to ask questions of the ancient texts that enable us to see what the community behind the text looked like.

Returning to Kuhn's analysis of scientific knowledge, we must note that initially the paradigms in the natural sciences are simply presupposed: research seeks clarification and precision of measurement, as well as elimination of problematical aspects. These determine what is considered to be normative science. Then certain inadequacies of "fact" and theory appear, with the result that a paradigm comes to be seen as an anomaly requiring a change of paradigm, a change of observational and conceptual recognition, and a change of research categories and procedures. Such radical shifts are accompanied by resistance and professional insecurity. It is not the case that "theories emerge to fit the facts that were there all along. Rather, they emerge together with the facts they fit from a revolutionary reformulation of the preceding scientific tradition." The result is that paradigm testing takes place as a "competition between two rival paradigms for the allegiance of the scientific community." Yet proponents of competing paradigms fail to engage each other because of disagreement about the problems that a paradigm is to resolve. Although new solutions often use the vocabulary and apparatus of the old, they do not employ them in the traditional way, so that new relationships among the factors have to be developed. Kuhn illustrates this point by contrasting the space concepts of Euclid and Einstein, concluding that "the whole conceptual web has to be shifted and relaid; a whole new way of regarding the problems and factors in their solution emerges." The tensions are increased because proponents of competing paradigms are operating in different worlds, so that "the transfer of allegiance from paradigm to paradigm is a conversion experience that cannot be forced."[17]

In a 1969 postscript, Kuhn remarks that he has been using "paradigm" in two senses: a detailed model on which research is based and the worldview implicit in the model. He suggests, therefore, that those who hold incommensurable viewpoints be thought of as members of different language communities, and that their communication problems be analyzed as problems of translation. "In the metaphorical sense no less than in the literal sense of seeing, interpretation begins where perception ends. . . . What perception leaves for interpretation to complete depends drastically on the nature and amount of prior training and experience." As a result, debates over competing paradigms turn, not on logical process, but on premises. The postscript ends with a series of questions addressed to "corresponding communities in other fields" (which should include religious studies): "How does one elect or is one elected to membership in a particular community? What does the group see collectively as its goals; what deviations, individual or collective, will it tolerate?" Kuhn's concluding observation is that "scientific knowledge, like language, is intrinsically the common property of a group or nothing at all. To understand it we shall need to know the special characteristics of the groups that create and use it."[18]

Barry Barnes, a sociologist at Edinburgh University, has written an insightful analysis of scientific knowledge and its similarities to sociological theory, in which he shows the fallacy of the assumption that scientific knowledge is objective and purely descriptive. Instead, he declares, "A scientific theory is a metaphor created in order to understand new, puzzling, or anomalous phenomena, either in terms of a familiar, well-ordered part of an existing culture, or in terms of a newly constructed representation or model, which our existing cultural resources enable us to comprehend and manipulate." When redescription becomes necessary, the metaphors may submerge or die. "Science may be regarded as a loosely associated set of communities, each having characteristic procedures and techniques to further the metaphorical redescription of a puzzling area of experience in terms of a characteristic, accepted set of cultural resources." Scientists teach neither rules of rationality nor general scientific method, but "make their judgments with a consciousness shaped by models and exemplars of their research tradition." Barnes sees two factors operative in the construction of a model in scientific research. The stock of available resources, is a function of the milieu and the range of an actor's experience within it. Accepted knowledge or standards of judgment depend on the milieu and may also depend on the actors' social roles and the concerns and interest of the groups to which they belong. The initial model will be modified or even replaced in light of research; the general pattern of the culture will determine the flow of the "and so on" effect. For all its appeal to internal standards and procedures, scientific knowledge will never be free of the effects of the culture in which it arises.[19]

In *Ways of World-making*, Nelson Goodman offers an evaluation and description of the procedures of scientists that, while similar to those given above, is somewhat more iconoclastic in tone. Comparing scientists with artists and other people in their daily pursuits, he asserts that "the scientist is no less drastic, rejecting or purifying most of the entities and events of the world of ordinary things while generating quantities of filling for curves suggested by sparse data, and erecting elaborate structures on the basis of meagre observation. Thus does he build a world conforming to his chosen concepts and obeying his universal laws." The result of this procedure is that "truth, far from being a solemn and severe master is a docile and obedient servant. The scientist who supposes that he is single-mindedly dedicated to the search for truth deceives himself. He is unconcerned with the trivial truths he could grind out endlessly; and he looks to the multi-faceted and irregular results of observations for little more than suggestions of overall structures and significant generalizations. He seeks system, simplicity and scope; and when satisfied on these scores, he tailors truth to fit. He as much decrees as discovers the laws he sets forth, as much designs as discerns the patterns he delineates." It is Goodman's opinion that "even if the ultimate product of science, unlike that of art, is a literal, verbal or mathematical denotational theory, science and art proceed in much the same way with their searching and building.[20]

Two other perceptive studies of models and methods in the natural sciences are those by Richard Bernstein and Ian Barbour. Bernstein discerns a similarity between Thomas Kuhn's approach to knowledge and that of Aristotle, who differentiated *phronesis* from other modes of knowledge (*episteme* and *techne*) as a "form of reasoning which is concerned with choice and which involves deliberation." Integral to this mode of knowledge are the interpretation and specification of universals that are appropriate to a particular situation. The result is that knowledge thus perceived is "involved in theory-choice," which is a "judgmental activity requiring imagination, interpretation, the weighing of alternatives and the application of criteria that are essentially open." Such judgments need to be supported by reasons, which themselves change in the course of scientific development. "Thus it is not a deficiency that rational individuals can and do disagree without either of them being guilty of a mistake." After summarizing with approval Richard Rorty's declaration that it is an illusion to think there is a permanent set of ahistorical standards which the philosopher or epistemologist can discover and which will unambiguously tell us who is rational and who is not, Bernstein goes on to reject the "false dichotomy: either permanent standards of rationality (objectivism) or arbitrary acceptance of one set of standards or practices against its rival (relativism)." He continues, "To acknowledge that in the future there will be modifications of the standards, reasons and practices we now employ does not lead to epistemological scepticism but only to a realization of human fallibility and the finitude of human rationality." When he shifts his focus from scientific understanding to hermeneutics, Bernstein comes back to what he calls the "intellectual virtue," *phronesis*, which he sees as communal rather than individual, in that universals and ethical principles are shared within the interpreting community.[21]

Ian Barbour asserts that "scientific models are products of creative analogical imagination. Data are theory-laden; comprehensive theories are resistant to falsification," and the drive for comprehensiveness is evident among positivistic philosophers and natural scientists. Models are experimental, logical, and theoretical, leading to a theory that accounts for observable phenomena but is subject to critical realism. Barbour compares paradigms employed by the scholar in religious studies with scientific ones, which "are not falsified by data, but are replaced by promising alternatives. Commitment to a paradigm allows its potentialities to be systematically explored, but it does not exclude reflective evaluations." What is distinctive about the religious models is their subject matter: awe and reverence, mystical union, moral obligation, reorientation and reconciliation, key historical events, order and creativity in the world. These models "evoke the communal adoration, obeisance, awe, devotion, ecstasy, courage," which are "the emotive and conative dimensions of human experience" that distinguish religious experience from philosophical speculation. "It is through these models that we see ourselves and all things, that our experience is understood, and that our total environment is illuminated, with the result that there are disclosed to us otherwise unnoticed parallelisms, analogies, patterns among the data which reach us through observation and experience."[22]

For the scholar in the field of religious studies, paradigms define a coherent research tradition, articulating the types of questions that can legitimately be asked, the types of explanations that are to be sought, and the types of solutions that are acceptable. In short, they determine how one sees the world. Choice of paradigm rests not on absolute rules but on such criteria as predictability, accuracy, simplicity, and fruitfulness. Barbour rejects both the positivist theory of experience (the private, subjective awareness of sense qualities produced by physical stimuli from the external world) and the corresponding notion about God as something that is inferred without being experienced. Instead, he insists that the experience of God is expressed in ways analogous to the experience of other selves: through various media of language and action, which are interpreted by those sharing this experience. Members of a religious community understand themselves to be dealing with God, but faith is trust that is tied to experience and personal involvement, and therefore subject to critical reflection. His criterion for evaluation of the noncognitive functions is the degree to which they fulfill social or psychological needs and provide ethical criteria. For the cognitive functions, Barbour prescribes simplicity, coherence, extensibility, and comprehensiveness. Although subjective features are more evident in religion than in the natural sciences, the objective factors include common data, cumulative evidence, and criteria that are not dependent on the paradigm. In contrast to naive realism, instrumentalism (religion as a useful fiction), and functionalism (religion as a sociological product), he calls for critical realism and what Robert Bellah has called symbolic realism, which expresses feelings and attitudes even while organizing and regulating the flow of interaction between subjects and objects. To this approach to the symbolic world, critical realism adds the analysis of the social context of the religion, as well as its function, shared values, and critical diagnosis of class and social structure, both within and outside the religious community.[23] Thus Barbour comes out methodologically where Bernstein and Kuhn do: with the community as the locus of critical inquiry.

Knowledge as a Social Construct

Alfred Schutz, whose education in Germany was strongly influenced by Max Weber and Edmund Husserl, was deeply affected on migrating to America in 1939 by the pragmatic, humanistic theories of John Dewey and William James. Out of this intellectual mix emerged his view of knowledge as a social construct: "The world of daily life is the organized world, the intersubjective world," experienced and interpreted by our predecessors, which we have to modify by our actions or which will modify our actions. Each person is in a "biographically determined situation, which provides his space, role, status and moral or ideological position. It has a history, a sedimentation of all previous human experiences, and especially of those perceived and experienced within the society in which the individual resides." These features of the socially constructed understanding of the world do not determine in any absolute sense what one thinks or does, but they do predict how one is likely to respond to the world. Those who decide voluntarily to adopt another "knowledge" must learn and appropriate it. Members of the out-group, however, do not regard the articles of faith and the historical tradition of the in-group as self-evident, since their own central myths, as well as their process of rationalization and institutionalization, are different. Lacking a translation code, or refusing to use one, they consider another group's natural attitude—even when it in many ways overlaps with their own—as perverse and hostile. The members of one group may try to educate or convert the benighted, or declare war on them. Schutz epitomizes his view of knowledge as social: the world into which one is born and within which one has to find one's bearings is experienced as a tight-knit web of social relationships, or systems and signs and symbols, with their particular structure and meaning, of institutional forms of social organization, of systems of status and prestige, and so forth. The meaning of all these elements of the social world in all its diversity and stratification, as well as the pattern of the texture itself, is taken for granted by those living within it.[24]

The implications of this view of knowledge for historical understanding are profound. As Schutz and Luckmann have stated the case, "The transmission of subjective knowledge becomes objectivated and socialized in signs, which process leads to idealization and anonymization." They mean by this that what is initially perceived as personal knowledge comes to be expressed in general terms that are assumed to be universally recognized as valid ("Everyone knows that . . . "). But this leads to articulation of that shared knowledge in general, impersonal terms, which are treated as being universally valid and are stated in abstract formulations, often through the specific authority of a legendary or historical knowledge, or the anonymous authority of the "forefathers." "It is thus . . . that knowledge comes to have an overwhelming and at the same time taken-for-granted independence, which in the end is based on the subjective results of experience and explication, but which contrasts with the individual and the subjectivity of his experience and situation. It need hardly be said that the social validity of such 'objectivated' knowledge can outlast its original social relevance."[25] The socially accepted symbol system may subsequently be altered under the impact of individual or corporate experience, or new knowledge may lead to a change in the system of signs or to its replacement by a new system.

Peter Berger has made important refinements in the descriptive analysis of sociology of knowledge, including a definition of the successive stages of such knowledge: externalization, the shaping of culture and society by language, symbols, institutions, and laws; internalization, the subjective identification of the self with the social world; and socialization, the transmission by society of its shared knowledge and meaning to a new generation, reinforced by the effort to conform that generation to social standards and institutions.[26] In Berger's earlier work written with Thomas Luckmann, there is a description of the nomic role of the symbolic universe constructed and affirmed by society, which "provides powerful legitimation for the institutional order as a whole as well as for particular sectors of it," including a society's history of its own origins and growth. The symbol system "locates all collective events in a cohesive unity that includes past, present, and future, so that the empirical community is transposed to a cosmic plane."[27] The process of legitimation of a "world" thus constructed begins at the intuitive level but moves in stages to the explicit level, by which the structure of reality as perceived by the group is objectified, affirmed, and justified. At the initial pretheoretical stage, the community names practices and institutions, thereby beginning the process of legitimating them. The second stage is that of primitive theoretical legitimation in the form of proverbs and aphoristic sayings that are assumed to be self-evidently true. The third stage involves direct theoretical legitimation in relation to specific institutional and conceptual features of the culture. The fourth and final stage is the integration of the various provinces of practice and meaning into a symbolic totality.

The import of these insights for historians is that historical analysis cannot rest content with the social description of such phenomena as economic factors, archaeological remains, social patterns, or even literary evidence, important as these features are. The primary aim of the historian must be to enter into the symbolic universe of the community that produced the material under examination, and to do so with the intent of identifying shared assumptions as well as the group's explicit claims, norms, and institutional forms.

The import of these insights for cultural anthropologists is similarly evident. The title of one of Mary Douglas's books, *Essays in the Sociology of Perception*, shows this, although her analyses of culture lack the important dimension of the dialectic between subject and object in the individual's relationship to culture and society that is central for Berger. More explicit evidence of the impact of Berger's approach is to be found in a volume written by four cultural anthropologists, in which the majority of the attention is given to the work of Berger. Although critical of what they perceive as Berger's view of culture as an expression of subjective attitudes and values of the individual, they welcome the attention given by him to patterns, rules, and relationships at the cultural level, which, while not socially determined products of the culture, gain plausibility in that they are reinforced by the social group. Central are the individual's needs for meaning and order. Culture is a set of classifications that permit the individual to make sense of the world and to function within it. Also central are the concepts of identity, institution, world-view, spheres of relevance, and categories of explanation. In concluding their critical review, the anthropologists state that "an elementary task of cultural analysis must be the study of symbolic boundaries, for these constitute the essence of cultural order." These boundaries not only exist as conceptual distinctions in person's minds but are also publicly visible in the manner in which social interaction occurs, in discourse, and in tangible objects. Resources are expended in creating and maintaining them, and many social activities should be understood as efforts to sharpen eroded boundaries and redefine cultural distinctions, and as symptoms of ambiguous frameworks. The central questions concerning cultural boundaries are, How are they defined and How do they serve to define (or redefine) the culture?[28]

Clifford Geertz has long been operating with a view of culture akin to that traced above. For him culture is "an historically transmitted pattern of meanings embodied in symbols, a system of inherited conceptions expressed in symbolic forms by means of which men communicate, perpetuate and develop their knowledge about and attitudes toward life." Quoting Suzanne Langer, Geertz affirms that "the concept of meaning in all its varieties is the dominant philosophical concept of our time. . . . Sign, symbol, denotation, signification, communication are our [intellectual] stock-in-trade." Social anthropology, especially that part concerned with religion, must take this seriously into account.[29] In a more recent essay, "Common Sense as a Cultural System," Geertz observes, "Common sense is not what the mind cleared of cant spontaneously apprehends: it is what the mind filled with presuppositions . . . concludes." Common sense is "as totalizing as any other: no religion is more dogmatic, no science more ambitious, no philosophy more general." The qualities of common sense are naturalness, which represents matters as they are, with an air of "of-courseness," and which rests not on philosophical naturalism but on shared assumptions of life and the world as experienced within a particular culture; practicalness, which is to know everything your mind provokes you to know about the world as experienced, and to arrange it in categories; thinness, as contrasted with intellectual analysis, which assumes that the world is what the wide-awake, uncomplicated person observes it to be, described in terms that seem to be self-evident and often expressed in gnomic utterances (epigrams, proverbs, obiter dicta, jokes, anecdotes) rather than in formal doctrines or theories; and accessibleness, by which "any person with faculties reasonably intact can grasp [these] common-sense conclusions," and once they are stated in a sufficiently unequivocal mode, "will not only grasp but embrace them." Thus "common sense is open to all, the general property of at least, as we would put it, all solid citizens."[30]

This basic understanding of the socially shared view of reality is evident in surveys of the field of anthropology, such as Maurice Freedman's *Main Trends in Social and Cultural Anthropology*, which highlights the importance of assumptions from sociology of knowledge and the legitimation of the history of the culture.[31] Similarly, in *Cultural Models in Language and Thought*, Dorothy Holland and Naomi Quinn assert that the order perceived in the world, including the social world, "is there only because we put it there." Such "culturally constituted understandings of the social world" show that people impose order on the world and that their orderings are shared by others. Much of what one knows and believes derives from "these shared models that specify what is in the world and how it works."[32]

In *Meaning and Moral Order*, Robert Wuthnow is properly critical of sociologists of knowledge for their primary emphasis on subjective meaning to the neglect of collective identities and symbols and on social structures to the neglect of the production and institutionalization of cultural systems.[33] But he does accept the basic assumption of a shared world, while urging those analyzing cultures to take into account the concrete manifestations of the social environment: social language, respected cultural authorities, important historical events, and social embodiments. Not merely the ideological trends, but the distinctive forms that the intellectual assumptions produce are to be examined, including texts and institutions. In a more recent work that bears the significant title *Communities of Discourse*, Wuthnow describes cultural change as taking place in three stages: production, which is diverse and offers alternatives; proliferation of charismatic figures, which encourages some of the alternatives and results in both structural and intellectual ambiguities; and institutionalization, as systems of routinization and communication develop, leading to dissemination and study of the basic ideas and making possible emancipation from the original social context and a challenge to the establishment. Major movements build on intellectual precedents, but the creative work of leaders is essential, since they sharpen rhetorical modes in their critique of accepted values and assumptions. The raw materials of social experience are put in a new symbolic framework in which, through figural formulations, problems in the present are linked with possibilities in the future. The factors indicating these changes include the prospect of transformation of the environment and both institutional and wider social resources. The new vision is opposed to the established order, not to replace it, but to provide a conceptual space for new modes of behavior.[34]

Implications for the Study of Christian Origins

The intended use of these sociocultural insights in the following historical analysis of postbiblical Judaism and Christian origins is not simply to replace the now widely discredited categories of nineteenth-century history of religion—such as Palestinian and Hellenistic Judaism, and Jewish and Hellenistic Christianity—with a new set of intellectual compartments into which the literary and conceptual evidence can be pigeonholed. Instead, my aim is to produce a new set of analytical modes and theoretical procedures by which the diverse and dynamic development of postexilic Judaism and the origins of Christianity can be illumined and more responsibly analyzed. The sociocultural approach leads a historical inquirer to ask appropriate questions that illuminate the texts and their origins, rather than providing an arbitrary and misleading scheme for classifying evidence.

When these insights from the social sciences concerning human communities, their leadership, and their sense of destiny are employed in historical study, new perspectives on the origins, dynamics, and diversity of religious movements emerge. These sociocultural analyses lead the historian to interrogate the evidence in fresh and revealing ways. The following questions are essential for the twin tasks of historical analysis and reconstruction:[35]

> *Boundary questions:* By what authority are the boundaries that define a group drawn? What are the threats to the maintenance of these boundaries? Who are the insiders? The outsiders? Can an insider become an outsider? Do

threats to the boundaries arise within the group or from without? What bounds of time and space does the group occupy? Which is the more important factor: group identity or the criteria for belonging?

Authority questions: What are the roles of power within the group and the means of attaining them? What are the structures of power within the group, including rank? How do the titles of leadership function in terms of authority and status? How is the leader chosen? Who is in charge? Can authority be transmitted to successive generations? If so, by what means?

Status and role questions: Are age groups or sex roles defined? Are there definable classes or ranks within the group? What are the attitudes expressed regarding wealth, buildings, clothing, and ritual equipment? If there is conflict within the group, what are the issues? Who has special privileges, and on what basis? Who performs rituals?

Ritual questions: What are the key formative experiences of the group, including initiation, celebration, and stages of transition? Who performs these rites, and what are the purposes of them? How are the rites transmitted to the successors? Is there evidence of changing attitudes toward the ritual in successive generations? In what direction is the change? To what extent and why has the group altered the traditional rituals? What language is used in rituals?

Literary questions and social implications: What genre does the group use for communication within its membership? With those outside the group, if any? What does the choice of genre imply? Does the author's choice of a specific genre influence the message he wants to communicate? If so, in what way? What are the themes of a text? What is its argumentative strategy? Who is supported? Who is attacked? Is there a canon of authoritative literature operative within the group? How is it defined? How does the literary organization of a communication serve to promote conceptual and social order in the group?

Questions about group functions: What helps or hinders the achievement of the group's aims? What are the dynamics of the group? What are its goals? What are the tensions within the group? What are its tensions with the surrounding culture? Who are the chief enemies? Does the group use body language? If so, in what way? What does it imply? Are there problems of cognitive dissonance within the texts produced by the group, or between its texts and its experience?[36] How are these problems handled? What are the ritual means of establishing and reinforcing group identity?

Questions concerning the symbolic universe and the social construction of reality: What are the shared values, aspirations, anxieties, and ethical norms of the group?

What is disclosed about the symbolic universe of the group by its shared understandings of supernatural beings (good and evil), miracles, and healing techniques? How does the group understand history and its own place within history? What is the group's view of time? How does it perceive the essential being of God? The divine actions, both within the cosmic structure and among human beings? Are there dualistic elements in the group's perception of reality? Do these good/evil factors assume political, moral, social, or cultural forms? What are the dominant symbols for the group and its place in the universe? In what distinctive ways does this group employ symbols that it shares with other groups? What are the distinctive symbolic features of the group under scrutiny? What are the boundary factors in the group's life that are important for the maintenance of its identity?

These questions are not always directly raised or explicitly addressed by the documents produced in postexilic Judaism and early Christianity. Yet the responsible historian must inquire along these lines and seek answers to them at the level of assumptions. The questions do not exhaust the field of inquiry for the biblical interpreter, essential though they are as a point of entry into ancient communities. Rather, they arouse in the investigator a sensitivity to the often unspoken but powerfully operative factors in terms of which the explicitly theological dimensions of the writings can be more fully understood, such as the nature of the human situation, the problem of evil, the divine purpose for humanity and for the cosmic order, and the identity and function of the agent (or agents) of God through whom that purpose is to be accomplished. None of the factors is ever present in a fixed, unchanging form, since the human circumstances in which the community exists and the divine word is responded to are always affected by changing social and cultural forces.

Varied as the answers to the questions are in relation to postexilic Judaism and early Christianity, there are certain convictions of these movements that seem to have dominated despite cultural and social change and the resultant changes within the Jewish and Christian communities. These convictions include: that there is an antecedent divine purpose for the creation and for humanity; that this purpose has been disclosed to and through divinely endowed agents and messengers; that suffering has a significant role within the divine purpose; that the divine purpose will be fulfilled by or for a community of the committed, rather than by or for isolated individuals; and that the achievement of the divine purpose will include God's calling to account human beings in general.

Accordingly, the interpreter must seek to maintain a balance between questions and answers shared by a range of groups and the diversity of responses that emerge from each group and distinguish it from other groups. Models of community and modes of renewal are often shared—with important differences—by several groups in both Judaism and Christianity around the turn of the eras. My first task (chapter 1) is to examine the diverse responses of Jews, in the period following their return from exile in Babylon, to the challenges and opportunities that they perceived to reconstitute themselves as God's people. Then I shall raise the same kinds of issues in regard to the origins of Christianity. After analyzing early Christian literature in terms of the five models of community evident in the Jewish sources, we shall see how these models were altered as the movement evolved toward more formal structures and organization.

Models of Community in the Literature of Postexilic Judaism

The return of the tribes of Benjamin, Levi, and Judah from exile in Babylon with the support of the Persian rulers appears to have been a protracted process extending over more than a century: from the initial stages in the reign of Cyrus (ca. 538 B.C.E.) through the reign of Darius (521–485), until three phases of reconstruction of the city of Jerusalem were carried out under Artaxerxes I (in 445–424 and in 434–426) and Artaxerxes II (404–358). The responses to and interpretations of these restorative developments for the sociopolitical life of Israel as well as the central importance of the Temple are variously depicted in the literature of Judaism down to and beyond the destruction in 70 C.E. of the far grander Temple that was built by Herod.

In the postexilic writings included in the Hebrew canon—both the historical and the prophetic writings—a favorite image for the renewed covenant community is the city, often referred to as Zion. At times the emphasis is on the social structure of the renewed society of God's people, and in some of the writings it is the cultic aspect of the life of the community that is central. For example, although the accounts appear in a somewhat confused sequence in the canonical books of Ezra and Nehemiah, the mixed status of the Israelites who had remained in the land of Israel during the exile is apparent in the reports of their having intermarried with other regional peoples and in the ability of the leaders of the long-term residents of the land of Judah to challenge the right of the returning tribes to rebuild the city and the Temple (Ezra 4; Neh. 2). The identity of the people of God and the question of the authority and strategy for renewal of people and shrine are paramount, as the ongoing situation is depicted in these biblical writings. These issues were to continue to thwart and divide the heirs of the heritage of Israel for the next four centuries, as control of the region passed into the hands of

Alexander and his successors, the Ptolemies and the Seleucids (fourth to second centuries B.C.E.) and then as it was seized by the Romans in the later first century B.C.E. The persistent questions that were heightened following the failure of the two Jewish nationalist revolts of the first and second centuries C.E. were, How are God's people to regain and maintain their identity as heirs of the covenant and By what means or agents will that renewal be accomplished?

The Image of the City Where God Dwells among His People

Isaiah's prophecy of the renewal of Judah pictures that event in terms of the redemption of Zion (1:17). This involves the elevation (whether physical or symbolic is not clear) of "the mountain of the LORD's house" (2:2–4) and the coming of nations in peace to worship the Lord there. What would today be called Israel's international relations problems are solved by the turning of the nations to the worship of Yahweh. Similarly, in Zech. 8:1–8, God's restoration of his people is linked to the rebuilding of Jerusalem, where God will dwell in their midst.

This image of the city as model of covenant renewal receives greater attention in the later prophecies of Isaiah 40–66. In Isa. 40:9–11, Jerusalem-Zion becomes the messenger of God to his people, assuring them of his plan for their corporate renewal. Cyrus's role as "the anointed" of God is to "build my city" and "set my exiles free" (45:13). So powerful is this symbol of the city that even the doubters and willful among Israel, though they do not trust God's promises for the transformation of the people, persist in "calling themselves after the holy city" (48:2). The promises of renewal of the covenant community are explicitly addressed to Zion, Jerusalem, and "the holy city" (52:1–9). When Israel returns to the land, even foreigners share in the rebuilding of Jerusalem (60:10–14), so that Zion and Jerusalem are the dominant symbols of the return and redemption of God's "holy people" (62:1–12). Depicted through the image of a woman in labor, Zion will give birth to the renewal of the people of God (66:8).

The same themes pervade the Psalms. Variously referred to as Zion, the holy city, the holy hill, or simply Jerusalem, the city is the symbol and locus for the accessible presence of God among his people (Ps. 3, 15, 46, 76). At times the rebuilding of the city is predicted in psalms that likely reflect the exilic period (Ps. 51, 69, 102). Others promise the reestablishment of God's kingship in Zion, either through God's son (Ps. 2) or by God's direct rule (Ps. 48). The specific source of God's power and mercy in the city is the sanctuary (Ps. 20), or "the hill of the LORD" (Ps. 24).

That this imagery of the city as a symbol of divine judgment and renewal goes back to the time of the exile is evident from the prophecies of Jeremiah, where the impending fall of Jerusalem is the primary sign of God's judgment on his people, just as the restoration of the city is the sign of their redemption. In Jer. 19:1–15, the leaders of the city—elders, priests, and prophets—join in the breaking of the jug, which symbolizes the disaster that God is bringing on his people ("upon this city," 19:15). Repeatedly, the predictions of the capture of the city by Nebuchadnezzar and its consequent destruction are presented as signs of God's judgment on Israel.[1] Conversely, the promises of restoration of the covenant people are articulated in terms of the rebuilding of the city,[2] especially in Jer. 31:31–39, where the vivid assurances of renewal of the covenant with Israel end in a description of the extent of the city of Jerusalem. Similarly, in the protoapocalyptic Isaiah 26, the ultimate blessing of God's people is depicted in terms of the strengthening and rebuilding of the city.

The agent of this covenantal renewal is for Isaiah and Second Isaiah primarily God himself. The human instruments by which stability and integrity will develop in the renewed community are the judges and counselors (Isa. 1:26), such as one finds in the Deuteronomic strand of Torah (Exod. 18:13–17; Deut. 16:18–20). In Isa. 45:13, Cyrus is God's "anointed" to rebuild the city and set the exiles free. But it is God who is the redeemer and liberator of Israel (48:2–22), and Zion is commissioned to proclaim this news to Judah as a whole (40:9–11). It is the Lord who will comfort his people. They will see God's salvation, and it is he who will go before them as they return (52:1–12). He will be their savior, and the agents that will rule over them are the personifications of Peace and Righteousness (60:1–22). God will establish Jerusalem (62:6–7) and will extend prosperity to his people, comfort them, and effect fiery judgment on hostile nations (66:12).[3] The only human role indicated is that of the messengers, or "sentinels," who are to announce to the city what God is going to do, so that they may be called "The Holy People, the Redeemed of the LORD . . . a City Not Forsaken" (62:12). Similarly, in Zech. 8:1–17, it is God who is the active agent, dwelling in Jerusalem, saving his people, enabling them to live in the city, and purposing their good there. In Jeremiah, just as Nebuchadnezzar was the instrument of God's judgment on his disobedient people (19:1–15; 21:6–10; 25:28–29), so it is God who will punish the very nations who effected the punishment of Israel (25:15–38) and who will finally restore his people (30:19–20) and put his law in their hearts (31:31–35).

In this prophetic tradition of the renewal of the city of God's people, there are a few strands that point enigmatically to human agents through whom the redemption or guidance of the new community will occur. For example, in Jer. 30:21, there is mention of a "prince" and "ruler" who will come among the people, presumably to guide them in the way of the Lord. This is the negative corollary of the role of Nebuchadnezzar as the instrument of God's judgment on the disobedient nation. Yet the overwhelming emphasis, as in the protoapocalyptic oracle of Isa. 26:1–21, is on the direct action of God, who will "ordain peace," increase the nation, and slay its opponents.

A Temple Cult–oriented Community

A significant number of Jews from the time of the Babylonian exile forward perceived the central model for God's people and for the maintenance of the relationship between them and God to be the Temple and its cultus. Only when the Temple cultus was being fully and properly carried out could the real Israel participate in the life God intended for his people. This point of view is evident in such postexilic biblical writings as Ezekiel, as well as in such later documents as 1 and 2 Maccabees, 1 Esdras, and the Dead Sea Scrolls.

Ezekiel's Vision of the New Temple

The concluding section of Ezekiel is dated by the writer to the fourteenth year after the fall of Jerusalem and the exile to Babylonia, which would be 573–72 B.C.E. The vision of the new Temple to be built in Jerusalem is linked with what is foreseen as a concurrent renewal of the land of Israel. The vision includes detailed measurements and architectural features (e.g., gates, vestibules, courtyards) as well as major components of the Temple: nave, holy place, and sanctuary. When completed, the divine cloud of glory will return to the Temple from the east. The new altar and the dedicatory offerings to be presented there are described in detail (Ezek. 43). Only those of the people of Israel who are ritually pure and who are obedient to the law will be permitted to enter the Temple. Conversely, foreigners and violators of the law will be rigidly excluded.

Those Levites who were formerly disobedient but now are truly penitent, however, may take part in the service of the Temple, though in servile and custodial roles. The faithful Levites, on the other hand, will become the functioning priests there. The land and what it produces are to be divided in such a way as to guarantee support for the Temple, for its priests and for the offerings there (45:1–9). This latter theme is taken up and expanded in Ezek. 47:13–48:35, where the reapportionment of the land is detailed. Regulations are set down for weights and measures as well as the presentation of offerings and preparations for festivals. Symbolically, a river is depicted as streaming forth from the Temple and flowing to the east, where it renews the Judean desert and transforms the Dead Sea into a freshwater lake filled with fish (47:1–12). It is not by chance that the Dead Sea community set up its headquarters on a bluff overlooking the ravine through which water drains from the Temple mount and east Jerusalem into the Dead Sea.

Significantly missing from this vision of the renewed Jerusalem is any mention of a king (*melekh*) or a ruler of Davidic descent. A "prince" (*nasi*) is described as having special access to the Temple (45:7–8), and property is allotted to the "princes," but these rulers are by no means autocrats or monarchs. Instead, they are warned against oppressing the people or taking land from anyone (46:18). They are pictured as simply agents or administrators of the ultimate authority, presumably God.

The outlook of this section of Ezekiel corresponds closely to that of the holiness code in Lev. 18–26, which emphasizes sexual, ritual, and moral purity of the people (Lev. 18–20; 26), but which also details the holiness of the priests (Lev. 21) and the offerings to be presented in the sanctuary (Lev. 22), as well as the festivals that the priests are to lead the people in observing (Lev. 23–24), including the sabbatical year and the Year of Jubilee (Lev. 25). Clearly, the major emphasis in these documents falls on the proper maintenance of the cultic life of God's people rather than on personal appropriation of the legal code in its social and moral dimensions.

1 and 2 Maccabees

Although the historical achievement of the Maccabees can be viewed as primarily that of securing—for about one century (165–63 B.C.E.)—political independence for the Jews, the major concern with which 1 Maccabees opens is that Antiochus IV's policy of forced hellenization has resulted in the profanation of Jerusalem and especially of its sanctuary (2:6–12). To attain the semblance of political freedom, however, the contestants for power feel that they must gain the support of other political and military powers in the Mediterranean world, including the Syrian rivals for the Seleucid throne. Most dramatic are the efforts of the Jews to outflank the Hellenistic rulers by alliances with Rome (8:1–32) and the Spartans (12:1–23). Yet when Jonathan identifies himself as the leader of the people, his role is not that of the king but of the high priest who presides over the council of elders, *gerousia* (1 Macc. 12). Similarly, as evidence of Simon's success in freeing the land of foreign domination and restoring peace and prosperity, we read, "He made the sanctuary glorious, and added to its vessels" (14:27). Simon is identified as "the great high priest" who presides over "the great assembly [*synagoge*] of the priests." Even the account of an invasion of the land focuses on "the sanctuary." Victory results in Simon's designation as "leader and high priest" (14:35), a title that is expanded and confirmed repeatedly in the document (14:35, 38, 41, 47; 15:2; and even by the Romans in 15:15, 21). Similarly, records of the activities of John Hyrcanus (who was in power 134–104 B.C.E.) are "written in the chronicles of his high priesthood" (16:23–24). The central focus of divine action and power in behalf of God's people is represented in 1 Maccabees through the role of the high priest.

Similarly, 2 Maccabees in its summary history of Israel concentrates on the desecration of the Temple and its subsequent purification (10:1–8). Just as the author's major concern is for "the consecrated sanctuary" (15:18), so the celebration of the defeat and dissection of Israel's enemy, Nicanor, takes place in the sanctuary (15:28–33).

1 Esdras

In highlighting the reforms instituted by Josiah the king (about 621 B.C.E.), the author of 1 Esdras recalls the establishment of the worship of Yahweh in Jerusalem by King David and the subsequent building of the Temple there by Solomon (1:1–5a). The emphasis in this historical description is not on the achievement of political power but on the ritual carried out in the Temple and the ministry of the Levites there (1:5b–21). The decline and corruption of the Judaic monarchy (1:25–56) are seen as divine judgment on the people's failure to maintain proper standards of ritual and ethnic purity (1:57–58). Similarly, the major theme in Cyrus's proposal and subsequent support for the return of the people of Judah to their land is said to be the rebuilding of God's house in Jerusalem (2:1–15).

In 1 Esd. 4:42–62, Zerubbabel is given authority by the Persian king to return to Jerusalem in order to rebuild the city and the Temple. In the list of those accompanying him on his return, special attention is given to the Temple servants, the priests and the Levites (5:24–46). The ritual and festival cycles are begun while the reconstruction of the Temple is being launched (5:47–71). With the support of the prophets Haggai and Zechariah, the Temple is completed (6:1–7:15).

When Ezra leads a group of the returning exiles (8:1–9:55), he is identified as "a scribe skilled in the law," but his official title is "priest and reader of the law of the Lord" (8:8–9). In his priestly capacity, he is authorized to appoint judges and to enforce obedience to the law (8:23–24). Ezra designates a special group of priests and Levites to oversee the safe return of the sacred vessels to the Temple (8:54–60). On the arrival of Ezra, the appropriate sacrifices are offered (8:61–67). The resident regional officials honor "the people and temple of the Lord," but the priests and Levite who were already living in the land have not maintained a separate ethnic identity and are called by Ezra to repentance and rectification of their ritual violations. Their penitence is joined by other representatives of the resident Jews (8:71–96). The pure priests and Levites take the leadership in enabling the people to regain purity and to maintain it (9:1–54). As Ezra reads the law of Moses to the people gathered in the forecourt of the Temple, he is designated as "chief priest and reader."

The Ritual Purity of the Law-abiding Community

The answer to the questions posed earlier in this chapter about covenantal participation and divine agency for renewal that appears to have dominated from the fifth century B.C.E. onward—with significant variations in specific details— was that for God's people to be renewed, they must become fully obedient to the law of God.

Ezra and Nehemiah

As set forth in Ezra and Nehemiah, the predominant assumption among what seems to have been the major portion of those concerned for recovery of the Israelite tradition in the period immediately following the exile was that to gain renewal the Jewish people must resume performance of the sacrifical and festival acts prescribed in the law, observance of the sabbath, and total abstinence from intermarriage with the indigenous tribes of the region (such as the Ammonites and the Moabites; Neh. 13:1–3; Ezra 9).

The Temple was to be rebuilt and its annual cycle of feasts resumed under the supervision of the priests, the Levites, and other designated workers. The priests and Levites, who were to be "learned in matters of the commandments of the Lord," were to ensure that the people obeyed the laws (Ezra 8:15, 29–30), a role in which they were to be assisted by magistrates and judges appointed by the priests (7:25–26). The magistrates and judges were to be responsible for identifying and punishing disobedience to the law. The books of Ezra and Nehemiah (which are part of the larger corpus of the revised history of Israel composed during the exile in what is now known as 1 and 2 Chronicles) perceive the exile as punishment for failure to fulfill the legal obligations of the covenant, and they see in the restoration of the people to the land the challenge and obligation to obey those laws now. Central for the community is conformity to the legal tradition, which now is recognized by scholars to have received canonical form through scholarly, priestly editing during the Babylonian exile[4] but which was then simply assumed to have been given by God to Moses in the same form in which postexilic Judaism possessed it. The intermediary through whom the law was given was a human figure: Moses. The transmission of the divine message to Israel, as described in Exod. 19–40,[5] including the initial giving of the covenant and its renewal following Israel's reversion to idolatry, is simply presupposed in Ezra and Nehemiah as recounted in the Pentateuch.

In the era of these two leaders in the recovery of the legal tradition there were several types of agents—all of them human in origin and status—whose roles were to transmit, interpret, and enforce the law, as I have noted: priests, Levites, and magistrates and judges. In addition, support was given to the enterprise of recalling the people to obedience to the law by the two prophets named in the account: Haggai and Zechariah (Ezra 5:1). With the encouragement and generosity of the Persian monarchs—toward the restoration of the city and the sanctuary, including the return of the sacred vessels taken from the Temple by the Babylonians (Ezra 1:5–11; 5:13–17)—the project was carried through, and the cultic basis of the relationship of the covenant people to God was restored.

1 Baruch

Although this document claims to have been written by Jeremiah's secretary (Jer. 36:4) from exile in Babylon and to date from after the fall of Jerusalem in 587 B.C.E., it seems to have been produced after the Jews had gained liberty in their land from Seleucid domination—that is, after 164 B.C.E. The main question addressed in this writing is, Why had such disaster befallen God's people? The answer was that the people had failed to obey "the statutes of the Lord" (1:18–20) and "the words of the prophets" (1:21). Baruch calls to God for the deliverance of the people from their enemies, which will serve as proof to the nations of the power and justice of the God of Israel (2:15). The people can be assured, however, that beyond the exile and other forms of punishment (which they have, in fact, already experienced) lies an era of restoration and of increase in the numbers of God's people (2:24–35). The agent of God through whom this renewal is to take place for the creation and for the people is Wisdom (3:9), which is personified and described in metaphorical language as coming down from heaven and living among the people of Israel (3:29–37) and then explicitly identified as "the book of the commandments of God" (4:1). To disobey wisdom leads to punishment, but not to destruction (4:5–20). Hope lies in penitence, obedience, and confidence in God's purpose to destroy the enemies—including the political power ("city"; probably Antioch, the Seleucid capital)—that have taken control of Jerusalem (4:21–35). Restoration of Jerusalem and its faithful people is certain (4:36—5:9). The law was the instrument for establishing the community of God's people, and is to be the agent of its renewal.

Tobit, Judith, and the Additions to Daniel

In the post-Maccabean period, stories were told of the ways in which God preserved those who were obedient to the law, even to the extent of enabling them to overcome the machinations of the demonic powers. The literary style of these narratives was influenced by the so-called Hellenistic romances, which were engaging tales written not merely as entertainment, but as propaganda for a religion.[6] In Tobit, the central figure is a man who is depicted as living during the exile under the Assyrians, though the events described fit in the period of Seleucid domination of the Jews (early second century B.C.E.). This man of courage resisted pressure from the Hellenistic rulers to conform to their cultural and religious standards, and thereby preserved his marital, ritual, dietary, and cultic purity. In addition, he performed acts of charity and piety, such as giving a proper burial to the body of an Israelite (1:3–2:10). The plight of God's people is said to have been the result of their failure to obey the law (3:1–6). The cure of Tobit's blindness is the consequence of his good works, and particularly of his having jeopardized his own purity by burying the exposed corpse (12:11–15; cf. Num. 19:11–13). An angel, Raphael, intervenes to restore and reward Tobit for his fidelity to the law.

The story of Judith is told in a fictional and anachronistic setting, ostensibly in the time of the Assyrian invasion of Palestine (4:3; late eighth century B.C.E.), but it then reports the recent return of the Jews from captivity in Babylon (which would have been late sixth century). The sacred vessels brought back to the Temple from Babylon have been newly consecrated. The people have humbled themselves and gathered in the sanctuary, where the priests are offering the appropriate sacrifices (4:9–15). The prosperity of God's people depends directly on their obedience to the law; if they remain obedient, they will be invulnerable, and the Lord will bless them.

Judith is a paradigm of piety (8:6). The welfare of the people requires them to abstain from worship of false gods and to maintain the sanctuary and its altar (8:18–24). Judith repeats these principles to the Assyrians, but then asserts that

Postexilic Judaism

her people have disobeyed and are therefore vulnerable to subjugation by their enemies. They are said to have taken for their own use tithed items, which should have been reserved for the priests. She affirms that after the people have been chastised for their disobedience, Holofernes will acknowledge the power of the true God, and she will lead him to Jerusalem, where he will be crowned (11:11–19). Having taken up residence among the Assyrians, where she survives by eating only the food she brought with her from the besieged city, she maintains her purity to the point of beheading Holofernes when he makes a sexual advance. The formerly hostile Ammonite neighbor, Achior, is converted and circumcised when he sees how God has used Judith to defeat the enemies of the people of Israel. The Assyrians are scattered and killed, while the people return to Jerusalem to join in the proper worship of God (15–16): "When they arrived in Jerusalem they worshipped God . . . the people were purified, they offered their burnt offerings, their freewill offerings and their gifts" (16:18). As in the next model I shall examine below, the cultus is understandably a major factor in obedience to the law, but in this story the emphasis falls on Judith's maintenance of her personal purity.

In the additions to Daniel, the historical plight of the covenant people is again seen as a consequence of disobedience to the law. The result has been that "there is no prince, no prophet, or leader, no burnt offering, or sacrifice, or oblation, no incense, no place to make an offering" before God (Song of Three Children, 15). Yet there is a prayer for acceptance by God on the ground of the contrition of the worshipper as a replacement for the legally prescribed offerings.[7] The Temple and the throne of God are not on earth, but in heaven. The writing is addressed to all who are "humble and holy in heart." Those who worship the Lord are urged to bless and thank him (Song of Three Children, 28–34, 65–68). Similarly, in Bel and the Dragon, Daniel gives no direct indication of involvement in the cult, but asserts simply that he worships, not the idols, but the living God who made heaven and earth (5, 25). The primary feature here is devotion to the God of heaven and faithful obedience to him, rather than participation in the cultus at the Jerusalem Temple.

The Pharisees

Until the last quarter of this century, most scholarly study of Judaism in the postexilic period and after—as well as of the origins of Christianity—assumed that the rabbinic methods and practices as documented in the Mishnah and Talmud were the continuation of beliefs, practices, and institutional forms that originated during the Babylonian captivity and were given Palestinian form and substance under Ezra and Nehemiah in the fifth century B.C.E., and that they prevailed in the period from the second century B.C.E. to the beginning of the literary formation of the Mishnah in the second century C.E. A telling critical review of this theory has been offered by Jacob Neusner in *Ancient Judaism: Debates and Disputes*.[8] As noted above in the introduction, Neusner's appropriate replacement for the term "normative Judaism" is "formative Judaism," which has become widely used since it highlights the process of change that Judaism was undergoing.[9] Other scholars continue to offer more traditional reconstructions of these developments, such as that of Shaye J. D. Cohen who does however take into account archaeological and textual evidence as it bears on the issue of historical analysis of Judaism in this period and by no means simply reproduces the older views.[10]

Neusner's analysis and conclusions have been strongly influenced by the work of his teacher, Morton Smith, whose observations about Judaism in this period were set forth in several forms, including a seminal essay, "Palestinian Judaism in the First Century."[11] Smith's understanding is that when Josephus refers to the Pharisees as a "school of thought" or as a "philosophy,"[12] he is using a suitable term, since the movement was developing a mode of appropriation of the historical and scriptural traditions of Israel, rather than a separatist sect. Neusner builds on the evidence from Josephus to sketch the earlier political phase of Pharisaism. Following the death of the Hasmonean king Alexander Jannaeus in 76 B.C.E., his successor, Alexandra Salome, turned to the Pharisees for assistance in governing the land of the Jews. This group seized the opportunity to coerce the populace into obedience to Torah as they understood it. When Alexandra died in 67, the struggle for power within the Hasmonean family led to the formation of an alliance by one wing of the family with the Idumean family of Antipater. In 63, the Romans intervened, installing Antipater's son, Herod, as puppet king of the Jews. Thereupon, the Pharisees shifted their political strategy, concentrating instead on more peaceful and voluntary ways of promulgating their aims for defining the people of God through their interpretation and application of the law of Moses. They began developing a broad base of support for their point of view through the formation of informal, house-based meetings for the study and appropriation of their legal tradition.

Two major features of Pharisaism are evident from this period: First, a central place was given to informal meetings in homes, where study and appropriation of the scriptures culminated in table fellowship. Second, guiding their grasp of scripture and shaping their common life of informal study and devotion was the aim of appropriating and observing strictly—but in a personalized way—the cultic and dietary laws set out in the Mosaic tradition (including those originally intended for priestly performance) as an essential means of gaining and maintaining purity for their adherents as the true people of God. There is no evidence of doctrinal debates among them or with outsiders, or of ritual regulations for their religious gatherings and their shared meals. The architectural and institutional formalization of the synagogue took place only in the second and third centuries C.E.[13]

In the earlier time, the Pharisees saw themselves as representing a mode of philosophy comparable to what was being proclaimed in the Greco-Roman world, since they claimed to be building on the wisdom traditions of Israel, as Morton

Postexilic Judaism

Smith noted in his essay. Smith pointed to Deut. 4:6 as articulating the significance of the law for those within and outside the community: "You must observe [the statutes and ordinances] diligently, for this will show your wisdom and discernment to the [non-Israelite] peoples, who when they hear all these statutes will say, 'Surely this great nation is a wise and discerning people.'" What was distinctive about this wisdom was the claim of the Pharisees that they drew on oral traditions that went back to Moses, and that observance of this "philosophy" reinforced their identity as God's people. Although one cannot be certain of the origins of the term "Pharisees," if it was derived from *perushim* (separate ones), it pointed to the conviction of this group that they possessed special wisdom in the form of legal requirements that established them as the distinctive people of the covenant.

In spite of the claim of Mosaic origins for their "wisdom," Jewish thinking about God and the world in this period was widely and significantly influenced by Stoic philosophy, with its speculations about human capacity for awareness of moral principles inherent in the universe (i.e., conscience), the divinely determined cycles of the ages of history, and the divine ordering of the world and of moral accountability, including future rewards and punishments (as I shall discuss below).

The Pharisaic movement flourished alongside the Temple cultus, unlike the Dead Sea community, which looked for the expulsion of the incumbent order of priests and the reconstruction of both the Temple and the city of Jerusalem, as the Temple Scroll attests. While making no radical break with the established Jewish leaders, the Pharisees interpreted and appropriated the law of Moses in a personalized (but not individualized) way, including the cultic regulations, which provided the traditional symbols for their voluntary gatherings in homes for table fellowship as God's pure and obedient people.

The Sadducees

Reports about and references to the Sadducees in Josephus, the New Testament, and the rabbinic traditions of the second and subsequent centuries C.E. are incomplete and ambiguous, or even at some points contradictory. It is probable that their name derived from Zadok (1 Kings 1:26), whose heirs they claimed to be in the interpretation of the law according to the priestly tradition, even though they were not all priests.[14] In this role that the Sadducees chose, they differed from and competed with the Pharisees, who were a lay movement wholly independent of priests and Temple. If this role for the Sadducees as promoters of the proper understanding of the cultic system is historically correct, it could account for the sharp denunciation of them in the Mishnah and Talmud by the rabbis, who regarded themselves as the true and proper heirs of the priestly role of legal interpretation.

The Dead Sea Community

Geza Vermes has offered a well-documented and persuasive reconstruction of the movement that produced the Dead Sea Scrolls.[15] The group probably existed in two forms, in gatherings in towns and cities of Judah and in the monastic core that lived at Qumran by the Dead Sea. In both situations, the priests had the central role. The Community Rule (1 QS) provided the regulations for the leadership of the withdrawn group, while the Damascus Document (CD) offered the guidelines for the lay groups. For the true Israel—which the community as a whole considered itself to be—the leaders were the sons of Zadok, who was high priest when the central cult was established in Jerusalem in the time of David (2 Sam. 15–20) and Solomon (1 Kings 1:8, 39–45). In the War Scroll (1 QM; 4 QM), twelve chief priests are to preside over the community, assisted by the Levites (1 QM 2:1–3).[16] But the already existing community at Qumran consisted of twelve men and three priests, who were to be "perfectly versed in all that is revealed of the Law" (1 QS 8:1–4). Ultimate authority throughout the movement rested with the priests, and every group of ten members had to have a priest or Levite (CD 13:3–7). The leader of each congregation in the towns and cities was a priest, as was the "Guardian of All Camps," who was the overseer of the entire movement and all its component groups.

As for the future hopes of the community, the Temple Scroll describes the rebuilt Temple and city, and provides detailed cultic regulations for sacrifices and festival days. Special blessings are promised for the high priests and for all the priests in the appendix to the Scroll of the Rule and the Messianic Rule. The worship of the group as a whole is referred to as "the Temple of the Kingdom." Of the two messianic figures mentioned in these eschatological documents—the Star of Jacob and the Son of Levi—it is the priestly figure who has priority of honor. It is he who first partakes of the messianic banquet of bread and wine. The overarching instruction for the community is that it walk according to the law of the sons of Zadok (the priests).

Although in the period around the turn of the eras there is no radical distinction between the law-abiding model and the Temple cult–oriented model, there is a significant difference in primary focus and emphasis. In the former model, the chief characteristic of the community is ritual purity at the personal level as qualification for participation in the people of God. For the second model, the major attention is given to the proper maintenance of the priestly cult as the guarantee of divine presence and proper relationship between God and his people. A corollary of this cultic emphasis is the dominant theme that the fulfillment of God's purpose for the covenant people will be experienced in a renewed Temple, administered by the properly prepared and fully obedient priesthood and participated in by a pure community. Heavy emphasis falls on the cultic purity of the people who seek to participate in this eschatological access to the God of the covenant, and on the complete fulfillment of standards by the priesthood, whose members serve as mediators between the holy God and his obedient, purified people. The persistence and attraction of this view of the covenant people is now abundantly attested through the Dead Sea Scrolls, which document in illuminating detail the appeal that this understanding of God's people into the first century C.E.

The Community of the Wise

Under the joint impact of the attention given to the law by Ezra following the return from Babylonian exile, the deepening permeation of the Middle East by Hellenistic culture and philosophy in the fourth and third centuries B.C.E., and Jewish loss of political identity following the decline of the Hasmonean dynasty, Judaism in this period sought new ways of reclaiming and reinterpreting its traditions. One of the most potent strategies employed in this situation was to claim and demonstrate that the Creator had given special wisdom to his covenant people. By studying and appropriating this wisdom, they could assure stability in an uncertain world and enduring participation in the purpose of God. Abundant documentation is available for the variety of ways in which Jewish thinkers and writers sought to promote the concept and experience of a community grounded in this divinely provided wisdom.

Ben Sira: Those Who Love the Law

According to Ben Sira,[17] Wisdom is the first of all created beings (1:4–10); she is given abundantly to those who love her, and especially to those who obey the law (1:26). Indeed, those who love the Lord will be filled with the law (2:16), and will be eager to learn more about it (6:18–37). The community of the wise will honor the priests and make the appropriate offerings, showing kindness to the poor and the sorrowing while avoiding conflict with the rich and powerful, with sinners or murderers (9:1–13). Instead, they will consult with the wise and have fellowship with the righteous, who obey the law (9:14–10:5). The reward of this search for wisdom, which will be found by holding to the law, will sustain the true seeker and bring joy and an enduring reputation (14:20–15:10). It is God's wisdom by which the creation was ordered from the beginning. Insight into this truth and an understanding of God's works, as well as an eternal covenant with commandments for a life of love and obedience, have been granted to humans (16:24–17:14). Although all nations have rulers, Israel is unique in that its people are accountable to God alone, who will reward or punish them according to their deeds, while forgiving the penitent among them (17:25–18:14).

Interspersed with the moral exhortations that run throughout the book, Ben Sira keeps describing the special place of wisdom in the life of God's true people. Wisdom, which is the fear of the Lord, is manifest through obedience to the law (19:20–30). Keeping the law results in control of thought and action, in contrast to the boorish ways of the fool (21:11–28). Wisdom personified, who came from the mouth of God, was assigned a dwelling place in Israel: in the tabernacle on Mount Zion, where she flourished and was fruitful (24:1–34). In a pair of images, wisdom is the Book of the Covenant but also the stream that will fructify the people and prepare them for the future ("like prophecy"). God will care for the community of the wise and provide stability for them, because they obey his law (32:24–33); he will restore them to Jerusalem, the city of his sanctuary, and will "fill Zion with celebration" of his wonderful deeds. The result will be that all the earth will know that the Lord is God (36:1–17).

God's wisdom is also manifest through the glory and order of the creation (39:12–35; 42:15–43:33). The climax of this hymn of praise is the assertion that "the Lord has made all things, and to the godly he has granted wisdom." This wisdom is also evident in the course of history, during which God has raised up leaders for his people: Moses and Aaron are the ones through whom the law was given that enlightens Israel (45:3–17). Ecstatic praise is offered to God for Solomon, who is called here "the wise son" (47:12–22). The last to be praised is Simon, the high priest (220–196 B.C.E.) who had restored and improved Temple and city, thereby uniting the people in the worship of God (50:1–21). What is probably the original conclusion to Ben Sira's text (50:27–29) offers the promise what whoever lays to heart the things recorded in this book "will become wise," and "the light of the Lord [will be] his path."

The appendix to the work emphasizes seeking for wisdom (51:13), resolving to live according to wisdom (51:18), and the soul's grappling with wisdom (51:19). In finding wisdom, enduring understanding is gained as well (51:20–21). It is this promise and potential which are the dynamic resource for the community of the wise.[18]

Wisdom of Solomon: Wisdom Enters the Holy Souls

In language and concepts, the Wisdom of Solomon shows the profound influence of Hellenistic culture on the writer and, presumably, on the community of his readers.[19] The opening appeal is not to his own group, however, but to "the rulers of the earth," that they should seek the Lord "with sincerity of heart" (1:1). They are addressed again in Wisd. of Sol. 6:1–11, where they are warned of the severity of judgment that will fall on them if they fail to find wisdom and seek only to exercise their power. Judgment is, however, inescapable for those earthly rulers who abuse the righteous (1:12–16) and thereby have made a covenant with death. They live for the pleasure of the moment, exploiting the poor and the helpless, since they have totally misunderstood God's purpose in the creation of human beings. Although the righteous "seem to have died," they are actually in God's hands and will have an eternal role when God's rule dominates the world (3:1–9). "God's grace and mercy are with the elect, and he watches over his holy ones," but the ungodly, who seem now to prosper, are doomed to destruction (4:7–15). The wicked powers cannot understand why the faithful who have died are now "numbered among the sons of God." Yet the latter will live forever and be rewarded by God, who will destroy their enemies (5:15–23), including the proud earthly rulers who have abused God's people (6:1–11).

Using imagery similar to that found in the Greco-Roman Isis literature, Wisdom is depicted as an attractive and gracious woman (6:12–16). To love her is to seek instruction and to keep her laws (6:17–20). In the author's choice of illustrative accounts of the historical experience of God's people in the Pentateuch, heavy emphasis falls on Israel's struggles in and deliverance from Egypt, which may be an indication of the Egyptian (Alexandrian?) provenance of this work.

Writing as Solomon, the author promises to portray the role of Wisdom from creation throughout the history of God's people (6:21–25), but first he describes how he sought and found her (7:7–14). In depicting her role as revelatory agent of God, he borrows technical terms from the Platonic and Stoic philosophical traditions as he describes her role in the order of nature and as the instrument of disclosure of the very being of God (7:15–8:21). Wisdom must be sought from God: she will be sent to earnest seekers. She is God's holy spirit (9:1–18). She it was who worked in the human scene of history to achieve God's purpose and to establish the faithful community: through Noah, Abraham, Jacob, Joseph, and Moses (10:1–21). It was she who enabled Moses to achieve the liberation of Israel from Egypt and to enter the new land, and who effected judgment on the wicked and idolaters who resisted God's purpose for his people (11:1–19:21). The history of the covenant people is the supreme testimony to the power and purpose of divine wisdom. The errors of the ruthless, scheming earthly powers stand in sharpest contrast to God's exaltation of the people who perceive and obey his purpose.

Compared with the wisdom of Ben Sira, a significant shift is evident in the perspective of the community that stands behind the Wisdom of Solomon. The emphasis in Ben Sira on the specifics of obedience to the law as the sign of wisdom within the community has been replaced by a more intellectual and theoretical approach that stresses the universality and timelessness of the divine purpose embodied in the eternal wisdom disclosed to the community. To express these cosmic truths, the author borrows freely from the culture of his contemporaries, the Hellenistic philosophers. The historical situation of the writer may be the mid-first century B.C.E., when the Romans assumed control over the eastern Mediterranean world, imposing their military might, culture, and religious traditions. This document would provide encouragement to the threatened Jewish community, but would also serve as an effective witness to the Roman intellectuals as to the breadth and depth of the Jewish understanding of God and his working in the world.

Apocalyptic Wisdom

The crisis in Israel that precipitated the formulation of an apocalyptic worldview and produced the first documents in that genre—Daniel and 1 Enoch—was a combination of two factors: an aggressive policy of the Seleucid ruler, Antiochus IV (175–163 B.C.E.), coercing Jews into conformity with Hellenistic culture in the service of consolidating his control over his kingdom; and profound disillusionment among many Jews with the Maccabean leaders, who were successful in military opposition to Antiochus, but who thereupon adopted secular and ruthless strategies to enforce their positions of power among their own people. Yet the crisis of the Maccabean era did not create this mode of understanding God's purpose for his people. Indeed, antecedents for this movement within Judaism go back to the mid-third century B.C.E., as Martin Hengel has pointed out.[20] It seems to have been then that conventicles were formed by those who sought to celebrate and appropriate for their own time the prophetic tradition.

Protoapocalyptic Writings: The Isaiah Apocalypse and the Zechariah Apocalypse

Inserted within the prophecies attributed by scholarly consensus[21] to the eighth-century-B.C.E. prophet Isaiah of Jerusalem (Isa. 1–35) are oracles that in style and content seem to come from a later period and resemble the perspective and rhetorical style of apocalyptic: Isa. 13–14, 24–27, and 30:19–26.[22] Michael Fishbane has shown that the central concern in transmitting a prophetic tradition was the relevance of the message for the changed conditions of the people of God, rather than preservation of the actual words of the original prophet.[23] What we might call supplementation and alteration of the words of the prophet were regarded by the editors in later centuries as demonstrations of the significance of the prophet's message in the people's new circumstances. Thus, following the exile of the northern tribes of Israel by the Assyrians, the subsequent exile of Judah by the Babylonians, and the disappointing results of Judah's return to the land by the Persians, the promise of renewal was not abandoned but recast in a cosmic framework. Not merely God's people, but also the whole of creation are to be transformed in fulfilment of the prophetic promises initially pronounced by Isaiah of Jerusalem.

Isaiah 13–14 describes the divine destruction visited on Babylon (13:1) and Assyria (14:24–25), which will be accompanied by geological and astral disturbances as the wrath of God is poured out on the enemies of his people. In addition to the restoration of Israel to the land, God will bring along with them proselytes ("aliens") to join the community of God's people (14:1–2). The powers of evil, here represented by the names of the Canaanite deities "Day Star" and "Dawn," will be cast down from the heights, and God will exercize control over all the nations and their rulers (14:12–21, 26).

The prose section in Isa. 30:19–26 is widely regarded as a commentary on 30:18, which calls for patient waiting for God's deliverance of his people. The difficulties they experience ("the bread of adversity, the water of affliction," 30:20) are part of the divine plan for their renewal. Their "teacher"—who could be God or a prophet or a divinely endowed interpreter of God's message for his people—will show them the way they are to take. The world of nature will be renewed, with unprecedented luxury combined with cosmic bounty as the Lord "binds up the hurt of his people" (30:26).

Isaiah 24 depicts the utter desolation of both the created and the social order that will sweep the earth and bring an end to "the city of chaos," which is apparently a symbol of the pagan powers (Assyria and Babylon) that have harassed God's people. But the punishment extends to the powers of evil and the disobedient "host of heaven" and will continue until "the Lord of Hosts" assumes power in Jerusalem in the presence of the elders of his people (24:23). God's triumph over the enemies of his people and his care for the poor and oppressed will lead even some from among the Gentiles to trust in Israel's God (25:1–5). Unprecedented plenty and rejoicing on "the mountain of the Lord" will be shared by those who have "waited" for him to come to their aid (25:6–9). Conversely, Israel's enemies will be ground down in defeat (25:10–12). Using the imagery of 2 Isaiah, this oracle describes the joy and peace that characterize the life of the renewed people, and then contrasts the hopeless doom of the wicked with the divine deliverance of the faithful, using imagery drawn from the pangs of childbirth (26:18) and promising life for the dead (26:19). After a brief, vivid picture of the defeat of the serpent-dragon symbolizing the powers of evil, the oracle builds on the image of Isa. 5:1–7, in which Israel is depicted as God's unfruitful vineyard, promising now that God will protect it and cause those who "make peace" with him to bear fruit that will fill the earth (27:1–6). The punishment of those who exiled and oppressed Israel will be greater than God's chastising of his people. The suffering of the latter accomplished expiation of their sins (27:9), but the destruction of the capital of their oppressors and its land will be total and without compassion. The final lines of this apocalypse promise restoration of both the exiles by the Euphrates and those Jews living in lands of the dispersion, such as beside the Nile (37:12–13). All will be brought back to their own land to worship God on Mount Zion.

Similarly, in Zechariah 9–14, there is an expansion and modification of the prophecies of Zechariah, which are explicitly linked with the Persian rulers' facilitating the return of the Jews from exile in Babylon (Zech. 1:1; 7:1). While the first section of this book (Zech. 1–8) focuses on the rebuilding of the Temple and the restoration of the monarchy (6:9–14), the apocalyptic portion (9–14) begins with a description of the punishment that God will bring on the cities of Syria and the Mediterranean coast—presumably referring to the takeover of this part of the world by Alexander the Great in the later fourth century B.C.E. (Zech. 9:1–8). In contrast, the Messiah is depicted as an agent of peace among the nations of the world (9:9–10). God will bring his people back from the lands where his judgment has scattered them (Zech. 10:9–12). Both pagan rulers and the leaders of God's people fall under judgment for their exploitation of the people under their authority (Zech. 11). The liberation and vindication of God's people will be accompanied by punishment of the surrounding nations that have harassed Israel, while Jerusalem will be the scene of the outpouring of God's compassion and healing on the faithful and penitent and on their leaders ("the house of David," 12:7–10). The land will be purged of idolaters and false prophets (13:2–6). Only a third of those who claim to belong to God will be acknowledged by him (13:7–9). The final scene is that of God bringing to an end the attack of the nations on Jerusalem and its people. The terrain itself will be transformed, and God's rulership will be established over all the earth (14:1–9). All nations will be invited to come annually to Jerusalem to participate in the festival of booths,[24] and the nonparticipants will be punished (14:16–19). The city and all its vessels for containing food and drink will be holy (14:20–21), thereby demonstrating the accomplishment of God's purpose to fashion a holy people.

These late additions to the prophetic writings show that God's purpose for renewal of his people will benefit the faithful and obedient, not only among birthright Israelites, but also among Gentiles who turn in faith to the God of the covenant. Crucial in preparing for the coming of this new era of liberation and holiness are the priests, but especially the prophets or oracles through whom the redefined message of Israel's destiny is communicated.

Early Apocalyptic Writings: Daniel and 1 Enoch

In the first six chapters of Daniel, the stories of Daniel's courage and the ensuing divine deliverance show how God preserves his people when they refuse to submit to non-Israelite rulers' efforts to impose practices in violation of the traditional Jewish law.[25] Although it was Cyrus who first seized power over the Babylonians, Daniel cites Darius for his testimony to the universal sovereignty of the God of Israel (6:26–27). The second half of this apocalypse (Dan. 7–12) offers visions of the end of the present age, which culminate in the triumph of God's purpose in the destruction of the wicked powers (Antiochus IV), the emergence of God's agent for the renewal of his people and of divine rule over the world ("one like a son of man," 7:13), and the vindication of the faithful community ("the saints of the Most High," 7:18, 23, 27). Insight as to what God is about to do is given only to the elect, obedient people of God, and is communicated through the angel Gabriel (9:22–23). The difficulties and sufferings experienced by the covenant people are the consequence of their disobedience to the law of Moses (9:11). Initially, the visions and the explanation of them are granted to Daniel alone (10:7–14, 21; 11:1–12:13), but he then passes on this revelation to the faithful remnant of God's people. The final battles take place on two levels: the angels battle the cosmic powers of evil, but these are symbols for the successive oriental and Hellenistic rulers who have oppressed Israel. A crowning feature of the divine vindication that is promised is the resurrection of the dead and the glorification of the faithful (12:2–3). These insights Daniel is to keep secret until the time of the end (12:4). Meanwhile, there is an appeal to the people to gain and maintain their purity. The contrast in comprehension is clear: "None of the wicked shall understand, but those who are wise shall understand" (12:10). Wisdom here is a matter of secret disclosure reserved for the elect and holy.

The so-called Book of Enoch (or 1 Enoch) is actually a collection of writings attributed to Enoch, the righteous one who was taken up to heaven according to Gen. 5:18–24. Based on the fact that portions of this material found at Qumran date back to the third century B.C.E. and that portions appear in such second-century-B.C.E. writings as Jubilees, it is evident that the Enoch tradition antedates the book of Daniel. Later sections of 1 Enoch, however, are perhaps contemporary with Daniel, and the much-discussed Similitudes of Enoch (37–71), no fragments of which were found at Qumran, may be as late as the first half of the first century C.E.[26] Of the four remaining sections of 1 Enoch, the oldest seems to be the Book of Watchers (1–36). There the major concern is with the final judgment of the wicked and the vindication of the righteous that will occur when God comes as judge of all. The criterion for judgment is obedience to the law.[27] God gives wisdom to the just so that they will know what he expects of humans and what he is going to do in order to set right the creation. The watchers seem to be the failed leaders of God's people; Enoch alone has the truth, because he was righteous and was taken up to God in order to receive a revelation of God's plan for his people.

The Astronomical Book (Enoch 72–82), which is also pre-Maccabean, gives details of the movements and the timing of the heavenly bodies, which serve to attest the certainty of God's control and plan for the history of the cosmos and of his people. The Book of Dreams (83–90) offers an allegorical sketch of biblical history, including the rule of seventy shepherds, an era that is divided into four periods and culminates in the deliverance of the small lambs (= the faithful) through the agency of the "great horn," probably a reference to Judas Maccabeus, who accomplished the liberation of Israel from Hellenistic rule in 165 B.C.E. The Epistle (91–108) is composite, including not only woes against the sinners and exhortations to the righteous, but an Apocalypse of Weeks (93:1–10; 91:11–17).[28] There history is divided into ten periods, or "weeks," of which the first six trace the origins of Israel, the giving of the law, and the progressive disobedience of the people. The depths of apostasy appear in the seventh week, which ends in divine deliverance of the faithful and elect. In the eighth week, the wicked are destroyed, in the ninth, the divine judgment on the wicked world is announced, and in the tenth week, the corrupt watchers fall under the divine curse. In place of this degeneration of the created order, God will establish in the end the new heaven and the new order of righteousness. Sinners will be burned with fire, but those who love God will be changed into the people of light (108:1–15).

The Similitudes of Enoch (37–71) echo the main themes of the rest of this Enoch literature: wisdom comes only from God, and is reserved for the elect and faithful (37:1–38:6); doom is to fall on the earth, the wicked, the evil angels, Satan, and the earthly rulers (65:1–67:13). All the secrets about these future events have been revealed to Enoch in heaven; he is to convey to the elect the promise of peace and union of God's people (71:1–17). What is distinctive in this section of Enoch is the role of the Son of Man, who is God's agent to accomplish this plan of cosmic renewal (46:1–8; 48:1–10). His identity ("name") is known only to God

(69:16–29), but Enoch is enabled to see him already enthroned, as well as God's heavenly place for the righteous community (70:1–4). Although the Similitudes of Enoch share with the rest of 1 Enoch and Daniel the belief that God is disclosing his purpose to the faithful remnant of his people and promising them a new life in the renewed creation, only in the Similitudes is there a special agent who will have a distinctive role in this renewal of God's sovereignty. As in Daniel, the human leaders who are harming and seeking to corrupt God's people are to be judged and replaced by God's own agent.

Later Apocalypses: Jubilees, 2 Enoch, 2 Baruch, and 4 Ezra

The qualities of apocalyptic that are discernible in such basic examples as Daniel and 1 Enoch include pseudonymity, claiming to be a revelation granted by God to a heroic figure of the past; the private nature of the revelation, first to the chosen intermediary and then to the elect minority among those who claim to be God's people; the review of world history in periods as determined by God; and the aim to warn, instruct, and encourage the faithful people.[29] All these features are present in the representative apocalypses here discussed, which date from the first century B.C.E. to the late first or second century C.E.

Since the discovery of fragments of Jubilees among the Dead Sea Scrolls, as well as quotations from and allusions to it in the Qumran writings, it has been reasonable to assume that this work was produced between 175 and 100 B.C.E. In Jubilees is emphasized the distinctiveness of Israel from all other nations: chosen by God (1:28), selected over all other peoples (2:21), marked by circumcision (15:11) and by participation in the sabbaths and festivals, and ruled by God alone (15:32). The strategy of the book is evident from its extended title quoted in the Damascus Document: "The book of the divisions of the times according to their jubilees and weeks." God's control of history and the creation is evident in his detailed ordering of the times and seasons. The book claims to have been written by Moses after he copied down the law of God at Sinai. In it is sketched the history of Israel from the day of creation to the new creation, when the powers of evil will be overcome, the true sanctuary will be built in Jerusalem, and the lights there will symbolize the healing, peace, and eternal blessing of Israel (1:1–29). In the divinely determined history of the people of God, the northern tribes appear only as villains, while Levi (the priest) and Judah (the king) are the representatives of leadership for the covenant people. The dominant feature of this book is that God is in total control of time, and hence of the events that will bring about the defeat of his enemies and the accomplishment of his purpose for the faithful remnant of his people.

Second Enoch is the name given in modern times to a document that seems to have been written while the Temple still stood and its program of sacrifices was being carried out by the priests. This fits the injunction to go to the Temple three times daily (2 Enoch 51–52). As in Jubilees, the chronology of human history is divinely determined (35), and God has disclosed his purpose to Enoch, who was taken up into the divine presence and given books in which to record the divine plan: the boundaries of the heavens, the movements of the heavenly bodies, the heavenly spaces, the cycles and seasons, the plants, and the elements (36–40). But all humanity is depraved and awaiting judgment, from which only the faithful will be delivered as they come to understand God's purpose through Enoch's books (41–44). Meanwhile, the obedient are to persevere in spite of assault and persecution, so that they may share in the final endless age (49–50), which will be free of darkness and corruption (65). Emphasis falls on the priestly role, as fulfilled by Methusaleh (69) and by the series of successors of Melchizedek, which will culminate in a great archpriest, the Word and Power of God, who will serve as king and priest over the renewed earth (71).

Second Baruch, or the Apocalypse of Baruch, comes from the time after the destruction of the Temple in 70 C.E., but the basic themes of the earlier apocalypses are sounded. Baruch has been given insight into the divine purpose at work in Israel's past history (the four successive kingdoms, 35–43), and how the culmination will come in the kingdom of the Messiah, which will last forever. The faithful will be vindicated, and are now instructed how they are to behave in the transition from present disaster to future blessing when God's servant assumes control (53–76). Israel—minus the apostates—alone has access to the Mighty One, to his revealed plan for history, and to his law, which is to guide his obedient people (85).

Fourth Ezra in its present form seems to include a later introduction (1:1–2:48) and an appendix (15:1–16:78), which may come from as late as the third century C.E.[30] Central in the basic document are the questions, Why does God allow evil and How long will he permit it to operate? The answer to these questions is to be found only in the future, when God acts directly in history, destroys the enemies of his people, and places in authority his son, the Messiah, whose reign will last for four hundred years (7:26–44). Then all humans will be called to account. Reworking Daniel's visions of four kingdoms, the four kings here depicted are the three Flavian emperors (Vespasian, Titus, and Domitian), to be followed by the "Lion" (= Messiah), also pictured as the man from the sea (13:25–56). Ezra has been granted this role as mediator of the divine revelation because he searched out God's law and devoted his life to wisdom and understanding. As in 2 Enoch, the role of Moses is linked with that of the seer of the end time (14). The people are summoned to discipline their hearts and minds so that they may be delivered by God as they pass through the time of unprecedented stress that lies ahead. In addition to the twenty-four public books (the Jewish scriptures), Ezra treasures the seventy secret books that are for the wise alone (14:45). Punishment lies ahead for the wicked and the indifferent, but vindication for the disciplined and faithful (15–16). Wisdom here is not human understanding, but the consequence of divine disclosure.

Included among the Dead Sea Scrolls were portions of the Book of Enoch.[31] But in the unique apocalyptic material from Qumran there is an even more radically separatist view of the consummation of the divine purpose than in most other apocalyptic writings. In the Qumran documents, the community is represented as convinced that God had called its members to make known to the elect alone the divine plan for the renewal of the people of God and for the accomplishment of the divine purpose in the world. The Damascus Document (CD 1), which is likely the earliest of the group's surviving documents, describes the infidelity of Israel as a whole ("they were unfaithful and forsook him"), which led to God's punishment of them through the exile in Babylon ("He delivered them up to the sword . . . [and] gave them into the hand of Nebuchadnezzar"). But it also reports how God had given to a "remnant," who had been "groping for the way," both insight into and a leadership role in achievement of his purpose through the Teacher of Righteousness who would "guide them in the way of God's heart."

Although the message of God's purpose was to be proclaimed diligently and was to be made available to "simple folk,"[32] the insights it contained would be grasped and become normative only for the members of the new community: "Hear now, my children, and I will uncover your eyes that you may see and understand the works of God, that you choose that which pleases him and reject that which he hates, that you may walk perfectly in all his ways and not follow after the thoughts of the guilt inclination and the lust of the eyes. For through them, great men have gone astray and mighty heroes have stumbled from former times until now. Because they walked in stubbornness of heart the Heavenly Watchers fell; they were caught because they did not keep the commandments of God." After noting that from the first only a minority (including Noah and Abraham) obeyed God, and after recounting the consequences of the apostasy of the majority of the covenant people, the rule continues: "But with the remnant which held fast to the commandments of God he made his covenant with Israel forever, revealing to them the hidden things in which all Israel had gone astray. He unfolded before them his holy sabbaths and his glorious feasts, the testimonies of his righteousness and the ways of his truth, and the desires of his will which a man must do in order to live."[33]

There follows a contrast between the priests and Levites on the one hand, who forfeited their relationship with God, and the "sons of Zadok" on the other, who are the true "elect of Israel." What is called for among the people, therefore, is penitence—an emphasis echoed in Dan. 9:4–29. The successive epochs of wickedness are running their course (1 Enoch 90:6), containing seven weeks of years in 1 Enoch 93 and seventy weeks of years in Dan. 9:24–27. Changing the image of the divinely determined sequence of the ages, the successive oppressive kingdoms of the world are to be replaced by the kingdom or rule of God (Dan. 7:1–27), which is to be assigned to "one like a human being" (in contrast to the wild beasts that symbolize the world empires) or to "the holy ones of God."

Social Aspects of Jewish Apocalyptic

A recent scholarly project analyzing the literature regarded as apocalyptic offered the following definition of an apocalypse: "A genre of revelatory literature with a narrative framework, in which a revelation is mediated by an otherworldly being to a human recipient, disclosing a transcendent reality which is both temporal, insofar as it envisages eschatological salvation, and spatial insofar as it involves another, supernatural world."[34] David Hellholm's proposal for an addition to this definition makes an essential point: that this type of literature is more than an individual authorial pastime. As Hellholm suggests, apocalyptic is "intended for a group in crisis with the purpose of exhortation and/or consolation by means of divine authority."[35]

George Nickelsburg has offered an extended series of questions that should be addressed to all documents regarded as candidates for the Jewish apocalyptic genre.[36] They may be summarized (partly as questions, partly as statements) as follows: Does the author employ vague and stereotyped language, or can we infer the kind of political, economic, cultural, and religious circumstances that created the sense of alienation, deprivation, and victimization reflected in the writing? Is there evidence of political persecution or economic oppression? Are the culprits Jews or Gentiles? Is the issue the Temple, the priesthood, the calendar, or some specifics of the law? Are these factors linked with known historical situations? How does the author respond? What attitudes and behavior are enjoined—waiting, cursing, pacifism, retreat, militancy, gathering the community? Is the community seen as "the righteous," in contrast to "the wicked"? Are they the elect, the eschatological community? Are they the sole locus of salvation? If so, what led to this community definition and organization? Is a new Temple needed? If so, why? What is the strategy envisioned to achieve these ends? What is the dynamic of an apocalyptic community? What is its leadership structure?

Approaching these matters interrogatively rather than with preset categories enables one to avoid coercing the evidence. It also helps to discern the different ways in which apocalyptic documents function, given the different nature of the communities in which they were produced. One might underscore the importance of community definition, which must itself be regarded as a line of development rather than a fixed entity. These data and methodological guidelines will shape my inquiry as, in the following chapters of this study, I turn to examine the range of models of community evident within the New Testament and other early Christian literature.

Prophecy and Consummation of Divine Purpose in Hellenistic and Roman Culture

The wider Greco-Roman world provided abundant analogies to these developments within Judaism, as David Aune has shown.[37] The Pythian oracles were not addressed simply to the immediate situation, but pointed to meanings reaching far into the future. Plato, Aune notes, regarded the *theomanteis* (inspired mantics) and the *chresmodoi* (oracle singers) as instruments through whom the gods spoke and was convinced that prophets were necessary to interpret their utterances.[38] From the fifth through the second century B.C.E., there were mediums who revealed the unknown in a state of possession. The modes of communication included oracular questions and responses, riddles, beatitudes, and letters. Their aims were conveying information and confirming both persons and statements. In the fifth century B.C.E., Herodotus knew of collections of oracles, and such sources are quoted by Pausanias and Plutarch.

I shall consider below how one of the major modes of oracular communication was adapted and exploited by the Jews: the Sibylline Oracles. But it is important to examine some material from Greek sources that resembles Jewish apocalyptic in significant ways. Walter Burkert states that apocalyptic is thoroughly operative in classical Greek literature,[39] although this conclusion is denied by some. In Plato's *Republic*, an ultimate system of the universe, with rewards and punishments, moves toward the overcoming of the powers of evil. Although this fulfillment is seen as taking place without direct divine intervention, it moves in an unalterable circle that includes justice and necessity. Later Greek thinkers foresaw cycles of rebirth of the natural order, although only the Stoics predicted that the cycles would end in *ekpyrosis* (cosmic conflagration). Burkert believes that Hesiod's notion of successive ages of history shared with the author of Daniel an Aramaic source, for which he finds documentation in an inscription from Deir Alla (ca. 700 B.C.E.). J. Gwyn Griffiths's essay "Apocalyptic in the Hellenistic Era" points to documents that share basic features with apocalyptic, including the third-century-B.C.E. Demotic Chronicle (which describes the destiny of Egypt in the Persian and Ptolemaic periods), the second-century-B.C.E. Archive of Hor (which combines astronomy and astrology to foretell the future), and the second-century-B.C.E. Oracle of the Potter, which describes the military, political, and natural woes that Egypt will suffer, culminating in the fall of Alexandria and the coming of a savior-king, son of Isis and Horus, who will bring peace to all the earth.[40]

The mid-third-century-B.C.E. Babylonian priest-historian Berossus has been characterized by Jonathan Z. Smith as an astronomer, astrologer, apocalypticist related to the Babylonian sibyl, and historian "of the cosmos from creation to the final catastrophe." Scribal intellectuals like Berossus filled "an invaluable role in the administration of their people in both religious and political affairs." They were guardians of the cultural heritage, intellectual innovators, world travelers who brought about a cross-cultural flow of wisdom, lawyers, doctors, astrologers, diviners, magicians, scientists, court functionaries, linguists, exegetes, and so forth. Their religious and nationalistic outlook was placed in a cosmic setting through the appropriation of traditional mythology and its transmutation into a view of creation moving through divinely determined cycles, culminating in a process of decline, and returning to watery chaos and ultimate renewal. In the Potter's Oracle, the early form of expectation that the king will bring order out of chaos and thus recreate the world has been replaced by the vision of a king sent by the goddess (Isis), in whose hands is all historical action. By incorporating the notion of the divinely determined cycles of years, there is set forth a new portrait of a cosmic renewal, details of which have been disclosed through the wisdom granted to the chosen agent of the divine.[41]

Astrology

According to Josephus,[42] it was Berossus who in the mid-third century B.C.E. introduced priestly astrology to the Greeks, establishing a school at Cos, although Josephus also claims that Abraham was knowledgeable in astrological matters. While the oldest extant horoscope dates from 410 B.C.E., astrology seems to have reached its peak in the Hellenistic-Roman period, when Chaldean astrologers explained Alexander's successful invasion of the Middle East on astrological grounds.[43] The two goals of astrology were mystical participation in the universe and scientific and mathematical knowledge of it. Stars and planets influenced every facet of life: family, love, prosperity, journeys. By the first century B.C.E., the leaders of Rome—Caesar, Pompey, and Crassus—gained support from astrologers, fostering the belief that the stars and planets controlled human destiny. Posidonius of Apamea combined this view with an affirmation of the Stoic notions of *ekpyrosis* and *palingenesia* (rebirth), a thesis incorporated in the Fourth Eclogue of Vergil. Octavius was able to exploit the appearance of a comet to show the assumption of Julius Caesar into heaven and the divine approval of his own accession to power. As Cranmer has phrased it, "'Scientific' astrology provided humanists with the link between mundane causality and the cosmic laws which regulated the movements of the stars and ruled the universe."[44]

In the Jewish literature of the Hellenistic-Roman period, there is evidence of contradictory attitudes toward astrology. In the Testament of Solomon there is a warning against astrology as the work of demons, and the houses of the zodiac are their dwelling places (2:2), while the thirty-six heavenly bodies are the loci of demonic activity in the world. In 1 Enoch 8:3, astrology is denounced as having been taught to humans by fallen angels. But the Astronomical Book contained in 1 Enoch (72–82) uses features of the zodiac, and the Treatise of Shem (late first century B.C.E.) advocates astrology, with its twelve chapters corresponding to the zodiacal houses.[45] Documents from Qumran show the influence on individuals of the position of the stars at their birth (4 Q 186).[46]

The Sibylline Oracles

As noted above, the Jewish Sibylline Oracles represent a borrowing of a genre highly regarded among the Greeks and Romans.[47] These writings show an expectation of disaster to be followed by a world transformation, although they do not develop the schema of a succession of kingdoms or epochs, as in apocalyptic literature. They emphasize elements common to Hellenistic religions and Judaism, and are critical chiefly of idolatry and immorality. They expect a savior king and the renewal of the purified Temple, in which potentially all seeking people of the world can participate.[48] Book 3 of the oracles pictures Cleopatra as bringing to an end the Ptolemaic line, to be replaced by the Romans, while Book 5 was written between the destruction of the Temple and the Bar Kochba revolt—probably before 115 C.E.[49] The attitude toward the Gentile culture moves from an optimistic apologetic for Hellenism to a nationalist hatred of the dominant power and a hope of divine deliverance by sources outside history. Yet even in their bitterness toward Rome, the oracles continue to use the images of politics and nature drawn from Greco-Roman culture and to see continuity between this special revelation and what God has disclosed to the wider world. These books end with a cosmic conflagration rather than a cosmic renewal. The earlier universalistic affirmations are replaced by the expectation of divine intervention to vindicate God's people, even while hoping that interested Gentiles may see the truth of these visions and share in the ultimate vindication.[50]

The Cynic Tradition

In a study of Cynicism, Ragnar Hoistad points out a number of features that have counterparts in the apocalyptic expectations expressed in post-Maccabean Jewish documents such as Daniel, as well as in the gospel portraits of Jesus.[51] This study has been largely ignored by scholars exploring the links between Cynicism and early Christianity.

The evidence Hoistad adduces shows the inaccuracy of the current effort of some scholars to portray the Cynics as antisocial critics of the values of the sociopolitical establishment, expressing their criticisms in clever aphorisms.[52] Hoistad documents from Crates (late fourth century B.C.E., a pupil of Diogenes) the central concern of the Cynics for sociopolitical values. The ruler is to be primarily an instructor (*paidagogos*), who derives his highest ethical values on the basis of his own self-chosen poverty, a prerequisite for inner freedom. This Cynic saint is a reconciler and spiritual guide, whose punishment of evil is not performed in a spirit of proud superiority. Instead, he calls the people to a new kingdom, an ideal community in which there is no war or wickedness, and to a simple way of life in accord with strict moral demands. The king abases himself, aware that his protests and criticisms will result in physical abuse and suffering that he must endure. In his severe moral struggle, he takes the role of a servant, becoming—paradoxically—a poor and suffering king, but he remains confident that he will at last be raised above all the adversities that plague the social world around him.[53]

Roman Stoic Speculation about the Future

Concurrent with the life of the Qumran community from mid-second century B.C.E. to around 70 C.E. is the Latin literature that shows in detail how Stoic thinkers were wrestling with many of the same issues dominating the writings of the Jewish apocalyptists. Two well-known writers of this period exemplify the efforts of leading Roman thinkers to deal with the issue of divine purpose and action in human history in terms of Stoic philosophy: Cicero and Seneca. Both were involved in the struggles at the political center of the Roman Empire: Cicero at the time of its establishment, and Seneca when a leadership crisis arose at the end of the Julio-Claudian succession of emperors. Both were central wisdom figures at the heart of the developing empire.

The importance of the issue of a divine purpose at work in human history is highlighted in Cicero's treatise *On the Nature of the Gods* and is then more directly addressed in his work *On Divination*. Although he asserts that he does not share the conviction that the divine purpose for the world is disclosed through oracles, dreams, and other modes of divination, he documents fully how deeply engrained these beliefs were in the minds of Stoics in the first century B.C.E. Balbus, who represents the Stoic position in *De natura deorum*, first makes a case for the rational ordering of the universe by the gods. In the course of describing the spherical form of the divine nature, he pictures the movement of the world as also spherical, and corresponding to it is the "great year" when the heavenly bodies complete their prescribed courses and return to their original relative positions. Only humans have been granted the gift of prophecy and divination. Through auguries, oracles, dreams, and portents, "the power or art or instinct has clearly been bestowed by the immortal gods on man, and on no other creature, for the ascertainment of future events" (2.65). Oracles, including the sibyllines, show that the gods disclose the future as a warning and a counsel to humanity (2.3–4). The stars are divine, possessing consciousness and an intelligence that is evident in their orderly motion. Divine nature is spherical and its motion is rotary, which accounts for the return of the heavenly bodies to their position at the beginning of the era (2.15–20).

In *De Divinatione*, Cicero notes the universality of the belief that the gods communicate concerning the future through divinatory signs, as is evident among Assyrians, Babylonians, and Greeks. He describes the importance of the augurs in Rome since its founding by Romulus, the appointment of supervisors for the sibylline oracles, and of *auspices* on all important state issues. He recalls the belief in this phenomenon of divine communication by Socrates, Plato, and Aristotle, as well as the importance of the oracles at Delphi and Cumae for deciding state issues. Although he reports a scathing criticism by Cotta, he commends the Stoics for the skill of their arguments and leaves judgment about the truth to the thoughtful inquirer.

In the mid-first century C.E., Seneca shows no trace of skepticism or ambivalence about divine disclosure of the future. In *On Providence*, Seneca affirms the universality of divine order and explains human suffering and hardship as divine discipline, since "God hardens, reviews and disciplines those whom he approves, whom he loves."[54] In *To Marcia on the Death of Her Son*, Seneca describes how the world renews itself over and over within the bounds of time, with cyclic conflagrations and renewal of the creation (21:1–3). The soul struggles for release from the body in order to ascend to the place from which it came, a place of eternal peace, where all is bright and pure (24:5). In *On the Shortness of Life* (19.1), Seneca asks about the fate that awaits the soul "where nature lays us to rest when we are free from the body."[55]

The divine determination of the course of history is affirmed in Roman culture at the outset of the empire by Vergil, as I have noted above. In the *Aeneid* he traces the origins of Rome back to Troy, thereby demonstrating the continuity of the purpose of the gods in human history. More enigmatic but also more complex is his Fourth Eclogue, in which he describes the birth of Caesar Augustus as a divinely ordained child ("offspring of the gods, mighty seed of Jupiter") who in maturity will bring in a new and joyous era of human existence, recalling the reign of the Olympian deities. All this has been heralded through the sibyl at Cumae: the new age of peace, prosperity, and plenty is about to begin. The revelation from the gods voices the hope of cosmic renewal through a divinely chosen and empowered royal agent, in direct (though unconscious) analogy to the hopes of the Jewish apocalypticists.

Communities of Mystical Participation

If one understands mysticism to be knowledge and experience of God through contemplation, considerable evidence of this religious mode may be discerned in Judaism from postexilic times into the Roman period. I shall survey some representative examples in literature from this era.

The Song of Songs

The image of marriage for Israel's covenant relationship with God appears in its most familiar context in Hosea 1–3, where the point is the infidelity of Israel to Yahweh, as it is in Isaiah's and Jeremiah's description of the disobedient nation as a whore (Isa. 1:21; Jer. 3:1–5). In Proverbs 7, faithfulness to wisdom (which is embodied in the commandments) is contrasted with yielding to the blandishments of other claims ("seductive speech"). On the positive side, in Proverbs 8 Wisdom prepares a feast and sends out maidservants to invite "the simple" to come and share in the bounty. In Wisd. of Sol. 8:2, she is loved and sought as a bride. But in Song of Songs, where the terms for wisdom do not appear, the relationship depicted is purely erotic.[56] Detailed similarities between the imagery of the Song and that of Canaanite mythology have been demonstrated by Marvin Pope.[57]

In his study of Origen's homilies on the Song of Songs, O. Rousseau observes that the Tannaitic rabbis rejected the literal, erotic interpretation of the Song of Songs, insisting rather that it is completely holy: Israel is the nation chosen as the bride of God.[58] By the early third century C.E., Origen had adapted that view of the Song, interpreting the bride to be either the soul made in God's image or the church.[59] Even the location of the Song within the canon is significant, since it is the last of three works of Solomon ranging from moral discipline (Proverbs) through the world of nature (Ecclesiastes) to the contemplative realm (Song of Songs).[60] Indeed, the whole canon of scripture is structured by seven songs it contains, beginning with the Pentateuch and the historical works and reaching a climax in the Song of Songs.[61] The insights that this book provides are not for the immature but "solid food for the perfect." The fleshly are to be discouraged from reading the book, since Solomon here is pressing on "to the invisible and eternal teachings given to the spiritual senses" to fulfill the human longing for "the unseen things which are eternal [2 Cor 4:18]."[62] In his analysis of mystical knowledge in the works of Origen, Henri Crouzel observes that for this patristic philosopher-exegete, divine truth is accessible to humans only through scripture as a gift of divine light, and allegorical exegesis is the essential means by which human intelligence can attain to knowledge of the divine mystery.[63]

Finding the antecedents of Origen's interpretation in the work of Clement of Alexandria, Charles Bigg noted more than a century ago in the opening chapter of his classic study *The Christian Platonists of Alexandria* that Jews in that city were powerfully influenced by the three main modes of Greek philosophy: Platonic, Aristotelian, and Stoic.[64] Subsequent study has confirmed and more fully documented his thesis, but has also shown that this impact of Hellenistic culture on Judaism is evident in the Hellenistic-Roman period not only in Egypt but widely throughout Judaism, including Palestine itself.[65] Additional evidence of the use of allegory within Judaism of the second century C.E. is provided by 4 Ezra, where the Song of Songs is perceived as depicting God's choice of his people and the special covenant relationship with them (5:23–30). It is in the writings of Philo, however, that we find the fullest documentation of this cross-cultural phenomenon.

Philo of Alexandria

Philo regards as essential preparation for God's taking up his earthly dwelling place in the soul that foundations be laid "in natural excellence and good teaching," which he sees as provided by the basic curriculum of Hellenistic learning: grammar, literature, geometry, music, and rhetoric. The goal of education is not personal gratification or private illumination, however. Rather, when such a house is built, "laws and ordinances from heaven" will descend to renew human life, and a new mode of communal life will emerge, which will be characterized by love of virtue and true happiness.[66] The key to the attainment of peace and prosperity by a society is the individual whose mind is devoted "to nobility of character." When God grants such wisdom and power, "the righteous one is the foundation on which humanity rests."[67]

To attain such socially beneficial wisdom requires self-discipline, however. In his allegorical exposition of the migration of Abraham, Philo calls for self-examination by his reader: "Give heed to yourself!" (Exod. 24:12). He then urges, "Depart out of the earthly matter that encompasses you: escape, O human, from the foul prison-house, your body, with all your might and main, and from the pleasures and lusts that act as its jailers; every terror that can vex and hurt [these evil forces], leave none of them unused."[68] Instead, the wise one will go by the king's way, shunning the appeal of earthly pleasures.[69] In the search for wisdom, there will be times when it seems fruitless, but on other occasions the ideas fall as in a shower from above, "so that under the influence of the divine possession" one is "filled with corybantic frenzy and unconscious of anything, place, persons present, oneself, words spoken, lines written." Yet in this divine frenzy one obtains "language, ideas, an enjoyment of light, keenest vision, pellucid distinctness of objects."[70] When this kind of leadership is exercized, intestine warfare within the nation will end and the people as a whole will be filled with wisdom and understanding.[71]

The allegorical approach to scripture enables Philo to discern spiritual meaning even in details of patriarchal travel. Thus, Abraham's journey "through the country" (Gen. 12:6) on the way to his encounter with God at Shechem means "love of learning [that] is by nature curious and inquisitive, not hesitating to bend its steps in all directions, prying into everything, reluctant to leave anything that exists unexplored, whether material or immaterial."[72] Philo extols the Jewish group known as the Therapeutae as those who excel in this approach to life and reality: "A people always taught from the first to use their sight [who] desire the vision of the Existent and soar above the sun of our senses and never leave their place in this company which carries them on to perfect happiness."[73]

The allegorical details in Philo's works point up the nature of God and of the divine relationship to the covenant people—a hermeneutical method that he describes as "the scientific mode of interpretation which looks for the hidden meaning of the literal words," thereby escaping the difficulty of the literal acount. Thus the high priest, who cannot touch the dead body of even his kin, "is not a man but a Divine Logos and immune from all unrighteousness whether intentional or unintentional, since his father is God, who is likewise father of all, and his mother is Wisdom, through whom the universe came into existence."[74] Philo finds similar meaning for manna, an entity that Israel could not identify (the term means "What is it?" [Exod. 16:15]): "The Divine Logos, from which all kinds of instruction and wisdom flow in perpetual stream . . . heavenly nourishment," which falls from heaven as "ethereal wisdom upon minds which are by nature apt and take delight in contemplation [*dianoia*]."[75] What Israel will find when it enters the land—cities and full cisterns and crops that they did not build or till (Deut. 6:10)—are virtues and souls ready to receive wisdom, progress and growth in understanding, "and the fruit of knowledge [through] the life of contemplation."[76] The stairway reaching to heaven that Jacob sees at Bethel (Gen. 28:12) is not merely the physical expanse of the heavens but "the abode of the incorporeal souls, since it seemed good to the Maker to fill all parts of the universe with living beings." Some of these have material (earthly) tendencies, while others, escaping earthly life "as though from a dungeon or a grave, are lifted up on light wings to the upper air and range the heights forever." They are "viceroys of the Ruler of the universe, ears and eyes, so to speak, of the Great King," who by "ascending and descending" convey the divine message to human ears that are ready to receive it. Mixing his images, Philo describes God, who stands at the top of the ladder, as a charioteer or helmsman, "standing over bodies, over souls, over actions and words, over earth, over air, over sky, over powers discerned by our senses, over invisible things, over all things seen and unseen; for having made the whole universe to depend on and cling to himself, he is the Charioteer of all that vast creation."[77]

Erwin R. Goodenough's path-making study of Philo, *By Light, Light,* presents a sound analysis of this mystical understanding of God. The Absolute One has given form to matter and "radiates from himself a great stream of Light-Power," which is variously called Logos, Sophia, Virtue, and Spirit, and which is manifest in both creative and ruling functions, the lower aspects of which are evident in the material world to those with proper insight. This inner structure of the divine has been revealed by God to humans through Moses, and is embodied in the Ark of the Covenant, which represents the eternal divine laws (the tablets of Moses), the power of mercy (the mercy seat), and the creative and ruling powers (the two cherubim). The voice that spoke to Moses is the Logos. Through these divinely given means, humans can come to understand the nature of God, his purpose for humans and the universe, and how God's people are to live.[78]

Thus, Philo's mysticism is not a matter of personal isolation or of refuge from a hostile world. His aim was to renew the Jewish community by providing insights for interpreting the history and literature of Judaism. He saw the role of those who shared his insights as one of public responsibility—which he took on concretely when he led a delegation of Jews to Rome to petition Caligula to free Jews from the obligation to offer divine honors to him, as demanded by imperial decree.[79] Yet the mystical approach to knowledge of God and his purpose for his community was important for Jews in the period of our inquiry, and had important parallels among Christians in the later first and subsequent centuries. The center of this perception of the people of God is the community of persons who have discovered and disciplined themselves to attain these modes of understanding.

Merkavah Mysticism

Ezekiel's vision of the chariot, the dome of the heavens, the throne, and the glory of the Lord (Ezek. 1:4–28) seems to have fostered images of the divine throne such as were found among the Dead Sea Scrolls and at Masada in a group of liturgical songs designated by scholars as Songs of the Sabbath Sacrifice.[80] Apparently akin to the unpublished Qumran document 4Q Berakoth, the songs were used on the occasion of a ceremony of covenant renewal, embodying praise to God in the heavenly sanctuary. The thirteen songs in the group describe how God has established the angelic priesthood and how the purity of the priests and the sanctuary is maintained. There are descriptions of the heavenly temple that recall details from the biblical accounts of the temple of Solomon and the eschataological temple depicted in Ezekiel. The throne of God is pictured in terms of a chariot, and in the divine presence sacrifices and praise are offered. As Newsom notes, the aim of these songs is to convey a sense of being in the heavenly sanctuary and in the presence of the angelic priests and worshippers as a communal experience, as is also evident in the Qumran Hodayoth and in the Scroll of the Rule. An earlier translation of one of the fragments by Geza Vermes includes the following passages: "For he is the God of all who exult in everlasting knowledge, and the Judge through his might of all the spirits of understanding. . . . All the spirits of righteousness celebrate his truth, and seek acceptance of their knowledge by the judgments of his mouth and of their celebrations when his mighty hand executes judgments of reward." Echoing the imagery of Ezekiel, the service in praise of God is described as follows: "The cherubim bless the image of the throne-chariot above the firmament, and they praise the majesty of the luminous firmament beneath his seat of glory. When the wheels advance, angels of holiness come and go. From between his glorious wheels there is as it were a fiery vision of most holy spirits."[81]

The earthly worship of God by the community imitates and anticipates sharing in the worship of God in the heavenly sanctuary, which will be accessible only to the purified, sanctified members of the community. Unlike the mystics of Philo, these have not attained access to the divine presence through diligent study or allegorical interpretation of the scriptures (in conversation with the philosophical insights of contemporary culture), but by divine disclosure alone. The content of the revelation is the vast splendor of the divine realm and the glorious future, rather than perceptive understanding of the created order and of the place of humans within it. In contrast to Philo's sense of moral and social obligation to the wider world, the Dead Sea community was concerned for its own future, which involved the destruction of its enemies (the War Scroll) and the expulsion from the rebuilt city and Temple of the incumbent priests and of all who failed to meet the community's understanding of purity (the Temple Scroll).

3 Enoch

Michael Stone has noted that such works as the Enochic Book of the Watchers and the Angelic Liturgy from Qumran are the antecedents of the chariot texts that developed about 500 C.E. In the latter, the mystics visit the realm of the dead and receive meteorological and astronomical secrets, but the major appeal is the promise of participation in the divine.[82] Other scholars have noted that speculation about penetrating the hidden world and reaching the otherwise inaccessible divinity led to the creation of ecstatic hymns and of tests that were required of those who sought to make the celestial journey. Also included in these documents were theurgic practices borrowed from Egyptian, Hellenistic, and Mesopotamian magic, of which the later *Sepher Ha-razim* provides eclectic evidence.[83] Speculation builds on such features as the secret meaning of ten numbers in the Hebrew alphabet. The throne mysticism does not in itself effect union with God, but helps to prepare the seeker and his pupils for this ecstatic experience.[84] In an early study of Jewish mysticism, Gershom Scholem made the valid point that mysticism stands in tension with historical revelation, in that while revelation (as through Moses and the prophets) is a given fact of history, the source of religious knowledge and true experience bursts forth from the heart, so that the secret disclosure is the real and decisive one. The secret dimension of mystical knowledge lies not only in the content of the doctrines, which treat of deeply hidden matters of human existence, but also in the fact that the disclosure is confined to a small elite, who may impart this knowledge to their disciples.[85]

It is this disclosure of the divine purpose to the elect community that is noted by Ithamar Gruenwald in his important study *Apocalyptic and Merkavah Mysticism*.[86] The commentaries (Pesharim) found among the Dead Sea Scrolls claim to disclose the inner and true meaning of scripture, which is secret and available only to the members of the community through the "Teacher of righteousness." With the destruction of the Temple and the pagan rebuilding of Jerusalem, there was a crisis in expectation, for which apocalyptic had no adequate explanation. Hence it failed as a resource for Jews and was replaced by Merkavah mysticism, which looked beyond the earthly and temporal to fulfillment in the celestial realm. Documentation of this shift is found in 2 Enoch, the Apocalypse of Abraham, and the Ascension of Isaiah, who passes through the seven heavens and is given a garment of glory. Traces of this transformed mode of expectation (from temporal to cosmic dimensions) are to be found in the Tannaim and the Amoraim, and especially in the Hekhalot literature, with details of heavenly ascensions and secret keys to interpreting Torah.

Perhaps the most vivid documentation of this form of mystical insight and participation is found in what has come to be known as 3 Enoch. Dating in its present form from the fifth to sixth century C.E.,[87] this document appears to have drawn some of its material from the Babylonian Talmud as well as from magical material known otherwise from the sixth to seventh centuries C.E. Detailed references to features of Caesarea Maritima imply a Palestinian origin for some of the material. In the circles that produced 3 Enoch, interest has shifted from the historical concerns of apocalyptic to the mysteries of heaven and the throne of God, probably in reaction to the destruction of God's earthly dwelling-place, the Temple. God's presence is understood to be spatially remote and inaccessible to humans, since the cloud of glory has withdrawn from the inner sanctuary of the Temple.[88] The angel Metatron, who figures prominently in 3 Enoch, has features of the archangel Yahoel but also of Enoch, who was translated to heaven and hence is a human prototype of the yearning mystic.[89] Thus there is in this document no aim to improve the earthly life of God's people or to develop a synthesis of the best of human understanding and divine insights, as in Philo. The goal of this mystical literature is celestial escape.

Communities of Ethnic Inclusiveness and Cultural Adaptation

In his excellent survey of the history of Judaism in the Hellenistic-Roman period, Shaye Cohen shows that the dominant qualification for membership in the covenant community of Israel was birth to Jewish parents.[90] Exogamy with neighboring Semitic tribes was prohibited in Torah (Deut. 7:1–4; 23:2–9) and was reinforced by Ezra on the people's return to the land from the exile in Babylon and expanded to include marriage with any non-Israelites (Ezra 9:1–4). In the Torah tradition, however, there was another strand that made provision and laid down the rules for participation by non-Israelites in the worship of Yahweh (Exod. 12:48; Lev. 17:8), but it also specified laws that they must observe as aliens (*gerim*). These included abstinence from working on the Day of Atonement and Passover (Lev. 16:29; Num. 9:19) and from offering sacrifices to other gods (Lev. 20:2). Yet they were to be treated with love (Lev. 19:33) and could enjoy the protection of the cities of refuge (Josh. 20:9). When they fulfilled the law in offering sacrifices, they received divine forgiveness like the Israelites (Num. 15:14–15, 26). Their role in Israelite society could be enslavement, however (Lev. 25:44–45).

Solomon is famed for his fondness for wives from among alien and non-Israelite people (1 Kings 11:1, 8). But in the time of Ezra and Nehemiah, a major sign of what is considered true repentance on the part of the Israelites as covenant renewal begins is that they divest themselves of foreign wives (Ezra 10:2, 10–11, 14–18; Neh. 13:27). In the Book of Jubilees, intermarriage with a wife from outside Israel is a capital crime (Jub. 30). Yet there is also evident in some of the Jewish literature of the postexilic period a more open attitude, which is sketched here. This and related material will be analyzed in chapter 6, where the feature of inclusiveness will be the central focus.

Openness toward Aliens and Strangers in the Later Prophets
A basic shift in attitude toward aliens is apparent as early as the time of Ezekiel. His condemnation of idolaters among the Israelites is as harsh as his denunciation of aliens who worship false gods (Ezek. 14:6–8). But when the land is divided in the eschatological age, aliens are to share in the allotments with the Israelites and are to be treated as citizens (47:22–23). In Isa. 14:1–2, aliens will attach themselves to the house of Israel, but the predominant relationship will be

that other nations will become slaves of Israel. In the latter part of Isaiah, on the other hand, eunuchs and aliens who join themselves to the Lord will be brought by him to the holy mountain to share in the covenant renewal with Israel, with the result that the "House of prayer" will serve "for all peoples" (Isa. 56:3–7). Foreigners will help to rebuild Jerusalem and its sanctuary (Isa. 60:10), and people of all nations and languages will be brought there by God, with the result that "all humanity shall come to worship before [God]," and from among these alien nations there will even be chosen some to serve as "priests and Levites" (Isa. 66:18–23). The universal access to Yahweh in his sanctuary is likewise affirmed in the Chronicler's account of the dedication of Solmon's temple (2 Chron. 6:32–33).

Relationship with Gentiles in the Later Narrative Tradition

In the brief, vivid narratives included in the Hebrew canon (Esther, Ruth, Jonah), there is also an important theme concerning the possibility of Gentiles being included in the relationship with the God of Israel. The contrast between Esther and Ruth is illuminating on this issue of Gentile participation in the life of the covenant community. In Esther, a faithful Jewish woman is able to preserve her purity and her commitment to the tradition, even as the wife of a pagan ruler. Her fidelity is confirmed by subsequent events, and leads to reluctant cooperation by the Gentiles with the Jews out of fear (8:17). In the Book of Ruth, on the other hand, the heroine is a foreigner (2:10) who has sought refuge "under the wings of Yahweh" (2:12). She becomes the active agent by which her dead husband's posterity and heritage are maintained (4:10). Divine approbation of this procedure is granted when the eventual human product of Ruth's marriage is David (4:13–22). In the Old Testament Apocrypha, Judith is the one through whom a pagan ruler is converted to trust in the God of Israel (Jth. 14:10), and in the additions to Esther, King Artaxerxes' letter testifies that "Jews are governed by most righteous laws and are the sons of the Most High, the most mighty living God, who has directed the kingdom both for us and for our fathers in the most excellent order."[91]

Jonah, written in the style of a Hellenistic romance—as attractive propaganda for the worship of a deity[92]—moves through its fascinating narrative about the adventures and misadventures of a reluctant messenger, whose warning to the people of Nineveh of God's impending judgment leads to the penitent conversion of the king and populace. The result is the deliverance of the city. The assumption of the writer of Jonah is that it is not Israelite genealogical descent, but repentance and trust in the message from God that lead to a right relationship between creator and creatures. However surprised or even annoyed some pious Jews may be, the possibility of participation in the benefits of God's people is declared to be open to the penitent and the faithful apart from ethnic origins.

Two apologies for Judaism—4 Maccabees (second half of the first century C.E.[93]) and Josephus's *Contra Apionem* (early second century C.E.)—seek to convince Jewish and Gentile readers of the antiquity and inherent rationality of the Jewish religious tradition. Both are profoundly influenced by and committed to Stoic philosophy. The thesis in each case is that what pagan philosophy falsely claims to offer, Judaism embodies in essence.

Fourth Maccabees is a dissertation on the question, "Is devout reason (*ho eusebeis logismos*) absolute master of the passions?" From the outset, the text is filled with technical terms from Hellenistic philosophy.[94] The thesis is that the triumph of reason over the passions is best demonstrated by those Jews in the Maccabean revolt who accepted martyrdom rather than conform to the idolatrous decrees of Antiochus IV Epiphanes. In the course of his argument, the author defines reason as the mind making a deliberate choice to pursue the life guided by reason, which is acquired in its fundamental form through the law of Moses. He then enumerates the philosophical virtues that are fostered by the law: prudence, temperance, justice, and courage. The law enables one to overcome foolish ambition, vanity, false pretenses, pride, and backbiting. It is rationality (*sophrosune*) that is master of the passions.

God placed the mind (*nous*) in humans as the sacred guide over all, including the passions and other self-gratifying inclinations, and to the mind he gave the law. Those who live by the law will rule over a kingdom that is temperate and just, good and brave (4 Macc. 2:22). Accordingly, Eleazar's defense of his refusal to obey the demands of Antiochus is based on the reasonableness of the divinely given law, which prohibits idolatry (4 Macc. 5:14–38). Eleazar is portrayed as a philosopher, obedient to the philosophical insights communicated through the law: "O Law, my teacher; I will not forswear you, beloved self-control [*egkrateia*]; I will not shame you, philosophic reason, nor will I deny you, venerable priesthood and knowledge of the Law." It is through the law as the instrument of reason that the seven martyred brothers were able to remain true to their commitment (13:25–27). In the closing section, the author appeals again to "the offspring of Abraham, children of Israel" to "obey this Law and be altogether true to your religion [*eusebeite*], knowing that devout reason [*eusebeis logismos*] is master over all the passions" and over pains from within as well as those imposed from without (18:1–4). The divine reward for faithful obedience to reason through the law is a share in the celestial life of "the sons of Abraham . . . in the choir of the fathers, having received pure and deathless souls from God" (18:23).

The document known as Pseudo-Phocylides,[95] which also probably dates from the second half of the first century C.E., claims to have been written by a sixth century B.C.E. poet of Miletus and uses ionic hexameter. But its aim is to persuade Gentiles to be sympathetic to the religion of the Jews. It affirms that this religion is universal in outlook and that the life of moderation is humanity's highest goal.

Human life is cyclical: all go to Hades, but the soul is immortal and will triumph over death.

In the *Contra Apionem*,[96] Josephus depicts the Jews as having been admirers throughout history of good order in the world and as living under common laws in accord with moderation and such virtue as is in accord with nature (2.15). Moses had regard to true piety and exhibited virtue to a high degree. His view of God emphasized the divine as unbegotten, eternal, immutable, and superior to all mortal conceptions—all of which is compatible with the teachings of Pythagoras, Anaxagoras, Plato, and the Stoics (2.17). The virtues that Moses extolled—justice, fortitude, temperance, and the universality of the law—all lead to piety in relation to God. Further, Moses linked instruction with the practical exercize of virtue in the law, and he set forth a philosophy that provides in a unifying way both rules for life and a basic understanding of God (2.20).

The universe (*ta sympanta*) is in God's hands; he is the beginning, middle, and end of all things. "By his works and bounties he is plainly seen . . . but his form and magnitude surpass our powers of description." Hence no art or skill could fashion an image of God (2.22). His law is administered through the priests, for both the worship of God and "a strict superintendence . . . of the pursuits of everyday life" (2.21). Both cosmic order and moral dimensions of human life are encompassed in the law. Like Plato, Moses insisted that all humanity should learn and conform to the laws. Only in this way can the true commonwealth of all people be established (2.37).

Although the Greek philosophers dismissed or rejected the Jewish laws, Josephus insists that they followed Moses's principles of thought and action. Greek writers failed to mention Moses and the Jews either because the close nature of the Jewish community kept outsiders ignorant of these truths, or because they wanted to ignore these ancient insights that anticipated in many ways the views of their own philosophers. Nevertheless, "the multitude of humanity . . . have had for a long time to follow our religious observances, our mutual concern with one another, and the charitable distribution of our goods, our fortitude in undergoing the distress we are in on account of our laws. As God pervades all the world, so has our law passed through the whole world also" (2.40). Thus, the laws of the Jews "teach the truest piety in the world" (2.42).

Whether to encourage his Jewish contemporaries, who may have felt intellectually inferior to Greek philosophers, or to promote his own synthesis, Josephus likewise articulates a view of the people of God as specially favored by God's instruction through the law of Moses and as possessing a truth that is older and purer than that of the philosophers. The philosophical culture of the Romans, built on that of the Greeks, is by no means incompatible with the teachings of Moses. Rather, Moses is the key to discerning the truth of philosophy. The Jewish community that Josephus represents sees itself in this intellectually and religiously advantageous position. An analogous understanding was adopted by Christian intellectuals in the second and third centuries C.E., as some of the Apostolic Fathers and especially the Alexandrines (Clement and Origen) eloquently attest.

Methodological Implications

In the chapters that follow, I shall examine in detail the early Christian counterparts of the options chosen by various groups of Jews with respect to the modes of their identity as God's people and the agents by which their corporate aims were to be achieved. The Christian models will not correspond precisely to those I have described in Judaism of the period prior to the destruction of the city of Jerusalem and the Temple. But the Jewish models are both precedents and foils for the variety of ways in which the early Christians understood themselves to be the heirs of the covenant promises, and for the roles they saw Jesus fulfilling in what they regarded as his God-given task of establishing the new people of God.

The Community of the Wise   2

Both types of the community of the wise that one finds in Judaism of the postexilic period can also be discerned in the early Christian writings. First are those that build on perceptions of wisdom shared, in part, with the wider culture contemporary with the group, on the basis of which is affirmed an understanding of God's purpose to structure an ordered society of the wise and obedient. In contrast to this perception of wisdom is that of those who are convinced that God has vouchsafed to an elect community his purpose for them and for the creation—a purpose that will be fulfilled through conflict and suffering but will culminate in divine vindication. It is the second of these options that clearly dominates in most of the earlier Christian writings and that evidences kinship with the later prophetic and apocalyptic traditions of Judaism.[1]

As I noted in chapter 1, apocalyptic writings were intended for a community in crisis, with the aim of exhorting and consoling the members in view of present suffering and the promise of future vindication by God. To summarize the questions that are appropriate to address to an apocalyptic document: What were the political, cultural, and religious circumstances that led the community to a sense of alienation and victimization? Who were the culprits who brought on the crisis? How does the author respond to the critical situation, and what attitudes and actions by the community are enjoined? How does the community define itself as the "elect" or "righteous"? How is it organized? What are its goals and strategy for survival and propagation of the movement?

The New Testament writings that treat of these issues and thus exhibit the apocalyptic community model are the Q source, the Gospel of Mark, and the letters of Paul, as well as two of the latest letters in the New Testament: Jude and 2 Peter. Clearly, the Revelation of John is the only complete apocalypse in the New

Testament, but its community model builds on features that seem to have been synthesized with another type we have traced in the Jewish tradition: the Temple/priesthood model.[2] I begin with an analysis of the Q source, which consists of the material common to Matthew and Luke but not found in Mark.

The Q Source

There are five motifs that run through the Q tradition, with a single unit often including more than one of them. These recurrent themes are the prophetic word about God's coming rule, Jesus as revealer and agent of God, accountability before God and preparation for judgment, the privileges and price of discipleship, and the inclusion of outsiders in the new community. Far from being primarily clusters of sayings of timeless wisdom, as some contemporary scholars assert, the whole of Q pictures Jesus as the messenger and agent of judgment on the traditional community and of renewal of God's people. Careful analysis shows how these motifs intermingle in portraying the role of Jesus and in defining participation in the new community.

The Prophetic Word about God's Coming Rule

The opening pericope in Q (Luke 3:7–9)[3] pictures John the Baptist denouncing his Jewish contemporaries because of their claim that physical descent from Abraham is sufficient ground for their claim to be members of God's covenant people. Instead, he declares that the "axe" of God's judgment is about to fall on those who fail to produce the "good fruit" of obedience to God. Using images of trees to be cut down and chaff left from the harvesting of grain, he warns that fire will destroy those who make an unwarranted claim to belong to God. The issue here is the typical apocalyptic theme of redefining the covenant community. While seeking some form of miraculous evidence from God as to the divine intention ("a sign," 11:29–32), this "generation" of those who claim to be God's people fails to hear the call to repentance or the message of divine wisdom given through God's "greater" agent, as it was conveyed earlier through Jonah and Solomon. (I shall note below under the fifth Q motif, the inclusive community, how important it is that the respondents to Jonah and Solomon were non-Israelites.) The Pharisees are denounced (11:37–52) because their obsession with ritual purity leads them to neglect inner moral purity and to prize public esteem for their religious observances. They will reject God's messengers—the apostles and prophets whom Jesus will send—just as their ancestors rejected and killed those whom God sent among them, extending from the murder of Abel in the first book of the Jewish canon (Gen. 4:8) to that of Zechariah in the last of the historical writings (2 Chron. 24:20–21), which brings the Hebrew canon to a close.

In spite of these warnings about fierce opposition, the messengers whom Jesus commissions are to be fearless, confident that God knows and cares for those who stand faithful in testimony concerning him, his agent (the Son of Man[4]), and the

Spirit of God that is operative in the world. A similar prophetic warning is addressed to Jerusalem as the symbolic center of the traditional people of God (13:34–35), expressing God's continuing concern for them but indicating that their refusal of "the one who comes in the name of the Lord" will result in their ultimate alienation from God. The long epoch of "the law and the prophets" (16:16–17) has now culminated in the prophetic role of John, whose task is to prepare for the announcement of God's rule and the impingement of its powers upon the present situation. This message and these new evidences of God's rule evoke violence from human and demonic opponents (11:20), but the promises spoken in the law and the prophets will not fail to be fulfilled. God's message about the future of his people and of the creation is given to the faithful community through the ultimate prophetic agent, Jesus, whose message defines God's people in ways that are sharply critical of the traditional modes of Jewish piety. John is the essential preparatory figure, but the distinctive and consummating role in the carrying out of this new prophetic message is that of Jesus.

Jesus as Revealer and Agent of God

The Q version of the temptation of Jesus depicts the efforts of the devil to lure Jesus into misuse of his extraordinary powers (4:2b–13). Both the devil and Jesus appeal to scriptures in support of their respective positions. The devil acknowledges Jesus' unique relationship to God ("Son of God")[5] and invites him to demonstrate his capabilities, presumably to attract a popular following. What is at issue is the source of Jesus' authority, as well as the ends to which his capabilities will be used. In response, Jesus insists that the sovereignty of God and the triumph of his purpose are the only factors operative in the mission to which he is committed.

The request of the centurion that Jesus heal his slave (7:2–10) is presented as being based on the military official's sense that, just as he has authority to effect certain results, so Jesus has the authority to cure his ailing servant. It is at Jesus' command that the healing takes place. This is followed in Q by Jesus' response to the question from John the Baptist as to whether or not he is God's agent "who is to come" (7:18–23). Jesus' response points to the results of his work: the healings, the renewal of life, the raising of the dead, and the proclamation of good news to the impoverished and deprived ("poor"). This answer of Jesus consists of a pastiche of terms quoted from the prophecies of Isaiah (Isa. 29:18–19; 35:5–6; 61:1), which are uttered here in such a way as to point not merely to the fulfillment of prophecy but more importantly to an era of accessibility for the previously excluded to the benefits and renewal of life of God's people. That theme is further developed in the next Q pericope (7:24–35). After identifying John as the advance messenger who will prepare the Lord's way (Mal. 3:1), Jesus describes the negative reaction of his contemporaries, who scorn not only John's ascetic ways, but also Jesus' free and easy lifestyle and associations with those outside the pale of social and ritual respectability. The "glutton and drunkard" designation, which derives from Deut. 21:20, is an epithet attached to someone who is considered unworthy of membership in the covenant people and is to be executed by joint community action. When Jesus associates with outsiders and then justifies his iconoclastic behavior as being performed with divine authorization, as the Q tradition reports, the appropriateness of the official community's rejection of him as a subversive of covenantal integrity is obvious.

In other Q material, Jesus is pictured as enjoying a special relationship with God, which enables him and his community ("babes") to understand the purpose of God in ways that are hidden to the self-styled "wise" who comprise the official leadership (10:21–22). Yet he also is seen as sorrowful that the power structure of the traditional community ("Jerusalem") rejects God's summons to repent and return to the divine purpose, just as the message of the "prophets" and other messengers was met with violent opposition over the centuries. Only when the new age dawns will the leaders recognize that the one they rejected came "in the name of the Lord" (Ps. 118:26). Yet they will be as completely unprepared for the disclosure of God's agent of renewal ("the Son of Man") at the end of time as the ancients were when acts of divine judgment befell Israel (17:22–24, 26–29). On the other hand, those who remain faithful to Jesus during his time of severe testing will have leadership roles in the kingdom that God has covenanted[6] for his new people, and will share in the eschatological meal.[7]

Accountability before God and Preparation for Judgment

I have already noted that the message of John as the one who prepares for the coming of Jesus to his role in the eschatological purpose of God highlights the judgment that is to fall on the indifferent and the obstinate (3:7–10, 17). The other side of that message of doom is the promise of vindication for the community of the faithful and obedient. In Luke's version of the Beatitudes,[8] there is a sharp contrast between the present condition of deprivation and sorrow and the future time of joy and fulfillment of the divine promises (6:20–23). The judgment will result in the members attaining the blessings that God already has in store for them in heaven. In the present, however, they must continue to act with love and grace, even toward their enemies, since this is the gracious and generous way that God responds to a human race that is largely hostile and at best indifferent to his purposes (6:27–36). When the members of the community abstain from judging others, God will reward them richly in the age to come (6:37–46). Their critical powers are to be focused on their own moral condition, allowing the new life God has implanted within them to manifest itself in appropriately obedient ways. Meanwhile, they can be sure that when the judgment of God falls on the world, those who have given heed to God's commands through Jesus will survive the time of testing, in contrast to the disobedient, who will be destroyed in the river of judgment that will be poured out on the world (6:47–49).

The Community of the Wise

The message of the good news is to go out to everyone, but those towns that reject the gospel and its bearers will meet their doom in the day of judgment, as did the people of Sodom (10:11; Gen. 19). Those liberated from the powers of evil must continue in their penitence and fidelity, or their final condition will be worse than ever (11:24–26). In the day of judgment, non-Israelites who responded to Jesus' prophetic and sapiential insights into the purpose of God will condemn the present generation, since it has failed to trust in the agent of God, whose understanding of God's purpose transcends the wisdom of Solomon and the message of Jonah (11:29–32). Woes are pronounced on the Pharisees for their preoccupation with ritual purity and legal minutiae, while they condone moral corruption and ignore the love and grace of God. Their spurning Jesus is at one with the rejection of the earlier prophets by their contemporaries (11:37–52).

All human actions will be exposed and evaluated in the coming day of judgment (12:1–9). Those who acknowledge Jesus as God's agent ("Son of man") will be confirmed by him, and those who reject him will stand condemned in the last day. Meanwhile, his followers are to be obedient, diligent, and always on the alert for his coming, so that they can share in the eschatological feast (12:35–46). The careless and preoccupied will not be able to take part in these ultimate rewards. The conflicts that his people will experience will involve their own families, but their loyalty must transcend even these traditional social obligations (12:49–56). They must be prepared to make certain adjustments and settlements on minor issues so that they will be free to devote their energies to the most important business: preparing for the coming of God's rule (12:57–59).

The string of parables in Luke 13:18–30 focuses on the contrast between the present beginnings and the ultimate outcome: the seed becomes a tree; the leaven pervades the dough; those who now refuse to enter the door of opportunity will never have a second chance to share in the life of God's new people. Gathered in that new community will be the patriarchs of ancient Israel and the prophets, as well as many from various parts of the world, including those whom the pious traditionalists regard as outsiders. Judgment will fall without warning, and those preoccupied with ordinary human affairs—marrying, buying and selling, planting, and building—will perish when destruction comes on the evil of the world and the faithful are vindicated by God (17:22–24, 26–29, 35–37). The images of the divine judgment include the outpouring of the fires of destruction, the escape of the obedient, and the gathering of vultures around the corpses of the wicked. The theme of accountability to God at the eschatological judgment is sounded in the parable of the money given to the servants by the absentee ruler-designate (19:11–27).[9]

The Privileges and Price of Discipleship

The Beatitudes declare dramatically the reversal of condition that is in store for the followers of Jesus, who come from among the "poor" (those who lack privileges and are excluded from the standpoint of dominant Jewish society) but are to share in the bounties of God's coming rule (6:20–21). They now experience sorrow, suffering, hatred, and revulsion because of their choice of association with the Son of Man, just as did the prophets of God, but the new age will bring joy and reward (6:22–23). Their acts of love and generosity to others in need will be richly rewarded, and they will enjoy status as children "of the Most High" (6:27–38). They demonstrate dedication to the "teacher" who has brought them this wisdom from God, which includes insight about their own shortcomings, and the need for a forgiving attitude (17:3–4) rather than criticism of others (6:39–42). Their own inner condition will manifest itself in either good or bad deeds, and the norm for their behavior is to be what "the Lord" teaches them (6:43–46). Fidelity to his words will erect a firm foundation that will enable them to withstand the storms that lie ahead for God's new people (6:47–49).

A major cost of such discipleship will be the break with the stability and support of family, just as Jesus himself experienced initial rejection by his family (9:57–58). Customary obligations to one's family must yield in priority to "proclaiming the Kingdom of God," and there must be no looking back in longing to the traditional security of the home, since those who share in the work of preparing for the kingdom will experience conflict in their own households, not peace (9:59–62; 12:51–53; 14:26–27). The life of the community depends on God and his grace for supply of daily needs as well as for forgiveness (11:2–4, 9–13). To the faithful, God has given the light of wisdom, but their life must be characterized by obedience to that light, or disaster and darkness will come (11:33–34). Those who make public their commitment to Jesus as Son of Man will be affirmed by God in the day of judgment, but those who refuse to make that dangerous public commitment will be doomed (12:8–9). Life is to be lived in total dependence upon God, rather than in anxiety about daily needs: a share in the kingdom is a gift from God (12:22–34). Certainty and urgency about the coming of "the Son of Man" are to characterize the attitude and values of his followers, since his return will bring reward for the diligent and punishment for the indolent (12:35–46). The hard choice between serving God or material values is inescapable (16:13). Meanwhile, the faithful are to remain accountable for the responsibilities that they have been assigned, as the parable of the absent nobleman indicates (19:11–27). Yet at the return of God's agent in the end time, those who have faithfully endured the difficulties they experienced because of their association with Jesus ("have continued with me in my trials," 20:28–30) will be able to share in the kingdom of God that is to be established.

The Inclusion of Outsiders in the New Community

A pervasive feature of the image of the community in the Q tradition is the inclusiveness of membership, in sharp contrast to the careful—even forceful— delineation of boundaries of the covenant people in the Qumran and Pharisaic traditions, and later in the rabbinic documents of the second and subsequent centuries C.E. Setting the criteria for participation in God's people is central for Q, as is obvious from the fact that even before Jesus appears on the scene, John the Baptist is challenging the standard requirements for sharing in the benefits of the covenant, including genealogical descent from the patriarchs (3:8–9). The metaphors are mixed in this passage, but even a seemingly lifeless stone ('eben) can become a child (ben) of Abraham, the founder of the covenant people. Even the seemingly stable planting of God (Ps. 1:3), when it is unproductive like the vineyard of Israel (Isa. 5:1–7), will be cut down in judgment and burned (3:9), as will the worthless chaff among those who call themselves God's people (3:17).

I have already noted that it is the deprived who share in the blessings of the coming kingdom (6:20–23), and it is a hated collaborationist centurion whose trust in Jesus leads to the healing of his servant (7:2–10). Those who by standards of first-century Jewish piety were physically and socially disqualified from participation in the covenant people but to whom the prophetic promise of renewal was extended are precisely the ones on whom Jesus focuses his ministry in contrasting his mission with that of John (7:18–23). Also noted above is the shocking characterization of Jesus as a "friend of tax collectors and sinners"—that is, of those who violate the national, ritual, and moral standards of the biblical tradition (7:34).

As the followers of Jesus set out on their mission, they are to accept support and hospitality from whoever offers it, without care for moral or ritual qualifications, as is emphatically evident in the instruction to "eat what is set before you" (10:2–8). The ultimate destiny of the towns they visit rests, not on their religious or ritual standards, but on their response to the good news of the coming kingdom (10:9–12). It is not to those who pride themselves on the maturity of their religious insights but to "babies" that God discloses his purpose through Jesus (10:21). Those who are excluded from sharing in the covenant by reason of their ethnic descent, as well as their social and cultural heritage (the Ninevites and the Queen of the South), are the ones Jesus highlights from the Jewish biblical tradition as being among those who will join at the judgment in condemnation of "this generation" (= the traditional claimants to special covenant relationship) for their failure to respond to either the wisdom or the call to repentance that Jesus proclaimed (11:29–32).

The expectation that participation in the kingdom of God will be based on criteria other than those of traditional piety is set out in the story of those seeking admission to God's household in the end time (13:22–30). The participants will not be the ordinary, complacent pious folk, who indeed will be "thrust out." Instead, those who share in the eschatological feast will come from all over the world. The refusal by his Jewish contemporaries to heed the message of Jesus has occurred in spite of his longing to bring them into membership in his "brood" (13:34–35), where the criterion for participation is to acknowledge him as one who "comes in the name of the Lord," in the words of the triumphant victory described in Ps. 118:26–27. The Parable of the Great Supper (14:16–24) makes the point that the beneficiaries of the new age that Jesus brings are not the traditional pious, who are preoccupied with respectable daily routines, but those on the fringe of the covenant community (the poor and the crippled on the edges of society: "in the streets and lanes of the city") and even those who are complete outsiders ("in the highways and hedges"). This outreach to the lost and the excluded is pictured as an essential feature of the nature of God, portrayed in Luke 15:5–7 as the shepherd who temporarily abandons the main body of his flock in order to seek and find the lost sheep. The implicit criticism of the leadership of Israel is expressed in the final pericope of Q (20:28–30), where the members of the new community function as judges of "the twelve tribes of Israel."

Summary of the Q Source

The wisdom that is being conveyed to the Q community is by no means a collection of timeless aphorisms. Rather, it is an invitation to share in a new community that God is establishing through Jesus, which embodies a selective, radical appropriation of the prophetic traditions of Israel. These claims have judgmental implications for those who see themselves as standing in special relationship with God by virtue of their conforming to traditional legal, ritual, and ethnic piety. The criteria for participation in the new community emphasize the inclusion of those who would have been judged outsiders by pious standards of that time. There is a powerful sense of urgency about getting out the message of what God is doing through Jesus, and a conviction that only those who perceive Jesus to be God's agent of renewal of his people will share in that new epoch of God's rule.

In the Q material, there are frequent references to the suffering and death that are requisite for the messengers and the faithful as they look for the new order. But there is no doctrine of atonement and no indication of the crucifixion story in Q. The basic conceptual features of apocalyptic are in the source, just as the basic social characteristics of an apocalyptic community are evident there. Except for "Lord" and "Son of Man," messianic titles are missing from Q, but the importance of baptism as the rite of preparation for judgment and renewal is conveyed through Jesus' association with and affirmation of John the Baptist, just as participation in the eschatological meal points to the Eucharist, as it is elaborated in other New Testament writings. The questions raised at the opening of this chapter concerning characteristic apocalyptic features are addressed in Q, so that community definition is clear, as is the role of Jesus as God's agent to establish the new people of God. It is the latter who are the ones to whom God has revealed wisdom through Jesus concerning the fulfillment of his purpose for them.

The Gospel of Mark

Critical Theories about the Origins of Mark

In the second century C.E., it was affirmed that the Gospel of Mark was a record of the memoirs of Peter, written by his companion Mark for the church in

The Community of the Wise

Rome. Eusebius reports this tradition, attributing it to Papias (ca. 130), who later became bishop of Hierapolis.[10] A similar tradition is recorded by Clement of Alexandria (ca. 200) in his *Hypotyposes*. With the rise of critical historical studies of the New Testament in the mid-nineteenth century, however, the theory was advanced—and widely espoused—that Mark was the product of a synthesis of the traditions of the story of Jesus with the Pauline view of Jesus as Lord and Son of God. Propounded by Gustav Volkmar in 1857, it was adopted by such distinguished figures as Otto Pfleiderer, Johnannes Weiss, Adolf Jülicher, and Adolf von Harnack. Rudolf Bultmann asserted in *The History of the Synoptic Tradition* that Mark was the first one to present the life of Jesus in the form of an *euangelion*, which he accomplished by "impressing it with a meaning such as it needed in the hellenistic churches of Paul's persuasion" and linking it with "the christological kerygma of Christendom." the "Christ myth" was united with "the tradition of the story of Jesus."[11]

A much more nuanced and apposite view of the origins and intent of Mark is that of Martin Dibelius, who dubbed Mark "The Book of Secret Epiphanies," noting that the divine glory of Jesus is evident only within the circle of his followers and that divine confirmation of him takes place within that circle through the transfiguration.[12] I shall note below in detail how the special disclosure of Jesus' identity, of the import of his message, and of his ultimate vindication is given only to the inner circle of his followers. First, however, I shall consider some recent proposals advanced by scholars for the origins of Mark.

Theories about an Ur-Markus are problematical, as Helmut Koester has noted, since proponents want to discover a gospel that is more primitive "than any text which can be reconstructed on the basis of external evidence."[13] As I note below in the "Critical Note on Priority in the Gospel Tradition," comparative analysis of the synoptics points to the most plausible hypothesis: that what we know as Mark 1:1–16:8 was the basic source for Luke and Matthew.

Burton Mack has advanced a radical theory about the origins of Mark.[14] He is thoroughly skeptical about both the methods and the results of previous critical analysis of the evidence: "The origins of Christianity are known to lie on the other side of the limits set by the nature of the texts at the scholar's disposal and the nature of the history that can be reconstructed from them. Thus the methods of historical literary criticism, the hallmark of the discipline, are tacitly acknowledged to be inadequate from the start." The result is that Mack finds no firm evidence regarding the origins of Christianity. He perceives as the cause of this difficulty the fact that there have been two kinds of equally inconclusive modern scholarly quests, for the historical Jesus, and for the earliest christology. Mack's proposal is that all these allegedly primitive features were in fact the creation of early Christian mythologists; his program is to look for historical circumstances and social motivations that would have led the early Christians to construct the cosmic mythic drama that appears in the New Testament.[15] In a rhetorical question to which he expects a positive answer, Mack asks, "What if the divine picture of Jesus in the New Testament were less hermeneutical with regards to the historical Jesus and more the myth of origin for movements in need of rationalization?"[16]

Mack's avowed method is to combine sociological and literary approaches "in order to redescribe a certain set of entangled textual and social histories of importance for the composition of the Gospel of Mark" and to reconstruct "a history of sectarian formation . . . for the time between Jesus and Mark." He thinks that there is no need to take into account claims about miracles, resurrection, divine appearances and presences, or unusual charismatic phenomena. The early Jesus movement did not pass on a social history of its origins but rather "this myth of the historical Jesus as the account of the divine origination" of the movement.[17]

What is the evidence on which the reconstruction of this myth of origins builds? After considering the diversity of roles of prophets and messiahs in the Jewish traditions of the first and preceding centuries, Mack turns to analogies between Jesus and the itinerant Cynic philosophers, whose teachings he finds closer to the function of Jesus in the (hypothetically) older layer of the Q tradition than the prophetic role, and concludes that the real Jesus combined popular Hellenistic philosophy with ethical ideals drawn from the Jewish wisdom tradition. Accordingly, Jesus was a teacher, a sage, and a charismatic moral reformer. Initially his followers took no meals together and observed no ritual related to his death.[18] It was in the Hellenistic communities of Syria and Asia Minor that the cultic notions of Jesus as god and savior arose, and following the post-70 rupture of the Jesus movement with the synagogue, the Old Testament epic tradition and Torah as the source of ritual code were replaced by "a mythically imagined event": the crucifixion and resurrection of Jesus.

At a time when both Judaism and Christianity were struggling with the aggressive power of Rome and with internal difficulties, Mack maintains, Mark resolved these issues by defining his group apocalyptically, thereby severing ties with Judaism and with other kinds of Jesus movements.[19] The miracle stories were composed, not as reports of what Jesus did, but to portray him as the new founder "of the congregation of Israel," elaborating this role by the prediction of the destruction of the Temple and the rending of its veil. In the passion story, Mark combined prior characterizations with Hellenistic myths to portray Jesus as a king whose authority (miracle stories) and wisdom (sayings) are absolute. Composing his account in scholarly fashion, Mark superimposed on his myth of origins an apocalyptic script of divine intervention, with victory assured by the resurrection and the fulfillment of the kingdom yet to come. All such features of the early Jesus tradition as personal salvation and social reforms were sacrificed to Mark's desire for "sectarian existence . . . governed by absolute loyalty to a power effective only in events of vindictive transformation."[20]

According to this elaborate proposal, Mark is the inventor of historical Christianity. Continuities with Jesus of Nazareth are at most vestigial and of no sub-

The Community of the Wise

stantive significance. The fertile, if somewhat feverish, imagination of Mark contrived the myth that stimulated the historical emergence of the church. Mack's
thesis, however, is fatally flawed, since it ignores the indisputable literary evidence
from the letters of Paul that a Jesus movement was already operative in Syria as
early as the mid-thirties C.E., whose members claimed to be the true heirs of the
covenantal tradition, expected a new era to dawn within the present generation,
perceived the death of Jesus as the ground of divine-human reconciliation, and
believed God had raised him from the dead, celebrating this event in the form of
a shared meal of bread and wine. Mack's elaborate effort at mythic construction
may provide comfort to those modern scholars who are embarrassed by the pervasive apocalyptic features of the oldest Christian tradition, but it founders as historical hypothesis on the earlier evidence of features shared by the significantly
diverse documents—Christian, Jewish, and Roman—that report about Jesus, his
crucifixion, and the movement he launched.[21] Although one must take fully into
account the special interests of Mark and his community as well as the editorial
features he inserted in the tradition he utilized, the antecedent nature of much of
his material leads to a very different scenario for the context and origins of this
document. It is to that scenario that I now turn.

Two other views of Mark that differ from Mack and from each other are those
of Herman C. Waetjen and Martin Hengel. Hengel thinks Mark was written in
Rome after the death of Nero and Galba (68/69 C.E.) but before the Jewish War
under Titus. Further, he proposes that Mark 13 expects a Nero redivivus and that
this gospel reflects Latin usage at several points. He assumes a historical connection
between Mark and Peter but does not think that the gospel is slavishly dependent
on the Petrine tradition. It was composed for oral recitation in the assembled
Christian community, as evidenced by the short cola of its style.[22]

Waetjen combines insights from sociological and literary approaches and concludes that Mark is "an integrated narrative" with a coherent relation of its parts
and its own universe. Building on the sociological analyses of Gerhard E. Lenski,
Waetjen sees the stratification of power in Mark's picture of Galilee: at the bottom are the mass of peasants and artisans; above them are merchants, retainers,
and priests; at the top is the tiny governing class. Jesus is represented in Mark as the
new human being (huios tou anthropou = Son of Man, in traditional translation), as
prophet in the tradition of Elijah, and as forerunner of death and resurrection.[23]
Although this sketch of the socioeconomic situation in Galilee may be largely
accurate, the analysis does not take adequately into account the diverse cultural
situation, with strong Hellenistic influences, or the range of socioeconomic circumstances of the followers of Jesus—including members of a family financially
able to hire servants (Mark 1:20) and a tax collector. Nevertheless, Waetjen's study
is to be commended for its effort to take more fully into account the context in
which the Markan tradition about Jesus arose.

The Markan Community

In preparation for my analysis of the Gospel of Mark, I rephrase the questions formulated above to describe apocalypticism. How does the community to which the revelation has been granted define itself? What are the qualifications for membership? What are its insights and resources, and what are its prospects? What are the circumstances that gave rise to the new community? Who are the culprits who shaped its problems, and how has the community been victimized? What tactics must be adopted to confront and overcome the crisis of conflict? In response to the crisis, what attitudes and actions are to be adopted by the community? What are the guidelines for behavior of its members? What are the pitfalls and misjudgments to be avoided? What are the qualifications and tasks of the one whom God has designated as the agent of renewal?

Defining the Apocalyptic Community

The intent to locate the Jesus movement in the final stage of the prophetic tradition is explicit in the spliced texts quoted by Mark from Mal. 3:1 and Isa. 40:3, which place John the Baptist in the climactic role of preparing the way of the Lord (which here probably is intended to mean "the way for Jesus").[24] This is seen to have been announced in scripture, as the community can now perceive. Further links with the prophets of Israel are evident in both the attire and the diet of John (1:6). The "hairy mantle" recalls Elijah (2 Kings 1:8) as he summoned Israel and its rulers to account before God, being a characteristic feature of those who claimed to stand in the prophetic line, as the warning in Zech. 13:4 about prophetic pretenders shows. The importance of the link with Elijah is confirmed by Jesus' response to the question raised about that prophet's coming in preparation for the new age (9:9–13). John's eating locusts reflects Lev. 11:22. The summons to people to leave Judea and Jerusalem for the river Jordan involves the symbolic act of confession and ritual cleansing, as a sign of a new beginning for God's people (1:4–5). Yet his role is here depicted as primarily anticipatory: yet to come are "the mightier one" and the "Holy Spirit" by which the penitent will be renewed (1:7–8).

Given the dual significance of baptism as sign of personal and public commitment to God and as evidence of a new beginning for the covenant community, it is obvious why the author of Mark and the early Christian community as a whole took over these features from the baptist movement. The initial utterance of Jesus in Mark 1:14–15 builds on John's call to renewal by announcing that the new age is dawning and God's rule has drawn near. What is needed is a profound change in orientation and commitment (*metanoeite*) in response to the good news brought by Jesus.

In addition to their own trust in Jesus as God's agent of renewal of his people, his followers are summoned to abandon their families and means of livelihood in order to call others to share in the new community, thereby gathering humans, not fish (1:16–20). There is a clear implication that the disciples were not called from the lowest strata of Galilean society, since the family has "hired servants" who can carry on its business in their absence. The great diversity of social, physical, ritual, ethnic, moral, and economic status among those who respond in trust to Jesus in the Markan narratives clearly reflects the openness of the movement and especially the setting aside of the traditional lines by which covenantal participation was defined. Significantly, Mark's first story of Jesus restoring to health the ailing concerns someone possessed by a demon (1:21–27), a feature that recurs in the other Markan miracle stories (1:32–34, 39; 3:10–11; 5:1–20; and 9:14–29). This sets the healing activity of Jesus in the larger context of cosmic conflict, since the focus is not merely the restoration of individuals but the defeat of the powers of evil.[25]

Jesus' healing of the ill is a theme that runs throughout Mark (1:29–32, 2:1–12, 3:1–6, 8:22–26, and 10:46–52), and in some cases the symbolic significance and the link with prophetic tradition are obvious, as in the last two references, where the blind receive their sight (Isa. 35:5). In other healing stories, a crucial factor is ritual impurity, which Jesus overcomes by touching and healing the one who is sick (2:1–12; 5:21–43). Still more remarkable is the string of stories in Mark which report Jesus' healings and exorcisms among those who are wholly outside the traditional covenant community: the Gerasene demoniac (5:1–20) and the daughter of the Syro-Phoenician woman (7:24–30), as well as the deaf-mute and many others healed by Jesus in the region of Tyre and the Decapolis (7:31–37). Mark gives two accounts of Jesus providing food for the throngs that followed him (6:30–44; 8:1–10). In the first story, the hunger and remoteness of the crowd from sources of food and drink are depicted in words that recall Israel's uncertain situation when God is about to appoint a new leader (Joshua) for the nation wandering in the desert (Num. 27:12–17) and when the prophet Micaiah warns Ahab of his defeat and the scattering of Israel (1 Kings 22:13–18): "like sheep without a shepherd." Clearly, the force of these passages is to declare that the redefining of the covenant people of God will result in judgment on those who presently claim that special relationship. Conversely, both feeding stories recount God's supply of his people's needs in language that reflects the liturgical usage of the early church: "He took, he blessed [or gave thanks, *eucharistesas*], he broke, he gave" (6:41; 8:6–7). The former of these stories is located in predominantly Jewish territory, Galilee (6:1), while the second incident occurs during Jesus' journey into Gentile territory (8:1).

Those who respond to Jesus in faith and receive the benefits of his healings and forgiveness include a spectrum of types of people, many on the periphery of the Jewish community or in places of very low status. Thus Jesus chooses as one of his intimate followers a collaborationist with the hated Roman regime: Levi, the tax collector (2:14). This act of inclusiveness is matched and extended by the free associations Jesus has with "many tax collectors and sinners," for which he is challenged by the Pharisaic scribes (2:15–17). The visit to the region of the Decapolis, the contact with local residents, and the act of touching a Gentile demoniac living in a tomb (5:1–20) would all be violations of ritual and ethnic purity. But Jesus defies these restrictive standards in order to meet a basic human need for liberation from the powers of evil and renewal, as he does in the case of the request from the Syro-Phoenician that her daughter be healed (7:24–30). Ironically, an odd configuration of witnesses acknowledges Jesus as the agent of God at the time of his crucifixion, when his followers all flee: the Roman military officer (15:39); the women, whose courageous, faithful role stands in sharp contrast to their repressed status in contemporary Judaism (15:41; 16:1–8); and Joseph of Arimathea, who endangers his own standing in Jewish officialdom by providing a burial place for Jesus (15:42–47). Thus, according to Mark, there are for Jesus no ethnic or ritual preconditions for gaining access to his healing and other miraculous powers or for participation in the new community.

The powers of Jesus are described in Mark as extending beyond ministering to individual human needs to controlling natural forces, such as stilling the storm on the Lake of Galilee[26] and multiplying the loaves and fishes (6:30–44; 8:1–10), as well as foreseeing the future in relation to his own death and resurrection (8:31; 9:31; 10:33) and the destruction of the Temple (13:1–4). These insights and prophecies are shared with the new community in Mark's account.

The basic resources of the new people of God include the tradition that Jesus commissioned the original corps of disciples to be with him, as witnesses and hearers of his work, to go out and preach the good news, and to have authority to expel demons (1:14–15). But central to their discharge of these challenging responsibilities is the fact that a special revelation has been granted to them: "the mystery of the Kingdom of God" (4:10–12). To outsiders, his teachings come across as a series of impenetrable riddles. But what has earlier been disclosed only to the disciples is now to be declared to the wider public (4:21–25). The parables in Mark 4 point to the astonishing results from seemingly minuscule beginnings. Yet the meaning of these teachings is reserved for the inner circle of those who follow him (4:33–34). The boundaries of the community are not sharply defined, however, since "whoever is not against us is for us," and those who do good deeds in Jesus' name will be rewarded by God (9:38–41).

Other important resources for the community include insights given to his followers about his impending death and resurrection, as well as the promise of the members' preservation in spite of the dire judgment that is to fall on the world (13:20, 27). That he will soon die is foretold in formulaic style (8:31; 9:31; and 10:33) and in symbolic mode through his being anointed by a woman in Bethany (14:3–9), and through the institution of the Christian equivalent of the Passover celebrating "my blood of the covenant which is poured out for many" (14:12–16, 22–25). The divine origin of, and sanction for, Jesus' revelatory and redemptive roles for his people are given vivid expression in the transfiguration scene (9:2–8).

The presence of Moses and Elijah indicates that renewal of the covenant people is in operation, and the divine manifestation—which is akin to what these two experienced as they were called by God to renew his people—resembles the vision and transformation of Daniel in the presence of his uncomprehending companions (Dan. 10:2–12).[27] In Mark as well as in Daniel and in Paul (2 Cor. 3:7–18), the vision of God is linked with the promise of renewal of the covenant. As in Daniel, the informed elect are given assurance of the divine deliverer who will come when the faithful have passed through their time of tribulation (13:24–27). They are also assured that God will preserve them through this coming period of conflict and judgment on the wicked (13:19–20). These, then, are the solemn warnings, the insights about God's purpose, and the promises of divine preservation that are vouchsafed to the faithful and elect community. They are informed that the Temple will be destroyed, that the present age will end, and that Jesus' death and resurrection are guarantees of their own ultimate deliverance into the new era for God's people.

The Challenges and Responses That Shaped the Markan Community

The first encounter experienced by Jesus in Mark is his temptation or testing by Satan (1:12–13). That this was regarded as part of the divine plan can be inferred from the report that the Spirit (literally) "expelled" him into the desert and that the angels were on hand to support him (Ps. 91:11). His experience recalls those of Moses (Exod. 3) and Elijah (1 Kings 19:11–18) as they underwent struggles in the desert in preparation for their roles renewing God's people. The theme of conflict with the powers of evil is sounded as Jesus begins his public activity in Capernaum: his teaching is followed by the exorcism of "an unclean spirit" (1:23–26), and the summary of his activity and his "new teaching" is that "he commands even the unclean spirits" (1:27).

The human opposition that Jesus encounters in Mark comes chiefly from the religious establishment, including the scribes, the Pharisees, and later the Council (synedrion) and the political and military power of Rome with which the religious leaders cooperate. The opening scene of Jesus' public ministry at the synagogue in Capernaum includes a contrast between Jesus' authority and the scribes' lack of it (1:22). It is the scribes and Pharisees who object to Jesus pronouncing forgiveness of sins to the paralytic (2:6), inviting a tax collector to be among his inner circle of followers (2:16), and refusing to demand that his followers fast (2:18). Detailed accounts of controversies with the Pharisees are reported in Mark 7:1–23, 8:11–13, and 12:37–40, where the issues concern Jesus' negative view of ritual purity, his refusal to offer his critics any miraculous confirmation of God's support for him, and his criticism of their religious ostentation (12:37–40). Jesus takes issue with the dominant interpreters of the Torah on such questions as whether there will be a resurrection (12:18–27) and which is the chief commandment (12:28–34).

There is an indication that Jesus' family was also initially opposed to his public activity in behalf of the coming kingdom of God. They try to restrain him because some are charging that he is out of his mind (3:21). The effort to take him out of the public arena leads to his assertion that his true family is comprised of those who perceive and obey God's will, rather than his literal kin (3:32–35).

Confrontation over traditional interpretations of the law and the official institutions of Judaism occupies much of the last third of Mark. The critique of the Temple and of the offical mode of the covenant community is hinted at in 11:11 and then articulated in symbolic form in the cursing of the fig tree (11:12–14), with the explanation of the image in 11:20–25. Jesus' critique is enacted in the cleansing of the Temple (11:15–19), with justification offered for this audacious action by appeal to scripture (Isa. 56:7; Jer. 7:11), on the ground that the place where all people might approach and find God has become a commercial enterprise for the benefit of the religious establishment. The critique of the religious institution and its defining of God's people builds on imagery of Israel as vineyard in Isaiah 5, but moves beyond that picture to foresee the people's rejection and murder of the divinely sent agent of their renewal (12:1–12). The image shifts to picture new tenants of the vineyard, but also a new structure of God's people, which is likewise said to be in fulfillment of scripture (12:10 = Ps. 118:22–23). There is to be no political subversion or attack on Roman power, however (12:13–17), but God will establish the "Son of David" as "Lord," triumphant over the enemies of his people (12:35–37)—once more, in fulfillment of scripture (Ps. 110:1). What is pictured here is not a retreat into a sphere of detached individual or small-group piety, but a confrontation between the agent of God for renewal of his people and the incumbent powers, political and religious.[28] After announcing the impending destruction of the Temple (13:1–4), Jesus is quoted as warning of the conflicts and persecution his followers will experience at the hands of the religious and civil authorities (13:9–11), including betrayal by members of their own families (13:13). Building on details of the imagery in Daniel 9 and 12, the desecration of the Temple and the cosmic disturbances that accompany these catastrophes are described (13:14–19), but with the promise of the survival of the elect (13:20–23). The final denouement will come with the disclosure of the Son of Man and the assembling of the elect from across the world (13:24–27). The time of this is soon, but no human knows it precisely (13:30–32).

Community Attitudes and Actions in Response to the Crisis

Throughout Mark, there are detailed instructions and special insights as to how the community is to deport itself with respect to both inner relationships and external, largely hostile forces. The members' primary role is to imitate the activity of Jesus: preaching the good news, expelling demons and healing the sick, and calling others to follow (2:14). They also have Jesus as a model for radical reinterpretation of the Torah, even on such basic issues as sabbath observance (2:27–28) and divorce (10:1–12).

They are to be prepared for a wide range of responses, as symbolized by the diverse results in the Parable of the Sower (4:13–20), ranging from hostility to astonishing acceptance, and from tiny beginnings to impressive growth in the Parable of the Mustard Seed (4:30–32).

The members of the community are forewarned about the costs and temptations they will experience in their commitment to Jesus. They must be prepared to face scorn because of their association with Jesus and even the possibility of losing their lives for following him (8:34–38). Prime examples of failure to remain faithful are not only Judas, the traitor (14:10–11), but also the denial of Jesus by Peter (14:26–31). Total personal discipline is required of those who are to enter the kingdom of God (9:42–48). Their attitude toward others within the community is to be modeled after that of a servant, who seeks only to fill the needs of others rather than aspiring to personal preeminence (9:33–37). They are to fulfill their duties diligently within the community, since they do not know when "the master of the house" will return and call them to account (13:33–37). In the interim, through shared bread and wine they are to celebrate his act of self-giving on the cross, which is the ground for the covenant in which they now participate (14:22–25), while awaiting the imminent coming of the kingdom of God, which some of them will live to see (9:1).

Jesus' Role and Authority in the Markan Community

Mark's account of Jesus being identified as God's agent through the descent of the Spirit upon him and the voice from heaven acclaiming him as "my beloved Son" reports this as a private experience of Jesus alone.[29] The declaration is a composite of the divinely appointed and "anointed" regent (Ps. 2:7) and the servant of the Lord (Isa. 42:1), upon whom God's Spirit will be poured out and who will "bring justice to the nations." The outpouring of the Spirit upon Jesus recalls Isaiah 61, where it is "the anointed" who is empowered to bring "good news" of justice and comfort to the oppressed and the afflicted. Ironically, it is the "unclean spirits" who are the first in Mark to recognize Jesus as "Son of God" (3:11). Throughout Mark, the actions of Jesus are evidences of the divine authority that has been granted to him to prepare the creation for the coming of God's rule. In most cases, Jesus' role as God's agent of renewal of his people and of the creation is not explicit but inferential, with the responsibility resting on the observer—or the reader/hearer of Mark—to draw the conclusion as to who Jesus is and what the source of his powers is.

Jesus' calming the storm by his simple command, "Peace! Be still!" (4:39) and his ability to walk on the water (6:45–52) recall the divine command that puts the waters in their place at the creation (Gen. 1:1–11) and the defeat of Leviathan, the sea monster who came to be perceived as the embodiment of evil but whom

God would defeat in the end time (Ps. 74:13–14; 104:26).[30] The availability of God's liberating power over the demons extends beyond the Jewish community to the wider Gentile world in the story of the Gerasene demoniac (5:1–20), as I have already noted. The feeding of the five thousand in a "deserted place" (6:30–44) recalls God's provision of sustenance for his covenant people on their journey from slavery in Egypt to freedom in their new land (Exod. 16:1–36; Num. 11:4–9).

Jesus' position as the anointed of God has its origins and basic definition in the Jewish tradition, but it transcends traditional structures and expectations. His healings and exorcisms take place in Gentile territories as well as in predominantly Jewish districts (6:53–56). All these stories serve to show that Jesus' role as God's agent of renewal for his people includes both cosmic as well as personal dimensions, and that its benefits extend to all who are ready to receive them from him. The traditional human notion that personal prosperity is a sign of divine approval is forcefully challenged in the story of Jesus' encounter with the rich man who comes seeking assurance of a share in eternal life (10:17–31). Jesus tells him that prosperity is a problem for those seeking to enter the kingdom of God, and that riches and family resources must not be relied upon but given up if one is to place one's trust solely in the power and purpose of God.

The model for the suffering that the community must experience is Jesus himself, who repeatedly predicts his own suffering and death in the fulfillment of God's purpose through him as Messiah. The specifics of his suffering are detailed (8:31; 9:31; and 10:33–34), as well as the promise of God's vindication of him by raising him from the dead. Paradoxically, Jesus appears as Son of Man—the triumphant figure who in Dan. 7:13 and the Similitudes of Enoch 46–48 defeats the powers of evil and is a source of light and wisdom for the community of the faithful.[31] Although the logical (or theological) links between suffering or death and triumphant divine vindication are not spelled out in Daniel, they are implicit in Daniel's early stories that report how God delivered the faithful when they refused to compromise their convictions as God's people: in the lions' den, the fiery furnace, and other threats of death at the hand of the pagan ruler. It is in keeping with this understanding that Jesus is reported in Mark 9:12 as asking the rhetorical question, "How is it written of the son of man, that he should suffer many things and be treated with contempt?" Even with precedent and rationale for Jesus' suffering, the immediate prospect of it in the garden (14:32–42) and the actual experience of it on the cross (15:33–41) are depicted as involving him in personal struggle. Yet in both cases the narrative incorporates direct reference to scripture (Ps. 42:6; Ps. 22:1) as well as scriptural allusions (Mark 15:36; Ps. 69:21) in order to demonstrate that this seeming tragedy is part of the divine purpose. Jesus' role in his mission, in the defeat of the powers of evil, in the challenge to the religious authorities, in his open invitation for participation in God's people by outsiders— all these are correlated with scripture in Mark's account of Jesus' redefining and rebuilding the people of God.

The New Community and Jesus as Agent of Divine
Reconciliation according to Paul

Two powerful influences on the thought of Paul with respect to his under-standing of the role of Jesus and of the new community of the covenant are his Pharisaic background and the dominant philosophical modes of the first century C.E.: Stoicism and Middle Platonism. Paul's earlier commitment to the Pharisees had involved him deeply in the efforts of that group to define the people of God by direct appropriation of the whole range of Jewish scriptures of the time—law, prophets, and both wisdom and liturgical traditions.

The popular modern caricature of the Pharisees as nit-picking legalists has been effectively challenged and replaced by the scholarly analyses of the evidence in the extensive writings of Jacob Neusner[32] and in the historical studies by Shaye Cohen and Anthony Saldarini.[33] Although Paul mentions his earlier connections with the Pharisees only once in his preserved letters,[34] it is obvious that the more faithful image of the Pharisees as primarily concerned for the direct relevance of the scriptures to the daily lives of their segment of God's people fits well with the image of Paul that shines through his writings. Gathered informally in homes for study and devotion and sharing common meals, the Pharisees sought to draw and maintain the lines of ethnic and personal purity that they were convinced should characterize the true people of God. It is wholly appropriate to someone of such a background that in Paul's letters the dominant theme is, What qualifies one for participation in the covenant people? The reverse side of the image of Paul the (preconversion) Pharisee is evident in his original violent hostility toward the early Christian communities,[35] which, like the Pharisees, were meeting in homes, appro-priating the scriptures to define themselves and their roles in the purpose of God. From the outset, the Jesus movement violated the Jewish traditions of ethnic and ritual distinctiveness for God's people. This group of followers of Jesus was seen by preconversion Paul as giving precisely the wrong answers to the right questions, which were dominant among the Pharisees.[36]

The second powerful influence on Paul's thought derived from the ethos of the urban, strongly hellenized places where Paul lived in Syria and southern Asia Minor. If credence were to be given to the tradition in Acts that links Paul with Tarsus,[37] it would be easy to account for the pervasive influence of Stoic thought and terminology on him, since Tarsus in this period was a major center of Stoic learning.[38] But the impact of Stoic philosophy on Jewish thought in this period was so strong that Paul would have been affected by it, no matter where his place of birth and training. The themes Paul shares with the Stoics include the universal access to natural law, the human capacity (conscience) to grasp that law, the basic human virtues, moral responsibility and accountability, and life beyond death. I shall note some of these features in detail in the analysis of Paul below.

To this conception of universal wisdom, Paul added a crucial additional factor:

the wisdom that God through Jesus has now revealed to his people. These two factors are joined in the opening lines of his most systematic letter, to the Romans (1:16–20). The problem of human evil is not the result of ignorance, but of suppression of the universally available truth about God: the invisible nature of God, his eternal power and deity. To know God is a possibility for the human race, but its members have chosen instead to worship objects of their own fashioning and to exchange the truth about God for a lie. This violation of the divinely intended relation of humans to their creator was responded to by a divine decree that led to the shattering of human relations as well, and to moral corruption in spite of the common knowledge of human accountability before God. No humans have an excuse for the moral disaster in which they find themselves. This is the case with those in the Israelite tradition, who have the law given to them through Moses, but it is also the situation of all other humans, who have access through their conscience to the divine law of the universe (2:12–16). Those with the special advantage of access to the Torah have forfeited their favored position by their immoral behavior in defiance of the God-given law (2:17–24). A divine irony lies in the fact that the rejection of Jesus by the Jewish leadership in Jerusalem has resulted in making accessible to complete outsiders a share in God's people; that is, to the Gentiles (3:1–8). Yet all humanity, both Jews and Gentiles, stands under divine condemnation for having rejected knowledge of God and obedience to his moral demands (3:9–20).

Jesus as Revealer of Divine Wisdom

God has by no means abandoned the human race, however. He has established a new mode of disclosure of his will and purpose for the creation and for those who are now chosen to be his people. Through the gospel that Paul preaches, God has made known his purpose through Jesus "according to the revelation (apokalypsis) of the mystery which was kept secret for long ages but is now disclosed and through the prophetic writings is made known to all nations . . . to bring about the obedience of faith" (Rom. 16:25–26). Thus has "the only wise God" made known his mode of renewing the creation (16:27). True wisdom is now revealed through Jesus, but the wisdom of this age and its purveyors will be shown to be foolish and vain (1 Cor. 1:17–22). God has confounded the self-styled "wise"—Jewish and Greek—and confronts all humanity with the gospel of the crucified Jesus, which seems utter folly to the worldly-wise. Unlike the "wisdom of this age," which the human race has spurned or perverted, "the secret and hidden wisdom" that God has disclosed to the faithful through and concerning Christ is accessible through the work of God's Spirit, which alone can make it comprehensible to God's people (1 Cor. 2:6–13).

The essence of this divinely disclosed wisdom concerns Jesus Christ, who was revealed (apokalypsai) to Paul with the aim that he should become the prime instrument for proclamation of Jesus among the Gentiles (Gal. 1:15–16). Jews and Gentiles alike can leave their position as the immature under care of what would be called today a babysitter (*paidagogos*) and take their God-given place as mature "sons" and daughters in the new community. There all human-imposed distinctions are dissolved: "Neither Jew nor Greek, slave nor free, male nor female." Through Christ they become members of the new covenant community, in the tradition of Abraham (Gal. 3:24–28).

Although Paul does not elaborate the idea in his letters, he clearly regarded Jesus as the human embodiment of divine wisdom, in sharp contrast to what human wisdom claimed to offer: "God chose what is foolish in the world to shame the wise . . . what is weak, low and despised" (1 Cor. 1:27–28). But Jesus, who is "the source of life" for the new community, "has become for us wisdom from God, and righteousness, and sanctification, and redemption" (1 Cor. 1:30). Thus the wisdom that Jesus embodies consists not only in what insights he reveals about God and his purpose for his people, but also in who he is and what he accomplishes in order to carry out that divine plan of human renewal. It is to these dimensions of Jesus' role that I now turn.

Jesus as Agent of Reconciliation and Renewal

Paul's perception of the relationship of Jesus to God, while including such attributes of wisdom as preexistence,[39] lays emphasis on what Jesus has done for the renewal of his people and of the creation. Yet in several important passages in his letters, Paul implies or even affirms that Jesus shared in the divine nature prior to his appearance on earth as the child of Mary. This is implied in the metaphor of his foregoing riches (of divine resources and relationship) and accepting poverty (of human limitations), according to 2 Cor. 8:9. It is more directly stated in Gal. 4:4, where God is said to have "sent his Son," placing him under the human limitations of birth and subjection to the law of Moses, in order to make possible the "adoption" of human beings as God's children. But the idea of preexistence is explicit in the Christ-hymn of Phil. 2:6–11. There Jesus Christ's being "in the form of God" and sharing "equality with God" is contrasted with the servile role he assumed when he took on the likeness or form of a human being, which culminated in his death on the cross. God's reward for this act of total obedience is the ultimate bringing of all humanity to acknowledge him as Lord. Thus there are two roles in the Jewish scriptures that are seen as combined in Jesus: the eternal purpose of God to renew the creation (= wisdom) and the human agent through whom God's sovereignty is effective in the world (= God's Son, Ps. 2).

Other psalms that look forward to the fulfillment of God's purpose through human agents emphasize other features than the royal role. In Psalm 8, the basically limited capacities of humans (literally "son of man") are contrasted with the universal sovereignty that God has assigned to his chosen agent. In Psalm 110, the divine instrument through whom sovereignty is established over the world and its inhabitants is pictured as an everliving priest. Similarly, in Paul's letters, the eternal nature of God's instrument is secondary to the modes of powerful action by which the divine sovereignty is to be made effective in the creation. Throughout his letters, Paul's depiction of Jesus lays emphasis on these roles of renewal.

The Redemptive Roles of Jesus

As noted above, in 1 Cor. 1:30, Paul links Jesus' role as the embodiment of "wisdom from God" with three functions: "righteousness" (*dikaiosune*), "santification" (*hagiasmos*), and "redemption" (*apolutrosis*). The text quoted from Jer. 9:23–24 contrasts human boasting in supposed wisdom with God's salvific activity, and then describes true "circumcision" as of the "heart" rather than the "foreskin." Clearly the imagery in the prophet, as in Paul's thought, concerns a mode of spiritual priesthood that results in inward moral transformation rather than external ritual acts. It is this theme and these sacerdotal images that are of central importance for Paul, especially in Romans 3.

The mosaic of quotes from scripture by which Paul sets forth his universal indictment of the human race, Jewish and Gentile (Rom. 3:10–18), describes moral failures and violations, but the conclusion is that the whole *kosmos* is liable for punishment under the law (3:19–20). None are acceptable; none meet the moral standards; none really "seeks for God" (3:11). All "fall short of the glory of God," in that they fail to measure up to the glorious image in which God created human beings (Ps. 8:5–8), when he intended them to take responsibility for the creation. Instead, they have failed to achieve the status and purity (*dikaiosune*) that God purposed for them (Rom. 3:19–20). The human problem is not one of a failure to attain judicially defensible status, as the usual translation, "justification," implies. Paul is emphatic that evaluation of humans by legal standards only confuses the issue: not by "works of law." Instead, what God has accomplished through Jesus provides acceptability for his people at both the personal and the communal level.

This inference is confirmed by the imagery of two other crucial terms in this section of Romans (3:25–26): liberation (*apolytrosis*) and expiation (*hilasterion*). The former term is used in the Septuagint for the freeing of a female slave to return to her family (Exod. 21:8) and for the restoration of Nebuchadnezzar to sanity and his royal role (Dan. 4:34–36). In both cases, the liberating act results in an achievement of intended status. Here the freedom provided through Jesus is available on the basis of trust (*pistis*) in what God has done, and the legal obligations are set aside. This does not mean that God is indifferent toward human sin, however. The other image in this passage makes clear the cost at which this liberation has been made possible: it is God who provided the expiatory sacrifice (*hilasterion*) that removes sin as a barrier between humans and their God. Unlike the argument of the Letter to the Hebrews (see below), Jesus *is* the sacrifice, and God exercized the priestly role of setting forth this efficacious offering. In Rom. 4:25, Jesus is said to have been "given over" as a sacrifice in payment for the "trespasses" of his people. Here the image recalls the offerings on the Day of Atonement (Lev. 16:1–34), when the ground of Israel's relationship with God is renewed by the sacrifice that makes "atonement for the people of Israel . . . for all their sins."

In his letter to the Galatians, Paul implies a more active role for Jesus, who is said to have given himself for his people and their sins. In Phil. 2:5–11, Paul blends active and passive roles for Jesus when he pictures him as "taking the form of a slave" and becoming "obedient unto death." In spite of these differences in detail, it is clear that Paul is using priestly imagery to depict the function Jesus had in bringing God's people into right relationship with their Lord and creator, through sacrifice for covenant renewal. That is the implication of Rom. 4:25, where Jesus is said to have been "handed over" as a sacrifice, as a way of "dealing with our transgressions." Above all, the repeated motif of Jesus accomplishing reconciliation between God and his disobedient and estranged people—Paul calls them "enemies"—occurs at crucial points in Paul's arguments (Rom. 5:10–11). In 2 Cor. 5:18–19, it is God himself who through Christ launches this dynamic of reconciliation. The terminology and imagery of Israel's cultic traditions are adapted and transformed by Paul, in that the reconciling sacrifice is human and the initiative in providing it is divine. Those who put their trust in this provision for expiation of sins and renewal of covenantal relationship are the new people of God who share in these benefits.

The Renewal of the Creation

In Genesis 3, the consequence of the sin of Adam and Eve is the cursing of the serpent, the travail of childbirth, and the struggle of humans to provide for their own basic needs. Paul D. Hanson has shown that, as the later prophetic tradition of Israel moved in the direction of apocalyptic, there was increasing attention to the cosmic accompaniments of God's renewal of his people, and God is portrayed as divine warrior, engaged in combat with superhuman powers. These features are evident in Isaiah 56—66 and especially in Zechariah 9–14, where Yahweh's defeat of his enemies and the renewal of Jerusalem and its temple include the transformation of even the topography of the area (Zech. 14:1–21).[40] Ernst Käsemann has called attention to the importance of the theme of cosmic conflict and renewal in the literature of Jewish apocalyptic, citing 4 Ezra 7:11–12[41] and 2 Baruch 15:7,[42] to show that the renewal of the creation will be a benefit for the faithful people of God in the age to come.

It is this hope, conceived and expressed in a variant mode of Jewish apocalyptic, that Paul declares has been assured by God through Jesus' death and resurrection. The cosmic dimensions of this mode of expectation are elaborated in later writings attributed to Paul, such as the Letter to the Colossians. All things are to be reconciled to God, earthly and heavenly (Col. 1:20). But in Rom. 8:38, Paul declares that none of these powers of evil will be able to frustrate God's loving purpose disclosed and effected through "Jesus Christ our Lord." In Rom. 8:18–25, Paul offers an elaborate account of the correlation between the redemption of

God's new people and the liberation of the created order from its bondage to the powers of evil. Indeed, the creation is depicted as "longing eagerly for the revealing [apokalypsis] of the children of God." It is currently in a state of "travail," subject as it is to these demonic forces that cause decay and thwart freedom. The presence of the Spirit within the people of God gives them hope and promise of ultimate liberation and vindication. They can be confident that no matter how potent these evil forces—death, principalities, and powers—now seem to be, Christ's resurrection from the dead gives his people assurance of ultimate defeat of these potencies and of a share in the triumphant liberty and fulfillment of God's purpose for the faithful.

Jesus and the New People of God according to Paul

Paul uses two major Old Testament figures—Abraham and Adam—to depict the role of Jesus in accomplishing God's plan for renewal of his covenant people; both of them have major implications for the understanding of this new people.

Abraham: The Father of All Who Believe God's Promise

The biblical tradition about Abraham shows that both circumcised Jews and uncircumcised Gentiles have equal opportunity to share in God's promise for his people. It was before Abraham was circumcised that he trusted in God's promise that he would have a son in spite of his inability to have one by Sarah. It was Abraham's trust in God's word to him that led to his entering a right relationship with God (Rom. 4:3; Gen. 15:6). This ground of acceptance by God is confirmed in the psalmist's pronouncement of God's gracious forgiveness (Rom. 4:6–7; Ps. 31:6) and in the establishment of the aged, humanly speaking heirless Abraham as the progenitor of the whole family of faith, both Jews and Gentiles (Rom. 4:17: Gen. 17:5). He did not waver, but was "fully convinced that God was able to do what he had promised" (Rom. 4:20–21). Similarly, the new people of God are those of whatever race or human qualification who trust in the new promise that God has given by allowing Jesus to be the sacrifice for "our trespasses" and then raising him from the dead. On this basis, God accepts those who trust him in a right relationship as members of the community of faith (Rom. 4:24–25).

Jesus: The New Adam as Prototype of God's People

Adam's role as the "type of the one who was to come" is largely a matter of contrast. Through Adam came sin and death, which permeated the whole of humanity, even before the law was given through Moses, among those who did not have a direct command from God as Adam did (Rom. 5:12–14). In an earlier letter, 1 Corinthians, Paul had offered a similar set of contrasts between Adam and Christ (1 Cor. 15:45–49). Adam was a "living being" shaped from "dust" (Gen. 2:7), and all humanity has borne his image, whose sure end is death. Christ is "a man from heaven" and a "life-giving spirit," who makes possible sharing in the kingdom of God. The contrasts are multiplied in Rom. 5:15–21. Judgment and death fell on the human race because of one archetypal sin of Adam. The gift of grace and human renewal is now available for all humanity through the obedience of Jesus. The giving of the law only heightened the consciousness and the activity of sin, but God's free gift leads to forgiveness and "eternal life" for the "many" who will accept it in faith.

The consequences for moral transformation and renewal of life are vividly described in Rom. 6:1–23. The rite of baptism symbolizes identification with Christ in death, burial, and resurrection. This is not merely an external ritual, how-ever, but leads to moral renewal through liberation from the deadening power of sin and to the new life that God provides. Responsibility still rests on members of the new community to refuse submission to the impulse to sin and instead to be fully obedient to the "new standard of teaching" established through the work of the Spirit among God's people. Those who were once "slaves of sin" are called now to become "slaves of righteousness," which will lead to their moral transformation into the holy people of God and their participation in the life of the age to come.

Implicitly, or perhaps unconsciously, Paul employs a metaphor that is akin to the Adam and Eve story to describe the basis of life for God's new people. In Rom. 7:1–25, the image changes to that of a marital relationship terminated by death.[43] Paul's point is that death through the "body of Christ" and the subsequent share in his resurrection free God's people from submission to sin and enable them to live by the power of the Spirit (Rom. 8:1–17). This new life is to be lived, not in dependence upon frail, flawed human resources ("the flesh"), as was the tragic case with Adam, but in sole reliance on the power, insight, and direction that God pro-vides for his people through the Spirit. The intimacy of the new relationship of the community to God is dramatically evident in Paul's instruction to address him by the Semitic term of childlike affection, "Abba." Compensating for human weak-ness in matters of morals and personal commitment are the compassion and insight provided by God's Spirit (Rom. 8:26–27).

The New Relationships of God's People

Paul describes the transformation of a range of relationships for the members of the new community, with traditional Israel, with the secular authorities, and with the diverse members of the new people of God.

Perhaps Paul's most radical statement on the issue of the relationship of the new community to the traditional definitions of Israel appears in Gal. 3:28, where he declares: "There is no longer Jew or Greek, there is no longer slave or free; there is no longer male or female; for all of you are one in Christ Jesus." From his extended and somewhat convoluted discussion in Romans 9–11, however, one can see that Paul continued to struggle with the question whether there was still a place in God's purpose for his historic covenant community, Israel.[44] Physical descent from Abraham and exercise of the human will are not the ground of right relationship with God. Rather, it is achieved by the sovereign mercy of God, which he chooses to disclose through certain human instruments (Rom. 9:6–22). Those who are called of God include many who are not part of the traditional people of God; the group includes both Jews and Gentiles, though only a "remnant" of Israel will share in this community of faith and be called children of the living God (Rom. 9:25–27; Hos. 2:1, 25; Isa. 10:22). The ground of right relationship for both Jew and Gentile is to trust in God and his promise to his people, and specifically to see Jesus as God's agent of renewal rather than as a stone of stumbling (Isa. 8:14). The criterion by which anyone—Jew or Gentile—finds acceptance with God and membership in his people is trust in Jesus as Lord, whom God raised from the dead (Rom. 10:5–13). This message has proved to be offensive to traditional Israel, but it is the instrument of renewal for Gentiles who hear it as God's word of renewal of his people (Rom. 10:18–21; Deut. 32:21; Isa. 65:1–2).

This does not mean that God has abandoned historic Israel, however. But Israel's rejection of Jesus as Messiah has encouraged the outreach of the gospel to Gentiles. With an elaborate metaphor of branches from a wild olive tree grafted on a cultivated olive tree, Paul insists that the Gentile converts must live productive lives in the new community in order that eventually Jews will seek there a share in God's mercy (Rom. 11:25–32). He concludes the discussion of this issue with an affirmation that God's ways are "unsearchable" and "inscrutable" and then calls for the eternal glorification of God (11:33–36). The fact that many in Israel do not see Jesus as God's agent of covenant renewal does not impugn the fidelity of God, nor does it preclude the ultimate participation of many Jews in the new community. Although he cannot fully comprehend or explain the divine process, Paul declares that what God is doing through Jesus is the spreading of "the riches and wisdom and knowledge of God" (11:33). He is convinced that priority must be given to proclaiming the good news to Jews, which is "the power of God for salvation to everyone who has faith, to the Jew first and also to the Greek" (1:16).

Until God's ultimate plan of renewal is accomplished, the relationship of the new community to the Roman authorities is to be one of obedience and fulfillment of obligations (Rom. 13:1–7). This includes submission to secular agents, since their position of authority has been given them by God as a means of maintaining order and stability in the shared life of the empire. The officers will punish only those whose acts are antisocial and will even look kindly on good deeds done by members of the new community. Here again Paul is assuming the operation of that beneficial force, the law of nature, by which the "conscience" of Christians will lead them to obedience. Obedience to this authority is called for, since the authority derives ultimately from God.

Relationships within the community are described by Paul in connection with moral behavior and functions within the group. There is to be recognition as well as affirmation of diversity within the community. Different opinions are to be respected on matters of dietary rules and observance of holy days (Rom. 14:1–6). In spite of these diverse rules and convictions, all members of the group are to be accepted and affirmed. The chief goal is to seek for "peace and mutual upbuilding" (14:19). Even private matters of faith are not to be allowed to become issues that cause separation within the community; instead, all are to seek the welfare of others in spite of diversities, so that in unity they can join in glorifying God (15:1–6). They are to give equal recognition to the fact that what Christ has done confirms "the promises given to the patriarchs" and that the gospel can lead "Gentiles to glorify God" and give them hope (15:7–13).

In addition to the diversity of background and regulations among the members of the community, there are important differences in roles they are to follow for the benefit of the community as a whole (1 Cor. 12–14). The "spiritual gifts" all come from God, and their exercise is to be seen as God's way of caring for the needs of the community, both internally and in its ministry to the wider world. Building on the analogy of the human body, Paul affirms the unity of this body in spite of the diversity of roles fulfilled by its members. These include "the utterance of wisdom . . . and of knowledge," which confirms the picture of this group as the community of the wise, as well as prophecy and interpretation of the ecstatic speech that some members utter (12:4–11). All the roles are to be viewed with equal respect, even though some have leadership responsibilities as "apostles, prophets, teachers, administrators" (12:14–29). Love functions as both dynamic and lubricant to overcome differences among the members (13:1–12). Those gifted with ecstatic speech are not to take pride in their spectacular gift, but to recognize that its function is to enable them to speak to the members "for their upbuilding and encouragement and consolation" and to bring "some revelation [apokalypsis] or knowledge [gnosis] or prophecy or teaching [didache] (14:1–6). The overarching aim in the exercise of these charismatic gifts must be "building up the church" (14:12). The contribution of individual members—"a hymn, a lesson, a revelation, a tongue, or an interpretation"—must be done for the purpose of "edification." The same theme is sounded in Rom. 12:1–8, where the diversity of spiritual gifts (charismata) is affirmed, along with their significance for the life of the body as a whole. In addition, there is mention of the importance of financial contribution (12:8, 13) for sustaining the common life of the new community. In this way the members will experience renewal of the mind and demonstrate the will of God concretely in their common life (12:2).

The Revelation through God's Spirit

In 1 Cor. 2:1–13, Paul contrasts the resource of human wisdom with that which God provides through the Spirit. The latter is "secret and hidden," and therefore inaccessible to "the rulers of this age." Combining phrases from the prophets (Isa. 64:3; 52:15) and from an extracanonical apocalyptic source (possibly an Apocalypse of Elijah[45]), Paul declares that this wisdom has been "revealed" [apekalupsen] by God through the Spirit. Only by this means can humans "comprehend the thoughts of God," which are communicated in "words not taught by human wisdom but taught by the Spirit."

Paul's teaching about the nature of the resurrection in 1 Corinthians 15 culminates in an account of the ultimate victory over the power of death and the transformation of human nature. What Paul writes here (as in all his letters) is not simply the logical conclusion of an intellectual inquiry or inference from philosophical or scriptural principles. Instead, as he phrases it, "Lo, I am telling you a mystery!" This is wisdom reserved for the members of the covenant community.

Apocalyptic Letters: Jude and 2 Peter

Not only does the writer of the Letter of Jude share features of the outlook of earlier Jewish and Christian apocalyptic writings, but he alludes to one such document in verse 9 (Ascension of Moses) and quotes another in verse 15 (Enoch Apocalypse). The Letter of Jude was probably produced shortly after the turn of the second century C.E., and is obviously pseudonymous in its claim to have been written by a brother of Jesus (v. 1). What is important for our purposes is to see that the primary concern of the writer is not the vindication of God's people at the coming of the end of the age, as in the earlier Christian apocalyptic material, but the regrettable condition of the Christian community in the interim before the eschaton occurs. The problems are doctrinal and ethical: what is being taught does not conform to "the faith that was once for all transmitted to the saints" (v. 3). Faith is here conceived as a body of theological truth. There is also moral perversion in the community, exploiting the Pauline teaching of grace and freedom for sensual and personal gratification (v. 4). The writer warns of the precedents in the experience of ancient Israel for God's punitive judgment on his disobedient people, and shows that the irresponsible ones have chosen as their behavioral models Cain (Gen. 4:8–9), Balaam (Num. 22), and Korah (Num. 16). Their moral and theological apostasy is a sign of the "last days" (2 Tim. 3:1–5). Accordingly, the faithful are called to build themselves up in the most holy faith, which is a summons to doctrinal development and the formation of confessional criteria for gaining and maintaining status in the life of the church (v. 20). The apocalyptic hope of the community in Jude emphasizes judgment on the defectors rather than fulfillment of the divine purpose for the covenant community. The chief grounds for group identity are correct doctrine and moral behavior.

These features are even more clearly evident in 2 Peter, which is directly dependent on Jude[46] but intensifies the centrality of correct faith (1:1) and "full knowledge" of God and Christ. This perception of faith and practice is also informed by popular Stoic philosophy. Both these influences are demonstrated in the formal opening of the letter, which employs the technical vocabulary of Stoic thought as well as the Hellenistic pattern of linking logically a series of virtues: "Just as all things that have to do with divine power concerning life and religion have been granted to us through the full knowledge of the One who called us to share in his own glory and excellence, through which he granted to us precious and great promises, in order that through these you might become participants in

The Community of the Wise

the divine nature, escaping this world's desire for corruption. For this reason, pursue with every effort to multiply your virtue by faith, and by virtue knowledge, and by knowledge self-control, and by self-control persistence, and by persistence piety, by piety mutual affection, and by mutual affection love."

The outcome of this process of moral renewal will be—stated negatively—"you will not be ineffective or unfruitful in the full knowledge of Christ" (2 Pet. 1:8). What will preserve the faithful and enable them to enter the future kingdom is a mix of correct behavior and authentic beliefs, once they are established in the truth (1:10–12). Confirming the truth is God's voice from heaven at the transfiguration of Jesus, which matches the prophetic words that have now been fulfilled. These are not to be interpreted privately, but will be confirmed through the Holy Spirit, in spite of the perversions of the truth by false teachers, who promote their destructive heresies and are doomed to destruction (1:16–2:3). The irrationality of the apostates is matched by their self-indulgent way of life. Because they have turned from the true knowledge of Christ, their final condition will be abysmal and irrevocable, described in an expansion of Prov. 26:11 (2:4–24). Even though the predictions of the end of the age have not yet been fulfilled, this delay should not raise doubts about the certainty of these prophecies. God's time cannot be reckoned by human computation, and the seeming delay allows more time for repentance. The vindication of the holy, as well as the cosmic renewal of the world, is sure to take place. The final appeal to the faithful to remain steadfast in the truth refers explicitly to the letters of Paul, which convey wisdom to the readers and are ranked in authority with "the other scriptures" (3:1–18). Meanwhile, the members of the community are to seek to grow in knowledge of God.

Here, as in Jude, the community maintains its belief in the coming end of the age, but the emphasis falls more on the judgment of the wicked and the apostates than on the fulfillment of God's purpose for his people or the renewal of the creation, as in the earlier Jewish and Christian apocalyptic. Yet the wisdom that has been granted to the elect and faithful community is the paramount factor in its relationship to God and the chief dynamic for its continued existence. Jesus is primarily the instrument of communication of the knowledge of God, in which the community is to seek to grow. It is in this sense that its members are a community of the wise.

Pure and Peaceable Wisdom: The Letter of James

Although the designation of the community at the opening of the Letter of James is "the twelve tribes in the Dispersion" (1:1), the orientation of the author and his readers is influenced far more by ethical issues derived from Greco-Roman culture than by the definitional question of the church's relation to Israel, as debated by Paul in Galatians and Romans. There are quotations from or allusions to scripture (canonical and extracanonical[47]) throughout James, for hortatory or illustrative purposes. But the major aim for the community expressed in this letter is epitomized in James 3:13–18. The highest value is wisdom. True wisdom will manifest itself in a good, or beautiful, lifestyle,[48] which is good works performed in a spirit of gentleness. This approach to life is contrasted with the flamboyant, selfish, gratification-seeking, boastful way of life. Instead of coming down from God and the heavenly realm, it is of this earth (*epigeios*), sensual (*psychikos*), and demonic (*daimoniodes*). James's description of the life produced by true wisdom employs terms that blend Jewish piety and Stoic morality: "pure, peaceable, gentle, willing to yield, full of mercy and good fruits, without a trace of partiality or hypocrisy." Such a life leads to a "harvest of righteousness sown in peace."[49] The encompassing term for the life of the community (1:27) is *threskeia*, "religion" or "worship," which is found frequently in literature and inscriptions from the Greco-Roman period. This "pure and undefiled religion" is to be characterized by works of mercy and maintenance of purity within the world.

The chief problem within the community is the tendency of some members to show partiality toward the rich among them (James 2:1–7). Indeed, the rich are directly and sharply criticized for the false values they have promoted and the injustices of their actions within society (5:1–6). The model for behavior of the members is not to be derived from the surrounding culture (*kosmos*), with its aims to gain material possessions, to fight and kill others, and to indulge one's passions (4:1–4). Humble submission to God and resistance to the devil, cleansing of the heart, and genuine penitence will lead to true piety (4:5–10). Concern for other members, rather than criticism of them, is enjoined. Boasting and egocentric pronouncements are to be avoided (4:13–17). Those who err are to be restored, rather than condemned (5:19–20). The chief moral qualities to be cultivated are purity, patience, steadfastness, compassion, kindness, and a sense of equality. The members must obey not only "the royal law" (love of neighbor, 2:8; Lev. 19:18) but also "the whole law" in every point, while at the same time showing mercy and abstaining from judgment of others (2:10–13). The models from the Old Testament, Abraham and Rahab, are those who not only trusted God but acted accordingly: they had both faith and works (2:22–26). Earnest efforts are to be made to restore erring members of the community (5:19–20). Prayers are essential in behalf of the welfare of others, recognizing illness and the need for forgiveness (5:13–18).

Although there is a strong sense of mutual responsibility within the community, there are only a few indications of leadership roles within the group. Elders and teachers are mentioned (5:14; 3:1), with solemn reminders of the responsibility that goes with taking on the role of teaching. The gathering of the community is described as both *synagoge* (2:2) and *ekklesia* (5:14). Missing from James are any references to the cross or the resurrection of Jesus, to the Eucharist or baptism, and to credal, hymnic, or kerygmatic formulae of faith. The nearest approaches to such confessional declarations are in James 1:1 and 2:1, references to James as "servant of God and the Lord Jesus Christ" and to believing in "our glorious Lord Jesus Christ."

The coming (*parousia*) of "the Lord" is expected and is important for James, and should be for his community as well (James 5:7–18). Patience and endurance are called for, with Job as the prime example of the latter (5:11). There are no details of the eschatological event itself, other than the certainty of judgment (5:9). There is no mention of the resurrection of the dead (as in 1 Cor. 15) or of the enthronement of Jesus (as in Mark 13:24–27). The main value of the *parousia* for James seems to be the theme shared by Jewish, Christian, and Stoic thinkers: the day of human moral accountability before the divine judge. Hence it serves as an encouragement to the faithful to be obedient in spite of difficulties, and as a warning to the rich and avaricious members of the community, whose moral priorities must be set straight. The *parousia* in not an imminent expectation as in Q, Mark, and Paul, nor is it an event derived from the tradition but postponed to the indefinite future, as in 2 Peter. Instead, it is a continuing expectation of divine moral adjudication that is to come.

Apart from the name of Jesus invoked by James and the confidence in his future coming in judgment and vindication, no salvific role is assigned to him in this letter, nor are his teachings appealed to directly as norms for the life of the community. As I have noted, "the wisdom which is from above"—presumably, but not explicitly, brought through him—is seen by James as consonant with many of the Stoic virtues, and the community is called to conform its way of life to this divine pattern. There is no place in this document for the apocalyptic mysteries. Rather, the emphasis is on the divinely disclosed pattern for moral accountability and communal responsibility, in accord with the wisdom from above.

Conclusions concerning the Community of the Wise

It is evident that the wisdom God has granted to his people is perceived in a variety of ways by different early Christian groups, as reflected in their literature. But in every case, that wisdom is to be regarded as a resource for a community as a whole rather than as private information for favored individuals. In the earliest form of the Jesus tradition (as evident in the Q source) the wisdom concerns the role that God has assigned to Jesus, calling his people to prepare in obedience for the coming of the new age, to abandon the ordinary human bases for stability and identity and rely solely on what God is disclosing and accomplishing through him. Present and prospective participants in this new community are not required to meet ethnic, ritual, occupational, or even moral qualifications. Instead, all who see in Jesus God's agent for renewal of his people and for triumphing over the powers of evil are invited to join. To them are granted the insights essential to understand who Jesus is, who they are, and what he is doing through them.

In the Gospel of Mark, there are explicit contrasts between public statements by Jesus and private explanations to his followers. Their roles as messengers and agents of God's renewing power are given more specific outlines than in Q, as is the warning of the suffering they must endure and the profound significance for covenant renewal of Jesus' suffering, death, and resurrection. The theme of divine judgment on the unheeding and hostile religious establishment is sounded. Disclosed to the community of the faithful is the sad destiny of the social and political establishment, with the assurance that beyond this impending judgment will come God's transformation of the social and political order—the kingdom of God—and the vindication of the new covenant people. At a number of points, Mark notes the sharp contrasts between the new people of God and the standards of the traditionalist leaders. It is only the former who share the God-given wisdom concerning God's purpose and strategy.

In the New Testament documents to which the earliest and most probable dates can be assigned—the letters of Paul—the themes sounded include the establishment of the new covenant people through the sacrificial death and divine vindication of Jesus in the resurrection; the blending of ethical insights drawn from the Jewish scriptures and from popular Stoic morality (e.g., conscience and natural law), which are to provide the norms for the new life in the community; and the power of the Spirit of God to provide insight and enablement for the life of the community. The factor of Gentile participation is handled explicitly by Paul, and the hope of world renewal shared by Stoics and pious Jews (with cultural differences in details) is communicated by Paul to the Gentile churches in such a way as to include its cosmic dimensions. He makes explicit the newness of this community, to which God has granted, through Jesus, the agent and embodiment of divine wisdom, his purpose for his people and for the creation.

In the late first, early second century writings Jude and 2 Peter, the apocalyptic expectation of the community is retained, but with important modifications. Overshadowing the importance of the turn of the ages as the time of God's vindication of the faithful (as in Q, Mark, and Paul), that cataclysmic eschatological event will effect the doom of the disobedient and the apostates. Insight concerning the divine judgment has been granted to the faithful community, which has maintained its integrity and special relationship to God by its fidelity to correct doctrine and to the scriptures. The expectation of imminent fulfillment of God's promise of vindication has been replaced by an acknowledgment of the inability of humans to calculate God's schedule. So long as the community retains its commitment to right doctrine, it can be certain of ultimate deliverance and, above all, of divine judgment on the defectors from the truth.

For the author of James, the wisdom vouchsafed to the community of faith is compatible with the teachings of the Jewish scriptures, as he makes explicit by his examples, but it is also compatible with Stoic moral philosophy, as he shows by his frequent use of the terminology and the rhetorical patterns of Hellenistic ethics. Although the author expects the *parousia* of Jesus, he does not place it within a larger framework of God's cosmic redemptive activity, as does Paul, or of divine vindication of Jesus as Son of man, such as one finds in Mark's gospel. Instead, the coming of Christ as judge is the early Christian equivalent of the widely held Stoic notion of moral accountability that will occur at the end of the present age. It serves as a warning to the morally irresponsible members of the community and as an encouragement to the faithful to persist in seeking ethical purity. The wisdom of God has disclosed the pattern for the moral shape of the life of God's people.

The Law-abiding Community   **3**

The varied and conflict-ridden history of the Jewish people in the four centuries beginning 200 B.C.E. resulted in a range of modes in which they came to understand themselves to be the people of God, culminating in the emergence of rabbinic Judaism in the second to sixth centuries C.E. The fundamental issue, for which many answers were provided in this period, was, What are the criteria for participation in the life of the true Israel, God's covenant people?

The Political Strategy for Jewish Identity

A major crisis precipitated in 168 B.C.E. by the decree of the Seleucid ruler of Syria, Antiochus Epiphanes, requiring all his subjects to acknowledge him as divine led to the Maccabean revolt. Antiochus's initial violation of the integrity of the Jews came when he offered the post of high priest to the highest bidder, Jason, who then encouraged the aggressive hellenization of Jerusalem by erecting a gymnasium there and by fostering a Hellenistic lifestyle in the holy city. Resistance to this forceful acculturation process led to Antiochus's decree in 168, which included the forbidding of circumcision, religious festivals, and observation of the sabbath. All copies of the law were to be destroyed, and an altar to Zeus was set up in the Temple in Jerusalem. Throughout the land, Jews were forced to participate in veneration of the Hellenistic deities.

Resistance to these policies, which threatened the identity of the Jewish people, was led by Mattathias, who launched a successful guerilla campaign under the leadership of his son, Judas (whose nickname was Maccabaeus, "the hammer"), against the Syrian oppressors. A peace treaty was agreed on in 165 B.C.E., and in December of that year Judas entered the Temple in Jerusalem, cleansed it, and reestablished the traditional worship and mode of life of pious Jews. It is this day of triumph that is celebrated today in Hanukkah (dedication), or the Feast of Lights. It appeared that the continuity of Israel as God's special people—controlling their land and maintaining cultic purity—was assured, although occupation of sections of the land by non-Israelites (Ammonites and Idumaeans) and the presence of Syrian troops in a fortress adjacent to the Temple resulted in a continuing low-level struggle for control. The successors of Judas—Simon (142–135) and his son, John Hyrcanus (135–104)—continued successful efforts to gain complete control of the land and to extend its borders to what they had been in the time of David.

At the turn of the century, however, the Maccabean ruler Alexander Jannaeus (103–76 B.C.E.) hired mercenary troops to attack fellow Jews who resisted his ruthless efforts to enlarge his own lands and power. The fact that the Maccabees assumed the roles of both high priest and king, even though they had no right to either title by hereditary descent, was a continuing source of alienation among Jews with a more traditional perspective. After a brief period of peace and conciliation under Alexander's widow, Alexandra (76–67), a fierce contest between her two sons for the throne and their separate appeals to the Roman military leader Pompey (then in Syria) completed the disillusionment of the people with this conflict-ridden political solution to Jewish identity. The coming of Pompey to Jerusalem with his troops in 63 brought to an end this century-long period of Jewish national independence.

Antipater, an Idumaean who served as minister to Hyrcanus II, son of Alexandra, worked closely with the Romans as they established control of the region. His son, Herod, was named king of Judea and Samaria and, after a period of struggle with local resistance groups, ascended the throne in 37 B.C.E., was confirmed by Augustus Caesar in 30, and ruled until his death in 4. By that time, Herod's kingdom had been extended to include his native Idumaea (an area east of the Dead Sea), Galilee, and territory north and east of the Sea of Galilee.

Herod actively fostered the hellenization of this domain by the rebuilding of cities complete with temples, baths, and gymnasia, and he gave support to the imperial cult. But beginning in 20 B.C.E., he ingratiated himself with the Jews in his kingdom and throughout the world when he greatly increased the sacred area on the eastern hill of Jerusalem and built there a new temple for the God of Israel. It was an architectural wonder, attracting many non-Jewish visitors. Yet the selection of the high priest was subject to Roman approval, and Herod's secret police sought to stamp out any Jewish dissent or nationalistic revolts.

At Herod's death, the territory he had ruled was divided among his sons.[1] The ineffectiveness of Archelaus's rule over the region of Judea soon led to the assigning of his territory to Roman procurators, the best-known of whom was Pontius Pilate (26–36 C.E.). In certain purely regional matters such as raising funds for the support of the Temple and the observance of indigenous customs, the Romans followed the older Hellenistic policy of establishing a council (*synedrion*) of wealthy and powerful local leaders, thereby creating at least the semblance of autonomy.

But Pilate's appropriating of funds from the Temple treasury to pay for building a new aqueduct and his ruthless repression of dissent led to his removal by the emperor. They also gave rise to a new wave of Jewish nationalism, which gradually rose to a significant level by the middle of the first century C.E.

Under the procurator Felix (51–60 C.E.), violence on the part of the Jewish nationalists was countered with fierce reaction by the Roman forces, which provoked further resistance, so that by the time of the last of the procurators—Florus (64–66)—the land was filled with revolutionaries and open fighting was common. The Jewish revolt of 66 was doomed before it began, however. Under the Roman military leaders Vespasian and Titus, the rebels were defeated, Jerusalem was severely damaged, and the Temple was destroyed. A second revolt during the reign of the emperor Hadrian in 130–135 resulted in the transformation of Jerusalem into a thoroughly Roman city, which was called Aelia Capitolina, and the erection there on the Temple site of a shrine of Zeus. For a time, Jews were forbidden to live in the city, and the priestly class simply disappeared. Excavation of the stronghold of Jewish resistance at Masada has shown dramatically the intensity of the Jewish efforts to regain political identity, but the failure was complete. Throughout the second century C.E., however, resourceful Jews began to develop another mode of gaining and maintaining identity that proved to be highly effective and enduring, as I shall note below. I shall now review the Jewish models for community described in chapter 1, adding some details to highlight the similarities and contrasts between certain of these Jewish options and the beginnings of the analogous Christian community.

The Cultic Model for Jewish Identity

The spectacular, world-renowned Jerusalem Temple and the economic success of the cult developed there seemed to point to this priestly enterprise as the powerful, logical, and historical model on which Jewish identity should rest. The priestly editing of the legal tradition of Israel—a process that may have begun during the exile in Babylon but flourished after the Persians encouraged Jews to return to the land and reestablish there the worship of their God—gave to the centrality of the cult documentary credibility and legitimacy. Herod's rebuilding of the magnificent structure and the effective collaboration between the Romans and the priestly families lent power and prestige to this enterprise. The carefully delineated sections of the Temple complex—the Court of the Gentiles, the Court of Women, the Court of Israel, and the inner shrines accessible only to priests and ultimately the high priest in the Holy of Holies—gave concrete expression to the special relationship of God to his chosen people through the priests and to his visible presence among them in the innermost sanctuary.

Support for the Priestly Establishment

Although there is no way to determine what portion of the Jewish people were loyal supporters of the Temple and its incumbent priesthood, it is apparent that the money expended by visitors from far away (for purchasing suitable offerings and for changing money into acceptable coinage for contributions) made the Temple function as the most important economic force in the entire region. The control of this enterprise by the priestly elite and their collaborators, with the direct support of the Romans, evoked a range of reactions. Many wanted to share in the tangible benefits of the operation. Others were content simply to take part in what were regarded as the essential cultic activities by which God's people gained and maintained a right relationship with him. Still others, however, while affirming that the Temple and its cultus were indispensable to carrying on that relationship, believed that the cult could not properly be carried out in this place built by Herod and maintained by the incumbent priesthood, who together had collaborated closely with the pagan power of Rome.

As I noted in chapter 1, the major group that supported the priestly establishment was the Sadducees. They claimed descent from the wing of the priestly tribe named by the prophet Ezekiel as the eschatological agents of God for the renewal of the covenant people in the new age that was expected to come soon (Ezek. 40:46; 43:19; 44:15). But because they were mainly members of wealthy, aristocratic families associated with the priesthood, they were eager to avoid direct conflict with Rome on political or cultural issues and seem to have had no interest in any radical transformation of the social or political system. Maintenance of the status quo was essential if the economic, social, and political advantages they enjoyed were to be preserved. Central to their religious convictions were the Temple and its cultus, reinforced by their understanding of the law of Moses. They rejected apocalyptic thought, as well as popular beliefs in angels, demons, and evil powers and the teachings of the prophets. For them, Torah was the basic authority as it found concrete expression in the Temple, the cult, and the priestly establishment.

Dissent against the Incumbent Priesthood: The Dead Sea Community

As I noted in chapter 1, the discovery and subsequent analysis of the Dead Sea Scrolls have provided detailed information about a cultic-oriented Jewish group that was convinced its founder, the Teacher of righteousness,[2] had been given information by God for establishing the truly obedient covenant community that would be vindicated by God in the future and established in Jerusalem in a rebuilt city and Temple.[3] There the people of God would live in purity, with access to the God who dwelt among them. Ruling over them would be two messiahs: the priestly messiah of Aaron, who would be higher in authority, and the royal messiah of Israel, who would restore the divinely sanctioned monarchy.[4] The only way that this obedient community could be properly established and continue as it awaited vindication was by withdrawing from life in Jerusalem and, like Israel in the days of Joshua, living on the eastern borders of the land of Judah on the edge of the desert. The chosen spot for this intermediate residence was a bluff overlooking the northwestern end of the Dead Sea, adjacent to a wadi through which today a seasonal runoff of water from the Jerusalem area flows down to the Dead Sea, but which is described in Ezekiel 47 as a perennial river flowing from beneath the rebuilt Temple of the end time. The scrolls were found in caves in the sides of the wadi and nearby, apparently hidden there as news came of the approaching Roman legions, on their way from Syria to put down the Jewish revolt of 66–70 C.E. On the bluff were found the ruins of the community center, including a common room for dining, with dishes stored in an adjacent pantry, and the remains of writing tables and inkwells where the documents of the community were produced.

The huge literature on this material produced in recent decades includes editions of the documents and interpretations of them.[5] Although there are thousands of fragmentary manuscripts from the Dead Sea caves still awaiting decipherment and publication, the basic pattern of the life and thought of the community has emerged clearly, based on the longer scrolls that have already been published and carefully studied. Among the community writings are the Scroll of the Rule, which recounts the founding of the group, its rules for common life, and its future destiny under God; special commentaries on the scriptures, showing how their hidden meaning is reserved for this community and what regulations the members must observe; the Copper Scroll indicating the treasures of the community and where they are hidden; and the Temple Scroll, which describes in detail what the rebuilt Temple and city of Jerusalem will be like, and who is qualified to live and worship there. Thus, in addition to the divinely achieved renewal of the Temple cult and its priesthood, the detailed rules are set forth by which the community is to live for the present and the future, until the coming of the two messiahs. Central to the ongoing life of this community were two features: gatherings at which the personal meaning of scripture and the group's traditions were explored and appropriated, and a meal of shared bread and wine, in anticipation of the ultimate meal that would be enjoyed when the two messiahs come at the end of the current age.

The fate of this group is unknown, but its library gives vivid and detailed insight into the extent and direction of this dissenting movement in Judaism in the first century C.E. Important to note are the voluntary basis for participation and the confidence that the purpose of God for his people was in process of achievement for and through these members.

The Move toward Personal Appropriation of Tradition

As I have already noted in chapter 1, in recent decades, Jewish scholarship has engaged in a radical rewriting of the history of the Pharisaic movement and the subsequent rise of what is commonly known as rabbinic Judaism. In the analysis of the Mishnah and the Talmud, which developed during the period from the second to the sixth centuries C.E., most scholars formerly took as historically reliable the traditional rabbinic assumptions that the rabbis' mode of interpretation of the law of Moses was to be traced back through oral tradition to the time of Moses, and that the personal appropriation of cultic tradition evident in the rabbinic sources—which was to be carried out without reference to the actual operation of the Temple and its priesthood—had been operative throughout the post-Maccabean period. Concurrent with the functioning of the cultic system, it was claimed, was the voluntary worship of God carried out by individuals or by small groups. It was this worship that survived the catastrophe of the destruction of the Temple and the termination of the priestly function.

The Pharisees

According to the research of Jacob Neusner,[6] the Pharisees began as a political movement in opposition to the Maccabean despots, but with the takeover of the land by the Romans in 63 B.C.E., they shifted their aims from politics to personal piety. The self-designation of the group highlights its sense of special relationship to God and the necessity of maintaining ritual and dietary separateness if it was to gain and retain its position as God's special people.

The most important feature of this movement for the subsequent historical development of rabbinic Judaism was that the center of piety was now located in small groups that assembled voluntarily, seeking piety, knowledge, and commitment. Also important was the fact that, although members of the group may well have taken part in the official cult system at the Temple while it was still standing (prior to 70 C.E.), their identity and the dynamic of their common life was based on their shared experience, through which the relevance and import of the biblical tradition were explored and appropriated.

Small Group Gatherings

As can be inferred from the Book of Daniel, as early as the reign of Antiochus Epiphanes in the first decades of the second century B.C.E., there were Jewish groups that sought to distance themselves from the struggle for political or military power of the kind led by the Maccabees, and claimed instead that God had given their faithful, seeking group insights into how the divine plan for the renewal of the world and the vindication of the faithful was to unfold. They designated themselves "the people of the saints of the Most High" (Dan. 7:27) and expected to be the corporate agents of divine rule in the renewed world order at the end of the present age. To them alone was given cryptic but detailed insight as to how God would overcome the idolatrous pagan powers and establish his rule on earth, an event that was soon to take place (Dan. 8–12). Confirmation of these promises was given to Daniel in the form of a vision of a celestial being who gave him encouragement to endure the difficulties he and his people were confronting and assurance of the ultimate triumph of God's purpose for them (Dan. 10).

The term that came to be used for such pious groups that met to discover and appropriate the promises of God for renewal of his people was (in Greek) the ordinary word for a gathering: *synagoge*. In the earlier stages, the synagogues were informal and spontaneous in origin. In Palestine and in the diaspora, Jews gathered in private homes or, if space was not adequate, in public halls. Archaeological excavations of ancient synagogues in Palestine show that the oldest structures erected specifically for purposes of religious assembly date from the third and fourth centuries C.E. These structures replaced, or in some cases were simply modifications of, homes where the informal gatherings first took place. Where the structures were adaptations of private homes, the shifting of walls and the enlargement of doors into the street manifest the process of adaptation from informal gathering place to a site of more formal religious gatherings.[7]

Significantly, the inscriptions found in the early synagogue buildings are in Greek. The fifth–sixth century C.E. synagogue buildings in Palestine have no iconographic decoration, however, and their inscriptions are in Hebrew or Aramaic. On the other hand, the earlier synagogues, in addition to their Greek inscriptions, have as their characteristic decorative feature a central floor mosaic consisting of the signs of the zodiac, with Yahweh represented in the center driving the chariot of the sun. Unmistakably, the cosmic role of the God of Israel was being interpreted and represented visually by the adaptation of the zodiac as the symbol for the divine ordering of the universe, an artifact of the Hellenistic period, possibly under Persian influence. Earlier—in the first and early second centuries C.E.—synagogues in Palestine and across the Mediterranean world were far removed from this formal, stylized meeting hall. Instead, the word *synagoge* did not refer to a building as such, but to an informal small-group gathering, which would most likely take place in a private home.[8]

Developments toward Formal Synagogues and the Judaism of the Mishnah and the Talmud

In the period following the failure of the First Revolt and accelerating in the time after the Second Revolt, the Jewish leadership not only fostered what had earlier been this more private, purely voluntary religious style, but also began moving toward systematization and formalization by building on the antecedents in what had been Pharisaism. The leaders of the earlier informal discussion groups may once have been called by the general term of respect, "rabbi." But now this term became the formal title for the organizers of the synagogue movement and their alleged predecessors. In the meeting halls, increasing attention was given to such symbolic details as the shrine in which the Torah was located. The group definition became sharper and the requirements for participation more specific.

Analogous to the architectural and decorative developments was the formalization of the conceptual base for the rabbinic movement, which is evident in the emergence of the Mishnah and the Talmud. Jacob Neusner has superbly summarized the nature and origin of the Mishnah. He dates its beginnings to around 200 C.E., following the failure of the two Jewish revolts, the destruction of the Temple and its priesthood, and the bitter end of the hope for eschatological renewal through a messiah and an end time.[9] Composed in an age in which the Romans were systematizing their laws into codes, the Mishnah offers a systematic account of the life of the people of Israel living in their land. Its sixty-three tractates cover six kinds of activity: economy, and specifically agriculture, including the provisions of rations for the priests; the observance of holy days and seasons, with special attention to what should happen in the Temple; the status of women; civil, commercial, and criminal laws, with a government based on the Temple and a king; the cultic rules for the Temple and regulations for its upkeep; and special rules for dealing with the unclean. Since Temple and priesthood no longer existed, the attention given to the Temple and the cultus is purely symbolic of the divinely ordained order for God's people.

The real concern in the synagogue movement was for the sanctification of the covenant people, rather than for their political deliverance and reestablishment within history. Messiah does not appear as an eschatological figure, and the rules set forth for the pious life only occasionally are correlated with scripture. It is likely that the Mishnah was codified under Judah the Patriarch (ca. 180–230), who was recognized by the Romans as head of the Jewish community and who developed this document as the legal code for the administration of Jewish life. The use and interpretation of this code over the next centuries made it enduringly relevant and useful for guiding the common life of the people. By 600 C.E., the Mishnah was adapted through ongoing use and intepretation into two other codes in two different locations: the Talmud of Palestine and the Talmud of Babylon. In the Talmuds, the rabbi is no longer merely the interpreter of scripture and the laws supposedly derived from it. He has become the basic authority for applying the Mishnah, which is now regarded (through the theory of oral law stretching back to Moses) as the other half of Torah. Both the written Torah and this codified interpretation of it are traced back to the revelation by God to Moses at Sinai. Together, with the Mishnah and Talmud interpreting the written law, they provide the ground for Jewish identity in the rabbinic period.

Thus, institutionalization and formalization of Judaism in the post-Temple, postnationalistic period are dramatically evident in the literary and architectural remains from the early centuries of the common era.

Shared Jewish and Gentile Insights into the Divine Purpose

I noted in the introduction that since the early nineteenth century, when scholars under the influence of Hegel's dialectical reconstruction of history and human thought posited the existence of two kinds of Judaism—Palestinian and Hellenistic—the study of both Judaism and Christian origins has tended to make sharp distinctions between these two supposedly different modes or spheres of Jewish thinking in the Greco-Roman period. Careful analysis of the texts from this era, however, together with extensive archaeological finds from sites dating before and after the turn of the era, has shown how deeply Judaism was influenced by Hellenistic thought and culture—not least in Palestine itself. I have also noted how the emergent institution of the synagogue used the Greek language and adapted the Hellenistic signs of the zodiac as a symbol of Yahweh's control of creation and history, going so far as to represent God driving the sun chariot.[10] This borrowing from Greco-Roman culture provides vivid expression of the Jewish concern in this period for correlating personal life with chronological and cosmic order, and doing so along lines developed in the wider Greco-Roman culture.

The extensive writings of Philo of Alexandria, as well as such shorter works as the Wisdom of Solomon and 4 Maccabees, show how broadly and deeply Jewish writers in this period were combining insights from the biblical tradition with concepts and aspirations in the Hellenistic philosophical tradition.[11] The importance of such Stoic concepts as conscience and natural law constituting the internal agency by which the divine moral demands are communicated is apparent in writings such as the Testament of the Twelve Patriarchs.[12] Platonic terminology concerning the creation and sustaining of the universe appears in writings such as the Wisdom of Solomon, and 4 Maccabees retells the story of the Maccabaean revolt in terms of Stoic endurance and the resulting moral renewal. All these Jewish documents are concerned to show how God's purpose is discernible in the history of his people, and the intellectual framework in which that claim is made is influenced substantively by concepts and a worldview derived from Hellenistic philosophy.

It is the works of Philo, as I have noted, that provide the fullest documentation of a synthesis of the scriptural tradition with an eclectic philosophical system combining features of Platonic ontology and Stoic ethics.[13] By his allegorical method, Philo is able to expound the history and laws of Torah in such a way as to locate the essence of these writings in concepts and religious aspirations that are identical with those of the Hellenistic philosophers. Often overlooked by biblical scholars is evidence of the correlation between Jewish and Greco-Roman thinkers: Stoic writings by leading Roman thinkers such as Cicero and Seneca in the centuries before and after the turn of the eras foresees an era of cosmic renewal which, while different in detail from Jewish apocalyptic, shares with that literature many of its hopes and aspirations.

Interests shared between Jews and the wider Greco-Roman world did not flow only in one direction, however. The attraction of thoughtful non-Jews to Judaism has been documented by the discovery of inscriptions that attest the phenomenon of Gentiles associating themselves with Judaism as "worshippers of God" (theoseboi) or as "proselytes." Some scholars have sought to dismiss the "God-fearers" as a fiction of the author of Luke-Acts that both the pious and other scholars have taken as fact. But the occurrence of the term in a list of benefactors of a synagogue in Aphrodisias shows that the term was used by Jews with reference to Gentiles who were drawn to Jewish beliefs and practices. It was also used by Gentiles in

The Law-abiding Community

recognition of the authentic piety of Jews. A long-known text from the theater at Miletus in Asia Minor refers to a section of the seats as "the place of the Jews, who are also called God-fearers."[14] Similarly, an inscription from the third-century-C.E. synagogue in Lydia mentions a God-fearer, Eustathius, who was a benefactor of the synagogue. Alan Segal describes the synagogue membership in the diaspora as including proselytes and "God-fearers in the process of converting."[15] The dynamic for this kind of conversion did not come from the converts alone through their attraction to the ethical monotheism of Judaism, but from Jews as well, who sought by apologetic means to make an appealing case for the Jewish tradition as freshly perceived and outlined in the literature of this period. The mounting evidence of the widespread use of Greek among Palestinian Jews in the first two centuries of the common era shows that there was no linguistic gap inhibiting the proselytizing process.[16] I shall note below the attention given to this factor in the Gospel of Matthew.

The Overarching Question: Covenantal Identity

The basic question that lies behind and penetrates this diverse range of responses to the political failures of Jewish nationalism and the intense encounter with Greco-Roman culture in this period is, What is the divinely intended model for those who want to appropriate the tradition of covenantal identity that was set forth in the law and the prophets and struggled over in the ensuing centuries as history moved into the period of Roman political and cultural domination? The factors involved in reaching answers to this question included the origins of the covenant with Abraham and his descendants, the manifestation of God's purpose in the history of his people, the moral basis for the life of the covenant people, access to God, the possibility of a role in the divine scheme for non-Israelites and their culture, the future accomplishment of the divine purpose for the people of the covenant. These factors provide the basic framework within which dramatic answers to the question—couched in specific terms that reflect debate with emergent rabbinic Judaism—are to be found in the Gospel of Matthew.

The Structure and Strategy of the Gospel of Matthew

Matthew set out his case for Jesus as God's agent for the renewal and redefinition of his people Israel in a document whose structure and strategy can be discerned through careful analysis of its distinctive details.[17] Throughout the gospel there is evidence of continuing dialogue with and challenge to the early phases of emergent rabbinic Judaism. The concerns of these movements are shared; the solutions offered are often radically different. The significant features of Matthew can be conveniently grouped under the headings context, constitution, confrontation and competition, consolidation, and consummation.

The Context for the Coming of Jesus

Matthew establishes the basic context for his portrayal of Jesus and his report of Jesus' message at the outset of his gospel in presenting the genealogy of Jesus. The two figures highlighted there are the prototype (though not actually the first) of the kings of Israel, David, and the ultimate ancestor of the covenant people, Abraham. In the account of the descendants of Abraham, a crucial event is highlighted: the deportation of Israel to Babylon (Matt. 1:11–12, 17). Thus the focus is on the origins of the covenant people, the apex of their achievements in David (through whom the twelve tribes were consolidated and the central shrine established in Jerusalem), and the nadir of Israel's history in the Babylonian exile. The scriptural base for the geneaology is evident when one compares Matt. 1:2–6 with 1 Chron. 2:1–15, 1:3–6 with Ruth 18–22, and 1:7–12 with 1 Chron. 3:10–19. That these crucial events did not happen merely by chance is further indicated by the strict chronological intervals between them: "fourteen generations," twice the sacred number seven.

Another vital aspect of the divine preparation of the context for the coming and career of Jesus is his birth to the Virgin Mary. The conception of Jesus occurs through the Holy Spirit and in fulfillment of scripture (Isa. 7:14).[18] A messenger from the Lord confirms this understanding of the event to Joseph in a dream (Matt. 1:20, 24), which is for Matthew a major medium of divine communication. These two themes of scripture fulfillment and of divine messages through dreams run throughout Matthew's version of the birth and childhood of Jesus. Through dreams the magi are warned not to return to Herod (2:12) and Joseph is instructed to "flee to Egypt" to escape Herod's decree (2:13), then to return to the land of Israel (2:19), and to settle in Galilee rather than in Judea (2:22). Fulfilling scripture are the place of Jesus' birth (Mic. 5:1, 3), the splendid gifts brought by the magi (Isa. 60:6), the return of Jesus from Egypt (Hos. 11:1), the lament over the death of the children killed by Herod's decree (Jer. 31:15), and the residence of Jesus' family in Nazareth (Matt. 2:23).[19] Jesus' subsequent move from Nazareth to Capernaum, with its ready access to wider Jewish and Gentile territories—including "Galilee of the Gentiles" (4:12–16)—is presented by Matthew as the prelude to the bringing of light to those "who sat in darkness" (Isa. 9:1–2).[20] Throughout his gospel, Matthew makes frequent explicit, as well as implicit, references to the fulfillment of scripture. What God is doing through Jesus is not shattering the biblical tradition but bringing it to its intended consummation.

A unique dimension of the divine preparation for the coming of Jesus is the visit of the *magoi*, led to Bethlehem by a moving star, which for Matthew affirms the validity of the Gentile interest in a mix of astronomy and astrology, as well as the potential for Gentiles to come to God through his chosen agent, Jesus, before whom these visitors "fell down and worshipped" (Matt. 2:11).

Matthew repeats twelve times the formal claim that what has happened through Jesus took place "in order to fulfill scripture."[21] All of these claims are unique to Matthew. Cumulatively, they seek to prove that the career of Jesus, from his birth to a virgin through his betrayal by one of his own close followers, is to be seen as the working out of a divine plan, discernible by the community of faith to which these insights have been granted by God.

The Constitution of God's New People

The Divine Preparation for the New Covenant (Matt. 3–4)

Matthew makes more explicit than the other gospels the claim that John the Baptist's activity to renew Israel is an essential preparation for achieving the over-arching purpose of God to redefine the new covenant community, which is not limited to Israelites pious by traditional standards. With superb irony, it is the "chief priests and the scribes" who inform Herod that the one to be born in Beth-lehem will be "a ruler who will shepherd [God's] people Israel." Their words allude to Mic. 5:2, but they also echo the promises to David concerning his ultimate suc-cessor (2 Sam. 7:12; Ps. 89:4). John's role as major challenger of the prevailing views is expressed both symbolically and directly in Matthew. This is in fulfillment of the scripture (Matt. 3:3; Isa. 40:3), as John helps prepare for the coming of the Lord (= Jesus). In Matt. 3:4, the garb of John is depicted in terms that mirror those of Elijah (2 Kings 1:8), the critic of Israel's royal establishment in his day. The pen-itent candidates who seek baptism as an expression of their yearning for a new relationship to God include not only pious Jews ("many Pharisees and Sadducees," 3:7) and those from Jewish territories, but also those from "all the region around the Jordan" (3:5–6). Most revolutionary in John's message is the claim that bio-logical descent from Abraham is not an adequate factor for assuring a share in the life of the age to come, but that "God is able from these stones to raise up [true] children to Abraham" (3:9). The radical selection process by which they are to be chosen is compared to the gathering of the wheat and the burning of the chaff (3:12).

In Matthew's account of the baptism of Jesus (3:13–17), distinctive details include John's assertion of his inferiority to Jesus, the latter's insistence that through the rite one must "fulfill all righteousness," the fact that the dovelike Spirit not only descends on Jesus but "alights" on him, and the words of the heavenly voice con-cerning God's Son, speaking not as a private word to him but as a public announce-ment: "This is my beloved Son." John uses the technical term from the formula for Christian baptism, *diakoluo*.[22] Thus this event of Jesus' baptism is the prototype for admission to the new community. In what follows in the gospel, Matthew sets out in detail what constitutes true righteousness.

Only in Matthew do we read that the devil's testing of Jesus includes visits to "the holy city" (4:5)[23] and to "a very high mountain" (4:8). There seem to be inten-tional parallels throughout Matthew with the story of Moses, who had his crucial encounter with God on Horeb/Sinai (Exod. 3:1–4:20), where he struggled with God concerning his role in behalf of God's people and where later he transmitted to them the covenant with Yahweh (Exod. 19 ff.). The duration of the temptation for forty days matches the similar experiences of both Moses (Exod. 24:18 ff.) and Elijah (1 Kings 19:8). It is on a mountain that Jesus conveys to his disciples the basic pattern for their obedience as members of the covenant people—the so-called Sermon on the Mount (Matt. 5–7). It is in the "desert" (*eremos*) that, like Moses, he feeds the hungry with food from God. He retreats to the hills after his engagement with the throngs (14:23), who seek him out to heal "the lame, the blind, and the dumb" (15:29–30)—precisely those who, as Jesus had earlier informed the questioners from John the Baptist, were his special concern (11:4–6), using terms from the apocalyptic portions of Isaiah (29:18–19; 35:5–6) that had provocative implications for Jews oriented toward ritual and ethnic purity. It is on a mountain that his transfiguration occurs (17:1), and from a mountain in Galilee that he commissions his followers to "make disciples of all nations" (28:16–20).

Another kind of symbolic parallel between the role of Moses as agent of the old covenant and Jesus as founder of the new is the fact that the teachings of Jesus in Matthew are grouped in five major sections, each of them demarcated by a concluding phrase, "When Jesus had finished": 7:28–29, following the Sermon on the Mount; 11:1, following the instructions to the disciples; 13:53–58, at the conclusion of an extended series of parables; 19:1, after instructions concerning life within the new community; and 26:1, at the end of Matthew's extended version of the apocalyptic discourse. This is Matthew's equivalent of the Pentateuch, with the account of the preparation of Jesus for his role as essential introduction in chapters 1 through 5, and the narrative of his trial, death, and resurrection (following the last section) as the concluding events through which the new covenant community is constituted. In between each of these five discourse sections, Matthew has placed stories about Jesus and reports of his teachings that add essential details to the depiction of his role as the agent of God for covenant renewal. Thus, throughout Matthew there is a pair of recurrent questions central to my analysis of postbiblical Judaism and the New Testament: Who is this agent of God through whom covenantal renewal is taking place, and what are the criteria for participation in that new community of God's people?

The Code for the New Covenant People (Matt. 5–7)

The Sermon on the Mount, which is constitutive for the life of the community, is set forth with a mixture of continuity and sharp contrast with the Mosaic code as the rabbinic movement was coming to understand it in the later first century C.E. This is made explicit in Matt. 5:17–20, with its insistence that the "righteousness" of the new community must "exceed that of the scribes and Pharisees." The difficulty is not with "the law and the prophets"—which are to be preserved completely—but with the incapacity of the self-styled official interpreters of the law to bring out the fulness of its meaning and moral demand, as Jesus has been sent by God to do (5:17). The commandments are to be obeyed, and instruction concerning them is to be a major responsibility of the members of the community (5:19). Their role as bringers of new vitality to human life ("salt of the earth") and as "the light of the world" is demonstrated and confirmed by the good works they do, thereby bringing "glory to [their] Father in heaven"[24] rather than to themselves (5:13–16).

The specifics of their moral obligations according to this understanding of God's law for his people are set forth through a series of antitheses, by which the traditional scribal interpretation ("you have heard that it was said," followed by a direct quotation from the law of Moses) is contrasted vividly with the new insight that Jesus has brought ("but I say to you"). The issues include attacks on others in the community (5:21–26), sexual misdeeds (5:17–30), divorce and remarriage (5:31–32), taking oaths (5:33–37), retaliation against antagonists (5:38–42), and loving one's enemies (5:43–48). Assumed to be in power here are the pre-70 institutions and officials of Judaism as permitted by the Romans: the judge, the officer, and the council (5:22–25). The rules for the community are set forth, not in terms of legal guidelines, but as a transformation of attitudes through self-discipline, integrity, generosity, and love toward one's assailants or opponents. The model for the behavior of God's people is the very nature of God, whose gracious provision of sun and rain benefits even the evil and the unjust (5:45). The call is to emulate the perfection of God, the heavenly Father (5:48). The ethical norms and rules of the Mosaic code are simply transcended in this new mode of moral responsibility that Jesus sets forth.

Three of the major forms of Jewish piety in the rabbinic tradition are giving alms, praying, and fasting. Matthew reports Jesus dealing with these issues, mostly in material found only in this gospel. All three of these practices are commended, but it is essential that they be performed with the sole purpose of helping to meet the needs of others (alms, 6:1–4) and of confirming one's personal relationship with God (6:5–8, 16–18) rather than as opportunities for pious ostentation. In each case, there is a promise of God's recognition and reward when the motivation for these acts is correct. In the middle of this section is Matthew's version of the so-called Lord's Prayer, which appears in its shorter, Q form in Luke 11:2–4. In Matt. 6:9–15, the liturgical features of the prayer are developed, with emphasis given to the contrast between what obtains in heaven and how God's people now live on earth. It is when the rule of God, which is now sovereign "in the heavens," becomes effective throughout the creation and on earth that the kingdom will have "come." Appended to the prayer is an expansion of the saying from Mark 11:25 about God's forgiveness, to which Matthew's version (6:15) adds a warning that those who refuse to forgive others will forfeit God's forgiveness. Again, the basic ethical orientation concerns the nature of God and his dealings with humans.

The emphasis continues to be on inner moral condition as the dynamic for moral action, as well as on the promise of heavenly recompense for a life of obedience. Priority is to be given, not to assembling tangible wealth on earth, but to amassing moral merits in heaven (6:19–21). Crucial for the life of obedience is insight, which alone can illumine the inner life of faith (6:22–23). Service to God must be one's exclusive aim (6:24). There should be no anxiety about daily needs, since God—whose care for the creation is evident even in the transitory beauty of the natural world—is fully aware of human necessities. Those who are preoccupied with daily necessities are characterized as being "of little faith."[25] To the call for giving priority to seeking God's kingdom (as in Luke 12:31), Matthew adds, "and [God's] righteousness" (6:33), which refers to the new mode of life that Jesus is here pictured as setting forth. There is no place for anxiety about daily needs (6:34). One can be confident that God will meet the requests of his people (7:7–11). The basic rule for behavior is to do to others as you would want them to do to you—a principle that Matthew links with "the law and the prophets" but is actually found in the Jewish wisdom tradition (Tob. 4:15; Ben Sira 31:15) and in a negative version ("Do not do to others what you do not want others to do to you") in early rabbinic tradition (attributed to Hillel). The generosity that is to be characteristic of God's new people is an exact reflection of the nature and activity of the loving God.

Matthew also includes solemn warnings against wrong relationships and false claim to a share in the common life. The spiritual treasures of God's people ("what is holy," "pearls") are not to be thrown out before the unworthy ("dogs," "swine"). Those who irresponsibly seek admission to the community are "many," but only a few are willing to undergo the strict discipline "that leads to life" (7:13–14). Those who merely call on the name of the Lord and utter prophecies or perform exorcisms in his name, while failing to do God's will in terms of moral obedience and renewal, do not qualify to "enter the kingdom" (7:21–23). The final tests of fitness to enter the new rule of God are the inner transformation that produces good deeds (7:15–20) and the ability to endure the fierce difficulties that will beset God's people. Only those who fully understand and accept Jesus' reinterpretation of the law of God for his people—the "wise" who "build on the rock"—will survive the judgment that is to come (7:24–27).

In the stylized statement that marks the end of this major discourse and the transition to the next narrative section of Matthew (7:28–29, leading to 8:1–9:35), the authority of Jesus evident in his teaching is contrasted with that of "their scribes." This latter phrase obviously implies that the new community has its own members, who are assigned the task of analyzing and interpreting to others the relevance of the scriptural tradition for the common life of the group. I shall note below the similar recurrent references to "their synagogues," indicating that the followers of Jesus have formed their own assemblies for worship and study.

Jesus as Agent of the New Covenant (Facet 1, Matt. 8–9)

Confirming and illuminating the instruction that Jesus has given in the Sermon on the Mount is Matthew's detailed account of the public activity of Jesus, drawn and adapted primarily from Mark, but with supplements from the Q source (8:5–13, 18–22) and from Matthew's own source (9:32–34). The accounts of Jesus' miracles are for the most part given in condensed versions,[26] but details are added in some cases to heighten the distinction between the traditional covenant people and the new community. In the story of the healing of a centurion's servant, Jesus deals directly with the military officer rather than through Jewish elders (8:5). The promise is given that participants in table fellowship with "Abraham, Isaac, and Jacob" in the "kingdom of heaven" will include "many from east and west"—that is, from outside Israel.[27] In Matthew's account of Jesus calming a storm, he is addressed as "Lord" and called upon to "save" the disciples, who are criticized as being "of little faith" (8:25–26). The story of the healing of a paralytic concludes with a note that glory should be rendered to God because he "has given such authority to humans" (9:8). The report of the healing of two blind men (9:27–31) is perhaps a variant of the healing of Bartimaeus (Matt. 20:29–34; Mark 10:46–52), and matches well with Matthew's added detail in the Beelzebul story (Mark 3:19–22) that the demoniac was also blind (Matt. 12:22). Blindness symbolizes for Matthew the inability of human beings, unaided by the power of God, to perceive the truth that Jesus has come to disclose. When the dumb demoniac is healed (9:32–34), in a distinctive Matthean account, the crowds attest the uniqueness of what Jesus has done: "Never was anything like this seen in Israel." As in Matthew's version of the Beelzebul story (12:24), it is the Pharisees who bring the charge that Jesus is in league with "the prince of demons."

The summary of Jesus' activity in Matt. 9:35–36 points up its three major dimensions: teaching in "their" synagogues—that is, those of the emergent rabbinic movement; preaching the gospel of the kingdom; and healing every disease and infirmity. To make explicit the intent of these activities, Matthew here inserts from the Markan tradition (6:34) the ground for Jesus' compassion on the crowds: they are shepherdless sheep, and thus in desperate need of becoming reconstituted as God's people. From the Q source (Luke 10:2) comes the appeal to God—based now on the metaphor of God's people as a vineyard—to help send workers out to accomplish the Lord's harvest.

The Messengers of the New Covenant (Matt. 10)

Essential to the constitution of the new people of God, therefore, are the preparation and commissioning of messengers to invite others to share in the new community. It is for this role that the twelve disciples/apostles (10:1–2) are commissioned and instructed in the second major discourse unit in Matthew (10:1–11:1). Matthew has here replaced the two separate accounts in Mark (Jesus' call of the twelve [3:13–19] and his sending of them [6:6b–13] with one extended description of their commissioning for the apostolic role. Unique in the gospel tradition is the limiting of the sphere of their preaching activities to the "lost sheep of the house of Israel," with specific exclusion of Gentiles and Samaritans. Since that limitation is repeated by Jesus in Matt. 15:24 and then violated by him when he heals the daughter of a Syro-Phoenician woman, as it is implicitly in the subsequent activity of Jesus among Gentiles and explicitly in the postresurrection instruction to the disciples (28:19), it must be seen here as an essential stage in the divine scheme but not as a permanent prohibition. The "lost sheep" are the confused and directionless traditional covenant people, and especially those dismissed to the fringe of that society: "Heal the sick, raise the dead, cleanse the lepers, cast out demons" (10:8). It is they who are to have the first opportunity to hear the good news, with its invitation to join the newly available "kingdom of heaven" that is now "at hand" (10:7).

The messengers are to launch their mission without advance financial support and to accept hospitality as it is offered when they move from village to village (10:9–11). Those who reject them and their message will be subject to divine judgment (10:14–15), and they are advised to exercise wisdom in the perilous undertaking to which God has called them (10:16). The opposition will include both religious and secular-political authorities: the local councils and leaders of "their synagogues" as well as Gentile rulers, before whom they will bear testimony (10:17–18). Through his Spirit, God will instruct them what they are to say (10:19–20). Their opponents will include members of their own families (10:21, 34–36), but they are to persevere in their mission until the coming of "the Son of man" signals the end of the present age and the beginning of the "rule of the heavens," when God's power and purpose will be in sovereign control of the world (10:23). Meanwhile, the disciples must bear testimony in the face of opposition, confident of God's preserving power (10:26–33) and ready to accept martyrdom ("take one's cross," 10:37–38), thereby to find true life (10:39). Those who respond with support, kindness, and encouragement to these messengers ("these little ones"), who are Jesus' true disciples, will receive a divine reward (10:40–42). Three terms indicate correlative roles in the community between Jesus and his followers (10:24–25): to Jesus as teacher, his people are to relate as "learners" (or disciples); to Jesus as Lord, they are to be servants; they are to acknowledge Jesus as "master of the household" (oikodespotes), rather than attributing his extraordinary powers to Satan (Beelzebul). The various roles and status of the messengers are indicated in Matt. 10:40–42, where the responses they receive from those to whom they go to bear witness are linked with their response to Jesus: prophets, those who do "righteous" acts, and "little ones," who are simply those who have learned from Jesus.

Jesus as Agent of the New Covenant (Facet 2, Matt. 11–12)

Drawing on the Q tradition, Jesus' role is once again (as in Matt. 3) redefined in contrast to that of John the Baptist (11:2–18). Jesus' response to being asked if he is "the one who is to come" is to point to his healings and his reaching out to those excluded in terms of traditional Jewish piety ("the poor"), in recognition that the inclusiveness of his activity in the name of God will be an "offense" to many. As I have noted above, his indication of those who benefit from his work is phrased in terms drawn from the eschatological and apocalyptic strands of the prophecies of Isaiah (Isa. 29:18–19; 35:5–6; 61:1). John is identified by Jesus as not merely "more than a prophet" (11:9), but as "Elijah," whose coming as a herald of the new age was predicted by Malachi (3:1; quoted in Matt. 11:10).

The violence of the struggles that will accompany the coming of God's kingdom is indicated, and the obtuseness and disbelief of contemporaries in reaction to his overtures to outsiders ("tax collectors and sinners") are depicted, culminating in their expulsion of him from the family of God's people and the call for his execution (Deut. 21:20–21). The failure of the cities of Galilee to discern the power and purpose of God in Jesus' "mighty works" done among them contrasts with the repentance that those works would have elicited in Gentile centers (11:20–24). God is disclosing his purpose through Jesus, not to those who pride themselves as being "wise and understanding," but to those who respond to him and his message with simple, childlike trust: "babes" (11:25–27). They alone will know the Father and his purposes for his people. In a uniquely Matthean saying, Jesus assures those who accept the difficult path of discipleship that they will be given rest for their souls (11:28–30).

The material assembled by Matthew from Mark and Q in 12:1–50 concentrates on the provocative nature of Jesus' activity and the mounting hostility toward him on the part of the religious leaders. The story of his defending his disciples' gathering grain on the sabbath is supplemented by a reference to a precedent: a priestly violation of the sabbath (12:5); by the astounding claim that "something greater than the temple [= Jesus] is here"; and by the prophetic pronouncement of God's preference for acts of mercy rather than sacrifice (12:7; Hos. 6:6). Similarly, the healing of a man with a withered hand on the sabbath is justified on the principle that "it is lawful to do good on the sabbath" (12:9–12). Matthew limits the ensuing conspiracy to "destroy" Jesus as violator of the law to "the Pharisees" (12:14).

Although the locus of Jesus' subsequent healing activity is not specified here in Matthew, the implication is that it includes areas where Gentiles live, as the extended quotation from Isa. 42:1–4 (LXX = Matt. 12:16–21) concerning Gentile responses to Jesus indicates. The final phrase is of basic importance: "In his name will the Gentiles hope." Conversely, the Pharisees conclude that Jesus' skill as an exorcist is the result of his being in league with Beelzebul or Satan (12:22–37). Jesus responds with the assertion that "the Spirit of God" is the source of his power, and warns that blasphemy against the Spirit will never be forgiven. His opponents are characterized as a "brood of vipers," denounced as rooted in evil, and warned of the consequences of their wicked accusations in the day of judgment. The warning against seeking for "signs" as a mode of divine confirmation is qualified by Matthew with reference to Jonah's experience in "the belly of the whale" as a sign of Jesus' impending death and resurrection. Thus, even before Jesus' initial prediction of his death and resurrection (Matt. 16:21), the reader is informed about what Jesus must undergo for the renewal of God's people to take place.

Two short pericopes offer further insights concerning participation in the new community. Matt. 12:43–45 makes the point that it is not sufficient merely to be liberated from the old forces that have shaped life before coming to Jesus: there must be a new spirit from God, or evil spirits will resume control. Matt. 12:46–50 claims that one's true family consists, not of ethnic kin, but of those whose sole aim is to "do the will of my Father who is in heaven." Once more, in this section Matthew has interwoven his major themes: the redefining of God's people and the role of Jesus in constituting this new people.

The Insights Reserved for the New Community (Matt. 13:1–52).

The third major discourse section in Matthew is composed of parables and private interpretations of them, reserved for the inner core of Jesus' followers. The parables are spoken to the throngs that line the beach (13:1–2), but the explanations are for the disciples only.

The Parable of the Sower, with its description of the range of results from the sowing of seed, is reproduced from Mark 4:13–20 without significant changes. The explanation of why Jesus speaks in parables is reported in a considerably expanded version, however (Mark 4:10–12; Matt. 13:10–15). The denial of access to these teachings is intensified in Matthew, as is the insistence that parables are used in order to prevent outsiders from understanding. This selective disclosure and divine concealment are in accord with the prophetic tradition, as the extended quotation from Isa. 6:9–10 indicates. It is the people's dullness and blindness that prevents them from grasping the truth as Jesus reveals it. In sharp contrast are the disciples, who do hear and comprehend what the prophets and righteous of the past were never privileged to hear.[28] The private interpretation of the Parable of the Sower derives from Mark (4:13–20), differing in a few details. The seed is "the word of the kingdom." The various modes of reception of the seed are described in terms of three types of individuals: one who receives the word with joy, but has no root and does not endure when persecution comes; one who is distracted by the cares of this world and delight in riches; and one who hears and understands, and bears fruit in varying degrees of abundance.

The distinctive Parable of the Weeds (13:24–30) compares the kingdom of heaven with the mixed results from the mingling of good and bad seeds sown in a field, the latter put there by "the enemy." The interpretation of the parable (13:36–43) explains that one must wait until "the harvest" (= *synteleia*, the consummation when the eschatological judgment will take place) for the sorting out of the mixed crop that is represented within the membership of the professing community. The "wheat" will be preserved, but the "weeds" will be burned. Although the professing community is pictured in this way as a mixture of good and evil, the removal of the latter is God's task, not that of the human leadership. An essential distinction—peculiarly Matthean—is apparent here: it is from "the kingdom of the Son of Man" that the culling out of the evil element will take place, but it is "the kingdom of the Father" into which the righteous are then to be admitted. The former pictures the mixed state of the new covenant people in the present order; the latter represents the ultimate condition of God's true people in the age to come. A similar symbolic picture of the mixed condition of the professing community and of the eschatological sorting out is based on the figure of the diverse kinds of fish drawn in by the fisher's net (13:47–50). In the latter parable, there is emphasis on the discarding of the unworthy members and the fiery and painful punishment they must undergo.[29]

The divine strategy of disclosing the purpose for God's people through metaphorical and symbolic forms of communication is affirmed in Matt. 13:34–35 and is confirmed by a quotation from scripture, which is actually from Ps. 78:2 rather than from a prophet. The variety of riches of divine knowledge is depicted under the two metaphors of hidden "treasure" and a search for a prize "pearl." Some of these special insights are old, and some are new (13:51–52). But all are vouchsafed only to the elect inner core of the new community.

Confrontation and Competition concerning the Covenant (Matt. 13:53–23:39)

I have noted the explicit and implicit challenges by Jesus in the preceding parts of Matthew to both the leadership of Israel and the dominant ways of understanding the covenant. These challenges include the description of Israel as a shepherdless people (9:36), the implicit contrasts between the Jewish gatherings for study and worship ("their synagogues") and those of the early Christians,[30] and Jesus' criticisms of synagogue practices and the interpretation of scripture.[31] It is in this section of Matthew that these issues are presented most sharply and with the most direct criticism of the leaders of the synagogue movement. They are present in the material recounting Jesus' activity, but they are supplemented in the central discourse section (18:1–35) by indications of how the new community is to establish leadership and procedures for its own organization.

Jesus as Agent of the New Covenant (Facet 3, Matt. 13:53–17:27)

Following Matthew's stylized transitional phrase "When Jesus had finished" (13:53), a series of pericopes—mostly Markan, but some uniquely Matthean—highlights how the last stage of Jesus' public activity involves mounting hostility from the religious authorities and challenges to the traditional understanding of the covenant through Moses, as well as to the emergent guidelines for covenantal participation in what became the rabbinic tradition.

Contrasting the astounding authority of Jesus with his humble and familiar origins, his neighbors are offended by his challenges to them and refuse to recognize him as a messenger sent by God. He acknowledges their rejection of his prophetic role and ceases his works of healing in their midst (13:53–58). Herod Antipas, tetrarch of Galilee, hearing of Jesus' extraordinary powers, mistakes him for a resurrected John the Baptist, whom he had executed (14:1–12). Brief accounts of Jesus' equivalent of Israel's covenantal bread from heaven (14:13–21) and the triumph over the waters in Exodus (14:22–33) make the implicit claim that Jesus is God's agent in forming the new covenant people. His ability to heal the sick, which was earlier pictured by Matthew as evident in the land of Syria (4:24), is now manifest in his own residential area, Galilee ("the land of Gennesaret," 14:34–36).

While omitting Mark's detailed explanation of the Pharisaic purity code (Mark 7:1–4), Matthew assumes that it is in effect and sharpens the criticism of this way of understanding obedience to God. Here Jesus attacks those who evade such explicit commandments as honoring one's parents by claiming that all their possessions have been dedicated to God and thus are not available for parental support (Matt. 15:3–6). The contrast between ostensible worship and true dedication to God is expressed in the quotation from Isa. 29:13 about those who teach human precepts instead of divine commands. The Pharisees' critique of Jesus' rejection of the principle of defilement by forbidden foods (15:10–11) is met by his denunciation of them as plants to be uprooted and as "blind guides" (15:12–14) and then elaborated by his tracing human defilement to what people do, think, and say, rather than to what they eat (15:15–20). The participation of people in the divine blessings across ethnic and ritual-purity lines is dramatically illustrated in the healing of the daughter of a Canaanite woman and of the "lame, blind, maimed, dumb" who come to him. The issue is highlighted when Jesus' claim that his activity is to be limited to "the lost sheep of the house of Israel" is challenged by this non-Israelite woman, and when those who benefit from his healing powers "glorified the God of Israel."

Although Mark's specification of Jesus' scene of action as Gentile territory (Mark 7:31) is omitted by Matthew, this gospel includes his version of the Markan report (Mark 8:1–10) of Jesus' feeding the hungry in the desert, which corresponds to the tradition of Moses and the manna. This is followed by a series of incidents in which the authority of Jesus is challenged by "the Pharisees and the Sadducees" (16:1, 6, 12). The request of the latter for a confirming sign from God is met by a second reference to "the sign of Jonah" (16:4), which here can mean only the call to repentance, although it could refer elsewhere to the resurrection (12:39–40). Jesus' critics are able to perceive signs of the weather, but not God's signs of what he is about to do. Their failure to discern the significance of the two events of his feeding the hungry in the desert as signs of the reconstitution of God's people is an indication of the worthless "teaching" ("leaven") which they promote (16:5–12).

The first clear declaration of the role of Jesus as God's agent of covenant

renewal and the first explicit indication of his death at the instigation of the religious leaders and his subsequent resurrection are now offered as he specifies his
destiny as "Son of the living God." Reported in a more abbreviated version in Mark
(8:27–31), only in Matthew is Peter's confession of Jesus as "the Messiah" followed
by Jesus' affirmation of the divine source of this insight and the assurance of the
establishment of the new community ("the church").[32] Perception of Jesus' messiahship has not derived from human informants ("flesh and blood"), but has been
revealed (*apekalypsen*) to Peter by Jesus' father (= God). The structure of the new
community which is being formed is indicated through the metaphor of its being
built on a rock, and the exercise of authority for admission and regulation of the life
of its members is given divine confirmation (16:17–19). This leadership role is further clarified in Matt. 18:18, where the question about members' obligations is set-
tled by the leaders, whose judgments receive divine confirmation ("bound . . .
loosed in heaven").

Jesus' messianic role is not to be made public (16:20) until the formal confrontation with the civil and religious authorities has taken place (26:57–27:26),
which event Jesus then begins to explain to the disciples as part of the divine
necessity (*dei*, 16:21). In spite of their initial incredulity as expressed by Peter
(16:23), the disciples are warned that they may be required to forfeit their very
lives for the sake of Jesus (16:24–28), though some may survive until his triumphant vindication when, as "Son of Man," he comes into his "kingdom" (16:28).
Divine confirmation of his role and vindication are given to the inner core of the
disciples in the transfiguration experience, which fills them with awe (17:1–8).
His salvific role in behalf of God's new people is confirmed by the presence of
Moses and Elijah at this event (17:3) and by his claim that the promise of the eschatological coming of Elijah (Mal. 4:5–6) has already been fulfilled through John
the Baptist (17:9–13). The demonstration of Jesus' power to accomplish human
renewal is given in Matthew's abbreviated version of the healing of an epileptic
boy by the expulsion of the demon (17:14–21). The disciples' inability to perform
such cures is explained in Matthew's version of this incident as a consequence of
their "little faith." With even "faith no bigger than a grain of mustard seed," they
could move mountains.

The core of disciples gathers in Galilee, which is the place where they are
told by Jesus to assemble and where they gather following his resurrection (26:32;
28:16). Meanwhile, they are to meet their obligations as pious Jews, as shown by
the instruction to pay the Temple tax (17:14–27) even though they are in fact
"free" from such humanly imposed regulations.

Consolidation of the New Community (Matt. 18:1–35)

In this, the fourth of Matthew's discourse sections, the issues are explicitly
rank and responsibility within the new people of God. The disciples are not to
strive for positions of power in their leadership roles, but to emulate the humble

status of children, thereby qualifying for honor when the kingdom comes in its fullness.[33] At the same time, attention must be paid to how one's behavior affects others within the community. There are three terms in Matthew for the humbler or immature members of the community: "little ones" (*mikroi*), "lesser ones" (*mikroteroi*), and "least" (*elachistoi*). In every case, there is an intended contrast between them and the prestigious or proud. To put a stumbling block in the path of one of the new or developing members of the community or to cause one of them to be tempted is to invite disastrous judgment from God (18:6–7). Indeed, each member must take care to control his urges in order to avoid the fires of divine punishment.[34] Instead, primary concern is to be given to these "little ones"[35] who are still growing into participation in the common life, just as the guardian angels assigned to care for them are constantly in the presence of God (18:10). Changing the image once more, the caring leader is compared with a shepherd who for a time leaves the safe flock in order to search for the erring sheep and then rejoices at their restoration (18:12–13). Just so, it is the nature of God to see that the marginal and immature "little ones" are loved, cared for, and sustained within the new flock (18:14).

The issue of settling disputes within the community is directly addressed in Matt. 18:15–20. Building on a Q tradition concerning repentance and forgiveness (Luke 17:3–4), Matthew here pictures Jesus as setting up stages in a process of adjudication. The first stage is a purely private interchange between the offended and the alleged offender (18:15). If agreement is reached, then fellowship is restored. If this fails, a few other members of the community are to be asked to share in the discussion, which introduces the legal feature from Torah (Deut. 19:15) of having testimony confirmed by "two or three witnesses." If the offender does not accept the results of this mode of conciliation, then the issue is to be brought before the entire community (*ekklesia*), and if this procedure does not produce confession and correction, then the member is to be expelled, as "a Gentile or a tax collector" would be excluded from Israel on ethnic and political grounds (18:16).[36]

The role of the community in settling internal disputes is then pictured as receiving divine confirmation. Using technical terms that are found in early rabbinic sources—binding and loosing—the promise is here given (18:18) that obligations agreed upon by the community are binding in the eyes of God ("in heaven"), and releases granted by the community also receive divine confirmation. This concept and terminology echo the words of Jesus in Matt. 16:19 about the authority that will be vested in the leadership of the church. At a more personal level, members are to be forgiving toward others in the community on an open-ended basis, rather than calculating and setting limits (18:21–22). The unique Matthean Parable of the Unforgiving Servant (18:23–35) warns that God will call to punitive account those who, having received full forgiveness of him, insist on holding others to every detail of their obligations. The divine quality of mercy as

The Law-abiding Community

disclosed preeminently through Jesus is to characterize all mutual dealings within the new community.

Jesus as Agent of the New Covenant (Facet 4, Matt. 19:1–23:39)

Following the typical Matthean phrase of editorial transition ("When Jesus had finished," 19:1), which brings to a close the discourse section on community formation, the gospel resumes following the basic pattern of Mark (at Mark 10:1–13:4), but with some important supplemental material (noted below) and with intense emphasis on the sharp differences between Jesus and the Pharisees. This latter factor increases the clarity of the Matthean picture of his community, which is being developed in conscious and sharp conflict with emergent rabbinic Judaism in the period after 70 C.E.

Here the issues of marriage and divorce are addressed in ways significantly different from the parallel passage in Mark (10:1–12). Before addressing the issue of the conditions under which divorce and remarriage are permitted (as in Mark), Jesus sets out the biblical basis of marriage, highlighting the accounts in Genesis 1 and 2, where the relationship is intended to be permanent. The focus then shifts to the legal permission to divorce one's wife, which is here said to be in violation of the principle established from the creation (19:8b). However, unlike Mark's version of this pericope, in which divorce and remarriage are flatly forbidden (10:10), the factor of "unchastity" is seen as providing adequate ground for divorcing the unfaithful wife and marrying someone else (19:9). Not only is there a specific legal loophole in Matthew's version, but appended to it is an utterly unique passage in which male abstinence from sexual activity is praised. Becoming a eunuch could be meant literally, but it is probably figurative here for refraining from sex, whether by innate inclination, by physical disability, or by personal choice "for the sake of the kingdom of heaven" (19:12). To possess this ascetic quality is here described as having "received" it—that is, from God.

Clearly, the celibacy of members of the community is here commended, but it is only one further piece of evidence for the ascetic mode of life that is being enjoined in Matthew. This theme is expanded in Matthew's fuller version of the young man who asks what is required to attain life in the age to come, and is told he must give up his possessions (19:16–30). In addition to the promises of renewal of family and possessions (as in Mark 10:29–30), Matthew reports Jesus predicting that participation of the inner core of this faithful followers in the rule by the Son of Man in the renewed world (*palingenesia*)[37] will involve authority over the reconstituted "twelve tribes of Israel" (19:28). The symbolic significance of Jesus having chosen twelve disciples for the inner core of his followers is evident in this link with the destiny of the true covenant people of Israel.

Amplifying the theme of judgment on God's people, Matthew includes a unique parable describing how the sovereign grace and generosity of God shatter the neat traditional assumption that divine compensation in the day of judgment will be exactly equivalent to one's moral performance. The familiar symbol of the vineyard for the covenant people (Isa. 5:7) and the calling to account on the day of harvest are now transmuted: all participants receive the same reward in the day of reckoning, regardless of the duration of their labors. The crucial factor is not human moral performance or common expectations, but divine munificence (19:15).

Small but significant modifications of the Markan account are found throughout this section of Matthew. After a slightly abbreviated version of Mark's third prediction of Jesus' arrest and crucifixion (Mark 10:32–34; Matt. 20:17–19), the request for special status of honor for the sons of Zebedee is verbalized by their mother (20:20) rather than by them, although Jesus' response is addressed to them (20:22 ff). Instead of the blind beggar at Jericho (Mark 10:35), two blind men are healed in Matthew's version of the story (20:29–34), which takes place when Jesus touches them, rather than merely by his word (Mark 10:52). Matthew's report of Jesus riding into the city involves two animals—an ass and a colt—in apparent conformity to the prophetic prediction (Zech. 9:9), which is quoted in combination with Isa. 62:11 (Matt. 21:2–5), and Jesus rides them both (21:7)! Mark's two stories of Jesus entering the Temple and cleansing its courts (11:11, 15–19) are combined into a single account by Matthew (21:10–17), in which Jesus is identified as "the prophet from Nazareth in Galilee." Although the quotation from Isa. 56:7 omits reference to the house of prayer for all nations (Mark 11:17), Matthew adds the details of Jesus healing the blind and the lame there, of his acclaim by the children, of the indignation of "the chief priests and scribes," and of Jesus' self-defense based on Ps. 8:2. Highlighted in these ways are the scriptural basis for Jesus' actions and the hostility of the official leadership of Israel. From his version of the cursing of the fig tree (21:18–19), Matthew omits the curious mention in Mark 11:13 that there were no fruit because "it was not the season for figs."

Once again, it is in the parables that the distinctive concerns of Matthew are most clearly evident. The Parable of the Two Sons, which is found only here (21:28–32), builds on the images of the son who worked in the vineyard (i.e., did his share in preparing for the renewal of the covenant people) and the one who did not. The condemnation of "the chief priests and elders" (21:23) rests on their failure to repent at the message of Jesus, while "tax collectors and harlots" enter the kingdom before them. The rejection of ritual, professional, or moral status as the precondition for acceptance with God is here stated in sharpest form, which fits well Matthew's version of the Parable of the Wicked Tenants (21:33–46). The murder of the son of the owner varies from Mark's account, in that the son is first "cast out of the vineyard" and then killed. The murderers are not merely to be destroyed (Mark 12:9), but are called "wretches" and are "put to a miserable death," while the vineyard is "let out to other tenants who will give [the owner] the fruits in their season." This point, which is repeated in verses 41 and 43, involves the kingdom being taken away from the leaders of historic Israel and "given to another nation producing its fruits." Clearly, the people—and especially the leaders—traditionally associated with God's covenant and its eschatological renewal (the coming of "the kingdom") are to be replaced by a redefined "nation" with a wholly new kind of leadership. Underscoring this point is the detail in Matt. 21:45 that the chief priests and Pharisees understand that Jesus "was speaking about them," though they fear the popular support of Jesus by those who consider him to "be a prophet" (21:46).

Similarly, Matthew's version of the Q Parable of the Banquet depicting outsiders' share in the eschatological joy (=Luke 14:16–24) is allegorized: the marriage feast is the consummation of God's purpose for his people; it is given by the king (God) for his son (Jesus Christ); the invitees who do not come—being preoccupied with regular business—maltreat and kill the king's servants; the king responds by sending troops to destroy the murderers and burn their city (the destruction of Jerusalem and the Temple by the Romans). The original invitees are said to have been "unworthy," but those who now come are a mixed group, including "good and bad": the new community is not comprised solely of the pure and faithful. The guest who lacks a wedding garment and is expelled represents those who come to share in the new community but lack the appropriate virtues for God's new people and thus are expelled from the presence of God. The invitation is broad ("many are called") but the worthy participants are "few."

The antagonists of Jesus who form the coalition to get rid of him include in Matthew 22 (as in Mark 12) Pharisees, Herodians, and Sadducees. Only minor differences from Mark's version are evident, such as Jesus' denunciation of his opponents as "hypocrites." The issues debated concern paying taxes to the Romans (22:15–22), belief in the resurrection (22:23–33), the greatest of the commandments (22:34–40), and the relationship of the Messiah to David (22:41–46). Significant is the final remark in this series of debates that from then on, no one dares to ask him any further questions (22:46), since his skill and insight in interpreting God's law are so extraordinary.

The challenge of Jesus to the scribes and Pharisees as those who would assume the leadership of the covenant people reaches a new level of intensity in Matthew 23, which builds on Mark and the Q source but now includes features of direct criticism of and contrast with inchoative rabbinic Judaism. The first criticism of these leaders points to their hypocrisy and their pious ostentation (23:1–12). Although they claim to be expounding the law of Moses, there is a gross disparity between the thrust of their moral demands—which are appropriate—and their behavior. The demands they place on others have no counterpart in a willingness to help others fulfill those requirements. Instead, their chief concern is to show off their piety through the garb they don—wide phylacteries to display their devotion to the law and broad fringes on their robes to display the distinctiveness of their religious commitment. They seek acclaim and preferential seating at feasts and synagogues, as well as honorific greetings in public. Three titles that they covet for themselves reflect developing patterns of status in the emergent rabbinic movement: "rabbi," which shifted from a term of respect to the honorific title of a recognized "teacher"; "father" as a designation of senior rank and broad authority; and *kathegetes*, authoritative guide or counselor, a designation which is now said to be appropriate only to Christ. The one fitting title and role for members of the community is "servant," and the only acceptable stance of the members toward each other is that of humble service.

There follows a series of "woes," which Matthew has adapted and expanded from the Q source (chiefly from Luke 11:39–52). The repeated phrase to characterize the "scribes and Pharisees" is that they are "hypocrites" (23:13, 15, 25, 27, 29). Their teaching creates barriers rather than access to the kingdom (23:13). They insist on such petty requirements as tithing spices, while neglecting the essential features that should characterize God's people: "justice, mercy and faith" (23:23). They stress ritual purity while ignoring inner moral purity (23:25–26). They glory in a show of external piety while harboring within themselves deadly features of "hypocrisy and iniquity" (23:27–28). They honor the memory of the prophets by building splendid tombs in their honor even while ignoring the prophets' moral demands (23:29–31).

Also denounced here are certain distinctive practices that flourished in the later rabbinic period. The first is the zeal of these leaders in trying to convert Gentiles to Jewish belief and practice: "proselytes." Another issue was that of determining which oaths were to be considered binding and which were merely a show of piety.

The concluding section of this critique of the Jewish leaders—after denouncing them as "offspring of snakes" and warning them of the danger of punishment in hell (23:32)—describes the cruel treatment that they will extend to the various types of leaders that Jesus will send among them: "prophets, wise men and scribes." These are pictured by Jesus in Matthew's account as authentic, reliable, and sent by God. Yet they will meet with hostility, persecution, and death at the hands of the leaders of the synagogue movement (23:34). Accordingly, God will hold the latter accountable for the murder of "all the righteous" whose blood has been shed on earth, beginning with Abel in the first book of the Hebrew canon (Gen.) and ending with Zechariah in the last book (2 Chron.).[38] The divine penalty will fall on "this generation," which is the post-70 era and its emerging rabbinic leadership.

The severe critique of the Jewish leaders gives way in Matt. 23:37–39 to Jesus' lament over Jerusalem, not merely as a city and the locus of the Temple, but as the symbol of God's people: scattered, lost, and desolate. Jesus conveys the continuing love of God in the open-ended promise that they can see Jesus again when they acknowledge him, in the words of Ps. 118:26, as the "Blessed One who comes in the name of the Lord."

Consummation of God's Purpose for His People (Matt. 24:1–25:5)

Matthew's introduction (24:1–3) to the apocalyptic discourse closely follows the Markan source (13:1–4)[39] but includes in the disciples' question to Jesus two technical terms that appear regularly in early Christian eschatology: "the sign of your coming (*parousia*) and of the close of the age (*synteleia*)." In the same way, the false claims of those who come in Jesus' name are said to include the explicit assertion "I am the Messiah" (24:5), and in Matt. 24:9 the hearers are warned that they "will be put to death" as well as being "hated by all nations." This phrase obviously implies the world mission of the church, which is made explicit in Matthew's addition to this pericope (24:14), where the scope of the witness is "the whole world" (*oikoumene*) and the witness is to be borne "to all nations." Expanded is the prediction of the internal conflicts that will characterize the community, including apostasy, betrayal, false prophecy, and waning devotion to the cause (24:10–12).

The Markan reference to "the desolating sacrilege" (13:14) is in Matt. 24:15 explicitly linked with the prophecy of Daniel (9:27; 12:11) and located in the Temple ("the holy place"). The warning to the faithful to flee as disaster approaches, the need to persevere during the time of tribulation, and the rise of false, wonder-working messiahs (24:15–25) closely follow Mark (13:14–23). A brief passage from Q (24:26–28) is matched in Luke 17:23–24, but there is added a direct reference to the *parousia* of the Son of Man. Similarly, in his version of Mark 13:24–27, Matthew makes a second explicit mention of "the sign of the Son of Man" (24:29–31) and adds the detail that the elect will be summoned by "a loud trumpet call," an image that recalls Paul's in 1 Cor. 15:52–53. Matt. 24:32–36 matches well its source, Mark 13:28–32, but Mark's ending to the discourse (13:33–37) is expanded and moved elsewhere by Matthew in his greatly extended version of the apocalyptic discourse.

Drawing from Q[40] and from his own parable source, Matthew further increases the references to the *parousia* and the "coming" of the Son of Man (24:37, 39, 42, 44, 50). As in Q, the emphasis is on the need to be ready rather than being preoccupied with routine household and personal obligations. As in Q, there is a promise of reward for the "servant" who faithfully discharges his duties, and of punishment for "the wicked servant"—presumably one with responsibilities within the community—who is preoccupied with his own affairs. To this irresponsible servant, Jesus assigns Matthew's favorite critical epithet, "hypocrite," and a place among those subject to protracted punishment (24:51).

Three parables bring to a close Matthew's version of the apocalyptic discourse: the Ten Maidens (25:1–13), the Talents (25:14–30), and the Last Judgment (25:31–46). The first and last appear only in Matthew. All three deal with the issue of how the community is to behave during the protracted interim before the end of the present age and the consummation of God's rule. Whatever the original form of these parables may have been, they now display unmistakably allegorical features. The story of the Ten Maidens focuses on the need to be fully supplied during the unpredictably long interval before the "bridegroom" returns, which means before the *parousia* occurs. This interpretation is confirmed by the fact that when the unprepared maidens seek admission to the "marriage feast," they address the bridegroom as *kurios* ("Lord," 25:11). The Parable of the Talents treats of the stewardship of those "servants" assigned responsibilities during the absence of their master.[41] Some have been bold and effective, while others have been timid and unproductive. The former are rewarded, and the latter "worthless servants" are expelled and sentenced to protracted punishment (25:29–30).[42] Both parables are addressed to those with leadership or service responsibilities within the new covenant community: How faithful will they be in discharging their duties, especially in view of the delay of the *parousia?*

The final parable in Matthew is more accurately designated as an allegory depicting the process of judgment of the world "by the Son of Man" when he returns in glory to establish the rule of God in the creation. Subject to this royal judicial review are "all the nations." The "sheep" placed on the right of the throne are invited to assume their share in God's rule now, and are told that this has been predestined for them "from the foundation of the world." The basis of their reward is their acts of kindness to the newly enthroned king, providing him food and drink, clothing and visits in prison. Their astonished question is, When did they perform such acts in his behalf? His answer is that, since they did such deeds for "the least of these my brothers and sisters," they did them for him. As I noted in my analysis of Matt. 18:6–9, the terms for "little ones" and "least" are Matthean favorites for indicating the humility and unpretentiousness of the members of the new community. Here the nations that receive divine commendation are those that have shown kindness to and supported these little ones, or "least" ones as they are called (25:40). The response of the wider world to the new people of God is the major criterion in the eschatological judgment of the nations as Matthew describes it. There are two kinds of eternal destiny that depend on the nature of the response: the blessed, who acted in support and generosity, are promised a life of eternal participation in God's new rule; the cursed depart into eternal punishment, which was prepared for the devil and his emissaries. Human destiny is determined by the ways in which the people of the world react to Jesus as represented by his struggling, suffering people: "the least of these" members of his new family. The consummation of God's purpose for them comes when they are vindicated and those who have aided them are rewarded, while those who have rejected them are punished.

The Crucial Events for the Launching of the New Covenant (Matt. 26:1–28:20)

In the account in Exodus of God's covenant with Israel at Sinai, the divine assurance to the people of Yahweh's continuing presence wherever they may go is based on the sacrificial altar that they are to erect "in every place where I cause my name to be remembered" and where "I will come to you and bless you" (Exod. 20:24). The correlative sacrifice on which is grounded the assurance to the new covenant community of God's presence and blessing is, of course, the crucifixion. Confidence in the efficacy of this sacrifice is given through the resurrection of Jesus from the dead. It is wholly fitting, therefore, that following the stylized transitional phrase "When Jesus had finished (26:1), Matthew reports Jesus linking the proximity of the Passover with the delivering up of the Son of Man to be crucified (26:2). The coalition of priests and elders conspires to have Jesus arrested and killed without public knowledge prior to the feast (26:3–4).

Yet the uncomprehending disciples do not grasp the significance of the woman's anointing Jesus, which he explains is being done in preparation for his burial (26:6–13). The ensuing account in Matthew builds on the Markan narrative (Mark 14:1–15:47), but with important modifications and additions. The official base of the conspiracy to get rid of Jesus is underscored by the detail that the conference "of chief priests and elders" took place "in the palace of the high priest" (26:3–4). The arrangement with Judas to betray Jesus includes the amount he was paid, "thirty pieces of silver," which also figures in the circumstances of Jesus' death and is seen as fulfilling scripture (see below; 27:3–10). Also added is the direct exchange between Jesus and Judas about Judas's role as traitor (26:25). In his account of the Last Supper, Matthew notes that the blood of the covenant was poured out "for the forgiveness of sins" and that this symbolic act will find its fulfillment "in the kingdom of my Father"—which is the eschatological kingdom, in contrast to the intermediate epoch of the church, designated by Matthew as "the kingdom of the Son of Man." Jesus' petition to escape suffering and death ("let this cup pass," 26:39, 42) is twice repeated, followed by a commitment to God's will.

Matthew's description of Jesus being taken captive by the crowd includes several distinctive features. Jesus addressed Judas as *hetaire*, which can mean "associate" or, more vaguely, "friend" (26:50). The companion of Jesus who cuts off the ear of the high priest's slave is instructed to put away his sword, since Jesus could appeal to God for angelic legions but must now accept his suffering and death in fulfillment of "the scriptures" (26:52–54). In Matt. 26:56, it is specified that the prophetic scriptures are now to be fulfilled. Omitted by Matthew is the detail about the young man running away naked (Mark 14:51–52). The hearing before the council is led by the high priest, Caiaphas, with scribes and elders; they "sought false testimony against Jesus," but only "two came forward" to bear testimony (26:59–60). Omitted in the prediction of the destruction and rebuilding of the Temple are the references to "made with hands" and "not made with hands" (Mark 14:58). Instead, Jesus claims the ability to destroy and rebuild "the temple of God" in three days, thereby emphasizing his divine prerogatives and powers (26:61)—a status further confirmed by his claim that from now on (*ap' arti*) he will be seated at the right hand of the Power until he comes "on the clouds of heaven." Again these subtle changes in the Markan source underscore Jesus' divine status and powers. His mocking tormentors ask him to identify who it is that struck him (26:67). After the leaders' joint decision to put him to death, he is turned over to Pilate, here identified as governor (*hegemon*, 27:2), the official agent of political authority.

Matthew's case for the innocence of Jesus is supported by his account of Judas's repentance of betraying "innocent blood" (27:3–10). The use of a bribe to buy burial space in a potter's field is pictured here as fulfillment of scripture, the quotation from which is a composite of texts (Zech. 11:12–13; Jer. 32:6–15; 18:2–3). Further confirmation of Jesus' innocence is provided through the dream of Pilate's wife (27:19) and Pilate's subsequent pronouncement and public act of washing his hands to show that he takes no responsibility for Jesus' execution (27:19, 24).[43] In contrast to his decision, the chief priests and elders ask for Jesus to be "destroyed" (26:21), and the people are said to take upon themselves and their descendants responsibility for his death (27:25). In contrast to Pilate's declaration of the innocence of Jesus, the one released by him at the request of the religious leaders is called "a notorious prisoner" (27:16). Matthew makes explicit the claim that Jesus is "the king of the Jews" (27:37). The derisive crowd at the foot of the cross challenges him, "If you are the Son of God, come down from the cross" (27:40), and then repeats this taunt (27:43). His cry from the cross, quoting Ps. 22:1, includes in Matthew's version a transliteration of the Hebrew, rather than the Aramaic as in Mark 15:34. At the moment of his death, Jesus does not merely expel his breath (*exepneusen*) but "yields his spirit" (*apheken to pneuma*, 27:50), which implies his active acceptance of death. Mark's account of the tearing of the Temple veil (Mark 15:38) is expanded to include the shaking of the earth, the splitting of rocks, the opening of tombs, and the return of the dead to life in "the holy city," where they are seen by "many" (27:51–53). Clearly, these details are intended to show the cosmic significance of the death of Jesus and its central importance as a harbinger of the resurrection—not only of Jesus, but also of those of the faithful community who have died. According to Matthew, it is the earthquake that leads the awestruck centurion to declare, "Truly this was the Son of God" (27:54).

The women who witness the death of Jesus and the subsequent events are said to be "many," with the result that the Jewish requirement of multiple attestation of testimony is met (27:55). Joseph of Arimathea is here identified as "rich" and as a "disciple of Jesus." The stone that has been rolled to close the entrance to the tomb is said to be "great," and, at the urging of "the chief priests and Pharisees," Pilate orders guards to be placed there to prevent Jesus' followers from removing his body and then claiming that he has risen from the dead. These guards seal the stone (27:62–66), which thereby heightens for the reader of Matthew the improbability that his scheming supporters have taken his body from the tomb. When the women arrive on the morning of the third day, they witness another earthquake and the descent of an "angel of the Lord," who removes the stone and whose appearance fills the guards with terror (28:1–4). When the latter report these events to the Jewish leaders ("chief priests" and "elders"), they are bribed to report that, while they slept, Jesus' followers removed his body (28:11–15). Matthew is adding to his case for credibility of the resurrection of Jesus by showing that even Jesus' enemies had to admit the inexplicable occurrence: the body of Jesus disappeared from a sealed and guarded tomb.

The women are reportedly invited by the divine messenger to see the empty tomb, and are instructed to tell the disciples that Jesus is going to precede them to Galilee, where they also will see him. Then Jesus meets the women—in an account unique to Matthew—and they touch his feet and worship him, while he repeats to them the message that the disciples will see him in Galilee (28:10). In this way, Matthew offers attestation that Jesus has risen from the dead, based on the experience of not only the disciples/apostles, but also of other members of the community. Galilee is where the disciples were first called by Jesus into his service, and it is there that they are to be commissioned for their now expanded role as worldwide witnesses.

Once more it is to a "mountain" in Galilee that the disciples are directed, and where they see and worship him, in spite of the continuing doubts of "some" (28:16–17). There follows the basic commissioning of the core of eleven disciples, based on the universal authority God has granted to Jesus in both the heavenly and earthly spheres. As a consequence of his status—risen from the dead and exalted into the presence of God—Jesus assigns them the task of going out to all the world in order to develop the new community. Their responsibilities are in three categories. They are to "make disciples," with participation in this role blending insight and responsibility now extended "to all nations," rather than limited to the people of Israel. They are to baptize the new members of the community, employing the trinitarian formula. Both the sacramental and liturgical aspects of this second charge show how far (in Matthew's view) the community has moved toward formal patterns and procedures, with specific rites and confessional modes as essential features of participation. Finally, the disciples are to instruct the members, requiring them to be fully obedient to the commandments of Jesus as he enjoined them on his followers.

The gospel ends (28:20) with the promise of Jesus' continual presence with the community until the present age comes to an end. We have seen that for Matthew the present age is "the kingdom of the Son of Man" (13:41), which is characterized by challenge to his followers as well as conflict and failure. Only those who remain faithful and obedient to the new covenant on these terms will be permitted to enter the ultimate epoch, "the kingdom of the Father" (13:43), when God will vindicate his faithful people and the divine rule will be triumphant throughout the creation. The terms for participation in this age to come are set forth by Matthew in concrete ways that in some respect resemble, but often stand in sharp contrast to, the perceptions of covenant participation and conformity that were simultaneously developing in rabbinic Judaism in the period following the destruction of the Temple. The failure of Jewish political and priestly structures resulted in a sense of urgent necessity for Judaism to provide instruments and guidelines for the post-Temple and postrevolutionary Jewish covenant community. It is this debate and competition that lie behind the development evident in Matthew: the formulation of the divinely established role of Jesus as Messiah and the structure—leadership and rules—for this new community, with its claim to be the true heir of God's promises to Israel.

The Law-abiding Community

The Community Where God
Dwells among His People

4

As I noted in chapter 1, in the prophetic and hymnic traditions of Israel—before, during, and after the Babylonian exile in the sixth century—a frequently recurring model for the renewal of God's people that was to follow the impending (or already experienced) judgment of God on the disobedient covenant community was the city. It was variously called: Zion, the holy city, the holy hill, Jerusalem, or simply "the city." What is implied in this term is not merely an urban or cultic center or even the capital and sanctuary of a fallen nation about to regain a new identity, but a community where in some special sense—even literally!—God is present, and from which the divine power and purpose are effective and operative in the world.[1] The emphasis on God's presence among his people is often linked with a variant version of the city as the model for the community: the Temple as the place where God dwells. Both these motifs—city and Temple—have their counterparts in the early Christian perceptions of the new covenant people, as is evident in the letters of Paul and in the gospel tradition as well as in the later New Testament books. It is through this new community that God's power and purpose are visibly at work.

Considerable evidence for use of the cultic model to understand both Christ and the early community comes from the letters of Paul,[2] and it is employed by later writers in the Pauline tradition as well. This claim is explicit in 1 Cor. 3:16–17, where the community is told, "You are God's temple, and God's Spirit dwells in you." The chief characteristic of this "temple" community is that it is "holy." Whether one prefers the reading of 1 Cor. 6:19 that speaks of the "body" as the temple or "bodies," the point is virtually the same: the members individually and corporately are the residence of the Spirit of God in the midst of his new people. This point is confirmed in 2 Cor. 6:16–18 by an extended composite quotation from the law and the prophets that elaborates on the claim, "We are the temple of the living God."[3] The image is further expanded in the post-Pauline Letter to the Ephesians, where the community is pictured in mixed metaphors as a building founded on Jesus, the apostles, and (Christian?) prophets that is now growing into a "holy temple" for a "dwelling place of God in the Spirit" (Eph. 2:20–21).[4]

In addition to using temple imagery, Paul speaks of the Christian community as "the household of faith" (Gal. 6:10), and in 1 Cor. 14:12, he pictures the use of the charismatic gifts as essential to the building up (*oikodomen*) of the church. The image of the house (*oikian*) also appears in Paul's theorizing about the "spiritual body," as he calls it in 1 Cor. 15:38–49, which in 2 Cor. 5:1–4 he describes as "a building from God, a house not made with hands, eternal in the heavens . . . so that what is mortal may be swallowed up by life." It seems, however, that here the "building" represents the new body of the individual, rather than serving as the image of the new community. In the Letter to the Ephesians, on the other hand, the goal of the church's ministry is to "build up the body of Christ," with the aim of achieving unity of faith and knowledge (Eph. 4:11–14).[5] The "head" of this new body is, of course, Christ, God's agent in the life of his people (Eph. 4:15). In Eph. 2:20–21, this image is mixed, blending the organic with the architectural. Christ Jesus is "the cornerstone" of a "whole structure" that is "growing into a holy temple" and into which the members of the community have been "built for a dwelling place of God in the Spirit."

Another important facet of Paul's use of cultic imagery appears in his descriptions of the death of Christ as a sacrificial offering, removing human sin as a barrier to right relationship with God (Rom. 3:21–26), or as the ground of divine-human reconciliation (2 Cor. 5:18–21). Similarly, Paul's readers are called to offer themselves to God as a "living sacrifice" (*thusia*), and this act of self-giving is characterized as a *logiken latreian*, often translated "spiritual worship" or "reasonable service." The phrase is not merely a metaphor for inward change, however, but implies an act of self-giving or sacrificial dedication. This mode of worship contrasts sharply with the traditional *latreia* of the "Israelites," which was based on the historic covenants, laws, and other grounds of group relationship to God with which Paul had formerly identified (Rom. 9:3–5): "Sonship, glory, giving of the law, the [traditional cultic] worship, and the promises."[6] From recalling the grounds of the old covenant—which he now views as ineffective—Paul proceeds to develop the argument that a genetic link with Abraham and the patriarchs is not the basis for participation in God's people (Rom. 9:6–13). The positive rationale for universal inclusiveness had been made by Paul earlier in Rom. 4:16–24, where Gen. 17:5 is quoted to show that from the beginning God intended the community of faith to be comprised of people from "many nations". Or, as Paul phrases it in Gal. 3:8, "all nations" (*panta ta ethne*) are to share in the blessing that God promised to Abraham and the community of faith (Gen. 12:3, 18:18). The climax of the role of Abraham as the progenitor of the community of faith comes in the account in Genesis

Where God Dwells among His People

22 of his willingness to sacrifice his son, Isaac, in obedience to the command of God. In Rom. 8:32, Paul implicitly contrasts Abraham's being spared the necessity of offering his son with the sacrifice made by God, "who did not spare his own Son, but gave him up for us all," thereby providing the ground for God's people to enter right relationship with him.

Paul also uses priestly language in describing the services that members of the community have performed for him and in behalf of one another (Phil. 2:25; Rom. 15:16–17).[7] In the latter passage Paul refers to himself as "a minister [*leitourgos*] of Christ Jesus to the Gentiles who performs a priestly service [*hierourgounta*] in behalf of the gospel of God."[8] Although these terms seem to be used in a metaphorical sense, given Paul's emphasis on Christ's sacrifice of himself, it is significant that he chooses cultic imagery to describe his own role and the community in whose service he believes God has called him.

Although the cultic theme is by no means dominant in the gospels, it does appear at some important points. In Mark, the climactic confrontation of Jesus with the religious authorities takes place when he cleanses the Temple (11:15–17). This prophetic pronouncement about the divine judgment that is to fall begins with the announcement of the destruction of the Temple (Mark 13:2). The rebuke of the status-seeking disciples in Mark 10:35–45 culminates in his prediction of his death as a "ransom [*lutron*] for many." In the infancy narratives of Luke, Zechariah hails God's impending redemption (*lutrosin*) of his people (1:68), and Anna the prophetess speaks to "all who were looking for the redemption [*lutrosin*] of Jerusalem." In John 1:29, Jesus is hailed as "the Lamb of God who takes away the sin of the world," and in John 10:11–18, Jesus presents himself as one who will "lay down his life" as a sacrifice for God's true people, the "sheep."

This cultic-sacrificial symbolism, which is a recurrent metaphorical or implicit feature in the gospels and some of Paul's writings, gains explicit significance when Paul uses it in depicting Jesus as the divinely provided atoning sacrifice and the new community as the temple of God in the passages quoted or referred to above. But in later New Testament writings, the model of the city and Temple as the place of meeting between God and his purified people becomes much more nearly central. I shall examine three of these: First Peter, which develops the Pauline tradition with its mix of apocalyptic expectation and accommodation to Greco-Roman culture; the Book of Revelation, which builds on the apocalyptic tradition, but with emphasis on city and Temple; and the Letter to the Hebrews, which employs the ontology of the Middle Platonic tradition to recast the central significance of Jesus as the archetypal priest and agent of divine access for God's new people. The first two examples were written around the turn of the second century, as the distinction between Christians and Jews became sharper and more obvious to outsiders, especially the Roman state, and as pressure increased on Jewish and Christian groups to formulate understandings of their respective movements that were appropriate in reaction to an increasingly militant imperial power. Hebrews, the third example of this model in the New Testament, which likewise dates from about the end of the first century, represents an effort to shift focus from the ephemeral earthly realm to the sphere of eternity, where ultimate truth (as it is perceived in the Middle Platonic tradition) is revealed. In all three cases, however, the sacrifice of Christ is central, and the people of God are called to accept responsibilities as the earthly community of worshipers, as well as to maintain their testimony within the wider culture.

Royal Priesthood, Holy Nation: First Peter

The First Letter of Peter, though attributed to Peter, shows by its relatively sophisticated Greek style and its dependence on the thought and terminology of Paul's letters, as well as by its lack of allusions to the career or teachings of Jesus, that it was not written by the Galilean fisherman who became an antagonist of Paul.[9] Throughout this letter, the imagery and structure of the community are presented in terms that draw on both cultic (Temple) and political (city) traditions.[10]

Cultic Imagery

After an implied comparison of the church to Israel, using the linked terms "exile" and "dispersion" (1:1) and making obvious reference to two of the major events in the history of Israel that forced the people to rethink their identity and the ground of their claim to a special relationship with God, the writer describes the new community in cultic language: "sanctified" and sprinkled with the blood of Jesus Christ (1:2). The people are summoned (1:15) to reflect God's holiness by their own holy manner of life, with direct reference to the commandment set forth in Lev. 11:44–45 and 19:2. Through obedience, they are to "purify their souls" (1:22). This is now made possible because they have been "redeemed," not with such humanly valued means as "silver and gold," but with "the precious blood of Christ, like that of a lamb without blemish or spot." These latter phrases recall the cultic regulations for renewal of the covenant under Joshua, according to Num. 28:3–11, where unspotted lambs are specified.

Sacrificial Imagery

In 1 Pet. 2:5, the new community is explicitly identified as a "holy priesthood," and its members are instructed to "offer spiritual sacrifices [*pneumatikas thusias*] to God through Jesus Christ." Thus the members of the group are not simply assigned to honorific posts as priests, nor are they to perform the traditional, literal sacerdotal functions by presenting to God physical items as sacrifices, in accord with the levitical regulations of ancient Israel. Instead, the expected mode of action seems to be like that called for by Paul in Rom. 12:1, where the members are called to present their bodies (= total selves) as a living sacrifice (*thusia*), which will be holy and which God will accept. The terminology is different, in that Paul calls this kind of self-giving a *logiken latreian* (reasonable or spiritual sacrifice), but the point is the same. Offering of the self to God is the exact counterpart of animal or other sacrifices to God in the old covenant, and hence a *thusia*. The one who makes such an offering is fulfilling a new kind of priestly function.[11] The designation of the new community as the "royal priesthood" (*basileion hierateuma*) is discussed below.

Architectural Imagery: The New Temple

Christ is portrayed in 1 Peter as having already been glorified by God in the resurrection (1:11, 21), but the full disclosure of his glory will take place in the future (4:13, 5:1), when his people will receive "the unfading crown of glory." The destiny of the community will be accomplished in a manner described by the author in architectural imagery: "Restore, establish, confirm your foundations" (5:10). Meanwhile, the members are to glorify God (4:16), Gentiles who see the good deeds of the members of the community will glorify God (2:12), and through their devotion to Jesus Christ, God will be glorified (4:11). Instead of the belief of the ancient Israelites that God was visibly and powerfully present only in the innermost court of the Temple, the service of God in behalf of his people, the oracles of God that convey his purposes to them, and even the manifestation of the divine glory are said to take place in the life of the new community.

A second important theme in 1 Peter related to the image of the Temple emphasizes the newness and the vitality of the structure and the corporate unity of God's people: the living building. An image widely used by the author of 1 Peter is that of "glory," which carries the symbolic meaning of the presence of God, traditionally in the inner space of the Temple, the Holy of Holies. In this letter, it occurs with connotations that closely resemble those found in Paul's employment of this image, especially in 2 Cor. 3:7–18, where the contrast is offered between the fading glory of God that Moses experienced in his encounter with Yahweh at Sinai (Exod. 34:29–35) and the permanent and surpassing splendor of God disclosed in Jesus Christ. In 1 Pet. 2:4–5, the link is made between Christ as "the living stone" and his people, who are to be "living stones." Together they constitute a "spiritual house" in which "spiritual sacrifices" are to be offered to God through Jesus Christ. Christ is the cornerstone of this new structure, although he also serves as a "stone of offense" to those who reject him. All of these pictures of Christ are drawn from the scriptures: Isa. 28:16, the laying of the cornerstone in Zion; Ps. 118:22, the rejected stone that has become the head of the corner; and Isa. 8:14–15, God's plan for renewal that becomes a stone of stumbling for his disobedient people.

Christ's sufferings in the flesh delivered him from sin (4:1–6). Just so the people of God are to overcome the "human passions" and "live in the Spirit like God." Jesus' obedience unto death (in Paul's phrase, Phil. 2:8) is not merely a divine cultic transaction to deal with sin, but also an eternal model of the way in which God's people are to live in accord with the divine will. As God vindicated Christ through his experience of suffering, so his faithful people should endure the difficulties they undergo in assurance of ultimate joy in God's presence (4:12–13).

The Holy Nation, the Royal Priesthood

In 1 Pet. 2:9–10, the author collocates a series of images of the covenant community drawn primarily from the biblical traditions of Israel. Each of the images serves to provide an additional facet of the new people of God.

A Chosen Race (*genos eklekton*)

In contrast to the use of *genos* in the Septuagint version of the Pentateuch, where it designates forms of life in the creation or refers to the departed members of one's family (Gen. 25:17), *genos* is used in Jeremiah to designate the offspring of Israel who do not share in the covenantal blessings (Jer. 31:36–31). In Second Isaiah, on the other hand, the term is found in connection with God's renewal of the earth, symbolized by springs and rivers in the desert, which are described as gifts of God to "my chosen nation." In the Servant Song of Isaiah 42,[12] the servant is told that God will call him "in righteousness," will grasp his hand, will confirm him, and will give him as a covenant to the people, and a light to the nations (*ethnon*).[13] The same basic point is made in Isa. 49:6, where in the Septuagint the role of the servant (*pais*) is "to raise up the tribes of Jacob and to restore the dispersion of Israel." The text continues, "See, I have placed you as a covenant of the people, as a light to the nations, as salvation to the end of the earth." In both these quoted passages, the covenant is made with *ethnos*.

A Royal Priesthood (*basileion hierateuma*)

In the Septuagint version of Exod. 19:6, where God is instructing Moses on Mount Sinai about the importance and the value of Israel's keeping the covenant, the special relationship of this people to Yahweh is epitomized in the two phrases "a royal priesthood" (*basileion hierateuma*) and "a holy nation" (*ethnos hagion*)—precisely the terms used in 1 Pet. 2:9. In Exod. 23:22, these terms are repeated, with the addition of a third phrase in 1 Pet. 2:9 to describe the people of God: *laos periousios*. This passage in the Septuagint, which has no counterpart in the Hebrew text, reports God as declaring: "If you indeed give heed to my voice and do all the things which I commanded you, and keep my covenant, you shall be the people of my special possession [*laos periousios*] from among all the nations. For all the earth is mine, and you shall be a royal priesthood [*basileion hierateuma*] and a holy nation [*ethnos hagion*]." What the author of 1 Peter is claiming is that these images of the covenant people have now been fulfilled in the new community called into being in the name of Jesus. I shall consider below the cultic significance of Jesus for this letter. The importance of identifying the people of God as a "holy nation" in the Hellenistic period is clearly indicated in the Wisdom of Solomon, where, in an extended retelling of the history of God's people (Wisd. of Sol. 10:1–19:22), the author characterizes Israel, enslaved by the Egyptians, as a "holy nation" (*ethnos hagion*) held in the power of "lawless men."[14]

In the historical books from Judges through Chronicles and Ezra, there is a persistent theme that Israel—in spite of its special relationship to Yahweh as the "holy nation"—in fact emulated the other nations, to the point of worshipping their gods and engaging in their idolatrous practices *(bdelugmata)*.[15] Jeremiah characterizes Israel as a disobedient nation, slated for divine punishment (7:28, 9:9, and 18:5–11, where the terminology shifts between kingdom and nation). The judgmental theme is epitomized by the prophet Haggai, when the priests have been asked about the people's ignoring of ritual rules and pronounce their behavior unclean: "So it is with this people and with this nation before me, says the LORD; and so with every work of their hand; and what they offer there [in the Temple] is unclean" (Hag. 2:14). Even more bitterly denunciatory is the pronouncement of Malachi (3:8) about the failure of God's people to fulfill their obligations through tithes and offerings: "You are cursed with a curse, for you are robbing me—the whole nation of you!"

In 1 Esd. 8:87–92, Ezra's prayer of confession acknowledges the dreadful range and depth of disobedience on the part of the people and their national leaders ("our kings") that has led to their exile and dispersion, from which they are now being called to recommitment and renewal in accord with the law of Moses. That hope was earlier made explicit in Jeremiah, where the assurance of God's renewal of the covenant with Israel (31:31–34) is confirmed by a divine guarantee that just as sure as the orderly movement of the heavenly bodies is the certainty that "the offspring of Israel" will endure "as a nation forever" (31:36). Similarly, Ezekiel asserted that the same "nation of rebels" who have continually "transgressed" the will of God (2:3) will be restored "from among the nations to which they have gone," and in place of divided Israel and Judah there will be "one nation in the land and on the mountains" (37:22–23). God will make "an everlasting covenant" with this nation, and the universal witness to this renewal will be God's presence among them and his sanctifying "Israel, when my sanctuary is among them forever" (37:27–28). The same dual hope of national restoration and the enduring presence of God among his people is expressed in Ben Sira 36:12–14:

> "Have mercy, O Lord, upon the people called by thy name, /
> upon Israel, whom Thou hast likened to a first-born son. / Have
> pity on the city of thy sanctuary, / Jerusalem, the place of thy
> rest. / Fill Zion with the celebration of thy Wondrous deeds, /
> and thy temple with thy glory."

It is concordant with this merging of political and cultural features for the renewal of God's covenant people that in 1 Pet. 2:9, the terminology for designating the new community combines regal and cultic functions. "Royal priesthood" *(basileion hierateuma)* implies a joining of the kingly and priestly roles, and fits well with the more political connotations of the correlative terms in this passage, "chosen race [*genos*], a holy nation [*ethnos*], God's special people [*laos*]." Yet the community is paradoxically called upon to be prepared to suffer, not to triumph through exercise of God-given power. In a hymnic passage (2:21–25) heavily dependent on the Suffering Servant poem of Isaiah 53, the writer calls on his readers to accept suffering as Christ did, even though he was free from sin or guile. In his death "on the tree"[16] he carried the sins of his people and made possible the healing of their mortal wounds (53:5) as well as their restoration to the flock of God, who is the true shepherd (53:6). The theme of Christ's death as God's way of dealing with the sins of his people is repeated in 1 Pet. 3:18, 4:1, and 4:13. Analogously, his people are to be prepared to suffer for reasons that from their perspective can only be viewed as unjust, yet in accepting this self-giving mode of life, they show that they are in full obedience to God.

A Holy Nation (*ethnos hagion*)

The term *ethnos* is central in the promise made to Abraham in Genesis 12, where Yahweh assures him not merely that he will have a son and heir, but that through him God will produce "a great nation," which will receive divine blessing and in which "all the families of the earth shall be blessed" (12:2–3). In the establishment of the covenant through Moses, the obedient people are promised that they will serve God as "a priestly kingdom and a holy nation" (*ethnos hagion*, Exod. 19:6).

God's Own People (*laos eis peripoiesin*)

In the language of the prophet Hosea (1:6, 9), this new community was formerly no people at all, but now it is "God's people." Recalling once more (as in 1 Pet. 1:1) the historical difficulties that Israel had experienced, they are addressed in 1 Pet. 2:11 as "aliens and exiles." The special relationship of this new people to God echoes the words of Mal. 3:16–18, where the reconstitution of God's people is described in terms of a "book of remembrance" in which the names of the members are recorded as God's "special possession." God will spare them as parents spare obedient children, and the difference between "the righteous and the wicked" will be clearly evident. A feature of this special relationship is set out in Hag. 2:9:[17] "Wherefore the glory of this house [the Temple] shall be great—the latter house more than the former—says the Lord Almighty, and in this place I shall give peace, says the Lord Almighty, that is, peace of soul in a special relationship [*peripoiesis*] to all who contribute to the erection of this temple."

The Role of Jesus as God's Agent of Renewal

Pictured as sojourners (*parepidēmois*) and as part of the "dispersion" of God's people—on analogy with the dispersion of Israel in the Greco-Roman period—the elect community is described in cultic language as chosen through the "sanctification" of the Spirit for obedience and "sprinkling of the blood of Jesus Christ" (1 Pet. 1:2–3). In 1 Pet. 1:15–16, the basis for moral renewal of the community is a call to be "holy" as God is—quoted from the Levitical code (Lev. 11:44, 19:2). Their redemption (*elutrōthete*) was accomplished through "the precious blood of Christ," who is here called a spotless "lamb" (1:19). Now their souls are to be "purified" (*egnikotes*, 1:22), preparing them for participation in the "holy priesthood" and for the offering of "spiritual sacrifices" (2:5).

The sacrifical suffering of Christ for the sins of his people—the righteous in behalf of the unrighteous—not only makes access to God possible for his new people, but also results in his being made alive in the Spirit (3:18) and thereby in their rebirth (1:3, 22). Both his suffering and his subsequent glorification were predicted through the prophets (1:10—11). The theme of Christ's suffering and the model it provides for his people are developed extensively throughout this relatively short letter. Christ's sufferings are predicted in 1 Pet. 1:11. Acceptance of suffering leads to approval by God (2:19–20). Those who suffer for righteousness' sake are blessed (3:14). Suffering for the right is God's will (3:17). Christ suffered for the sins of his people (3:18). His people share in Christ's sufferings (4:1). Like Christ, they are not to suffer as wrongdoers (4:15).[18] They are to suffer in accord with the will of God (4:19). They are witnesses to what Christ's sufferings mean (5:1). All of them must undergo the experience of suffering (5:9). After suffering, God will call them to glory (5:10).

The model for this depiction of the redemptive significance of the death of Christ is the Suffering Servant poem of Isaiah 53, to which there are repeated allusions in the hymnic passage in 1 Pet. 2:21–25 that details the meaning of his sacrifice.[19] His death also is pictured as having provided him access to the souls of the dead ("spirits in prison"), specifically to those who lived in ancient times and did not give heed to God's word (3:21). His triumph over death is given symbolic—and cultic—significance in that baptism, portrayed here as analogous to preservation of the faithful in the time of Noah, accomplishes cleansing of the "conscience" (3:20–21).

Mingling metaphors, the author of 1 Peter describes Christ as a "living stone" that is the basis for the "spiritual house" being constructed (*oikodomeisthe*, 2:4–5) and as the "chief shepherd" (*archipoimenos*) who serves as the archetype for those assigned to give leadership to "the flock [*poimnion*] of God" and to provide the members examples of proper behavior (5:1–4). When their time for enduring suffering is past, the God who called them through Christ will "restore, establish, strengthen" them (5:9–10). For the author of 1 Peter, suffering and sacrifice are not modes of ritual purification but a pattern of obedient life for the new community, for which the self-giving of Christ is the prototype. He is "the shepherd and guardian [*episkopos*] of their souls" (2:25). Life within the family [*adelphotes*] is to be characterized by love as well as by the acceptance of suffering (2:17, 5:9). In the inner life of the new community as well as in the divine action through Christ by which it was founded, the cultic image of suffering is paramount.

The Revelation to John: The City That Comes from Heaven

The Central Importance of the City

Although the Revelation to John is the only book in the New Testament that designates itself as an "apocalypse" (1:1), and although there is a clear and repeated indication that only the informed and elect will be able to comprehend the message of the book ("let whoever has ears to hear, hear"; 2:7, 11, 17, 19; 3:6, 13, 20 22), the model that best fits the picture of the community conveyed by Revelation is that of the city/Temple. Of the many references to "kingdom" and cognate terms,[20] only four use "king" as a title of Christ (9:11, 15:3, 17:4, 19:16), and only once is there mention of the "kingdom of God" (12:10) or the "kingdom of Christ" (11:15). In one passage "kingdom" is linked with the suffering of the faithful in the present age (1:9), and in another it is joined with the role of the members as priests (1:6), which has important implications for the symbolic images throughout the book.

By contrast, the terms "city" (*polis*) and "temple" (*naos*) occur respectively twenty-six and fifteen times in this book. When the author is depicting the present evil world order that the "city of God" will replace, he uses *polis* rather than kingdom to characterize it. Martyred saints lie in the streets of the great "city" (11:8), which is punished by an earthquake as a manifestation of God's judgment as a consequence of its wickedness (11:13). Here the "great city" is Jerusalem, designated "allegorically" (*pneumatikos*) as "Sodom and Egypt," because it was in Jerusalem that "their Lord was crucified" (11:8). Thus God's judgment on Israel for the failure to receive Jesus as his redemptive agent is seen as culminating in the destruction of the city of Jerusalem. The final encounter between the power of God and the forces of Satan is pictured as taking place at the end of the thousand-year interval during which the faithful martyrs are raised from the dead and rewarded (20:1–6). When Satan is released from prison, he leads the armies of the wicked gathered from across "the broad earth" to undertake a final, futile attack on "the [military] encampment[21] of the saints and the beloved city" (20:9).

The City as Symbol of Evil Power

Far more frequently, however, the "city," which is depicted as the focus of God's wrathful judgment, is portrayed as the center and structure of the powers of evil, repeatedly referred to in terms of Israel's traditional enemy, "Babylon" (14:8; 16:19; 17:5; 18:2, 10, 21). It is "outside the city" that God's wrath is depicted through the image of the blood of the wicked pouring out like wine from a wine press, creating a sea of blood that reaches to the bridle of a horse and extends for about two hundred miles (14:20). With mingled glee and lament, the fall of "the great city" is foretold repeatedly. From symbolic details that are included in the visions and oracles, it is clear that the city is Rome as the focus of human power, arrayed against God and his people. In Revelation 12 there is a vivid portrayal of the conflict between the purpose of God and the violent opposition from Satan. The woman "clothed with the sun" represents God's intention for the creation, and the child about to be born is the figure of Christ, through whom that purpose will be achieved. The multiple horns and diadems of "the dragon" obviously are adapted from the vision in Daniel 7 of the beasts that represent the successive world empires. The child, destined to be ruler of "all nations" (12:5), has been kept from destruction by being taken up into the presence of God. The final desperate efforts of the dragon to thwart God's plan for the renewal of the creation are detailed in Rev. 12:7–17.

The beast that is seen arising from the sea (13:1) with multiple heads, horns, and diadems is the human agent (Caesar) to whom Satan gives effective rule over human affairs. Although the beast speaks blasphemies against God (13:5), it gains control over the whole of humanity and is worshipped by all except those whose names have been written "in the book of life of the Lamb that was slain" (13:8). The "beast from the earth" is the agent that promotes and enforces the worship of the first beast and regulates commerce on the basis of allegiance to the emperor (13:11–18).[22] In the midst of these predictions of the religious manipulation of those subject to the Roman empire is the announcement of the fall of "Babylon the great," the city of Rome, which symbolizes and embodies the power of the pagan realm. There is no rest for those who worship the beast and its image (14:8–11). This theme is repeated in Rev. 16:19, where the pouring out of the bowls of divine wrath culminates in the shattering of the city by an unprecedentedly violent "earthquake."

Perhaps the clearest evidence that "Babylon" is an insider's code word for the doomed city of Rome comes in Rev. 17:1–6, where it is depicted as a "great harlot" with whom "the kings of the earth have committed fornication." That is, the regional rulers have sold their political and religious freedoms in order to get along with Roman dominance of the world. The depth of Rome's fornication is seen in the emperor worship that it fostered as a sociopolitical instrument to consolidate power, and in the shedding of the blood of the Christian martyrs. The seven-headed beast that the woman is astride is shown to be Rome by the link with the "seven hills" on which the city rests (17:9). Although the identity of the ten kings mentioned in Rev. 17:7 ("horns") and 17:12 cannot be determined with certainty, they appear to refer to successive emperors over the period of more than a century, probably from Octavian (30 B.C.E.–14 C.E.) to Domitian (81–96 C.E.). Their imperial line will be overcome by the Lamb, who is "Lord of lords and King of kings" (17:14). His subjects will be "the chosen and the faithful."

The final destruction of Rome is detailed in Rev. 18:1–24 with the account of the plagues and fire that fall on the city. There is a surprising note of sorrow or regret in the lament (18:10), "Alas, alas! O great city, O mighty city, Babylon! In one hour has your judgment come." Yet the great city will be thrown down with violence, and will be found no more (18:21). In foretelling and portraying the judgment of God on the enemies of his purpose, human and diabolical, the major image is that of the city as the target of divine wrath.

Temple Imagery

We have seen that the image of the city embodies the structure of human existence in the Revelation to John. It is not surprising, therefore, that the messages to the churches in the form of seven letters (1:4–3:22) are addressed in terms that specifically link them with the cities in which each church resides. The characteristics of each city are mirrored in the counsel given to each of the seven churches. Yet the details of description and prescription for the churches are not couched exclusively in the political imagery linked with the *polis*. Instead, great importance is attached to the modes of worship being carried on in each place, not only by the members of the community but also by the wider society as well. Essential to John's view of true and proper access to God and of the ground of right relationship between God and his people is the sacrifical role of Jesus. The temple is pictured as the point of meeting between God and his true people. All these sacerdotal and cultic images are reflected throughout the Revelation to John. The first direct description of the new community (1:5) concentrates on the sacrifice of Christ, by which his people are freed from their sins and transformed into a "kingdom, priests to God the Father." The image of the sanctuary that Jesus has made accessible by his death in behalf of his people pervades this book.

Anticipating the importance of worship in the new community, as well as within the cities where the seven churches are located, is the depiction of the latter as instruments for spreading the light of God, seven golden lamps (*luchnia*, 1:12), an image modified in Rev. 1:16–20 to picture the churches as "seven stars." Clearly this image builds on the importance of the lamp stand in the sanctuary of Yahweh in the biblical tradition. Of prime significance is the fact that the lamp stand is linked in Exodus 25–26 with the ark of the covenant and the table for the Bread of the Presence. It is repeatedly referred to in Exodus, Leviticus, and Numbers as a vital feature of the tent where God is present, serving as symbol of that presence and of the light he brings to his people. Special assignments are made to the Levites to care for the lamp stand.[23] David and then Solomon make specific provisions for the positioning of the lamp stand in the Temple as it is being planned and built, according to both Deuteronomic and Levitical traditions.[24] In the wisdom tradition, Ben Sira compares the beauty of a wife to the glowing light from a lamp on the holy lamp stand in the sanctuary of God (26:17), but in the prophetic writings the lamp stand in the Temple figures literally in both the judgment and the renewal of God's people, as when Jeremiah laments the fracture of the lamp stand and the removal of its fragments to Babylon (52:11–23).[25] Conversely, Zechariah pictures the lamp stand and the two olive trees as symbolizing respectively the eyes of the Lord and his two anointed agents[26] who look toward and work for the renewal of his people, following their experience of judgment in the Babylonian exile (4:2–11).

In the letters to churches, the problems and responsibilities of the communities are often set forth through commendations of the ritual condition of the members or through contrasts with the defective members and/or the wider society in which a community lives. Such a distinction between true and false claims and criteria for membership in God's people is evident in the warning to the church at

Smyrna against those who claim to be people of the covenant ("Jews") but are "a synagogue of Satan" (2:9). In the letter to the church at Philadelphia (3:9), a similar warning is voiced, and then linked with a promise that those of this erroneous persuasion about the people of God will be forced to grovel before those whom God loves, who have resisted all pressures to deviate from his purpose for them (2:10).

The significance for the seven churches of the cultic features of the city where each is located is most evident in the letter to the church in Pergamum (2:12–17), where the chief problem is the involvement of members of the church in pagan cults. The reference to "Satan's throne" can be understood in at least three different ways. It could mean the cult of Asklepios, the god of healing, for whom a major shrine was located in the city, to which large numbers of seekers of healing and renewal came. During the reigns of Domitian (81–96) and Trajan (98–117), Pergamum became the outstanding shrine of this healing god in the whole of the empire, and, as can be inferred from the writings of Aelius Aristides, a place where the idle rich sought not merely cures of ailments but solace and communion with the divine.[27] A second possible interpretation of the reference involves the monumental altar of Zeus that was erected in Pergamum by the local monarch, Eumenes II, around 180 B.C.E. in gratitude for his victory over the Gauls. Its splendid reliefs (which were reconstructed in the Pergamum Museum of Berlin) attest to the rich honors bestowed there on the chief of the Greek gods, and the important place that this city gave to the traditional Greek gods in the ordering of human affairs. The third interpretation derives from the fact that, from the time of the establishment of a Pergameme realm by Attalus I in the last quarter of the second century B.C.E., the rulers there looked to Rome to prevent the takeover of Asia Minor by the Seleucid rulers of Syria and the East. The traditional policy of ascribing divine ancestry to the regional dynasty fitted well with later claims by Rome of the emperor's divinity. When Rome took over direct control of this region in the first century B.C.E., Pergamum was a natural center for promoting the emperor cult. It is probably a blend of the second and third interpretations that lies behind the description of this city "where Satan dwells." It is there that John the seer perceives a counterfeit of the true house of God and of the divinely based worship of God through Christ. The warning here is against participation in these rites in honor of a false god through eating "food sacrificed to idols" (2:14).

Passing references to impure and corrupted models of the people of God are found in the descriptions of unworthy religious groups in Smyrna and Philadelphia as synagogues of Satan (2:9, 3:9). By contrast, those in Sardis who resist pressure to share in pagan worship are called conquerors and are given white garments as manifestations of their purity (3:4–5). The church at Laodicea, in spite of its claim to prosperity, is "wretched, pitiable, poor, blind and naked." The members are urged to accept the fiery trials that accompany fidelity, by which they may be refined like "gold," and to seek to obtain as divine rewards the "white garments" of purity (3:18).

When the seer is taken up to heaven into the presence of God and the Lamb (4:1–11), he beholds God enthroned and the living creatures who sing praise "without ceasing" to "the Lord God Almighty" and worship him. As this scene continues, there is mention of "bowls of incense" (5:8) and of the "altar" where the souls of the martyrs rest (6:9), both of which imply that the setting includes features of a temple as well as the seat of God's power ("the one seated on a throne," 4:2, 5:1, 5:13). Similarly, in Rev. 8:3–5, there is mention of the "fire and smoke from the altar," which represent the prayers of the saints, as well as the outpouring of divine judgment on the wicked of the earth. In Rev. 14:15–18, the messengers of God are described as coming forth from the temple and the altar of God to give instructions to God's agents of judgment on the evil world. In Rev. 15:2–4 (as in 4:6), there is mention of a "sea of glass," which implies God's ultimate triumph over the waters of chaos.[28] The calm sea is the gathering place of the nucleus of God's new people, as the prophet phrased it (Isa. 51:10): "Was it not you who dried up the sea, the waters of the great deep, and made the depths of the sea a path for the ransomed to cross?" Although the historical reference in Second Isaiah is clearly the crossing of the sea in the time of the Exodus, its symbolic significance here is God's defeat of the powers of evil and the renewal of his new covenant people. This sea stands before "the temple of the tent of witness," from which come forth the angels of divine judgment to put into effect the wrath of God on a disobedient humanity (15:5–8). All these visions and portents are disclosed "in heaven" (15:1) and point to the renewal of the creation that is to accompany the coming to earth of the holy city of God.

The Lion/Lamb Forms God's New People

The way in which Christ embodies features of both priest and sacrifice is evident in the opening part of Revelation (1:5–6), where he is described as the one "who loves us and has freed us from our sins by his blood." The sacerdotal theme is repeated in the next phrases, which describe the community as "a kingdom, priests to his God and Father." This image of Jesus in a priestly role is greatly elaborated in Revelation 5. The dominant representation of Christ is as the Lamb,[29] but he is also "the Lion of the tribe of Judah" (5:5), who has conquered the enemies of God. This blending of images—the Lamb as symbol of sacrifice and submission and the Lion as symbol of power and authority—is essential for the author of Revelation, not only in his portrayal of the salvific role of Jesus but also in his defining of the new people of God, as set forth in chapters 5–7.

As a consequence of the Lamb's acceptance of death as a sacrifice, he receives power, wealth, wisdom, might, honor, glory, and blessing (5:12). A different image of the effect of his sacrifice in Rev. 5:9 describes him as worthy to bring into reality God's purpose for his people, because he has "purchased them" or "set them free" for God (*egorasas to theo*) "by his blood." Still another cultic image is employed in Rev. 7:14–17 for the multitude "in white robes" that have been "washed in the blood of the lamb." The priestly dimensions of their role are implied in the depiction of them before the throne of God, where they "serve [*latreuousin*] him day and night in his temple," that is, in a cultic capacity. The combined roles of Jesus and his people take yet another symbolic tack in Rev. 7:17, where, before the throne of God, the Lamb becomes the shepherd of the community and leads them to "springs of living water." Those who participate in this new flock of God are said to have come from every tribe, tongue, people, and nation (5:9). In Rev. 7:4–12, where the redeemed people gather before the throne of God, their assembling is described in two stages: the 144,000, who are chosen and ordained ("sealed") out of the twelve tribes of Israel, and then the innumerable multitude "from every nation, from all tribes and peoples and tongues" (7:9). They join in praise to God "and to the Lamb" (7:10).

In contrast to the Antichrist, who is described in terms of the dragon and the beast, representing the idolatrous imperial cult with its pseudomessiah, Rev. 14:1–7 once more portrays the Lamb on Mt. Zion with the faithful remnant (the 144,000), who join the heavenly song that celebrates God's renewal of his people and the creation. The scene of cosmic triumph before the "sea of glass" includes the song of Moses (recalling the historical tradition of God's people) and the song "of the Lamb," which celebrates the triumph of God's purpose and invites "all nations" to join in the worship of God.

In the closing visions of Revelation, the images are again mingled. After the shout of praise to God for his triumph over the powers of evil represented by the empire and its idolatrous scheme of human subjugation (19:1–4), there is a description of the consummation of God's purpose for his people under the metaphor of the marriage of "the Lamb" and "the bride" (19:5–8). The latter image of the community of the faithful is repeated in the final scenes (21:9). A completely different image of Christ is offered when he appears as a triumphant rider on a white horse and is hailed by the multitude as "King of kings and Lord of lords" (19:11–16). Yet even here the cultic facets are evident in the mention that his robe has been "dipped in blood" (19:13). Other images include the "sword from his mouth" with which he pronounces judgment and his treading "the winepress" as he effects the judgment of God on a disobedient and rebellious world (19:15). The faithful martyrs who share in the millennial reign of Christ are described in Rev. 20:6 as "priests of God and Christ."

The Holy City

The climax of Revelation comes in the depiction of the renewal of God's people and of the creation that occurs when the holy city, the new Jerusalem, comes down from God out of heaven (21:1–22:5). The anticipation of this event is couched in similar imagery early in the work, when the hope and confidence of the author of Revelation about God's plan are formulated in terms of the "city of God" or the "new Jerusalem" (3:12). In the interim, before the judgment of the wicked and the vindication of the faithful are accomplished by God, the witnesses to God are to address their message to God's traditional people, here symbolized by the Temple at Jerusalem and the altar of God (11:2). The outer court of that structure was accessible to Gentiles, who are described as "trampling the holy city" (11:3) and who are not to be evangelized, as indicated by the instruction not to measure "the court outside the temple." This blend of political power and sacerdotal purity serves the author's portrayal of the present crisis that God's people face and the hope of future deliverance and renewal God is conveying to them. The human institutions as well as the divine ones that will replace them are pictured in Revelation in ways that combine political and priestly imagery. The community being constituted here is one that acknowledges the sovereignty of God, access to whom has been made possible through the divinely provided sacrifice, the Lamb of God.

In the final letter to the seven churches (to Philadelphia, 3:12), the faithful are promised that if they persevere in the face of opposition and martyrdom, God will establish them as "pillars in the temple of God." Each pillar will be inscribed with God's name and with "the name of the city of my God, the new Jerusalem which comes down from God out of heaven," as well as the "new name" of the holy one (3:7) who conveys the message to God's people. Before the new city comes to earth, however, some of the faithful are taken up to heaven to see it, as John is summoned upward by the heavenly voice that addresses him (4:1). There he is given insights and information about what God is going to do in the future. Transported in the Spirit, he sees the throne of God and the twenty-four elders who represent the people of God, as well as the living creatures that surround the throne and offer God ceaseless praise (4:2–11). The prophet is told to "measure the temple of God and the altar" and to take account of "those who worship there" (11:1). Clearly, this group is the representative sample of the complete covenant community that, as the previous verse indicates, is to include members from "many peoples and nations and tongues and kings" (10:11). A voice is heard from heaven that is compared with "many waters," with "thunder," and with the sound of "harps," and the 144,000 faithful who have been "redeemed from the earth" are called the aparche—first fruits, or down payment, or promissory deposit—on the complete number of God's people (14:1–5). Their being in the presence of God attests to God's preservation of his obedient people, just as it offers assurance to the suffering and oppressed of the majesty and power of God, which will overcome all obstacles and effect his purpose for his people and for the creation. In Rev. 19:1–4, the heavenly worship of God is depicted yet again.

In the last two chapters of Revelation, the ultimate consummation of God's purpose is described. In a variation on the bridal image in Rev. 19:5–10, where the community is prepared for marriage to the Lamb, here the city itself is "prepared as a bride adorned for her husband" (21:2). The main point of these images is that "the dwelling of God is with humans," and they shall be his people, whom he will free from all sorrow and pain (21:3–4). The descending city, "the bride, the wife of the Lamb," is described in detail, the central feature being "the glory of God," which is now available to all instead of being concealed in the innermost section of the Temple and accessible only to the priests on prescribed occasions. The importance of the new community is conveyed in the multiple use of the sacred number twelve, recalling the tribes of Israel and the twelve apostles (21:12–14).

Most remarkable is the declaration that there is no temple in the new holy city (21:22–27). God and the Lamb are resident in the new city, visible and accessible without priestly mediators, now that the way to God has been opened by the Lamb and his sacrifice. The radiant light of God's presence shines on the "nations" and even on their "kings," and is available at all times. Only those who "practice abomination or falsehood" are excluded, while all who "are written in the Lamb's book of life" may enter the city of God. From the throne comes forth not only light but the water of life and the fruits that bring about the "healing of the nations" (22:2). The priestly imagery continues to the end of the book in the pronouncement of the blessedness of those who "wash their robes" (22:14) and in the warning that those who tamper with the prophetic message of John will forfeit a share in "the tree of life and the holy city" (22:19). It is to this focus and source of purity and power that Christ has provided access, as John pictures it, and those who share in this ultimate order are the people who have responded in courage and trust to what God has done through Jesus and disclosed to the new community through John. The implied contrasts between the holy city and historic Jerusalem are moral, chronological, and spatial. Old Jerusalem is implicitly seen as destroyed for its disobedience and its failure to see in Jesus God's agent for renewal of his people. The coming down of the new Jerusalem will take place in God's time and will be the sphere of life for the new obedient community that saw in Jesus the Lamb of God. There is no hint in Revelation of a philosophical or ontological distinction between a temporal copy and an eternal model of *polis* along Platonic lines, such as I traced above in chapter 1 in the Wisdom of Solomon. In Revelation, reality is seen as moving within the temporal sphere, with the accomplishment of God's purpose for his people and for the creation soon to be disclosed from its heavenly place of origin.

The Eternal City: The Letter to the Hebrews

The imagery of the city of God is central for the Letter to the Hebrews.[30] Jesus is the agent of God through whom the new city is being prepared and who has already taken his place of honor in that city. The city is a symbol of the new community at two levels: there are mutual responsibilities for God's people as they prepare for "the city," and there is confidence in the future fulfillment of God's purpose for his people, which will take place in that city.

Polis *in the Greek Tradition*

Homer uses *polis* to refer not only to the acropolis[31] and to the city and its surrounding region,[32] but also to the whole community or body of citizens.[33] For Aristotle, *polis* is the entire state or community.[34] From classical times into the Hellenistic period, the kindred term *politeia* means the conditions and rights of citizenship, the constitution of a state, or more broadly, the government.[35] *Politeuma* is used for the body of citizens,[36] and in the Greek papyri and inscriptions from the Hellenistic era, it connotes the corporate body, or the association as a whole. Analogously, *politeuo* means "to be a citizen," and in the passive voice, "to be governed."

This is not merely abstract terminology, however; rather, there is a model of social and moral unity that is aspired to as the goal for the true *polis*. This was dramatically expressed around 100 C.E. by Plutarch in his essay *Of the Fortune or Virtue of Alexander the Great*.[37] After depicting Alexander as a philosopher in action who introduced "the barbarians" to Greek language and literature and to humane customs in place of such savage practices as eating the corpses of departed relatives, he describes how this philosopher king changed "the wild and brutish customs of many various nations," reducing them to order and government (1.4–5). Following the principles laid down by Zeno, the aim was to have all humanity live under common law, as fellow citizens, conforming to one manner of living "like a flock feeding together with equal right in one common pasture." For Zeno, this was a fanciful dream, but Alexander worked to bring into reality this image of a commonwealth. He believed himself to have been "sent from Heaven as the common moderator and arbiter of all nations . . . to bring all nations, near and far, under the same dominion" (1.8), to "subdue all the kingdoms of earth under one form of government and to make one nation of all humanity." In this way, one law would preside over the whole world, and one form of justice would illumine the world under a universal government, thereby "establishing peace, concord, and mutual community among all humanity" (1.8–9). In another treatise, *Of Common Conceptions, against the Stoics*, Plutarch describes the whole world as "a city" (409). Both the basic aspiration for the perfect "city" and the philosophical terminology by which its coming is described in the Letter to the Hebrews are powerfully influenced by Hellenistic philosophy, in both the later Platonic and Stoic traditions.

An essential factor that contributed to the early Christian appropriation and adaptation of this view of the *polis* was the intellectual tradition of Judaism most fully documented in the writings of Philo of Alexandria. As Goodenough noted, biblical stories are allegorically interpreted to demonstrate the truths of Hellenistic philosophy.[38] Thus, the six cities of refuge in Israel are the symbols of six emanations from ultimate Being (*to on*), beyond which humans may rise into the very presence of God.[39] Similarly, the cherubim represent the "highest and chief Powers: Goodness and Sovereignty." Between the two is the Logos, the fiery sword that is the symbol of reason. Through these powers, and ultimately through the Logos, one can ascend to God.[40] In his treatise *On Creation*, Philo pictures Adam as cre-

Where God Dwells among His People

ated in the image of the Logos, which is the essence of beauty (139). The descendants of Adam have degenerated, but he was not only "the original forefather [*archegetes*] of the race," but also the "unique citizen of the world [*cosmopolites*]." The world was "his city [*polis*] and dwelling place [*oikos*]." Philo assumed that there were "citizens" (*politas*) of this "city" (*polis*) and "polity" (*politeia*) before humans were created, and adding that "they might justly be termed people of the great city [*metapolitai*]" since they were enrolled "in the greatest and most perfect commonwealth" (*politeumati*).⁴¹ Although the details of this cosmic construction of human origins differ from those of the Letter to the Hebrews, the mode of contrast between the temporal and the eternal is remarkably similar, as I shall note.

For Jews, the central feature of the earthly holy city was, of course, the Temple (or earlier, the tent of meeting). According to Philo, God provided these earthly sanctuaries for humans, who are as yet unworthy of coming into the presence of ultimate Being. The rules given through Moses serve to "teach in advance one who would worship God that even though he may be incapable of making himself worthy of the Creator of the cosmos, he yet ought to try unceasingly to be worthy of the cosmos. As he participates in the imitation, he ought directly to become one who bears in mind the original pattern, so that he is in a sense transformed from being a human into the nature of the cosmos, and becomes . . . himself a little cosmos."⁴² The high priest must approach the divine nature to "be a creature bordering upon both natures [human and divine] so that, though human, he might appease [*hilaskontai*] God through some mediator [*dia mesou tinas*], and that God may have some agent of service [*hypodiakanos*] to use in abundantly extending his gracious acts [*charitas*] to humans."⁴³ Philo does not demean in any way the cultus carried out in the Temple in Jerusalem, but its eternal, transcendent meaning is what makes this earthly shrine and worship important.

The New Synthesis: The Eternal City and Jesus the High Priest

In the sophisticated opening lines of Hebrews (1:1–4) and throughout much of the document, the author uses terminology borrowed from the Jewish wisdom tradition and from Hellenistic philosophy to describe the mediatorial role of Jesus in the accomplishment of God's purpose in the creation and in the formation of his new covenant people. As "son," he stands in unique relationship with God. As "heir," he is to assume control of the universe. And he is the one through whom the "ages" of world history were framed. The wisdom imagery is paralleled in Greek philosophy as well as in Hellenistic Jewish writings. To speak of Jesus as reflection or image of the divine glory (*apaugasma*) recalls Wisd. of Sol. 7:25–26, where personified wisdom is described as "the breath of the power of God, a pure emanation of the glory of the Almighty . . . a reflection [*apaugasma*] of eternal light, a spotless mirror of the working of God, and an image [*eikon*] of his goodness." The "stamp" or "impression" of the nature of God carries similar connotations in Philo, *On the Virtues* (52), where Moses has received the "stamp" of the divine upon his nature.

In addition to displaying to humanity the nature and purpose of God, Jesus' central role for the author of Hebrews is sacerdotal, in that the climax of his work was to accomplish purification of sins. Having fulfilled this priestly function, he is now seated "at the right hand of the majesty on high" (1:3), where his eternal status is that of God's "son," superior to all the angels (1:5–14), and where he is addressed as "God" and rules forever in righteousness. It is significant that this description builds on concepts articulated in the Song of Moses and psalms linked with David—both of which concern renewal of the covenant between God and his people.[44] The priestly and royal roles are interwoven here.

The intermediary function of Jesus as priest is detailed in Hebrews, beginning with Heb. 2:3–8. The author stresses the full identification of Jesus with humanity, as well as his acceptance of his own death providing the fitting sacrifice for human sin. "A little [brachu] lower than the angels" (Ps. 8:5) is interpreted chronologically rather than ontologically, so that Jesus' position below that of the angels is only temporary. Because of his acceptance of suffering and death, he has already been "crowned with glory and honor." His suffering in behalf of God's people revealed him as the originator (archegos[45]) or archetype through whom the members of the community of the covenant gain their identity, which the author describes in phrases drawn from the Psalms and the Prophets.[46] He partook of human nature so that through his suffering and death he might effect "expiation" (hilaskesthai) for the "sins of the people" (2:14–17). The ability of Jesus as priest to identify with the redeemed people is elaborated in Heb. 4:15, where it is asserted that "he was in every respect tempted as we are, yet without sin."

In Heb. 3:1–6, the image linked with Jesus' role as "high priest" shifts to include a description of God's "house"—a term that could refer directly to the community or metaphorically to the sanctuary as the place where God dwells. But the import is the same in either case: the "house" is where God dwells among his people, and it has been built by God's "son." This message transcends the earthly sphere, and the hearers are invited to become participants in a "heavenly call" (3:1). This is not a summons to leave the earthly sphere immediately, but to relocate one's values and hopes to the heavenly (epouranios[47]) realm, where the priestly role and accomplishments of Jesus have already laid the basis for the ultimate achievement of God's redemptive purpose for his people and for the creation. An analogous kind of calling (klesis) is found in Stoic philosophers of the early second century in connection with the summons to share in the divine.[48]

In Hebrews 5–10, there are alternations between details of the priestly role of Jesus and ethical appeals to the members of the community he has founded. In contrast to the traditional priest of Israel, whose temporal and moral limitations enabled him to identify with the people as a whole and required him to offer sacrifices for dealing with his own sins as well as with theirs, Jesus as priest was without sin (4:15) but he experienced temptations, suffering, and death, and thereby learned obedience (4:14–5:4). Although he refused to "exalt himself" in this priestly role, God has designated him as "son" and "high priest forever" in the tradition of Melchizedek (Ps. 110:4). What Jesus provides, therefore, is not a representative divine residence in an earthly sanctuary, such as the tent or the Temple of Israel, but access to the very presence of God (4:19–20). This contrast of sanctuaries is developed along ontological grounds, setting forth the distinction between the temporal and historical limitations of the sanctuary of Israel and the eternal heavenly sanctuary into which Jesus has already entered (7:1–28).

A parallel distinction is made between the hereditary Aaronic priesthood in Israel and Jesus as high priest (7:1–14). The former is based on legal regulations and "bodily descent"—requirements that would have excluded Jesus from the role. The priesthood of Jesus is grounded in an eternal principle, thereby guaranteeing a "better covenant" (7:15–22). The author invokes the Platonic contrast between the temporal (kath'emera) and the external (ephapax), as it is evident in the succession and multiplicity of occupants of the priestly role in the history of Israel and the unique, paradigmatic, and unrepeated self-offering of Christ (7:23–29). Hence he is described as a high priest who is "holy, blameless, unstained, distinct from sinners, exalted above the heavens." The culmination of his eternal priesthood was his offering up of himself, whom God appointed as "a son made perfect forever." The earthly priests serve a "copy and shadow of the heavenly sanctuary," since those who built the original "tent" were told to copy the "pattern" (tupon), or ideal model in the Platonic tradition. Accordingly, the "divine service" (leitourgeia) Jesus accomplishes is far superior—not merely in degree but even in eternal essence— to that of historic Israel (8:1–7). This is what Jeremiah's prediction about covenant renewal was pointing to (8:7–12; Jer. 31:31–34). After detailing the liturgical practice prescribed for the tent/temple in the Mosaic code, which are temporary pending the final divine disclosure, the author pictures Christ as having provided access to "the greater and more perfect tent," which is not subject to human construction or to the limits of the created order. In this eternal sanctuary, he offered his own blood, thereby achieving an "eternal redemption" (9:6–12).

The contrast between temporal and eternal redemption is repeated in similar form in Heb. 9:11–10:22. Jesus entered the more perfect sanctuary, taking his own blood, and thereby mediated the new covenant. The old rites purified the earthly copies; Jesus' sacrifice purifies the eternal models. The old rites are constantly repeated; Jesus' offering of himself is "once for all." The old code is now obsolete; the new covenant provides access to the presence of God through the "flesh" of the human Jesus, which here represents the essential barrier that differentiates the creatures from their creator (10:20).

The effects of this cleansing sacrifice are not merely ritual, however. The human conscience is renewed, with the result that those who rely on this divine remedy are able to avoid sin (10:26–31) and are called to live by faith (10:32–39). Those who refused to seek relationship with God through the old covenant were punished, but a worse punishment awaits those who "spurn the Son of God, profane the blood of the covenant, and outrage the Spirit of grace" (10:29). Those who place their trust in this divinely provided mode of reconciliation and persist in this way of life will "receive what has been promised" (10:32–39). They must endure the present trials and difficulties in confidence that what God has promised through Jesus, "the coming one" (Isa. 26:20), will take place.

Faith, therefore, has two dimensions for the author of Hebrews. It is a mode of reliance on the unseen realm of eternal, archetypal reality, in contrast to the ephemeral, changing, human sphere, in which only shadowy copies of the real are evident; and it is a confidence that in the future these eternal realities will be the sphere of life of God's people in his presence. In short, faith is both ontological (drawing on Platonic tradition) and eschatological (building on Jewish prophetic and apocalyptic traditions). Those who lived in accord with the divine promise of a reality yet unseen are the heroes and heroines of faith, sketched in Heb. 11:4–38. They acknowledged the incompleteness of what they received from God, but looked forward to fulfillment of the divine promise in the "heavenly country"—the realm of the eternal (11:16). The faithful experienced all manner of disappointment, oppression, conflict, and even martyrdom, but they looked beyond this world to the better realm of divine perfection (11:39–40). Employing the image that I have proposed is constitutive for this letter, the writer declares the essence of Abraham's faith to be that "he looked forward to the city which has foundations, whose builder and maker is God" (11:10).

The climax of the disciplinary injunctions with which the letter concludes (12:1–13:19) comes in Heb. 12:22–24: "You have come to Mt. Zion and to the city of the living God, the heavenly Jerusalem, and to the innumerable angels in festal gathering, and to the assembly [ekklesia] of the first-born who are enrolled in heaven, and to a judge who is God of all, and to Jesus, the mediator of the new covenant, and to the sprinkled blood that speaks more graciously than the blood of Abel." The agent of fulfillment of God's purpose for his people and for the creation is Jesus, whose obedient life, suffering, and death constitute the archetypal sacrifice by which God's people are brought into right relationship with their creator. The image of consummation of that redemptive plan is not of isolated or separate individuals being admitted to the elect, but of a renewed and transformed people, depicted through the use of models drawn from the political and ritual usages of Jews and Gentiles in the Greco-Roman period. Also from this cultural resource are drawn the epistemological and rational assumptions as to what the enduring reality will be for this people: not historical, temporal, or recurrent traditional features, but the archetypal and eternal. The goal of existence for this community is not preservation of the historic heritage, but transport from the earthly to the heavenly sphere of ultimate reality. Yet that exchange of context for human life is seen as lying, not in a realm accessible through timeless mystical ascent and escape from the dimensions of temporality and struggle, but in the future for the persistent, perceptive faithful community. The letter ends, therefore, with concrete, pragmatic advice about how matters are to be handled within the community by leaders and followers during the period of indefinite extent when the community must live under the present circumstances of conflict and limitation.

The death and resurrection of Jesus, through "the blood of the eternal covenant," have guaranteed not only the future transformation of "the sheep," but also the effective power at work among them to make their lives "pleasing in [God's] sight" (13:20). Sufficient for the renewal of the life of this community are the archetypal sacrifice of Christ, the high priest, and the members' present access by faith to the heavenly "city of the living God" (12:22).

The Subsequent Impact of the City Model

In chapter 7, I trace some of the variety of ways in which the models of community developed in the second century toward institutional forms and authoritarian leadership. With regard to the city, the development of structure is evident as early as the writings of the Apostolic Fathers, where the authority of the bishops is a significant factor. For example, in 1 Clement 40:1–44:6, the divine origin of order within the church is traced, including both the priestly and the monarchic roles of the bishops based on the authoritative roles of priests. Levites, and tribal chiefs in the days of ancient Israel. So effective was this authoritarian system in the second and third centuries that, following the fierce competitive struggle for the office of emperor, Constantine turned to Christianity as offering the best option for stability and unity in the empire. As W. H. C. Frend has observed, there was no political structure in the ancient world to match "the vast ramification of Christian organization extending from Armenia to York. . . . Its adherents were drawn from town and countryside alike. . . . In its highest ethical appeal, its banishment of the blood and sacrifice from worship, and adherence to a God at once transcendent and active in the universe, Christianity presented in a coherent form ideas to which the pagan world was groping."[49] The dramatic triumph of this model occurred in the building of Constantinople as the combined center of monarchy and sanctuary.

The subsequent social, administrative, military, and moral decline of the empire, culminating in the capture of Rome by Alaric in 410, led Augustine of Hippo to write *The City of God*. Following the lead of Tyconius, a North African theologian who interpreted the biblical cities of Jerusalem and Babylon allegorically as symbols respectively of divine and human rule, Augustine wrote this monumental work contrasting the earthly city of human endeavor and the ultimate city of God. The purpose of God for the creation, hinted at in events of human history, had been cryptically and partially revealed since the days of Cain and Abel (who symbolize respectively self-seeking and obedient humans) but had been fully disclosed in the coming of Christ. While affirming the essential goodness of the creation and admiring the efforts of humans to accomplish good in this life, Augustine saw human envy and self-seeking as the fatal blight on the earthly city, of which Rome was the prime instance, since it accomplished its goals through conflict and human destruction. Nor was the church as human institution free of this fatal blight, since in it lived both saints and sinners. At their best, these earthly cities are partial indicators of the city of God that is beyond history, in which alone peace and justice will prevail.[50]

The Community of Mystical Participation   **5**

In the classical philosophical system formulated by Plato, two major concerns were how to understand and perceive the gods and the realm of the eternal, and how individual souls might move beyond the transitory sphere of human existence into that eternal realm. This analysis of the human situation in relation to the divine had a powerful and enduring impact on subsequent philosophical and religious thought in the wider Greco-Roman culture, including Jewish intellectuals in the second and first centuries B.C.E. and in the subsequent centuries into the Byzantine period. My investigation will require that I analyze the ways these concepts influenced the New Testament writers as well, especially their impact on the Gospel of John.

Historical inquiry in this field was long dominated by learned but simplistic assumptions that developed in the nineteenth-century history-of-religions scholarly tradition, of which Richard Reitzenstein's book *Hellenistic Mystery-Religions* is a prime example.[1] After surveying a wide range of materials from Greek, Roman, Iranian, and Egyptian sources over several centuries presenting evidence of mystical and other modes of religious speculation, Reitzenstein depicted mysticism as a unified phenomenon that culminated in Gnosticism in the second and subsequent centuries C.E. A similar early-twentieth-century mix of learned analysis of ancient sources and unwarranted generalizations about the shared features of the Greco-Roman mystery cults and early Christianity can be found in Alfred Loisy's book *Les mystères païens et le mystère chrétien*.[2]

These authors, and generations of scholars who accepted their hypotheses, ignored social and cultural developments in the Greco-Roman world during the period surveyed, including the important basic changes in Judaism that came with the rise and failure of the nationalistic revolts from the time of the Maccabees

(165–63 B.C.E.) to Bar Kochba in 132–135 C.E. They also ignored the mystical features of Judaism in the late prophetic and apocalyptic traditions, as well as the central theme in Greek and Roman philosophy of the ascent of the soul into the realm of the divine and of human accountability before the gods in a future day of judgment. Reitzenstein extrapolated backward from the Gnostic developments of the second century C.E. and following, thereby fashioning conceptual and cultural communities to the neglect of important differences between Gnosticism and the antecedent forms of mysticism.[3] To examine the New Testament evidence against this artificial and anachronistic construction would be insensitive and misleading. Careful attention to the range of evidence enables one to perceive the continuities as well as the important differences among the various mystical quests of Greco-Roman culture, postexilic Judaism, and nascent Christianity.

Intercourse with the Divine

Plato

For Plato in the *Symposium*, the ground and significance of knowledge of the divine is conveyed symbolically by the very name of the one whose discourse on the subject this philosopher reports: Diotima Mantinikes. Four Greek roots lie behind the name: honoring (*tima*) the gods (*dio*), divinely granted insight into the ultimate, triumphant truth (*manti, nikes*). The central agent is Love (*Eros*), who is a great *daemon*, midway between the divine (*theou*) and the mortal (*thnetou*). *Eros* interprets and conveys things divine to humans and things human to the divine (202–203): petitions and sacrifices from below, and instructions (*epitaxis*) and requitals (*amoibai*) from above. Through *Eros* are transmitted all divination (*mantike*) and the techniques of the priests for sacrifice, ritual, and incantations, as well as all soothsaying and sorcery (*goeteian*) and all intercourse between gods and humans, awake or asleep. Whoever is wise concerning these matters is a demonic man (*daimonios aner*). An an intermediary, Love is a friend of wisdom (*philosophos*, 204).

Human sexual relationship is a symbol of begetting on a beautiful thing by means of both body and soul, an ever-existent and immortal factor in human life (205C, 206E). The wise seek union with the beautiful, just as Solon begat laws (209E). No matter how beautiful the body of one's lover may be, one must move beyond the single example to the universal principle that it exemplifies (210). Beauty of soul is to be admired more than beauty in laws and observances, but seeing beauty in the abstract, ideal mode (akin to what might be called today the whole social-scientific realm of beauty) enables one to escape from slavery to a single example, "turning rather to the great ocean of the beautiful." This "wondrous vision" is gained when one moves beyond the particulars to the highest beauty, ascending the rungs of the ladder "from personal beauty to beautiful observances, from observances to beautiful learning [*kala mathemata*] and from learning to the study of the beautiful itself, so that in the end one comes to know the very essence of beauty" (210E–212A).

In the *Phaedrus*, Plato describes the realm of ultimate being, which is the region above the heavens (247). The twelve great gods ascend to heaven for a banquet with Zeus. That region is controlled by the colorless, formless, intangible being (*ousia*) with which all true knowledge is concerned, which is visible only to the mind (*nous*), the pilot (*kybernetes*) of the soul. The perception (*dianoia*) of the divine is nurtured on pure knowledge (*episteme*), and every soul that is capable of receiving such perception rejoices in seeing reality for a space of time. By gazing upon the truth, the soul is nourished and made happy until the cyclical revolution of the cosmos brings it back to the same place. In the course of this revolution, the soul beholds absolute justice, temperance, and knowledge, not such phenomena as have a beginning or are subject to change, and it feeds on eternal beings, after which it passes again into the heavens, awaiting the next revolution. If it becomes forgetful or distracted, the soul falls again to earth and takes on one of several roles: king, politician, gymnast, prophet or mystic, craftsman or farmer, sophist, demagogue or tyrant. Only the soul that has fullest perception of truth will enter the body of a philosopher. Souls return after a ten-thousand-year cycle to the original type of body in which they dwelt, except for honest philosophers and pederasts, who are spared the relentless cyclical pattern of existence. The rest are judged at the end of their lives, pay the penalty for their misdeeds, and then return to some human or animal body (249). Humans must understand a general concept that is formed by collecting into a unity by means of reason (*logismos*) the many perceptions of the senses. This unity is a recollection of those eternal realities the soul once beheld when it rose up to the realm of true being (*to on ontos*). It is the goal of the enlightened mind (*dianoia*) to take this flight, to perceive the perfect realities, to be initiated into the perfect mysteries, and to be truly perfect. All humans behold the realities (*to onta*), but only the few who can recognize them behind the imperfect earthly copies are able to soar to the state of perfection in which they achieve the highest vision of absolute beauty.

In the *Phaedo* (112–114), Plato depicts in detail the underworld and the fate of the dead. All souls are judged according to how they lived: the morally neutral go to the lake of Acheron, where they pay penalties for misdeeds; the hopelessly wicked are consigned to the pit of Tartarus forever; and the seriously wicked are thrown into Tartarus until they have been purified and then are transferred to the Acherusian lake, where they have an opportunity to make amends for wrongs done to others. Those who have rejected the pleasures and ornaments of the body and have instead sought learning and the adornment of the soul with the proper virtues—sobriety, justice, humanity, freedom, and truth—await a journey to the blessed realm of the pure (*eis aidou poreian*).

The mysticism in Plato's dialogues involves the diligence and the destiny of the individual. Those who responsibly avail themselves of the insights provided for all humans to behold ultimate reality, and whose perspectives on life and values are determined by these insights, are the ones who enjoy the renewal of happy existence, and possibly elevation to a place among the lesser gods. The decisive factors are the ability to fix attention on the eternal models and to conform one's life to these norms of justice and beauty.

Greco-Roman Mystery Cults

The yearning for the direct experience of God in personal rather than intellectual terms flourished during the Hellenistic and early Roman periods. This factor is evident in the popularity of the mystery cults, especially those linked with Demeter at Eleusis, Dionysus, Asklepios, and Isis. These cults were conveniently and appropriately classified by Lewis R. Farnell in his Gifford Lectures of 1920: heroes and heroines of divine or daimonic origin, sacral heroes and heroines, functional heroes and special gods (*Sondergötter*), the cult of Herakles, the Dioskuroi, Asklepios, epic heroes, ancestors, cults of historic persons, and individual belief in immortality.[4] Under the last category, Farnell discussed the mystical aspects of Plato's thought that I have just sketched.

Surprisingly little attention was paid by Farnell, however, to the cult of Demeter, which was centered at the great shrine in Eleusis, a short distance west of Athens, and was a magnet that attracted the famous and throngs of the anonymous from the mid-eighth century B.C.E. into the Roman period. Founded in response to a famine that struck Greece about 760, the observances in honor of Demeter, the goddess of fertility, were believed not only to assure the annual cycle of crop productivity but also to provide individuals access to some form of divine life. The legend on which the cult was founded, the various shapes that it took in process of development, and both the literary and archaeological remains of the cult and its famous site have been analyzed by George Mylonas.[5] The myth on which the cult was based told how Pluto had taken Persephone, daughter of Demeter, away to the underworld. The preoccupation of the fertility goddess with the search for her lost daughter resulted in the cessation of fertility of soil and crops. Finally Zeus ordered Pluto to return Persephone to her mother. Before taking her back, Pluto gave her some pomegranate seeds to eat, which assured that she would have to return to his realm for sustenance, remaining there for a third of each year. When she was with her mother, they dwelt among the gods on Mount Olympus, and the crops flourished; when she was gone, all fertility of the land ceased.

The mystery cult that developed on the basis of this myth has left behind no detailed literary evidence, but it seems to have given assurance to its initiates of a life beyond death in a realm of bliss and blessedness like the Elysian Fields of Homer. Further, it provided hope of present participation in the life of the deities through some kind of continuing mystical experience that was inaugurated when ritual initiation took place at Eleusis. The mystery attracted men and women, slaves and free, the humble and the powerful, and continued to do so until the cultural conquest of the Mediterranean world by Christianity in the fourth and subsequent centuries C.E. The emperors Hadrian and Marcus Aurelius added to the impressive structures that surrounded the shrine of Demeter. Cicero stated in his *De legibus* (2.14.36) that there was nothing in this world more excellent or divine than the Eleusinian mysteries.

The role of Asklepios developed along similar lines. Originally the agent who cured physical ailments and alleviated human suffering, this deity came to be regarded as the embodiment of wisdom (including knowledge of healing) and philanthropy in the root sense: love of humanity.[6] The response of his devotees is well epitomized in an inscription from the second century C.E.: "O Asklepios. . . . How shall I come into your golden house, O blessed one, O god of my longing, unless your heart is favorable to me and you are willing to heal me and establish me again in your shrine, so that I may behold my god who is brighter than the earth in springtime. You alone, O divine and blessed one, are mighty; you, who love compassion, the supreme gods have granted as a boon to mortals, as a refuge from their sorrows."[7] Asklepios is not ranked among "the supreme gods," but he is the one who supports and relieves those who are suffering. The relationship with the deity, though probably initiated through a priest or functionary at an Asklepion (a shrine dedicated to this god, where he was believed to be active in healing), seems to have been primarily individual, although one can sense from the writings of Aelius Aristides in the second century C.E. that devotees of Asklepios may have gathered informally around the shrines that honored him.

The cults of the heroes were often local and popular, showing neither systematic conceptual or institutional organization. Some were linked with shrines of deities, as Theseus was associated with Poseidon at Athens,[8] but there was no attempt to include the honored heroes among the gods. The heroes were immortal, but not divine. Their chief value seems to have been as the embodiment of ethical ideals or as models of human service. Their essential humanity was the ground of their appeal to successive generations.

The majority of people, who could not aspire to posthumous veneration as heroes, turned instead to the hope of individual immortality, to be gained and maintained through personal relationship with a deity. Among other major Greco-Roman options for such personal association with divinity were the cults of Dionysos and Isis.

In literature attributed to Orpheus but of unknown origin and indeterminate date, there is a myth that Zeus intended Zagreus, his son by his daughter Persephone, to become ruler of the universe. The Titans murdered and ate the child, but when they were killed by Zeus, their surviving offspring possessed something of the divine nature of Zagreus. After swallowing Zagreus's heart, Zeus begot Dionysos, who now displayed divine features. H. J. Rose has effectively summarized the cult that built on this myth. The chief end of humans is to be rid of the Titanic dimension of life and to preserve the divine element. Before each individual is a long series of lives, in this age and the next, during each of which one may be rewarded or punished for good and evil deeds in one's preceding existence. In the end, those who persevere may attain something like divinity and eternal happiness. The method to be used is the Orphic lifestyle, which is a mixture of ritual and abstinence, with some attention to ethical behavior.[9]

The dramatist Euripides (fifth century B.C.E.) describes in his *Bacchae* a group of women devoted to Dionysos (known in Roman culture as Bacchus) who, in an ecstatic frenzy induced by wine, seized, dismembered, and ate an animal they believed was attacking them, only to discover when they regained their normal condition that the victim was the son of their leader. Although Euripides has overdrawn the situation, eating raw meat was a way of sharing in the life of the god. So popular was the cult in Rome in the first century B.C.E. that the senate adopted a policy prohibiting the Bacchic worship and requiring families of the women devotees to punish them appropriately.[10] The appeal of ritual cults was the promise of direct access by seeking individuals into the ways and even the life of the gods. Their quest was fostered and confirmed by others who shared in this longing for participation in a life beyond present human limitations. The worship of Egyptian goddess Isis succeeded in combining these personal aspirations with a more reflective rationale for entering a sphere of life beyond common human limitations and frustrations. I shall examine below the well-documented development of the cult of Isis in the second century C.E., as attested in the writings of Plutarch. But first it is essential to consider how a human inhabitant of Egypt at the turn of the eras—Philo of Alexandria—synthesized the mystical dimensions of the Platonic tradition with his Jewish biblical heritage.

Philo's Mystical Journey

In his treatise *On the Cherubim*, Philo declares explicitly that disciplined study in the traditions of Greco-Roman learning is essential for the development of skills in insight, knowledge, and communication (98–107). The only fit earthly dwelling place for God is the human soul that is prepared to receive him; there alone God dwells invisibly. Preparation for his coming demands not only virtues (*aretai*) and noble actions (*kalon praxeon*) but disciplined mastery of intellectual methods and information: the *engkuklia*, basic scholastic learning. This learning, which will "adorn the whole house of the soul," includes grammar and literature, geometry, music, and rhetoric. Once the house of the soul is thus prepared, "the laws and ordinances from heaven will descend, to sanctify and consecrate" the mind and daily life of "the virtue-loving soul." The highest attainment for humans is not freedom, but to become "the slave of God," confessing that one has "the Lord of all for one's master."

By this means, the soul can be prepared to "depart from the father's house," which means to rise above a mode of life that is controlled by one's bodily urges and by the structures of one's secular social context (*On the Migration of Abraham* 9–11). Once one comes to know oneself and to be freed from dominance by society and myopic, selfish values, one is ready to heed the call: "Depart, therefore, out of the earthly matter that encompasses thee: escape, O human, from the foul prison-house, thy body, with all thy might and main, and from the pleasures and lusts that act as its jailers; every terror that can vex and hurt them, leave none of them unused. . . . Depart also out of thy kin, sense-perception. . . . But if thou desire to recover the self that thou hast lent [i.e., to inappropriate and unworthy controlling factors] and to have thine own possessions about thee, letting no portion of them be alienated and fall into other hands, thou shalt claim instead a happy [*eudaimonos*] life, enjoyed forever."

In the intellectual realm, Philo contrasts his frustration when trying to pursue certain philosophical themes with the sudden showering down on him of ideas: "Under the influence of divine possession I have been filled with corybantic frenzy and been unconscious of anything—place, persons present, myself, words spoken, lines written. For I obtained interpretative insight, ideas, an enjoyment of light, keenest vision, pellucid distinctness of objects, such as might be received through the eyes by most lucid showing." It is through this method that there "comes to pass seeing of the divine Light, identical with knowledge [*episteme*], which opens the eye of the soul and leads it to apprehensions distinct and brilliant beyond those gained by the ears." That is, the divinely granted insights utterly transcend the best that can be communicated through human teaching. The privilege of seeing what God has destined for his people is reserved "exclusively for the purest and most keen-eyed" (*On the Migration of Abraham* 46). For them, God holds out not only a life of contemplation and progress toward enjoyment of the "fair and beautiful," but also the gift of the *logos*, in two senses: excellence of reason for perceiving the noblest concepts and the ability to express them in clear and masterly fashion (72–73).

The benefits from this access to divine understanding are not limited to those who participate directly in it. Philo notes the occurrence in human history of "instances of a household or a city or a country or nations enjoying great prosperity through a single individual who has given the mind to nobility of character. Most of all has this been so in the case of one on whom God has bestowed, together with a good purpose, irresistible power. . . . For in truth the righteous individual is the foundation on which humanity rests" (*On the Migration of Abraham* 120–121).

Nevertheless, the highest good for the people of faith and wisdom is vision (*opsin*)—not that of the senses but that of the soul (*On the Contemplative Life* 10–13). Philo sets forth as a model of commitment to divinely given wisdom the Therapeutae, whom he characterizes as being "always taught from the first to use their sight" so as to behold "the vision of Being [*tou ontos*] and to soar above the sun of our [physical] senses and never leave their place in this company which carries them to perfect happiness [*teleian eudaimonian*]." They do not merely follow the counsel of others, but are "carried away by a heaven-sent passion of love [*erotos*], remaining rapt and possessed [*enthousiadzousi*] like bacchantes or corybants [*bakcheuomenoi kai korubantiontes*] until they see what it is for which they are longing [*to potheumenon*]."

The mystical experience itself is described in allegorical interpretations of the law of Moses in two other treatises of Philo, *On Flight and Finding* and *On Dreams*. In the first of these treatises, Philo interprets the six cities of refuge mentioned in Num. 35:12 as a metaphor for the threefold nature of the divine and the three central agencies of human existence (103–104). The former triad consists of the Logos of the Ruler and his creative and royal powers. He notes that both heaven and the entire cosmos are in consonance with these powers. The three central agencies of human existence, which is perishable and marred by sin, are divine mercy, enjoinment as to what humans should do, and prohibition of what is not to be done. The rule that one who has fled to a city of refuge can return to his native place only when the high priest dies (Num. 35:32) is interpreted figuratively rather than by the difficult literal meaning (*dysapologeton*): the high priest is perceived not as a human officer but as the "divine Logos" (108–115). He is free of all unrighteousness, "intentional or unintentional." The injunction to the high priest against defiling himself by contact with those outside his own family (Lev. 21:2) Philo understands to mean that the Logos is free of defilement because his father is God and his mother is Wisdom, "through whom the universe came into existence." The anointing of his head with oil means that "his ruling faculty is illumined with a brilliant light." The garments that the Logos puts on are the four elements (earth, air, fire, and water). The body is a member of the soul, and the mind of the wise one discerns virtues. The high priest's refusal to set aside his miter shows that the Logos never abdicates his viceregal reponsibilities for guiding the universe, just as his refusal to rend his clothes symbolizes his constant maintenance of the harmony of the universe. The high priest's abstinence from marriage to widows or harlots indicates his own unwavering devotion to God the Father.

Another image for the Logos in the treatise *On Flight and Finding* is manna.[11] Although initially it was not recognized for what it was (Exod. 16:15), it came to be seen as "the Divine Word from which all kinds of instruction and wisdom flow in perpetual stream" and as "heavenly nourishment." Mystical participation in this divinely provided resource is described as follows: "This divine ordinance [*syntaxis*] fills the soul that has vision alike with light and sweetness, flashing forth the radiancy of truth, and with the honied grace of persuasion imparting sweetness to those who hunger and thirst after nobility of character." Analogously, the fertile fields and cities described to Israel as Moses prepares the people to enter the promised land (Deut. 6:10–11) are images for virtues, generic ("cities") and special ("houses"): cisterns represent wisdom, vineyards and olive groves symbolize progress and growth, and "the fruit of knowledge is the life of contemplation [*bios theoretikos*]." The result will be "unmixed gladness as from wine, and intellectual light as from a flame which oil feeds" (176).

It is in *On Dreams* that Philo gives some of the most vivid details of the mystical experience itself, culminating in the vision of God. Building on the vivid account of Jacob's dream (Gen. 28), he describes the air itself as the stairway to heaven, since it is the abode of incorporeal souls (133–149). Because the souls are invisible, some consider the air to be untenanted, but it has a population like that of a city, the inhabitants of which are imperishable souls equal in number to the stars. Some that are materially inclined descend to the earthly region, while others ascend. The latter, regarding the body as a prison or a tomb, seek escape as from a dungeon and sail to the upper air, where they "range the heights forever." Beings that "are of perfect purity and excellence, gifted with a higher and diviner temper, have never felt any craving after the things of the earth, but are viceroys of the Ruler of the Universe, ears and eyes, so to speak, of the great king, beholding and hearing all things." Philo notes that some philosophers call such beings "daemons," but he prefers to designate them as "angels or messengers," since they do God's bidding and report the children's needs to the Father. Both God's "chastisements" and his "benefits" must be conveyed to us through his designated aides (*hyperetais*). These divine agents—"words of God" (*hoi logoi tou theou*)—move up and down through the universe, disclosing what is immortal to mortals and "condescending out of love for humanity and compassion for our race," among whom they are "helpers and comrades, that with the healing of their breath they may quicken the soul into new life." Philo appeals to the human soul to purge itself of all that is unworthy and prepare for the indwelling of the divine: "Be zealous, therefore, O soul, to become a house of God, a holy temple, a most beauteous abiding place. . . . Perhaps the Master of the whole world's household shall be yours, and will keep you under his care, to preserve you forever."

The mystical goal for Philo is to become indwelt by God, who will transform and purify one's life. Aiding in his spiritual quest are the beneficial activities of the souls of the faithful departed, who serve as God's agents of renewal and enable the pious seeker to perceive and comprehend the encompassing, universal purpose of God. The individual searching for God's truth is able to escape from the impurity of this world and from inner evil impulses, and to live obedient and radiant in the light of the direct knowledge of God.

Plutarch and the Role of Isis

In his excellent survey of the Middle Platonists, John Dillon shows how Plutarch combines with his basic Platonic orientation features from both Stoic and Pythagorean philosophy.[12] Plutarch describes the coordination (*synentasis*) of psychic and bodily actions, comparing the human soul to a string instrument, whose performing quality depends on how carefully it has been tuned. All souls incarcerated in human bodies have the potential for becoming daemons, disembodied souls of the dead that are forces of good or evil in the world. Good daemons play the role of assisting the minds of humans to gain liberation from the body for a time. Most minds resume the cycle of reincarnation, but a few achieve permanent status among the divinities.

Plutarch's treatise on the cult of Isis (*De Iside*) contains a rich and comprehensive exposition of the potential for liberation of the soul and attainment of divinity.[13] Plutarch asserts that behind the multiplicity of regional names of the deities there is a single set of divine beings. The depictions of them are symbolic; for example, Hermes is portrayed as a shepherd, caring for the lambs in his flock (354E–355C). Osiris is seen as a king, establishing laws and instructing humans how to raise crops and honor the gods (356B), and is linked with the constellations (359D). On learning of Osiris's death, Isis is guided to his coffin by "the divine spirit of rumor" (*pneumati daimonio phemes*, 357A). Plutarch scorns the notion that these deities are divinized humans, suggesting instead that they are deified daemons, which are more powerful than humans yet share in their struggles and experiences and range in behavior from virtue to vice (360E). Because of their virtue (*arete*), Osiris and Isis were transformed into deities (*theous*), just as were Herakles and Dionysos (361E). After noting the correspondences between mythical struggles and those evident in natural phenomena (meterological, astronomical, and seasonal changes), Plutarch suggests that conflicts in nature are manifestations of a basic polarity in the cosmos. Here he notes dualistic schemes in Persian religion, as well as in the philosophies of Heraclitus, Empedocles, the Pythagoreans, Plato, and Aristotle (363–370). Osiris is the "lord of all the best things" and therefore the image of mind and reason and of cosmic order. Typhon, his enemy and would-be destroyer, is irrational passion, subject to death and disorder (371). Osiris represents foresight, power, and procreation. It is he who guides the cycles of the stars and the seasons, who loves the good and fosters growth and truth, and who enables what is spiritually intelligible and orderly to triumph over the powers of evil, which are symbolized by his own death.

Isis's offspring by Osiris include not only Horus, but also Apollo, whose "procreation, which occurred when the gods were still in the womb of Rhea, suggests symbolically that before this world became manifest and was completed by the *logos*, matter—which by its nature was incapable of itself to do so—brought forth the first creation." Plutarch then summarizes Plato's description of the creation in the *Timaeus* (50 CD), where Plato calls "what is spiritually intelligible" (*noetou*) the form (*idean*), the pattern (*paradeigma*), and the father; on the other hand, matter (*hulen*) is designated as mother and nurse and is seen as the seat and place of creation. What is produced is called the offspring (*engonon*) and the creation (*genesin*). After outlining other myths of creation, Plutarch warns against treating them as statements of fact or as stories picturing the fertility cycles of the Nile (377B), insisting that the myths must be interpreted as symbolic vehicles giving access to truth (375D). Osiris, whose name is linked by Plutarch, with *hosios* (holy) and *hieros* (priestly), is the agent who brings to light matters pertaining to the heavens, with links to the world above as well as to the world below (375). Isis, whose name is

Mystical Participation

declared to be akin to *ousia* (being), is identified with Being, the well-ordered and the useful in the cosmos (*kekosmnemenon*, 375–377), where everything is determined by one *logos* and one providence (*pronoia*). One must avoid superstition (*deisdaimonia*) and atheism (*atheoteta*).

Philosophy provides a guide into the mysteries. Even traditional religious rites are to be viewed as responses to a useful purpose (*logos*). Indeed, there is no human quality more divine than *logos*, and no greater driving force toward true happiness (*eudaimonia*). Plutarch affirms the Pythagorean view that associates the gods with the numerical and geometric patterns evident in the world (= *kosmos*, 382A–E). He regards the robes of Isis and Osiris as symbolic of mystical access to the divine: Isis's variegated robe represents the whole range of the cosmos: light and dark, day and night, fire and water, life and death, and beginning and end. Osiris's robe, which is worn only once, symbolizes light, the origin of everything, and the primal event, and thus represents "understanding of what is spiritually intelligible, pure and holy," which, "having shown through the soul like lightning, affords only one chance to touch and behold it." Plutarch asserts that Plato and Aristotle "call this branch of philosophy that [which is] concerned with the highest mysteries, in that those who have passed beyond conjectural, confused and widely varied matters spring up by force of reason [*logos*] to that primal, simple and immaterial element; and having directly grasped the truth attached to it, they believe that they hold the ultimate end [*telos*] of philosophy in the manner of a mystical revelation."

Although Osiris reigns over the dead, he lives far removed from the earth (not under it), in a realm undefiled by any being subject to decay or death (382F–383A). Human souls freed from the body—where they had only a dim vision of the divine achieved by understanding gained through philosophy—pass over to the formless, invisible, dispassionate, and holy kingdom. God is their leader (*hegemon*) and king. They behold and insatiably desire ineffable and unutterable beauty—Isis, who fosters and fills the world with all the beautiful and good things that share in the creation. As in the thought of Philo, the mystical goal of the philosopher as understood by Plutarch is to gain understanding of the true nature of the universe and a vision of ultimate reality. Unlike the actual Isis cult described by Apuleius in his *Metamorphoses*, there is for Plutarch no role for a continuing community of devotees of the goddess or for an ongoing cultus in her honor. Instead, he pictures the mystical ascent of the individual into the presence of the supreme deity. Others are invited, even urged, but none are needed to assist the solitary seeker to achieve that goal.

Merkavah Mysticism

In his classic study of Jewish mysticism, Gershon Scholem noted the important difference between revelation conceived as taking place once for all in a historical situation (as at Sinai) and revelation that "bursts forth from the heart," illuminating other revelations not fully comprehended in the past. "The secret revelation is to [the mystic] the real and decisive one. And then the substance of the canonical texts . . . is melted down and given another form as it passes through the fiery stream of the mystical consciousness." The secret features of the mystical include "the most deeply hidden and fundamental matters of human life," accessible only "to a small elite of the chosen who impart the knowledge to their disciples."[14]

With the prevailing mood of disillusionment following the fall of the Maccabean king-priests to the Roman invaders and Rome's subsequent domination of the priesthood until the destruction of the Temple in 70 C.E., there was a surge of reflection by many Jews about intermediaries between God and the faithful remnant of his people. This led to speculation about angels and demons, building on Ezekiel's visions of the heavenly realm and on the special relationships with God enjoyed by Enoch, Moses, and Solomon.[15] Hopes of penetrating the hidden world and reaching the "ever-inaccessible divinity" inspired the writing of ecstatic hymns and the description of techniques required of those who would make the mystical journey, as well as to adaptation of theurgic practices from Hellenistic, Egyptian, and Mesopotamian sources.[16]

Ithamar Gruenwald proposes that a major factor in the rise of apocalypticism was theodicy: whatever had been concealed from human understanding concerning the injustice that seemed to dominate the world was now revealed for the knowledge and benefit of the just, since God's purpose in the world was about to be consummated. These secrets, which had been disclosed to the legendary sages of antiquity, were concealed in books that at the present eschatological turning point were available to the faithful.[17] Thus the *pesharim* among the Dead Sea Scrolls are not merely commentaries on scripture, but claim to disclose the inner meaning of scripture to the elect and enlightened Qumran community. The "One who teaches it rightly" (usually translated as "Teacher of righteousness") has alone been given the true interpretation of prophecy and the timing of the end of the age. In addition to Daniel and later portions of the traditional prophets, the major documents of apocalypticism before 70 C.E. include 1 Enoch and the Similitudes of Enoch. Writings after the fall of the Temple seek to explain how God's living presence could be found after the divine dwelling in Jerusalem was destroyed. Thus in 2 Enoch, the hero ascends through seven heavens into the presence of God. In the Apocalypse of Abraham, the patriarch ascends to heaven on an angel's wing, hears a celestial song, and is granted a vision of God (based on Ezekiel). The prophet has a similar experience in the Ascension of Isaiah.

In the Hekhalot literature, the early elements of which date from the second century B.C.E., the main subjects are heavenly ascensions, revelations of cosmological secrets, and secret methods of studying and mastering Torah. Unlike apocalyptic as such, the Hekhalot specify what a mystic must do, including prayers, incantations, fasts and diets, use of magical names and seals, and ritual cleansing of the body.[18] The ascents are achieved on ladders or in chariots.[19] Historic figures from scripture serve as paradigms for these ascents to the divine presence, but the details of technique and the mystical process show the influence of pagan syncretism as well as magical technique on this type of Jewish thinking.[20] The chief beneficiaries of this mystical mode seem to be the actual participants, though they perhaps share the heavenly secrets with associates or pupils. Some scholars propose a distinction between the later mystical texts, which emphasize participation in the divine, and the older documents, such as the Book of the Watchers (in Enoch), which concern the fate of the fallen angels and the disclosure of meterological and astronomical events.[21] Yet in both types of literature there is a notion of an elect minority of pious, seeking individuals to whom knowledge of the divine purpose and nature has been granted. No indications are given in the Merkavah texts of the import of these personal mystical experiences for the wider Jewish community, either for the mystics as a whole or for a more encompassing people of God.

The Johannine Mystical Community

The analysis of the Gospel of John offered here seeks to demonstrate features of this writing shared with the mystical philosophical and religious literature of the Greco-Roman world sketched above, but also to point out distinctive elements of this work differentiating it from that literature as well as from the other writings that came to be included in the New Testament. The perspective on the elect community represented initially in the New Testament by the Gospel of John subsequently underwent significant changes. I shall also examine some of the literature produced by Christians or by related groups in the second and third centuries C.E. that was never accepted as authoritative by the main body of the church. And finally, I shall survey the commentary on the Gospel of John produced by Origen, himself a scholar in the Alexandrine tradition that had produced Philo.

As I shall indicate in some detail, several features of John's portrayal of Jesus and the community he is calling together differentiate this book from the philosophical and mystical writings sketched above in this chapter. They include claims that the redeemer figure also had a central role in the creation of the world ("all things were made through him," John 1:3), that this revelatory figure is a human being whose parents and siblings are known and whose experiences included actual suffering and death, and that an essential feature of his revelatory role is his forming a community, rather than providing an escape for favored individuals from involvement in the ceaseless round of human existence.

The Role of the Logos in Creation

The Logos is portrayed in the Gospel of John as an eternal and essential instrument of God, rather than a remedy introduced after the initial plan for the creation failed to produce the divinely desired results. The creation story of Gen. 1:1–2:4 emphasizes God's speaking, both to accomplish creation of the universe and its earthly inhabitants, human and animal, and to bestow blessing and responsibility upon humanity, created by God's word in God's own image (1:26–28). Similarly in John 1:1–3, *logos* connotes not merely the expressed word of God but also the reasoned divine purpose that lies behind and informs the utterance.

In his commentary on the Gospel of John, Raymond Brown traces the background of *logos* from Heraclitus through the Stoics, noting Philo's fondness for the term—more than twelve hundred times in his extant writings! In the Hebrew scriptures, "word" (*dabar*) is used with reference to a spoken word, a thing, an affair, an event, or an action. The phrase "Word of the Lord" (*dabar Yahweh*) is not only a message from God but also the purpose and the power to carry it out (Hos. 1:1; Joel 1:1). The "word" gives life (Deut. 32:46–47); it carries the power to heal (Ps. 107:20); it is the agent of creation (Ps. 33:6), as well as the power to achieve divine ends (Isa. 55:11; Ps. 147:15, 18). In the Septuagint, similar roles are assigned to "word," which is rendered at times by *logos* and at others by *hrema* (Wisd. of Sol. 16:12, 26, 9:1; Ps. 147:15, 18). Similar functions are also attributed to Wisdom, which is never explicitly identified with the Word of the Lord, although the two are in parallel in Wisd. of Sol. 9:1–2. In Ben Sira 1:1, Wisdom comes from the Lord and remains with the Lord forever. In Wisd. of Sol. 9:9, Wisdom is the agent of creation and is described as *monogenes* (the only one of its kind), just as Jesus is in John 1:14 and 18. Like Jesus, who "came to his own, and his own people did not receive him" (John 1:11), Wisdom "tabernacled in Jacob" (Ben Sira 24:8–12) and experienced rejection (Ben Sira 15:7; Enoch 42:2; Bar. 3:12). Brown also notes that Wisdom is identified with Torah in postexilic Jewish literature (Ben Sira 24:23–24; Bar. 4:1). In John 1:17, however, there is a contrast between the law, which came through Moses, and "grace and truth," which came through Jesus Christ. Like Jewish writers of this period, the author of the Gospel of John is powerfully influenced by Greek philosophical and religious concepts, although he adapts them to his own purposes and employs them to make his own distinctive points.[22]

Analogous to the multiple connotations of *logos* is the multilayered meaning of *arche* ("beginning"). The opening phrase of John 1, "in the beginning" (*en arche*), implies not only the initial moment in a temporal sequence but also the originating divine plan and purpose in terms of which the creation of the world took place. It is not surprising that Origen devotes a large section of the opening book in his commentary on John to unpacking the implications of this phrase, showing that it connotes the point of departure to a new goal, the chronological starting point, the initial substance from which other substances are fashioned, the archetype from which subsequent copies are made, Jesus as the prototype of the new people of God, the active principle by which the divine intentions are carried out, and the divine wisdom in which the potential for renewal of the creation is eternally resident and active. The last point is made in the opening verse of John where the continuing presence of the Logos with God is affirmed and the link between what the Logos is to accomplish and the essential nature of God is asserted.[23] This primal role of the Logos in the purpose of God is reaffirmed in John 1:2, and its com-

Mystical Participation

prehensiveness is declared in John 1:3, where positive and negative corollaries affirm its function in the entire process of creation.

The role of the Logos includes far more than effecting the creation of the universe, however. The Word also is intended to communicate "light" of the knowledge of God and his purpose for the creation to all humanity. Even though the darkness of ignorance and evil seek to thwart the divine radiance, that "light" continues to shine and is not overcome (1:5). Every human has the potential for benefiting from the divine enlightener and agent, the Logos, through whom the ordered universe (*kosmos*) was fashioned, and yet the world does not recognize the Word or the role begun and continued through the Logos (1:10). Even then the Logos appears in human form (as John depicts this development, beginning at 1:14 and continuing throughout his gospel), his own human kin—the people of Israel—will on the whole not accept him as agent and messenger (*logos*) of God. Those who do accept him as the light sent from God—no matter what their ethnic origins or previous personal commitments ("not of blood, or of the will of the self, nor by male choice," 1:13)—will qualify to become members of God's family (1:12).

This understanding of the *logos*, while showing kinship in many basic ways with that which I have sketched in Greek philosophy of this period, is distinctive in at least two major ways. Unlike the Platonic tradition, which holds out a promise of escape from the ceaseless cycles of existence in the earthy sphere, the Logos through whom renewal of human existence is promised is also the agent through whom the universe was brought into being. I shall trace below the import of John's declaration, "The Logos became flesh" (1:14), but here we should note that John pictures the Logos as bringing the tangible world under control rather than providing an escape. The second distinction comes from the fact that the elect few who perceive the Logos in the Platonic tradition are represented as wise individuals whose insights deliver them from the wearisome, meaningless rounds of human existence. Throughout the Gospel of John on the other hand, as I shall note, the call is to participate in a new mode of communal life, in the new people of God.

The Logos Has Become Human in Jesus

In addition to the more theoretical notion of the word become flesh in John 1:1 and 14, the term appears throughout John with at least three different connotations. In John 17:20, for example, *logos* is used for the message about Jesus that his followers spread abroad. More difficult to differentiate sharply are those passages where *logos* refers to what Jesus speaks and the broader concept of God's word in the world. Yet in every case, "logos" is not a rational principle but a divine communication conveyed in humanly comprehensible terms.

The less ambiguous occurrences of the term appear with reference to what Jesus speaks. It is through the "word" of his teachings that his disciples come to understand the scriptures after the resurrection and to believe "the word which Jesus had spoken" (2:22). During his public ministry, it is through his "word" to the Samaritans that many of them come to trust him as "the Savior of the world" (4:41–42). Similarly, Jesus' "words" (logoi) in Jerusalem at the Feast of Tabernacles, with the explicit claim to be fulfilling the scriptures,[24] elicit strong and mixed responses: some acclaim him as "the prophet" (the eschatological prophet announced in Deut. 18:15) and some as "the Christ," even though his place of origin is said to be Galilee rather than Bethlehem (John 7:42; Mic. 5:2–5), while others want to arrest him. That it is the implicit and explicit force of what he says (logoi) that evokes these varied reactions becomes even clearer in John 8, where vindication and knowledge of "the truth" are promised to those who "continue in my word" (8:31), and those who "keep" Jesus' "word" will never experience death (8:51–52). Conversely, those in whom his word finds no root and who "cannot bear to hear" his word are children of the devil and devoid of the truth. The divisive impact of Jesus' word among the Jews is indicated again in John 10:19. Those who have responded in various ways to the "words" (bremata) of Jesus will be judged "on the last day" through the instrument of his "word" (logos, 12:48).

The reliability of Jesus' "word" is highlighted by the claim that those who love him will "keep" his word, and thereby experience the love of God the Father. His own people will find cleansing through his word (15:3). In John 18:32, Jesus' "word" announces in advance what the mode of his death will be: that is, the Roman mode of crucifixion rather than the Jewish mode of stoning. It is Jesus' "word" in which he claims to be the Son of God that leads Pilate to agree to his execution (19:8, 13). Jesus' predictive "word" also announces that all his faithful followers will be preserved through the time of difficulty that he and they are to experience (18:9), and in the epilogue to John's gospel, one of his followers is promised that he will survive until Jesus returns in glory (21:23).

Yet Jesus' "word" is also linked with the word of God, who "glorifies" Jesus, whom Jesus "knows," and whose "word" Jesus "keeps" (8:55). The logos is thus the ground of Jesus' relationship to God in terms of both essence and obedience. Analogously, God's people, to whom his "word" came in the past, are called "gods" (theous, John 10:34–35, Ps. 82), but they forfeited that status through their disobedience. Jesus, on the other hand, has a right to that title, since he is fully obedient to the divine logos. The ultimate and enduring truth is God's "word" (17:17).

This "word" is also being proclaimed by Jesus' followers, who are given assurance that those who trusted in and obeyed ("kept") Jesus' word will respond similarly to theirs (15:20). In his final prayer before the trial and crucifixion, Jesus expresses hope that God will maintain the unity of those who respond in trust to the "word" of his followers—a unity analogous to that which obtains between God and his incarnate logos (17:20–23).

Jesus' Union with God

A central aspect of this unity for the author of the Gospel of John is evident in the careful distinction he makes between eternal being and transitory existence, using forms of the Greek verb *eimi* to describe the former, and of *ginomai* to depict the latter. This difference is apparent in the opening lines of the prologue of John, where the eternal status of Jesus is described through the repeated use of *en* (was): in the beginning was the Word, and the Word was with God, and the Word was God (1:1–2). The contrast is sharp and explicit in John 1:2, where the Word's being (*en*) "in the beginning with God" is differentiated from the process of creation "through" the *logos*, by which everything came to be or was made (*egeneto*). The difference between being and becoming is also powerfully evident in the Septuagint, where the ineffable name of God, Yahweh, which is disclosed to Moses on Sinai, is rendered in Greek as *ego eimi ho on*, "I am he who is" (Exod. 3:14). Throughout the Gospel of John, Jesus is identified with ultimate being by the ascription to him, and by his appropriation to himself, of titles in which "I am" is central. Unlike Jesus, John the Baptist responds to questions from the Jewish leaders about his identity in a most emphatically negative way ("he declared publicly, he did not deny, but declared publicly," 1:20) that he is not the Messiah, using the full term: "I am not the Christ" (*ego ouk eimi ho christos*).

In response to the remark of the Samaritan woman about the coming of the Messiah (4:25), Jesus affirms, "I am [*ego eimi*] he—the one who is speaking to you" (4:26). Similarly, in seeking to overcome the fears of the disciples when he comes walking across the stormy Lake of Galilee, with the waters of chaos as symbols of the powers opposed to God and his purpose in the world,[25] Jesus calls to them, "It is I [*ego eimi*]; do not be afraid" (6:20). From this point on in John's gospel, Jesus defines his identity through combining the "I am" (*ego eimi*) designation with symbolic representations of the roles he fulfills for the benefit of God's new people. In four passages, the symbols are given extended exposition: Jesus, the bread of life (6:22–59); Jesus, the light of the world (8:12–58); Jesus and God's flock (10:7–30); and Jesus and the true vine (15:1–17). Other depictions of Jesus' role and identity are given in vivid but more compact form, as in John 11:25 ("I am the resurrection and the life") and in John 14:6 ("I am the way, the truth and the life").

Jesus the Bread from Heaven

An insightful survey of the theme of bread from heaven theme has been offered by Peder Borgen.[26] In his treatise *On the Change of Names*, Philo contrasts humanly attained wisdom, which, however admirable, is ephemeral, with archetypal wisdom, which is immortal and unchangeable. The former is the highest human achievement; the latter is the supreme gift of God. Jacob ("supplanter") is the one who challenges and replaces faulty human modes of thought and behavior, but in his role as Israel, he—like Abraham before him—is enabled to behold ultimate being (*to on*) with clear vision. The humanly inquiring mode of existence and its ephemeral results are contrasted by Philo with the vision of God granted to Moses and Abraham when, through the agent of God (*hyperetes tou theou*) that is the Logos, the foundation of the future for God's covenant people is laid. Everything below this level of being (*to on*) is unstable and impermanent (*On the Change of Names* 77–87). True wisdom is communicated, not by the humanly wise (*sophistes*), but by God, who grants true virtue without limit, perfect and complete. It is given entirely by God's own initiative (*autourgos*); the bread God sends from heaven (Exod. 16:4) is heavenly wisdom (*ten ouranian sophian*), granted only to those who yearn for true virtue (*arete*). The effort of Stoics to foster morality through instruction in the virtues and natural law—which was promoted by Seneca and Epictetus in the later first century C.E.—is noble but inadequate. Only wisdom above can accomplish enduring human renewal. This "bread from heaven," or manna, though potentially available to all Israel, is apprehended and experienced as mystical illumination only by those properly prepared to receive it (*On the Change of Names* 257–260).

The only extended sequence of miracle stories that appears in both John and the synoptics is found at John 6:1–25: the feeding of the thousands, Jesus walking on the water, and the subsequent healings by the lake.[27] John's version of the feeding story corresponds to those in the other gospels in the following details: the location by the lake; Jesus climbing a mountain; the shortage of bread for the crowd; the boy with the loaves and fish; the five (or four) thousand men in the crowd; Jesus' instruction to them to sit; the remaining fragments that fill twelve baskets.[28] Also remarkable is the use in John of technical terms shared with the eucharistic traditions preserved in Paul and the synoptic gospels:[29] "He took, he blessed/gave thanks, he broke, he gave" (6:11). In John 6:15, the explicit link between this act of feeding and Jesus' role as king has equivalent features in the other gospel accounts of the Last Supper (Mark 14:25; Matt. 26:29; Luke 22:18).

The assigning to Moses of the roles of prophet and king in postexilic Jewish literature has been amply documented by Wayne A. Meeks. This theme appears in the works Philo and Josephus and in other noncanonical Jewish writings.[30] Josephus also describes the leaders of insurrections in Palestine during the reign of Nero who sought to build a popular following by claiming to be prophets and promising divine confirmation through miracles (*Wars* 2.258–263). It is fundamental, therefore, that Jesus is shown by John to have redefined in nonpolitical terms the kingdom God is establishing through him. The miracle of feeding the crowd is not to be seen as divine qualification for political leadership.

It is also evident in John's account that the bread from heaven Jesus provides is not to be equated with a proper understanding of the law of Moses. The shocking nature of Jesus' challenge to the Jewish law has already been evident in his welcoming of the Samaritans among his followers and in his declaration that Jerusalem is not the central locus for the worship of God "in spirit and truth" (4:20). Now his instruction is that, unlike eating manna (which merely extended the earthly

Mystical Participation

lives of the participating Israelites, 6:49–50), eating his flesh and drinking his blood are essential for sharing in eternal life, for continuing relationship with God through him, and for participation in the resurrection of the dead (6:53–56). To drink blood or to eat meat with blood still in it was prohibited by Mosaic law (Gen. 9:4; Lev. 10:16; Deut. 12:15–16). To eat human flesh was simply unthinkable.

The symbolic meaning of this passage can be understood therefore, as pointing in two directions that are not mutually exclusive. Eating and drinking the "flesh and blood" of Jesus indicate full participation in the life he offers to his new people, including both suffering and blessing, as demonstrated in his own earthly career. At the same time, the corporate symbolic action by which that total commitment is demonstrated is participation in the Eucharist. As noted above, terminology from this tradition has been incorporated by John into his version of the story of bread from heaven as a sign of Jesus' messiahship, by sharing in which one can find true life through his name (20:30–31). If the "bread from heaven" is not wisdom or insight into the law, neither is it a primarily individual spiritual experience. Rather, it is a corporate sharing in the obedient life, the fidelity unto death, and the divine vindication through the resurrection that is seen by John as constituting the role of Jesus as model and uniting force for his people, now symbolized in the Eucharist.

Jesus the Light of the World

The extended section from John 8:12 to 9:41, although recounting conversations Jesus had with various people, is actually an elaborate setting forth by symbol and direct affirmation of the meaning of Jesus' claim in the opening verse, "I am the light of the world." The imagery of light recalls the initial divine acts of creating and ordering the universe in Gen. 1:1–19 as well as the guidance into the life of obedience that God provides for his people: "For with you is the fountain of life; in your light we see light (Ps. 36:9). "Your word is a lamp to my feet and a light to my path" (Ps. 119:105). It is also a common motif in the Prophets for the renewal of God's people: "The people who walked in darkness have seen a great light" (Isa. 9:2). In imagery clearly akin to this section of John, we read in 2 Isa.: "I will lead the blind by a road they do not know, by paths they have not known I will guide them. I will turn the darkness before them into light, the rough places into level ground" (Isa. 42:16). To gain access to this light, one must "follow" Jesus (John 8:12).

The Pharisees' challenge to this claim by Jesus is based not only on the ground of its substance but on the fact that it is the testimony of an individual and therefore lacks the multiple witnesses required by the law of Moses (Deut. 17:6, 19:15). Jesus' response is to claim an origin that authenticates his testimony ("whence I have come and whither I am going," 8:14). Judging in this context does not refer to rendering legal decisions but to having true insights and evaluations, and in these matters Jesus' declarations rest on the testimony of his Father, whom his critics do not know (8:18–19). The intended claim—to be from God—remains implicit thus far. In the next phase of the conversation (8:21–30), there are somewhat clearer indications of Jesus' origins: where he is going, his opponents cannot come; they are from below, he is from above; they are of this world (*kosmos*), he is not. To the Christian reader of John, the unmistakable import of Jesus' claim comes in his utterance that all will die in their sins who do not recognize that "I am" (*ego eimi*, 8:24). Yet the inherent dual meaning and unbelief on the part of the opponents in response to his insights (judgments) and declarations to the world are evident in their continued failure to identify who the "Father" is who sent him into the world. The factor of his death is included by the unseeing opponents (8:22) and affirmed in Jesus' prediction of the ambiguous event: the lifting up of the Son of man (8:28), which was announced earlier (3:14) and linked with Moses (Num. 21:5–9), and which points to both his crucifixion and his exaltation as the ground of participation in God's people (3:15).

The issue of the identity of those are able to see who Jesus is (that is, continuing in the truth and enabled thereby to enter the life of freedom, 8:30–32) becomes explicit when the opponents claim to be children of Abraham but are told that they are indeed children of the Devil (8:33–47). Their false understanding of Jesus and of God's purpose through him manifests that they are descended from "the father of lies." If they were children of the truth, they would discern who he is and the truth of his words. Their erroneous understanding of God's purpose for his people is evident when they link the destiny of "Abraham and the prophets" with the common human experience of death and reject Jesus' claim of entering the glorious destiny that God has prepared for him. Jesus declares that Abraham himself was able to see and to rejoice in this future "day" when God's purpose through Jesus would be consummated (8:56), and then goes on to contrast Abraham's mode of being in the realm of the ephemeral and transitory ("before Abraham came into existence," *genesthai*) with his own participation in the eternal ("I am" [*ego eimi*], 8:58). The violently hostile reaction of the hearers shows that they get the point of Jesus' radical claim of sharing in the life of God.

The symbolic force of Jesus as light of the world is implicit in the story of his restoring the sight of a man born blind (9:1–12). In response to his disciples' traditionalist question about the moral responsibility for this man's blindness, Jesus reaffirms his role—"I am the light of the world" (9:5)—and then proceeds to give sight to the blind man.[31] That the acknowledgment of God's power through Jesus to effect such a transforming illumination is a divisive issue among the Jews is evident in the refusal of the parents to offer an explanation of their son's recovery that would give credit to Jesus. At stake are acquiescence in Jesus' having performed this act on the sabbath (9:16) and the policy of the Jewish leaders that those who publicly acknowledge (*homologese*) Jesus to be the Messiah are to be expelled from the synagogue (*aposynagogos*, 9:22). The definition of the community of faith is emerging here in explicit contrast to the traditional community of law-abiding Israel. Sharply different from the leaders' hostile reaction to Jesus is the declaration of the healed man that Jesus is truly "devoted to God" (*theosebes*) and that it is God who has empowered him to perform this act of healing. Jesus identifies himself as "Son of Man" to the formerly blind man, who trusts and worships (*prosekunesen*) him (9:35–38). The final ironic note in the symbolic tale is Jesus' denunciation of the Pharisee's claim to be able to see as self-deceived and blind (9:39–40). The declaration that Jesus is "the light of the world" (9:5) has two radical implications. First, Jesus is *the* light, an exclusive claim implying that all other persons and modes that purport to bring knowledge of God to the world are false or grossly inadequate. Second, the light Jesus brings is accessible to the whole "world" (*kosmos*), not merely to the ethnically and culticly separate group that comprises the faithful of Israel. That Jesus makes such claims within the courts of the Temple, where the God of Israel was believed to dwell among his people, intensified the hostility of his Jewish hearers (8:59).

Jesus the True Shepherd and the Flock of God

The next set of symbols in John describing the role of Jesus and the participation of his people in the new community is sheep and shepherd (10:1–18). The metaphors that portray the role of Jesus are mixed: the sheepfold, the gate, and the shepherd. Others have come in the past claiming to be the leader of God's people ("the shepherd of the sheep"), but they have not taken on their role as God intended: they have "climbed in by another way" and are thieves and robbers (10:1). The "gatekeeper"—that is, God, who is ultimately in charge of the welfare of his people—gives the true shepherd access to his flock (10:3). The divinely approved shepherd knows and calls by name and leads out from the traditional people of God those who are truly "his own sheep," and they recognize "his voice" and are prepared to follow him.

In John 10:7, the image shifts, portraying Jesus as the "door" by which alone entry is possible to the flock of God. In contrast to previous claimants to this role, who exploited, slaughtered, and in crisis abandoned "the sheep" to attackers (10:8–9, 12–13), Jesus provides them life by laying down his own in their behalf (10:10–11, 17–18). The mutual knowledge between shepherd and sheep is the counterpart of the knowledge of the Father and the Son (10:14–15). The potential participants in the new flock of God include those now regarded as outsiders ("not of this flock"), which would point to Gentiles as well as to those of Jewish ethnic background who are regarded by pious Jews as unworthy and to be expelled from the community. It is the decision of the shepherd that results in Jesus' death rather than a fate that others impose on him, just as it is within his power—given to him by God—to take up his life again (10:18) and to grant his flock eternal life and total security in the hand of God (10:28–29).

The Jewish response to these claims is depicted as bitter and hostile, dismissing Jesus as demon-possessed and "mad" (10:19–21). The issue as to whether or not he is God's Messiah is articulated in a setting that is both historically and symbolically relevant to the definition of God's people: at the feast commemorating the rebuilding of the Jerusalem Temple, and in the portico dedicated to the builder of the original Temple, Solomon (10:22–23). The debate becomes more heated when Jesus declares his oneness with the Father, expressed in the terminology of ultimate being: "I and the Father are one" (*ego kai ho pater hen esmen*, 10:30). Understandably, this claim evokes an even more hostile reaction from the Jewish leaders, who accuse Jesus of "blasphemy" since he makes himself God (*theon*, 10:33). His response is to claim that God "consecrated him and sent him into the world," that he is "doing the works of the Father," and that God is in him and he is "in the Father" (10:36–38). In terms of both being and function, the unity of Jesus and God are affirmed here. The reaction of his Jewish hearers is to try to arrest him (10:39), thereby getting him out of the people's sight and hearing. Yet in spite of this official opposition, Jesus' own "sheep" continue to hear his voice and follow him (10:27), and are preserved forever in the sphere of loving care here represented as his own "hand" or the "Father's hand" (10:28–29).

Jesus the True Vine

In Psalm 80, there are two images depicting God's relationship to his covenant people: the flock and the vine. Both are followed by petitions to God to renew Israel (80:3, 19). The image of the vine traces Israel's history from the Exodus ("a vine out of Egypt") through settlement in the land of Canaan and the subsequent period of expansion and destruction, ending in an appeal for renewal and a promise of fidelity to God. In Isa. 5:1–7, unfaithful Israel ("it yielded wild grapes") is warned of divine neglect and impending punishment. The misdeeds of the people are then specified: greed, gross indulgence, and exploitation of other Israelites (5:8–23). The same image of wicked deeds produced by the favored nation appears in Jer. 2:20–21. In the song of Moses (Deut. 32:32–33), Israel's enemies are pictured as "the vine of Sodom, . . . the tendrils of Gomorrah." As Raymond E. Brown has noted,[32] plants and vines appear in the Prophets and later Jewish literature as symbols of participation by the covenant people in the consequences of disobedience (Ezek. 17:1–21) or in the divine blessing (Ezek. 17:22–24).

Philo (in *On Drunkenness* 222–224) warns that no good plant producing fine fruit can grow in the soul of the wicked, but that what grows there will "be the bearer of bitterness and wickedness and villainy, or wrath and anger and angry moods." He prays that in the lives of the faithful there may be "the trees of right instruction [*paideia*], producing fruits of genuine worth . . . and powers of reason which will beget good deeds." Conversely, in his treatise *On Noah's Work as Planter*, Philo says the mind that "has entered the way of good sense" and pursues it will become a tree bearing fruits: "instead of passions freedom from them, knowledge [*episteme*] instead of ignorance, and good things in place of evil" (98). To foster greater production of the good, the process of pruning must be carried out (104). After dividing into two sentences the injunction against eating fruit in the land until three years have passed (Lev. 19:23) and interpreting them allegorically, Philo declares that fruit produced by education (*paideia*) in the truth that transcends the three stages of time—"past, present and future, that is, all eternity"—is wholly pure and needs no cleansing (113–116). According to Philo, the divinely provided fruit of virtue and true piety is produced in the lives of the wise and faithful by the work of the Logos.

In John 15:1–2, Jesus' declaration of his identity (*ego eimi*) includes his own role as "true vine" and that of the Father as the one who guides the growth of the vine, but he then goes on to describe the place of God's people in this vital relationship. The "true," or, more appropriately, "real,"[33] vine is Jesus, which implies a contrast with false claimants to identity as God's people. The branches of the "real vine" are those that bear fruit, thereby bringing glory to God (15:7). Those that do not bear fruit are pruned and discarded, enabling the fruitful branches to become even more productive. What bearing fruit involves is not directly stated, but the references to being "made clean by [Jesus'] word" and to abiding in him (v. 4) and in his love (v. 9), when combined with the instructions to obey the Father's commandments (v. 10) and the subsequent specification of Jesus' commandment to "love one another" (v. 12), imply that the fruit to be produced is the life of mutual love within the community. That love is not merely attitudinal, but involves willingness to die in behalf of others, as Jesus himself did (v. 13). Thereby the members of the community show that they are true "friends" (*philoi*). The ultimate ground of this relationship is Jesus' choice and designation of them as his people with the aim that their lives be characterized by love for one another (vv. 14–17).

This love is contrasted in John 15:18–16:4 with the hatred that Jesus evoked from the world (*kosmos*), which was turned against God as well and which his people will experience on his account. Jesus' exposure of the world's sin evoked that wholly unwarranted hatred, as was predicted in scripture (Ps. 35:29, 69:5). The Paraclete, or Spirit of truth, whom Jesus will send will confirm his people's testimony as to who he really is and will strengthen them so that they can remain faithful in spite of expulsion from the synagogues or even martyrdom. The image of the vine, therefore, is a vivid symbol of the living, enduring relationship between God and his people through Jesus, which is to be characterized by fidelity and loving obedience.

Jesus the Resurrection and the Life

Jesus' role as agent and symbol of triumph over death, while set out most completely in John 11, is already anticipated in the earlier parts of John. In the prologue, Jesus is said to be the one in whom is life, which is the light of humanity (1:4). Those who trust in the Son have eternal life (3:15–16, 36). The "living water" Jesus provides will be a wellspring of eternal life in those who experience it

(4:14). Those who hear and heed his word have eternal life, and will not come under divine judgment (5:24). He calls his people to share in the "bread of life" that he offers (6:33) and embodies (6:35). Those who follow him will "have the light of life" (8:12). To his sheep, Jesus gives "eternal life" (10:28). The benefits he offers to his people are explicitly linked in John 5:25–29 with the resurrection, which is pictured as already present in the experience of his people ("the hour is coming, and now is when the dead will hear the voice of the Son of God, and those who hear will live"), but it is also linked with the future event "when all who are in the tombs will hear his voice and come forth . . . to the resurrection of life [or] the resurrection of judgment." The eschatological hope of resurrection is still affirmed, but it is balanced by the promise of new life in the here and now for the community of faith. It is this double import of the resurrection that is unfolded in John 11:1–44.

The story of the death and resurrection of Lazarus is told in John in a way that is significantly different from the stories of Jesus raising the dead in the synoptic tradition, where the action is seen as an extension of Jesus' power to heal and restore. There is an intentional double meaning in Jesus' declaration, on hearing of Lazarus's illness, that it is not "unto death" (11:4). The literal meaning could be that Lazarus will not die, but Jesus is pointing beyond death to renewal of life. The drama of the story is heightened by Jesus' intentional delay in reaching the home of the ailing Lazarus and his sisters (11:6). The symbolic import of what is to happen is hinted at in the contrast between those who walk in the dark and those who have the light within them (11:9–10). In describing Lazarus's death, he uses the term "fallen asleep,"[34] with its distinctive early Christian eschatological implication that those who have died are in a condition from which they will soon be delivered at the triumphant coming of Christ in the new age.[35] Like Jesus' promise to wake him, this is heard as a literal description of sleep and awaking. In seeming contradiction, Jesus then announces that Lazarus has died, and notes that there are benefits in the fact that he had not been present to heal this ailing friend. The situation is perceived by Thomas as an instance of martyrdom that he and the other disciples may be called to undergo (11:11–16). The reality of Lazarus's death is indicated by the fact of his burial and by the expectation of the stench from the decaying corpse. Up to this point, the sisters' view of the situation rests on their belief that, had Jesus come more quickly, he could have healed their brother. Now they have only the traditional Jewish view of a resurrection at the end of time as the basis of hope of seeing their brother alive again (11:17–24).

Jesus' self-affirmation in response to this assertion of Jewish piety embodies a major transformation of resurrection belief. Jesus declares that he is "the resurrection and the life" and goes on to claim that those who trust in him, even though they may die, will share in the resurrection, as will those who live until that new era comes (11:25–26). Martha not only affirms this claim, but utters her confession that Jesus is in fact the promised "Son of God who is coming into the world"

(11:27). He does not merely announce the life of the age to come: he is its embodiment. Ironically, the opening of the tomb and the summoning of the dead Lazarus from it (11:28–37) are followed by the plot of the religious leaders to have Jesus put to death. The assumption of these leaders is that if Jesus is allowed to continue, both the sacred site (*topos*) and their identity as the people of God (*ethnos*) will be destroyed. Yet many of the Jews were convinced that God was the source of life and power behind Jesus' healing acts (11:45, 12:11). Unwittingly, the leaders' plot will result in the redefining of God's people, including the "gathering into one God's children who are scattered abroad" (*ta dieskorpismena synagoge eis hen*, 11:52). Thus, in a variety of forms and images, the Gospel of John depicts the role of Jesus as constituting God's new people.

Jesus the Way, the Truth, and the Life

Another symbolic representation of this role arises when the Greeks come seeking to "see Jesus" (12:20–21). Their quest is seen as the decisive indicator that God's purpose is coming to maturity, so that Jesus' impending death and resurrection will result in the conversion of many, within and outside the traditional covenant people. This divine action will "bear much fruit," since many—both Jews and Gentiles—will choose to join the new community. Indeed, when Jesus is "lifted up from the earth"—pointing to both his crucifixion and his exaltation to God—he will "draw all" to himself. Once more the Jewish leaders are quoted as speaking unwitting truth in their satirical remark: "Look, the world [*kosmos*] has gone after him" (12:18). Many of the leading Jews are said to have believed in him, but "for fear of the Pharisees" they made no public confession of their faith, lest they be expelled from the synagogue (12:42, expanded in 16:1–4). The unbelief with which Jesus was greeted is perceived as the fulfillment of scripture concerning divine blinding (12:38–40; Isa. 53:1, 6:10). To reject Jesus and his word is to reject God and his purpose, and thereby to forego participation in eternal life (12:44–50). The theme that Jesus alone provides access to God is given its basic formulation in John 14:6: "I am the way, the truth and the life. No one comes to the Father, except by me." Taking the term "way" literally, Philip asks to be given more specific directions for finding the Father, to which Jesus responds by declaring categorically his oneness with God in what he says, does, and embodies (14:8–11).

The themes of the unity of Jesus and God and the comprehensiveness of God's provision for his new people are elaborated in the discourses of John 16–18. Jesus' departure will make way for a new God-provided resource in the community, the Spirit, or Paraclete.[36] The role of the Paraclete is instructional, informing the members of the community about God and Jesus and their own difficult but essential role in the world. The Paraclete will convict the world of its sin in rejecting Jesus and thereby rejecting God; it will guide the members into "all the truth"; it will glorify and proclaim God's truth as disclosed by and through Jesus (16:4–15). For the interim before Jesus' triumphant return, they will be comforted and supported by the Paraclete, and God will hear their petitions spoken in the name of Jesus (16:16–33).

Jesus' role as way, truth, and life is implicit throughout the prayer reported in John 17. The event that is pending—his crucifixion—is represented not as a tragedy but as the essential step toward his glorification of God and by God. The ground of hope for eternal life is the knowledge of God that is now possible through what Jesus did on earth, accomplishing God's work (17:1–5). The members of the new community he has founded have heard and kept his word, and Jesus prays that they may be kept faithful to God. Their faith will give them joy, even when he is separated from them and present with the Father (17:6–13). They must realize that, like Jesus, they "are not of this *kosmos*"—that is, their values, pattern of relationships, and aspirations are not taken over from the present human culture and social system (17:14–19). Above all, he prays that they may be unified—"perfectly one"—a situation that will be evident chiefly through the love they display[37] and will serve as the foundation for their testimony concerning Jesus and God's purpose in the world through him (17:20–26). The highest good will be for them to be one, as Jesus and God are one (17:21). As Jesus revealed the "name of God" (that is, God's nature and purpose) and continues to reveal it through his new people, so God's love will be in them and he in them (17:26).

The Mystical Community Develops the Need for Structure and Authority

The internal problems that surfaced in the subsequent shared life of the community of mystical participation are evident in the Letters of John. First is the emergency within the community of those who think life by the Spirit carries with it no moral requirements. The author of 1 John declares that members must not "walk in darkness" but "live according to the truth" (1:6). To maintain that those in the fellowship have no problem with sin is gross self-deceit and shows a lack of grasp of the truth (1:8). The author counters with a description of the process by which members can obtain forgiveness (2:1–2). Essential are obedience to the commandments and following the moral "way" that Jesus walked (2:3–6). To hate someone within the community is an indication that one is "walking in darkness" rather than in the light of the truth that Jesus has disclosed (2:7–11). An equally serious problem arises when the members "love the world" (2:15). Clearly, the connotations of this warning embody a different understanding than is expressed in God's love for the world in John 3:16. As noted in the previous section, the *kosmos* is here perceived as the dominant culture, manifesting its self-gratifying values and norms, as the mention of the modes of "lust" and "pride" shows (2:15–16).

The situation within the community has deteriorated to the point at which some who were ostensibly members have withdrawn, denying both the Father and Jesus as Son (2:18–25). The true members are to abide by their original confession of the Father and the Son, allowing their primary understanding of the Christian message to "abide" within them. Meanwhile, sin is not to be tolerated within the community; those who commit these evil acts are "children of the devil" (3:4–10). Love, not hatred, is to characterize all their relationships, as the supreme example of Jesus' death in their behalf evidences (3:11–18). This conscious commitment to love and truth will be confirmed by the confidence that God will place in their hearts and will be evident in the life of mutual love that characterizes them as members (3:19–24). The renegade former members are a part of the alien world, which gives heed to their perverted message. But the true community has access to God and lives by the principle of love set forth in God's gift of his Son as "the expiation for the sins" of his people (4:1–10). That love is to be the active principle in all the relationships within the community and is confirmed by the activity of the Spirit among them (4:13–21). Those who stand by their confession[38] of Jesus as Son of God in human form and who live in reliance upon the Spirit of God are already living the life God has promised (5:1–12). Their prayers are heard, including their requests in behalf of erring members, although the lives of God's people are not characterized by sin, as the errant former members claim (5:13–18). The letter ends with solemn warnings about the persistent "power of the evil one" and the necessity of focusing solely on Jesus and God, rather than on man-made "idols" (5:19–21).

The Second Letter of John reiterates the centrality of the commandment to love as the basis for sharing in the common life of the new community. But a revealing detail appears in verse 4, where only some of the "children" still "follow the truth." Clearly, many no longer do so. The chief criteria for identifying the outsiders are their failure to fulfill the commandment to love and their failure to "confess the coming of Jesus Christ in the flesh." The docetic heresy, which claimed that the earthly life of Jesus was only a kind of divine masquerade and that he never shared in the limitations of human existence (discussed below), is here linked with those who are deceivers and the Antichrist. What is essential is to hold correct doctrine (*didache*).

In 3 John, the movement toward codification of belief and practice has taken yet another significant step. The writer commends his readers because they "follow the truth" (v. 4) and support those itinerant Christian messengers who come to their community (vv. 5–6). The central importance of adherence to "the truth" is also evident in the support of Demetrius and the claim of John that his own testimony is "true" as well (v. 5). The ideal for the community as a whole is that its leaders and members may be "co-workers in the truth" (v. 8).

On the other hand, Diotrophes is called to account in this letter because of his persistent failure to acknowledge the authority of John. Not only does he seek to discredit John and his authority within the community, but he refuses to accept those authorized by John and wants to deny them the support of the community as a whole. The true and faithful members of the community are recognized here by John as simply "friends" (*philoi*). What seems implicit in these letters of John is the development of regional authority—what later come to be called dioceses—

where a single figure, who was later to be known as bishop (*episkopos*), has ultimate authority in matters of faith, practice, and leadership roles. Yet the attempt is made to preserve the spirit of spontaneous communal life, even in these letters dealing with issues of authority.

The Esoteric Logos

In a cultural milieu where the mystical philosophy and religious movements I have referred to earlier in this chapter were flourishing, it is understandable that similar developments would occur among the Christians. The varied results of this acculturation included portraits of Jesus as an esoteric figure as well as teachings that he vouchsafed only to enlightened insiders. Far from the sort of worldwide evangelism I have described in chapter 3 (on Matthew and the church as the true Israel) and will examine more fully in chapter 6 (on Luke and the ethnically inclusive community), I here examine briefly the proto-Gnostic and Gnostic documents which insist that knowledge of the truth about God is reserved solely for members of the in-group.

Jesus: The Divine Masquerading as Human

Ignatius, bishop of Antioch in Syria, was sent to Rome for trial during the reign of Trajan (98–117 C.E.) and was soon martyred there. In his extant letters to various Christian communities, he not only insists on the human, historical dimensions of the life of Jesus, but explicitly refutes those who want to picture Jesus as one who merely seemed to have taken on human form. Constantly repeating the emphatic adverb *alethos* (truly, openly), he sketches in his *Letter to the Trallians* Jesus' human descent from David, his birth to Mary, his eating and drinking, and his being persecuted and crucified and dying, the latter events having occurred in the presence of human and divine witnesses. He then proceeds to reject emphatically the view of those—whom he styles as unbelievers (*apistoi*)—who teach that Jesus' suffering was only an appearance or semblance (*to dokein*) of human experience. To accept this notion would make Ignatius' impending martyrdom an act of utter vanity.[39] The historical features of Jesus that Ignatius affirms elsewhere include not only his descent from David and birth from Mary, but also his baptism, his suffering, his crucifixion "in the flesh," and his being raised from the dead. None of these is mere appearance (*to dokein*), just as the resurrection of the faithful will not be in the mode of the disembodied (*asomatois*) or the lesser divinities (*daimonikois*). Jesus' association with his disciples after the resurrection was at the tangible human level, when they touched him and shared meals with him. Ignatius declares, "If it is merely in semblance [*to dokein*] that these things were done by our Lord, then I am also a prisoner in semblance [*to dokein*]."[40]

True Knowledge and the Knowers of Truth: Gnosticism

By the middle of the second century C.E., however, there were flourishing movements from Alexandria and Asia Minor in the east to Rome and Carthage in the west engaging in radical revision of definitions of the role of Jesus and of the community he had formed. His function was seen by these revisionists as conveyer of esoteric knowledge about God and the reality of the cosmos; the recipients of this *gnosis* were a self-proclaimed privileged minority.

The Origins of Gnosticism

Previously known largely from attacks on Gnosticism by scholars from the mainstream of the developing church in the second and third centuries, gnostic teachings were documented in detail with the discovery of a large collection of writings at the remains of a monastic settlement in Upper Egypt in 1945.[41] In spite of the scholarly reconstructions claiming to show that Gnosticism predated the rise of Christianity, all that can be demonstrated is that certain dualistic modes of philosophical speculation were operative in the second century C.E., of which the dominant example is what has been called Middle Platonism.[42] According to this intellectual perspective, the goal of human existence is to gain liberation from involvement in the material world, finding refuge in the realm of spirit and light. This mode of transmutation is evident in the versions of Christianity that were attacked by the leading Christian intellectuals of the second and third centuries C.E.

Chief among these early Christian apologists were Irenaeus (120–202) and Tertullian (160–230). In his huge work *Against Heresies*, Irenaeus emphasized the historical reality of the incarnation of Jesus, including his sufferings and death. He goes on to denounce those who consider the earthly career of Jesus as only a matter of appearance, affirming instead the full identification of Jesus with human flesh-and-blood experience in his birth, temptation, suffering, and death (5.1). He explicitly rejects the teaching of Valentinus (fl. 140–165) that the flesh of human existence is excluded from participation in salvation and that therefore Jesus did not, and did not need to, participate in that mode of humanity (5.2). Instead, Irenaeus insists that salvation is not an escape from the material world (5.4); indeed, the nails in Jesus' hands and the wounds in his side demonstrate God's concern for and his ability to redeem full humanity (5.7, 14). Those he is writing against are teaching that redemption consists in the release of the soul from the body, but Irenaeus counters this notion with an insistence that the human body will be raised in the end time, when the fulfillment of God's purpose and the reward of the faithful are achieved (5:31).

In several treatises attacking the positions of those he regarded as teachers of falsehood, Tertullian traces to Greco-Roman culture the origins of what he denounced as erroneous notions claiming to be the proper way of understanding Jesus and God's purpose in the world through him. "Heresies are instigated by philosophy," such as the Epicurean belief in the death of the soul, the broad-based philosophical denial of the restoration of the body, or Heraclitus's identification of the divine with fire.[43] Tertullian sees the secrecy of the Gnostic teachings as imitating the Eleusinian mysteries.[44] According to Valentinus, the birth of Jesus is not the result of human gestation but rather the passage of a divine being through Mary. What is represented to be Jesus in the gospel tradition actually consists of several beings, so that the superior Christ descended on the "animal and carnal" Jesus, only to depart from him when his revelatory work was completed.[45] Tertullian also attacks the teaching of Marcion (85–160) who differentiates two deities: the good god of spirit and the evil deity of the material world. Marcion has claimed that Christ was neither "the author nor the restorer" of human fleshly existence and should not be thought of as possessing a human, earthly mode of being or having experienced human birth to Mary. Tertullian declares in response that, contrary to the theories of Marcion, the death of Jesus was foretold by the prophets of ancient Israel and foreshadowed by such symbols as Moses raising the bronze serpent.[46] Hence, the Gnostic thesis under attack here is that divine self-revelation must take place within the structures and modes that characterize divinity, not humanity. The human aspects of the traditions about Jesus are purely symbolic, to be explained away through allegory and skillful interpretive methods.

The basic aim of the Gnostic theologians whom Irenaeus and Tertullian denounce as heretics, therefore, is to reconstruct a mode of Christian faith which is free of logical and philosophical paradoxes such as the one that "the Word" that "was God" at a specific point in human history "became flesh" and lived in a setting of human limitations (John 1:14), leading to suffering, death, and bodily resurrection. Another way of eliminating what the Gnostics regarded as embarrassing notions was to transform the evidence. This was achieved by rewriting the Gospels in such a way as to eliminate those features that were discordant with the dualistic philosophy. Three examples of this development are representative of the Gnostic effort and its results.

Typical Gnostic Documents

The Gospel of Peter, probably written in the mid-second century C.E.,[47] pictures Jesus as going through the experience of the crucifixion without feeling any pain (10) and as momentarily deprived of his power rather than abandoned by God. This is apparent when, instead of the quotation by the crucified Jesus from Ps. 22:1—"My God, my God, why have you forsaken me?" (Mark 15:34; Matt. 27:46)[48]—Jesus is reported as crying, "My power, O power, you have forsaken me!" (19). This term of address to God suits Gnostic thought well, but the identification of God with *dynamis* has neither place nor precedent in the Jewish[49] or canonical Christian traditions. The nonhuman nature of the earthly Jesus and his identification with heavenly beings is unmistakable in this gospel's account of the stone rolling away of itself from the entrance to the tomb of Jesus: "They saw again three men come out of the sepulchre, two of them sustaining the other, and a cross following them, and the heads of the two reaching to heaven, but that of him who was led by them overpassing the heavens" (39–40). The divine masquerade of

Jesus as a human who appears to suffer and die could scarcely be more dramatically depicted.

The Gospel of Thomas was long known from quotations in Greek dating from around 200 C.E., before it was discovered in 1945 as a complete text. It has been proposed—and accepted by some scholars—that in this gospel "many of these sayings are preserved in a form which is older than the forms of their parallels in the Synoptic Gospels."[50] Careful analysis of the document as a whole shows, however, that the tradition has been consistently modified and adapted—both in substance and in detail—to a view of Jesus and his role in the world that is compatible with the emergent Gnosticism of the second century and completely at variance with the apocalyptic view represented in the demonstrably oldest New Testament traditions: Q, Mark, and the authentic letters of Paul.

Missing from the Gospel of Thomas are references to basic features of the canonical gospel tradition: Jesus' relationship with his family and with John the Baptist, his conflict with the religious leaders of his day, and his sufferings and death. These are precisely the elements that are mentioned by Josephus and by the Roman historians in their passing references to Jesus.[51] Most tellingly absent from this gospel is any consideration of how the community of God's people is constituted, which we have seen to be the dominant concern in Jewish sources as well as in the early Christian writings. Similarly, there are no references to baptism or the Last Supper, both of which represent important aspects of Jewish community identity and participation in this period, as I have noted.

The major themes of the Gospel of Thomas—in consonance with which the older gospel tradition has been adapted or new sayings have been created—are self-knowledge, access to esoteric, revealed truth, overcoming one's human identity, and escape from the world. In contrast to these, the canonical gospel tradition emphasizes the knowledge of God and his purpose for the creation that Jesus has disclosed, the truth Jesus reveals to his followers, which they are charged to proclaim, finding one's identity in the context of the new covenant community, and the transformation and renewal of the created world that are to occur through Jesus.

The major emphasis in the Gospel of Thomas falls on the theme of self-knowledge. "The kingdom is within you and it is outside of you" (logion 3),[52] the goal of which is complete knowledge of oneself as a child of God. Reaching this goal brings knowledge of the knower by God; failure to reach it is described as poverty: "You are in poverty and you are poverty." The light of knowledge is internal, "within a man of light" (logion 24), and has the potential for giving light "to the whole world," but if it is rejected, "there is darkness." In spite of the lofty role of John the Baptist in the divine scheme, his status will be far exceeded by "the little one" who comes to "know the kingdom" (logion 46). Insight into these privileged "mysteries" is reserved for those who are worthy[53] to receive it. Even those who have a grasp of total knowledge—or knowledge of the ultimate deity—are fully lacking if they have not initially obtained knowledge of themselves (logion 67). One's eternal destiny turns on achieving this internal knowledge of oneself: "When you bring forth that in yourselves, that which you have will save you. If you do not have that in yourselves, that which you do not have in you will kill you" (logion 70).

In logia 5 and 6, the disciples are promised that whatever they now fail to understand will be disclosed to them. When they ask Jesus about the rules by which they are to live, they are told to be truthful and to avoid doing what they hate. But then there is the assurance that there will be complete disclosure of all the heavenly secrets. Revelation has been inaugurated, but fuller insights are yet to come as the disciples grow in knowledge, which is not to be proclaimed publicly (as the gospel is in the canonical tradition) but is to be reserved solely for the in-group.

Essential to attaining this lofty level of knowledge is overcoming human, personal identity. The reversal of human roles is indicated in logion 4, where the supposedly knowledgeable ("the man aged in his days") has to ask about the meaning of "life" from a "child of seven days"—that is, one regarded by the self-confident as immature and ignorant. These considered to be juvenile ("first," and thus at the bottom of the hierarchy of humanity) will turn out to be "last" and will ultimately be disclosed as those with true insight. They will become fully unified beings ("a single one"). What this involves is spelled out in more detail in logia 22 and 114: one achieves ultimate human unity by overcoming the distinctions that characterize ordinary existence. "When you make the two one, and when you make the inside as the outside, and the outside as the inside, and the upper side as the lower; and when you make the male and the female into a single one, so that the male is not male and the female is not female, and when you make eyes in place of an eye, and a hand in place of a hand, and a foot in place of a foot, and an image in place of an image, then shall you enter [the kingdom]." Not only sexual differentiation— which is part of the order of creation in the biblical tradition and is presented in the canonical gospel tradition as a continuing feature of the divine purpose for humans[54]—but also failure to conform to a model of solitary human existence are rejected in the Thomas tradition. In logion 114, the eradication of sexual differentiation specifies that every women must make herself male in order to become "a living spirit."

What is implicit here is a radically dualistic view of reality, in which the created universe is inherently evil and salvation lies in escape from and transformation of it. This objective is set forth in both explicit and implicit ways. The "world" as a whole is denounced by Jesus as "drunk" in logion 28. The inhabitants do not "thirst" for truth, but are "blind" in heart, and will depart from the world "empty as they entered it." Only if they reject the values of this world ("have thrown off their wine") will they be able to "repent" and turn toward the truth. Those who make this change will be a tiny minority (logion 29): "Blessed are the solitary and the elect, for you shall find the kingdom." They can make this shift because they originated from the kingdom: "You came forth hence, and shall go there again." The motif throughout the canonical gospels of the invitation by Jesus and his followers to ethnic, religious, and moral outsiders to share in the life of God's new people is the antithesis of the emphasis here on esoteric and exclusive information for the elect.

Pistis Sophia, dating from the latter half of the third century, evidences an even more distant kinship with the gospel tradition, in that it is concerned solely with the instructions that Jesus gives his disciples, seated on the Mount of Olives, on his return to them eleven years after his resurrection. The special revelation he brings is embodied in the great radiance that comes from behind the sun and transcends its light, descending upon Jesus. For a time he goes back into the heavens, but then he returns and begins the instruction of his disciples. He gives them the secret interpretation (*hermeneia*) of his words and of mystical letters. The Greek equivalent of the Hebrew name of God, IAO = Yahweh is said to show the following: *Iota* means "all has gone forth"; *Alpha* means "it will turn back"; *Omega* means "the perfection of all perfections will take place." In response to a question from his disciples about where he has been, Jesus gives them details of the journey he made through the various structures and levels of reality on his way to and from the presence of the ultimate God. Although there is mention of his crucifixion and his resurrection on the third day, the essential role of Jesus is to convey the secret revelation to the inner circle of his followers: "Thou Father of all Fatherhood of the Infinite, hearken unto me for my disciples' sake, whom I have brought before thee, that they may believe all the words of thy truth." The Gnostic recasting of the Jesus tradition has fully developed: Jesus is the conveyer of secret knowledge, and the community of the faithful is the elect group to whom cosmic disclosures have been granted to enable them to escape from involvement in the material world.

The Role of the Mystical Logos in the Early Christian Intellectual Community: Origen of Alexandria

The Christian intellectuals of Alexandria in the second and third centuries C.E. took over from the traditions of that city best represented by Philo the principle that sacred writings had two levels of meaning: the literal, and the spiritual or mystical. Origen, who at eighteen became the head of the Christian catechetical school, made a threefold distinction in his *De Principiis*: just as humans consist of body, soul, and spirit, so scripture has three levels of meaning. These are the somatic or literal sense, the psychical or moral sense, and the pneumatic or spiritual sense. The third one was for Origen a combination of critical intellectual perception, containing linguistic and philosophical features, with mystical insights. His homilies were aimed at the general reader or hearer, but his commentaries sought to disclose the fuller meaning of the text. Indeed, he shows little interest in the historical or literal meaning, but concentrates instead on the ultimate, transcendent significance.[55]

This interpretive strategy is evident from the outset in Origen's *Commentary on John*. In the first two books of this work—which are devoted to an exposition of John 1:1—he explains what it means to say that "the Logos was God." The Logos participates in God's divine nature, but the omission of the article (*theos en ho logos*, not *ho theos en ho logos*) shows that these terms are not interchangeable. All humans are created in the divine image, but Christ is the archetypal image of God and the agent of creation. Through him, humans may attain to the divinely intended relationship with God (2.2). Origen rejects the Valentinian view[56] that the world was not created through the Logos and that the life the Logos brings is not physical existence but only spiritual life. Rather, he insists, the higher life the Logos brings is the life according to reason and the fulfillment of divine reason within those who are open and receptive to it (2.19). The titles of Christ—light, resurrection, way, high priest, and especially Logos—are not intended as identifications of separate individuals, but point rather to the multiple roles and functions Jesus fulfills in the purpose of God (2.23–41). As Logos, Jesus takes away from his people all that is irrational, making them truly reasonable. As a result, they do everything—even eating and drinking—to the glory of God. Through the enlightenment the Logos brings, everything that is dead and devoid of reason is driven off, and he reveals to the community of faith and discernment the Father whom he knows (2.42).

In the opening books of this commentary, Origen sketches the community and the roles of its leaders. The church is the spiritual Israel (Rev. 7:3–4), and its leaders are the "priests": those who mediate between God and his people through the exposition of scripture, and especially of the Gospels. To grasp the meaning requires more than intellectual effort; it can be apprehended only if one has leaned on Jesus' breast and received Mary to be one's mother (John 13:23–25, 19:26–27). It is not physical or birthright relationships that are central for participation, but mystical communion and renewal (2.6). Central to the life of the community is the move beyond the "somatic," literal, historical, narrative description in the Gospels to the level of "pneumatic," spiritual insight. The goal in the study of scripture is to discern "all matters concerning the very Son of God, both the mysteries presented by his discourses and the enigmas which appear in the accounts of his acts." The somatic meaning is important, as when one must bear public testimony to belief "in Jesus Christ, and him crucified." But discernment of the spiritual meaning enables one to "partake of heavenly wisdom" (2.9).

This community of mystical participation shows clear kinship with the Jewish antecedents I sketched earlier, and the sharing of the aims and thought of the Gospel of John are evident, not only in Origen's commentary on that gospel, but also in his overall approach to the meaning of Christ and the resources and responsibilities of the community.

The Ethnically and Culturally   **6**
Inclusive Community

Ethnic and Cultural Exchange between Judaism and Greco-Roman Culture

Although the emphasis throughout the Jewish scriptures is on the unique relationship of Israel with God, which has been established by divine choice and is to
be maintained by preserving ethnic and ritual purity, there are important features
that offer a different point of view. In the Prophets, the Psalms, and especially
some of the writings of the Hellenistic period, there is affirmation of the divine
intent that people from other nations are to share in the blessings of God's people
and to join with them in honoring the God of Israel, who is Lord of all creation.
Further, there is a potent effort on the part of Jewish writers in the Greco-Roman
period to demonstrate the compatibility of certain traditional beliefs of Israel about
God and his purposes with insights expressed by philosophers and writers in the
wider Hellenistic culture. The reflection of the situation in which Jews found
themselves in the Greco-Roman period is evident in both the literary modes and
the technical terms derived from Hellenistic culture in which these beliefs are set
forth in Jewish literature. These efforts to achieve synthesis with the wider contemporary world during the centuries before and after the turn of the eras aim to
demonstrate the consonance of Jewish understanding with wisdom as it is evident
in various aspects of Greco-Roman culture.

Recent archaeological finds in Israel from the Hellenistic and Roman periods
have provided important evidence of this cultural synthesis, which continued as
late as the fourth century C.E. After reviewing some of the literary and cultural
attestation of this phenomenon from Jewish sources, I shall analyze in some detail
the clear testimony of the extension and adaptation of this development toward
inclusiveness as evident in early Christian sources—specifically in the Gospel of

Luke and the Acts of the Apostles. I have already noted in chapter 2 above similar evidence of Gentile inclusion and of Hellenistic cultural features in the Letters of Paul.

The View of Gentile Participation in the Purpose of God for His People in the Prophets and Psalms

A pervasive theme in the Jewish prophetic tradition announces the divine retribution that is to fall on "the nations" for their maltreatment and oppression of Israel. In both pre- and postexilic prophets, there are multiple oracles in which judgment is pronounced on Israel's hostile neighboring nations: Joel 3, Ezekiel 25–30, Amos 1, Obadiah 1–16, Jeremiah 25–27, 46–51, and Zechariah 12–14 are obvious examples. Characteristic of the hostile, scornful attitude attributed to Yahweh with regard to the other nations is the declaration of Jeremiah (25:15–33) concerning the "cup of the wine of wrath" that all the hostile nations are to drink, which will cause them to "stagger and go out of their minds." After a long list identifying these nations—the rulers and their people—the enemies of "the Lord of Hosts, the God of Israel" are told: "Drink, get drunk and vomit, fall and rise no more, because of the sword [of divine judgment] that I am sending among you" (25:27).

A similar bitterly hostile attitude is expressed repeatedly in some of the Psalms, where the nations are condemned on national, political grounds (Ps. 2) and are said to have "sunk in the pit they have made" (9:15). They are in an uproar of confusion (46:6) and their "counsel comes to nothing" (33:10). God "holds all the nations in derision" (59:5–8) and will pour out his anger on them (79:6–7), subjecting them to severe punishment (83). The enemies of Israel will be destroyed (108:8–13), with the result that their lands will be filled with corpses (110:6) and their kings will be slaughtered (135:10, 136:17). Vengeance will be executed on the nations and punishment on these hostile peoples (149:7).

A more constructive attitude toward the nations is also evident in the prophetic tradition. In Jeremiah, the hostility of the nations toward Israel functions as the agency for God's punishment of his disobedient people (1:13–19, 2:15–16). A similar opinion is expressed in Habakkuk 1: it is God who is raising up the Chaldeans (Babylonians) to effect judgment on erring Israel, since these people have been "established [by God] for punishment [of his people]" (1:12). Following Ezekiel's series of oracles of divine judgment on the nations that have oppressed Israel (25–30), there is a string of laments for Tyre (27–28) and Egypt (30–32), with the lamentations for the latter including sorrow over the decline of its impressive powers. Remarkable is the affirmation of the wisdom and skill evident in their political and economic strategies, as well as of the beauty of their culture, although they are nevertheless denounced for their pride and idolatry.

Another positive motif in the prophetic attitude toward the nations is evident in the role Jeremiah sees himself as being called to carry out: "a prophet to the nations" (1:5). This includes the expectation that when the covenant of God with Israel is renewed, "Jerusalem shall be called the throne of the Lord and all nations shall gather into it . . . and shall no longer stubbornly follow their own evil way" (3:17). When Israel will one day properly serve the Lord "in truth and justice," then "nations shall bless themselves by [Yahweh] and by him they shall boast" (4:1–2). They will be taught the might and power of God and acknowledge the divine name (16:19–21). In Mic. 4:1–4, when the Temple is restored in Jerusalem, peoples from many nations will came to this house of God "that he may teach us his ways" and that "we might walk in his paths." They will be transformed from agents of war into instruments of constructive productivity. A similar expectation is voiced in Hag. 2:6–7. In Zeph. 3:8–9, the nations are to be transformed and to call on the name of Yahweh.

These themes of Gentile participation in the worship of the God of Israel, which appear in the Prophets and are expanded in Zechariah, predominate in 2 Isaiah and in the later oracles as well as in the so-called apocalyptic section of Isaiah (21–35). But God's sovereignty over and recognition by all the nations are also pervasive themes in the Psalms. "All the ends of the earth shall remember and turn to the Lord, and all the families of the nations shall worship him" (22:27–28). All the earth is called to fear the Lord, and all its inhabitants are to stand in awe of him (33:8–9, 65:5–8). God's sovereignty is over all the nations (47:1–9), and God's holy mountain in Jerusalem is "the joy of all the earth" (48:1). All the nations join to praise and honor God (66:4, 8; 67:2–7). All of them bow before him and glorify his name (86:9), and his judgment, which is grounded in righteousness, will pervade and guide the world (96:3–13). They have all seen the victory of his purpose in the world (98:3) and will join in his worship (99–100). In response, God will welcome their worship and hear their prayers (102:15–22).[1] In the last of the Psalms, the universality of the worship of the God of Israel is enunciated: "Let everything that breathes praise the LORD" (150:6).

After the initial visions of the destruction of the hostile nations in Zechariah 1 and the promises of restoration of Israel (1:17), there is the prophecy that "many nations shall join themselves to the Lord on that day, and shall be my people, and I shall dwell in your midst" (2:11). Representatives of every linguistic group in the world will come to attach themselves to the Jews, saying "Let us go with you, for we have heard that God is with you" (8:20–23). Although, in the final stage of the restoration of Israel, the nations will form a coalition to destroy God's people, and even though the divine response will be one of punishment of these opposing powers (12:3–9, 14:2–12), those who survive this judgment will go up to Jerusalem yearly to worship "the King, the Lord of Hosts," and a plague will fall on those who fail to observe the Festival of Booths (14:16–19).

It is in Isaiah 40–66 that the potential for universal inclusion of the nations in the worship of the God of Israel is set forth in greatest detail. The prophetic description of the renewal of God's covenant with Israel in Isaiah 40–44 includes a prediction of the effective operation of justice in the nations and the attentiveness of Gentiles to God's law (42:4), as well as the appointment of Israel to serve as "a light to the nations" (42:6, 49:6–7). The result will be the acknowledgment by the nations that the only God is in Israel, and so kings and princes will prostrate themselves before the Holy One of Israel, and all humanity will know that God alone is Lord (49:26). The invitation to share in the life of God's people will be universal (55:1–5), and foreigners—even eunuchs—who seek affiliation with Israel will be confirmed and rewarded (56:3–8). When the renewal of Israel and Jerusalem take place, nations and their kings will come there to the light of God and will assist in the rebuilding of the city (60:3–12) and in the supply of basic needs for the people there (60:16), feeding their flocks and tending their fields (61:5). The wealth of the nations will pour into the city (66:12), where even Gentile kings will come to see the glory of God in the midst of Israel (62:2) and where all humanity will come to worship before Yahweh (66:23).

The Issue of Ethnic Inclusiveness in the Apocrypha and Pseudepigrapha

As I noted in chapter 1, openness to Hellenistic culture permeates the Wisdom of Solomon, which was written by an Alexandrine Jew about 100 B.C.E. Its message is addressed without specific reference to Jews, and the exhortation to seek wisdom is for all rulers: kings, magistrates, and princes of the people (6:1–21). These roles, which are assigned by God, must be discharged in accord with wisdom. The cosmic order and structures of the universe are described by Wisdom, who is herself depicted in the technical terminology of Hellenistic philosophy.[2] The virtues wisdom produces in humans are derived from that intellectual tradition: prudence, moderation, justice, and fortitude. Wisdom enables one to understand rhetoric, as well as to discern the past and the future and the outcome of the cycle of the ages—a theme important for Roman Stoics, as I have noted. Yet in the latter third of the book, it is affirmed that God's special favor is enjoyed by the land and people of Israel, and the earlier inhabitants of that land are denounced as cannibals and merciless murderers of their own children. It is to the sons of Israel alone that God "gave the sworn covenants of goodly promise" (12:19–22). Although there is the possibility for all humans to discern God in the order of the universe, the fact is that even eager seekers are distracted, with the result that they are doomed to identify as gods things that human hands have made (13:5–10). The result is that only God's people actually receive the light of knowledge of God and his purposes; all others stumble in darkness (17:1–19:22).

In the Wisdom of Ben Sira, the exclusiveness of the communication of divine wisdom is even more severe, even though the opening verses announce that God has poured out wisdom on all his works and lavished these insights upon his friends. It soon becomes clear that the only ones who are able to discern these divinely bestowed insights are those who are oriented toward the law of Moses: "Reflect on the precepts of the Lord; let his commandments be your constant meditation. Then he will enlighten your mind, and the wisdom you desire he will grant" (6:37). Although God deals with the whole range of human beings from the time of creation, it is with Israel that he has made "an everlasting covenant" and "revealed his commandments to them" (17:11). Perfect wisdom is the fulfillment of the law (19:17).[3] She dwells in Jacob, and in Jerusalem is her domain (24). Yet the main concern of this work is conformity to the personal and social precepts of the law, not to cultic obligations, so that keeping the law is more important than sacrifices and offerings (35:1–6). The highest of human vocations is that of the interpreter of the law (39:1–11). Although the glory of God is said to be revealed in the natural order—a primary principle of Stoic philosophy—it is only among those obedient to Israel's law that this truth is accurately discerned. Israel's neighboring peoples—the Edomites, the Philistines, and the Samaritans—are denounced with bitter hatred. The last of these are so despised that, although they are clearly indicated, they are not directly named (50:25–26).

From these Jewish wisdom writings, it is evident that the potential for universal discernment of God and his purpose through the cosmic order is frustrated by the lack of obedience on the part of non-Israelites to the specific precepts of Israel's law. This exclusivism is made even more explicit in the historical account of the Maccabean revolt, 1 Maccabees, where it is asserted that only those are to be preserved by God who obey the law in its full ethical, ritual, and sacrificial precepts.

A collection of documents that drew for both literary models and details of content on Greco-Roman sources and traditions is the Sibylline Oracles.[4] All these oracles claim to have been the utterances of an aged prophetess and to have their origins at Cumae in Italy, at Erythrea and elsewhere in Asia Minor, or in Persia or Babylonia. Oracles of this type include the official collection in Greek hexameter kept at Rome[5] and the Jewish oracles, which were preserved in Egypt.

The third of the Jewish Sibylline Oracles lists seven kingdoms that will shape the destiny of God's people, Israel, ranging from the kingdom of Solomon to the rule of "a king of Egypt, who will be of the Greeks by race," under whom "the people of God will again be strong" and will become "guides in life for all mortals" (93–95).[6] God will send him as "a king from the sun, who will stop the entire earth from evil war, killing some, imposing loyalty on others; he will not do all these things by his private plans, but in obedience to the noble teachings of the great God" (652–657). The result will be the cosmic renewal of the whole creation (669–701). Yet the focus of the worship of the true God will be the Jerusalem Temple, in the vicinity of which God's children will live in peace, rejoicing in the benefits that his grace supplies (702–704). The special role for Israel and its legal tradition is further affirmed, in that all humanity is enjoined to support the Temple and to "ponder the Law of the Most High God" (715–719). Accordingly, people from every land will share in the worship of the God of Israel in the Temple, which will be the only house of God then in existence. The result will be peace among all humanity, which will be symbolized and confirmed by the transformation of ferocious animals into harmless beasts (767–775).

In sharp contrast to this positive portrayal of the Gentile ruler and his role for Israel's renewal, Sibylline Oracles 4 and 5 are severely critical of the pagan powers and their monarchs. In Oracle 4, hostility is expressed toward Egypt (82–85, 484–496) and even more intensely toward Rome (162–178) because of the idolatrous claims of its leader (Nero). Other oracles in this collection also predict the doom of the Greek kingdoms and of Rome. In Oracle 4, which was written after the destruction of the Temple in 70 C.E. and the eruption of Mount Vesuvius in 80 C.E., there is a list of successive world kingdoms, ending with Macedonia (Alexander, or his successors?), toward which the oracle is most negative. Unlike in Oracle 3, temple worship—including that in Jerusalem—is linked with idolatry and rejected. The savior figure is not an earthly ruler but is of heavenly origin, although he accomplishes renewal of the earth (249–255, 420–427). These prophecies, with their despair of and hostility toward Gentile rulers, while not surprising, contrast the more vividly with the theme that I noted earlier in certain strands of the prophetic tradition, including some parts of the nonbiblical oracular material, where it is asserted that the pagan powers have an essential role in the renewal of God's people and that their subjects may share in the worship of the God of Israel.

An important document that gives evidence of more positive relationships between Jewish and Hellenistic intellectuals is the Letter of Aristeas. Probably written around 100 B.C.E., this letter describes the process and results of the decision by the Ptolemaic authorities of Egypt to ask the high priest in Jerusalem to set up a team of translators to render the Jewish scriptures in Greek. This was considered to be an essential item for the library in Alexandria, which had as its goal to include copies of all the books written throughout the world. Making the request for a translation of the Jewish scriptures, the librarian declares that all humans worship the same God, and that the differences consist only of the names assigned to the deity (16). The Ptolemaic king shows his approval of the project by releasing from slavery more than a hundred thousand Jewish prisoners, an action that he considers to be "a religous obligation to the Most High God, who has preserved for us [Egyptians] the kingdom in peace and highest renown throughout the whole world" (37). The letter to the high priest was accompanied by many costly gifts to the Temple (42). When the high priest complied with the request and sent seventy-two translators—six from each of the twelve tribes, as requested in the letter from Egypt—the king welcomed them with a series of splendid banquets, for which the food was prepared in accord with Mosaic dietary regulations (181, 184). An extended series of theological questions addressed to the translators by their Egyptian hosts points up the basic rational compatibility of their respective approaches to justice and order, cosmic and moral, at both social and individual levels (187–300). The king marveled at the genius of the Jewish lawgiver (312). Divine approbation for the enterprise is given positively by the fact that the whole translation was completed in seventy-two days with universal agreement, and negatively by the ailments with which those were stricken who misquoted or exploited the translated text (313–316). Equally as striking as any of the details of this narrative is the writer's assumption that pious Jews in Jerusalem would have the facility with Greek to undertake this huge translation and to engage in substantive discussion on philosophical issues with their pagan interrogators in Alexandria.

The Appropriation of Hellenistic Concepts and Literary Models for Communicating the Purpose of God for his People Israel

In addition to the adaptation of the Sibylline Oracles by Jewish writers around the turn of the eras, other Hellenistic literary forms were taken over and utilized by Jews for purposes of instruction and propaganda. For example, the writer Ezekiel composed in the second century B.C.E. a version of the story of the Exodus that he modeled in style and emphasis on classic Greek tragedy and that he called *Exagoge*.[7] More common among Jewish writers of this period is the use of a literary mode that has been called "the Hellenistic romance" by modern scholars, although, as I noted in chapter 1, it is not intended chiefly for entertainment.[8] Instead, the aim of this literature is propaganda for a religious group, as Douglas Edwards has persuasively shown in his study of *Chariton* by Xenophon of Ephesus, which like, Apuleius's *Metamorphoses*, seeks to promote the cult of Isis.[9] Examples of this enticing form of religious propaganda by Jewish authors include the books of Joseph and Asenath, Tobit, Judith, and Esther (especially in its longer Greek version).[10] The fascinating details of each story serve to persuade the reader of the reality and importance of the religious experience or mode of devotion that is being recounted.[11] Derived from Hellenistic culture, the genre has been adapted for distinctively Jewish purposes in these didactic narratives.

Other documents from this period give evidence of the intent to show explicitly the basic compatibility of Jewish piety and Hellenistic philosophy, especially Stoicism. Fragments by a writer named Aristobulus, which are preserved in Eusebius's *Praeparatio Evangelica* and his *Ecclesiastical History*, provide clear evidence of the efforts by Jewish intellectuals to correlate their traditions with the insights and structures of Hellenistic philosophy and science. The first fragment offers a correlation between the scriptural mode of dating the Passover and astronomical principles current in the Hellenistic world.[12] Three other fragments provide explanations for the anthropomorphisms concerning God and his activities that occur in the law of Moses. Thus, "the hands of God" is a metaphor for the divine power, just as a description of him as standing is a reference to his divine authority. Similarly, to depict him as resting on the sabbath is a figurative way of representing God's completion of the ordering of the creation. Aristobulus also claimed that Plato and Pythagoras learned their philosophy through access to a translation of the Hebrew scriptures into Greek centuries earlier than the Septuagint, with the result that "Plato imitated our legislation and . . . investigated thoroughly each of the elements in it." Similarly, Pythagoras "transferred many of our doctrines and integrated them into his own system of belief."[13] This matches the claim of Artapanus, an Egyptian historian of the second century B.C.E., in his *Judaica* (also quoted by Eusebius), that Abraham taught astrology to the pharoah of Egypt.[14] The significant feature of these materials is that an intelligent, educated group of Jews living in Alexandria in the Hellenistic and early Roman periods was concerned to demonstrate correlations between the learning of the Greco-Roman world and its own biblical traditions.

The intent of these apologetic analyses of Israel's past and of the biblical depiction of the God of Israel is nicely summarized by Aristobulus: "For it is agreed by all philosophers that it is necessary to hold holy opinions concerning God, a point our philosophical school makes particularly well. And the whole constitution of our Law is arranged with reference to piety and justice and temperance, and the rest of things that are truly good."[15] Significant in this claim is not only the general correlation of the religion of the Jews with Hellenistic philosophy, but also the use of the distinctive terms of Stoic virtue in which Aristobulus sees the aims of the law of Moses to be set forth. Similarly, in the *Testaments of the Twelve Patriarchs*, appeals to obey the law of Moses are intermingled with injunctions to exhibit piety (*eusebeia*), to live in integrity of heart, to be free of duplicity, to possess singleness of mind, and to avoid irreligion (*asebountes*). The Stoic orientation of this ethical system is confirmed by references to behavior that is "contrary to nature" and by appeal to the "conscience," for which there is no correlative Semitic term.[16]

The conceptual antecedents of a characteristic feature of Jewish apocalypticism that divides history into successive periods moving toward decline, as found in Daniel and the Sibylline Oracles, are evident in Greek writers such as Hesiod, whose *Works and Days* depicts the successive ages of human existence.[17] While the Jewish portrayals of the periods differ significantly from those in the Hellenistic writers, it is clear that the apocalypticists are offering their conceptual equivalent of this philosophy of history, which emerged in the Greek world. In chapter 2, I noted the correspondences between the Stoic expectation of a new era of moral rectitude in the future and the Jewish apocalyptic hope of salvation and renewal in the age to come.

Thus many Jewish thinkers of the Hellenistic era were vigorously and imaginatively engaged, not in denouncing the contemporary culture of the Mediterranean world as pagan or diabolical, but rather in establishing correlations between their traditions and what they regarded as the positive, enduring insights and hopes of their non-Jewish contemporaries. A prime representative of this undertaking is, of course, Philo of Alexandria, whose allegorical method enabled him to discern ontological and ethical insights in scripture that were shared with the philosophers of the Platonic and Stoic traditions. I examined his contribution in chapter 5 above in my analysis of the community of mystical participation. The

examples of Jewish appropriation of Hellenistic concepts and terminology that I
have adduced in this chapter are by no means exhaustive, but are offered rather
as representative of a significant trend within Judaism in the period prior to the
fall of Jerusalem and the end of its Temple and priesthood, which led to the rise of
a more exclusive mode of Judaism in the rabbinic period. Ironically, at the very
time that these strategies of cultural correlation were being abandoned by Jews in
favor of emphasis on the distinctiveness of Jewish identity, Christians were actively
employing methods of cultural synthesis. As noted at the beginning of this chapter, the two New Testament writings that best exemplify the attempt to depict the
Jesus movement as inclusive along ethnic, cultural, literary, and conceptual lines
are the Gospel of Luke and the Acts of the Apostles.

The Inclusive Strategy of Luke and Acts

Participation in the New Community as Portrayed in the Gospel of Luke

From the opening lines of the Gospel of Luke to the final page of Acts, the
author builds on the conviction that "the things which have been fulfilled among
us" (Luke 1:1) are founded on the traditions and institutions of Israel. The central
actors in the events that culminate in the birth of Jesus are depicted as "righteous
before God, living blamelessly according to all the commandments and regulations of the Lord" (1:6). The divine disclosure to Zechariah that his wife is to bear
him a son in their old age recalls the experience of Abraham (Gen. 18:11, 26:5),
and comes to him as he is discharging his traditional priestly duties in the Temple
(1:8). The child, John, is to be an ascetic in accord with the law of Moses (1:15;
Num. 6:3, Lev. 10:9, 1 Sam. 1:11). His role as preparer for one to come is like that
of Samuel, whose birth came as a special gift from God (1 Sam. 1:1–20) and
whose major achievement was to anoint David as king of Israel. John is to enter his
divinely assigned role "in the spirit and power of Elijah." His birth will bring fulfillment of promises God made to David (1:69), to the prophets (1:70), and to
Abraham (1:73). His role as preparer is essential for the realization of the "holy
covenant" (1:72). The one for whose coming he prepares will bring in the new
"day which will dawn upon us from on high" and will "give light to those who sit
in darkness and the shadow of death." The latter promise may well be a hint of the
light to the nations that will be brought through the one who is to come.

Similarly, the role of Jesus that is announced before his birth is pictured as
corresponding in detail to the Jewish scriptures. As Son of the Most High, he will
ascend the throne of David and will reign over the house of Jacob forever (2 Sam.
7:12, Isa. 9:6, Mic. 5), and there will be no end of his kingdom (Dan. 7:14). The
Magnificat that celebrates his birth (1:46–55) is a close match for Hannah's song
at the birth of Samuel (1 Sam. 2:1–10), and echoes other scriptures in its details.[18]
Zechariah's prophecy (1:67–79) also consists of echoes of scripture, especially
from the Psalms and Prophets.[19] The importance of this anticipation of the birth of
Jesus within the framework of Jewish hope is articulated in relation to Anna the

prophetess (2:36–38), who lives, worships, and fasts in the Temple continually. Having seen the child Jesus, she gives thanks to God and speaks about Jesus to "all who were looking for the redemption of Jerusalem." It is Jerusalem that will be the scene of the death and resurrection of Jesus, the outpouring of the Spirit, and the launching of the world mission of the church (Acts 1:8). But far beyond the geographical factor, in Luke's account the traditions and hopes of Israel are the starting point for the establishment of the new people of God.

Further, the law-abiding practices of the family of Jesus are made explicit in Luke's gospel: the circumcision, purification, and dedication of the child are all in accordance with the law (Gen. 17:9–14; Exod. 13:2, 12, 15; Lev. 5:11, 12:2–4, 8). All that is done is "according to the custom of the law" (2:27), and "when [the parents of Jesus] had performed everything according to the law of the Lord," they returned to Nazareth (2:39). It was their custom to go to Jerusalem every year to join in celebration of the Passover (2:41), and so they went when Jesus was twelve. Jesus is engaged there in listening to the teachers of the law, raising questions, and displaying his own astounding "understanding" of the law (2:46–48).

Yet the hopes and promises of renewal of God's people are by no means limited in Luke's account to the descendants of Jacob or to those who conform their lives to the law of Moses. The promises of God to Israel are not concerned solely with the future of that ethnically distinct group. Rather, what God has begun with Israel is to offer renewal for the whole of humanity. Accordingly, from the early chapters of Luke onward, it is clear that what is being inaugurated by God through Jesus is to be openness to participation by "all peoples" (2:30). The hope of "revelation to the Gentiles" expressed by the aged Simeon (2:25–35) incorporates insights from Second Isaiah (42:6, 49:6), but it is now asserted to be in process of actualization with the birth of Jesus. In the scriptural justification for the work of John the Baptist, Luke's account (3:4–6) goes beyond the passage quoted from Isaiah 40 in Mark 1:3 by including the promise that "all humanity shall see the salvation of God." In addition to the challenge John offers to the traditional Jewish supposition that descent from Abraham guarantees participation in God's people (3:7–9), he is depicted—only in Luke (3:10–14)—as offering repentance to the masses and inviting such obvious outsiders as soldiers and tax collectors (7:29) to share in the renewal.

The most dramatic evidence of the ethnically and culturally broad audience for Jesus' call to participation in God's people, however, appears in Luke's expanded and relocated account of Jesus' rejection in the synagogue at Nazareth. By placing it at the outset of Jesus' public activity[20] and quoting from Second Isaiah (61:1–2, 58:6), Luke combines a series of claims: A major focus of Jesus' attention in "preaching good news" will be those on the fringe of Jewish society: the poor, the blind, captives, and the oppressed. Jesus declares that this prophecy is already in process of fulfillment through him that very day. In justifying his outreach beyond the limits of traditional piety, Jesus recalls two examples from the prophetic tradition of Israel: Elijah's special help for the non-Israelite widow from Sidon (1 Kings 17:8–24) and Elisha's cleansing the Syrian leper (2 Kings 5:1–19). Similarly, in Jesus' answer to the question from John the Baptist as to whether he is "the one who is to come" from God to establish the new people of God, those whom he identifies as the beneficiaries of his healing and outreach—the poor, the maimed, the blind, and the lame—are precisely those pictured in the prophecies of Isaiah as sharing in the healing, renewing purpose of God (29:18–19, 35:5–6, 61:1).

Throughout Luke's gospel, Jesus is depicted as one with major concern for those religiously, physically, occupationally, or morally excluded from acceptance by the prevailing standards of Jewish piety. Material from Q is reported or adapted to make this point, as is material from Luke's own distinctive source. The Beatitudes, according to Luke, are addressed directly to those in special need—the poor, the hungry, the hated, and the sorrowful (6:20–23)—unlike Matthew's modification of these terms to make them apply to religious condition ("poor in spirit," "hunger for righteousness," Matt. 5:3, 6). Conversely, Luke alone adds to the Beatitudes Jesus' woes against those in socially secure situations: the rich, the full, and those who laugh and are well regarded (6:24–26). Special beneficiaries of his concern and healing powers are marginalized people as diverse as the widow whose son has died (7:11–17), the centurion whose servant is ill (7:1–10), the ten lepers in Samaritan territory (17:11–19), and the woman with an infirmity (13:10–17). Indeed, women figure importantly in the Jesus movement as Luke pictures it, from the wealthy group that provides financial support (8:1–3) to Mary and Martha, who provide housing and meals for Jesus (10:38–42), and the faithful ones who come to prepare the body of Jesus for burial (23:54–56, 24:10) and are rewarded by being the first to hear the news of Jesus' resurrection.

Having reported Jesus' sending the twelve out "to preach the kingdom of God and to heal" (9:1–6) in his own version of the Markan account (6:7–13), Luke describes the mission of seventy—or in some manuscripts, seventy-two—others who are to go before Jesus and prepare the way for his itinerant activity. The symbolic significance of the numbers is probably of prime importance for Luke: twelve corresponds to the number of the tribes of Israel, and seventy or seventy-two is the number of the other nations of the earth according to Jewish tradition.[21] That a mission to the Gentiles is ultimately in view is clearly implied by Jesus' subsequent judgment on the unresponsive Jewish cities (Chorazin, Bethsaida) and the prospect of a penitent reaction from such pagan cities as Tyre and Sidon (10:13–15).

The parables of Jesus in Luke likewise point to the inclusion of marginal people in the faithful community, and to the conviction that this corresponds to the purpose of God. In the Parable of the Good Samaritan (14:15–24), a member of the group despised by Jews for making what they considered to be a counterfeit claim to be the people of God acts in love and compassion to meet the continuing needs of the victim of a vicious attack. In the Parable of the Great Supper

(14:15–24), those who share in the joys of the new era are depicted under the image of a banquet as people who are indeed on the margin of Jewish society or even completely "outside the walls" of Jewish identity. Similarly, in reply to the hostile reaction to Jesus' practice of maintaining contact with sinful people and even violating dietary laws by eating with them, God is portrayed in Luke under a series of images of those who rejoice in the recovery of what has been lost. A shepherd takes the initiative and succeeds in recovering a lost sheep from his flock (15:1–70). A housewife concentrates her efforts and is filled with joy on recovering a lost coin (15:8–10). Then there is the unique Lukan parable of a father who rejoices at reconciliation with his alienated and disobedient son—a response that contrasts with the resentful older brother, who had maintained the family status quo. The implication is clear: Jesus' initiative in reaching out to the outsiders corresponds with the nature and purpose of God, but it is be resented and denounced by the traditionalists whose identity is based on the separatist features of Israelite law.

The same basic point is made in two vivid stories that Jesus tells only in Luke, The Rich Man and Lazarus (16:19–31) and the Pharisee and the Tax Collector (18:9–14). In the former, there is a pair of contrasts between the affluent life of the rich man and his state of torment in Hades, and wretched poverty and bodily ailments of Lazarus as opposed to his place of special honor in the life to come next to Abraham, the progenitor of the covenant people. After the rich man requests that Lazarus be permitted to bring him some relief from his torment and that someone be sent to alert his brothers of their destiny if they continue their self-satisfied, socially irresponsible way of life, he is told by Abraham that, though the brothers have the Law and the Prophets from which they could draw the proper insights, they would refuse to change their attitudes even if someone were to rise from the dead. Clearly, the indictment is aimed at those Israelites who are depicted as continuing to live in withdrawn contentment, even though God has attested the role of Jesus in covenant renewal by raising him from the dead. The other story contrasts the complacent sense of moral superiority of the Pharisee with the contrition and confession of failure on the part of the tax collector. The reversal of status of the two in the day of judgment ("humbled . . . exalted") is then specified (18:14).

An equally vivid point to Jesus' overturning the religious and social norms of his Jewish contemporaries is evident in the story of Zacchaeus (19:1–10). This man is not merely one of those Jews who contracted with the Romans to raise taxes from their own people: he is a chief tax collector. It scarcely need be added that he was "rich." Equally objectionable to pious Jews were the tax collectors' bid for service to an alien pagan power, the cost to local residents that was the collectors' source of income, the fact that, once having paid to the Romans the amount of the contractual obligation, they could keep the rest for themselves, and the fact that the transactions included taxes on ritually impure items in transit from Arabia or Mesopotamia to Mediterranean ports. It is at the home of such a person—objectionable on moral, ritual, and economic grounds—that Jesus is here pictured as inviting himself to stay as a guest. In such a relationship, Jesus would be violating the current Jewish standards of covenantal identity, but he compounds the controversy by affirming that this tax collector is indeed a member of the covenant community ("a son of Abraham"). Then he makes explicit that his role in the purpose of God—"Son of Man," which is linked in Daniel with the establishment of God's rule in the world (7:13–14)—is to "seek and save" those who have been excluded ("the lost").

Drawing on the Q tradition, Luke reports Jesus denouncing the Pharisees and the official interpreters of the Jewish law (11:37–52). Jesus notes not only the hypocrisy of his contemporaries, who, while honoring the tombs of the prophets, ignore their messages, but also the guilt of their ancestors, who killed those who spoke for God. The divine announcement that the Wisdom of God will "send them prophets and apostles, some of whom they will kill and persecute" cannot be documented in any surviving Jewish documents, although it is consonant with the declaration of Jeremiah that, since the days of Israel's Exodus from Egypt, the people have paid no attention to the messengers God has sent to them (7:25–26). Now, however, the indictment is much more severe: it is to "this generation" that responsibility is to be assigned for the rejection and death of all those in the biblical tradition of Israel through whom God was challenging his people.[22] God's judgment on the religious institutions of Judaism is further specified by the prediction of the destruction of the Temple, with no hint of its being rebuilt (21:5–6), and the desolation of Jerusalem at the hands of alien armies (21:30–24). Building on the Markan tradition (13:14–20), as does Matthew (24:15–22), Luke alone notes that this judgment will culminate when "the times of the Gentiles [will be] fulfilled" (21:24).

The involvement and perspectives of Gentiles and marginal Jews are given in greater detail in Luke's version of the trial and crucifixion of Jesus than in the other gospels. At the end of Pilate's interrogation of Jesus, the official pronouncement is, "I find no crime in this man" (23:4). That negative view of the charges brought against Jesus is confirmed by the Gentile-appointed ruler of Galilee, Herod Antipas, who is content to dress Jesus in mock-regal garb in response to the Jewish leaders' charge that he seeks to be their king (23:6–16). The opinion shared by both rulers is that Jesus is "not guilty of the charges against him" of promoting political revolution (23:13–16). Jesus is also exonerated by one of the criminals undergoing crucifixion beside him, who thereupon is promised by Jesus a place with him "in paradise" (23:40–41). Even a condemned criminal who is penitent is welcome among the new people of God. The onlookers most fully described in Luke's narrative of the crucifixion constitute a group that was marginal in the structure of the Jewish community: women, "the daughters of Jerusalem," who are there to lament his death and are warned of the consequential judgments that will fall on their people (23:27–32).[23] The Lukan gospel is consistent in its indications that the participants in the people of God in the new age are those on the periphery of the covenant, or wholly outside the covenant community as defined by the traditional standards.

Participation in the New Community as Pictured in Acts

The theme of the grounding of the new community in the scriptural traditions of Israel is emphatically operative in Luke's postresurrection stories, which explicitly insist on the continuity between what God promised his people in the Law, the Prophets and the Psalms and what he has now done for the renewal of the covenant through Jesus. The risen Christ calls the two disciples on the road to Emmaus "foolish and slow of heart," since they do not believe what "the prophets have spoken": that it was a divine necessity that he should first suffer and then enter his glory. "And beginning with Moses and all the prophets, he interpreted to them in all the scriptures the things concerning himself" (24:13–26). Later he explains to all the disciples that "everything written about [him] in the law of Moses and the prophets and the psalms must be fulfilled." But expanding and transforming this emphasis on the fulfillment of the promises to Israel is the pronouncement that, following his suffering and resurrection, "repentance and forgiveness of sins should be preached in his name to all the nations, beginning from Jerusalem" (24:44–47).

The Preparatory Events and Perceptions for the Inclusive Mission

The rationale for the world mission of the apostles is confirmed by word and deed in Acts. Following the instruction that their witness is to extend from Jerusalem to the ends of the earth (1:8), the Spirit is poured out on a throng including Jews and devout men "from every nation under heaven" (2:5). The miracle described as taking place on Pentecost is that all of them hear the apostles "telling in our own languages the mighty works of God" (2:11). It is also proclaimed by Peter as the fulfillment of the prophecy of Joel (3:1–5), when God announced that "in the last days I will pour out my Spirit upon all humanity." The potential inclusiveness of this opportunity is confirmed in the assurance that "whoever calls on the name of the Lord will be saved" (2:21). Peter's sermon asserts that Jesus' deliverance to death was "according to the definite plan and foreknowledge of God" (2:23). His resurrection from the dead is also said to be in accord with scripture, and Ps. 15:8–11 is quoted to show that his resurrection was indeed foretold. "All the house of Israel" should know that God has made Jesus "both Lord and Christ" (2:36). When the hearers ask what they should do, they are told to repent and be baptized in the name of Jesus Christ, assured that the promise of the Spirit is not only to them and their children, but also "to all that are far off" (2:38–39). How inclusive the participation is to be is not here indicated, but in Peter's sermon in the Portico of Solomon (3:12–26), he declares that, although he and his Jewish hearers are the children "of the covenant which God gave to their fathers," they must recall that God promised Abraham, "In your posterity shall all the families of the earth be blessed" (quoting Gen. 12:3).

The synthesis of grounding in the Jewish tradition and outreach to the wider Gentile world is dramatically evident in Acts 6 and 7, where a differentiation is made between the members of the new community who, like the original apostles, came from a traditional Jewish background and those whose cultural context was Hellenistic. The names of all seven of the latter are unmistakably Greek. Though the explicit reason for designating the seven is that they are "to wait on tables" (6:2), their qualifications are said to be that they are "full of the Spirit and wisdom" as well as "faith" (6:3–5), and the work in which they engage includes "signs and wonders" and debates in the synagogues concerning the role of Jesus in the purpose of God as set forth in the Jewish scriptures (6:8–15).

Called before the Jewish council and charged with speaking in the name of Jesus against the Temple and the law (6:14), Stephen, who is preeminent among the "deacons," sketched the history of Israel, pointing out how the leaders of the people have repeatedly misunderstood God's purpose and rejected his agents and how God's dealings with the leaders of his people have not been exclusively located in the land of Israel. Thus it was in Egypt that Moses was threatened by his people (7:23–29) and subsequently rejected by them (7:35–43). God was first resident among his people when they were in the desert, and even though Solomon built the house of God in Jerusalem, the prophet had the insight that God does not dwell in structures made by human hands (Isa. 66:1–2). The leaders' hostility toward Jesus is said to be in keeping with their ancestors' rejection and persecution of the prophets, and even though the people of Israel received the law, they have not obeyed it (7:48–53). This challenge to the chief symbols and substance of Israel's special relationship to God, which were also the chief source of national pride and regional income, results in the corporate act of executing Stephen by stoning as a major threat to the integrity of the covenant people as officially defined. Divine confirmation of the rightness of Stephen's interpretation of the purpose of God for his people is provided for him and for the reader by the final vision granted him of Christ exalted at God's right hand (7:54–8:1).

Before turning to the account of the conversion of Paul, whose effort to destroy the new movement is mentioned briefly in connection with the martyrdom of Stephen (8:3), it is important to note two other dimensions of the outreach of the new community beyond traditional Judaism: Philip's proclamation of "the good news about the kingdom of God and the name of Jesus" in Samaritan territory (8:12), and his role in the conversion of the Ethiopian eunuch (8:26–39). In Samaria, divine confirmation of Philip's gospel is provided—as in Luke's account of the ministry of Jesus—by signs and wonders performed through him. The conversion of Samaritans by the good news about Jesus is made public by their submission to baptism. The inspection team sent from Jerusalem by the apostles furnishes additional confirmation that this is God's work: those who received baptism are now given the Holy Spirit through the laying on of hands (8:16–18). The evangelism continues as the apostles return through the "many villages" along the road south from Samaria to Jerusalem (8:25).

Philip's next venture for the sake of the good news about Jesus (8:26–39) takes him down the "desert road" that leads to Gaza and the Mediterranean coast and then on to Egypt. There Philip meets a seeker of God returning from Jerusalem to his native Ethiopia, whose origin and physical condition call into question his participation in the covenant according to the dominant Jewish understanding: he is not a descendant of the sons of Jacob, and his castrated state would disqualify him from serving as a priest or approaching the altar of the God of Israel (Lev. 21:20–23).[24] His perplexity about the passage of scripture he was reading aloud as he moved along in the chariot—part of the poem of the Suffering Servant in Isaiah 53—provides Philip the opportunity to explain to him the redemptive significance of the death of Jesus. He comprehends the "good news," affirms it, and makes his commitment public and official by being baptized. This matches the promise in Second Isaiah that in the age to come eunuchs who "choose things that please me and hold fast the covenant" will gain recognition and acceptance among God's people (56:3–5). The Spirit transports Philip to the southern coastal strip, where he extends his evangelistic activity to Azotus (Ashdod) and all the other cities by the Mediterranean—earlier Philistine, and strongly Hellenistic in cultural orientation in this period—ending at the Roman capital of the land, Caesarea. There are now multiple precedents in the activities of the Jerusalem apostles for inclusion of non-Israelites in the new community, but it remains for the conversion of Paul to serve as the focal point at which the practice of outreach to the non-Israelite world will be formulated as an apostolic policy and the strategies to achieve this goal will be adopted.

Assisting in the effort to destroy the Jesus movement as a threat to the institutions of Jewish law and common life is Saul, whose subsequent transformation into a messenger of Christ to the nations of the world is both symbol and model for the divinely intended renewal of the community as a whole. In the letters of Paul, there is no indication of the specific locus of his having "persecuted the church of God violently and tried to destroy it" (Gal. 1:13) or the place where he had been trained in Jewish tradition so that he "advanced in Judaism beyond many of my own age among my people" (1:14). But in Acts 8:1–3, his participation in "ravaging the church" seems to have taken place in Jerusalem, and his authorization to discharge his murderous threats "against the disciples of the Lord" in Damascus was obtained from the high priest in Jerusalem.[25] It was to Jerusalem that the guilty members of the new community ("the Way") were to be taken, presumably for judgment and appropriate punishment (9:1–2). Similarly, there is no hint in Paul's letters of his having studied in Jerusalem with one of the pioneers in what was to become the rabbinic movement, Gamaliel, as he reports in Acts 22:3–5, when he recalls the authorization from the high priest and the council in Jerusalem for his attack on the new community in Damascus. Acts identifies Jerusalem as the base for his striking out against what he sees as a threat to the integrity of the covenant people. What Acts attests is not only his conformity to the Jewish rules for defining covenantal participation, but also his dependence on and support by the established authorities and defenders of that system.

The appearance of the heavenly light is followed by a voice asking Saul his reason for "persecuting me" (9:1–4). Responding to the unidentified speaker politely as "Sir" (kyrios), Saul learns that he is being addressed by Jesus, who is the real target of his persecution and whom he will soon identify as "Lord" (kyrios). Unable to see, he is led into Damascus, where Ananias, identified simply as a "disciple," has been instructed by a vision to place his hands on Saul to enable him to regain his sight. Ananias's reluctance to expose himself to this man armed with "authority from the chief priests" to capture and take back to Jerusalem those who have "called upon the name" of Jesus is overcome when he is assured that this former opponent is now to become a messenger proclaiming that name. Paul is to bear testimony before three types of people: Gentiles, kings (representing the civil authorities, with whom Paul deals extensively in the rest of Acts), and Jews, whom he engages in every city where he goes, including Rome itself (28:17–28). Ananias's apprehension about Saul's being bent on the destruction of the new community is initially shared by the members in Damascus (9:21), but Paul switches immediately to the role of confounding the Jews in Damascus by making a coherent case that Jesus was the Messiah (9:22).

When he returns to Jerusalem, the disciples are afraid to associate with this recent mortal enemy of their movement, but he "preached boldly in the name of the Lord" until the "Hellenistic" Jews there—apparently zealous to preserve the cultic boundaries of the covenant people to which they had committed themselves—begin plotting to kill him (9:29). The leaders of the new community are pictured as relieved when he decides to go back to Tarsus, and they help him on his way. Before Paul is to begin his vigorous and effective program of preaching and teaching among Gentiles, initially in Antioch, he is described as spending time in his hometown, while the churches in Jerusalem and Antioch are prepared by events in the region for the wider mission. Meanwhile, confirmation of the divine support for the work of the Jerusalem apostles is evident through the marked growth of the church "in all Judea and Galilee and Samaria" (9:31) and by the healing and restoration of life that occur through Peter (9:32–42). The result is that many "trusted in the Lord" in the coastal cities of Lydda and Joppa. It is in this vicinity that Acts locates the next major event in the spread of the new community into the ethnically wider Gentile world: the conversion of a Roman military officer through Peter.

Cornelius is portrayed in Acts 10:1–8 as a prime representative of Roman imperialism in the land of Palestine: a centurion of the Italian cohort. His unit is composed, not of regional recruits, but of those from the Roman homeland. Yet he has been prepared for a major personal transition, having become one who honors the God of Israel, together with his entire household. His consequent moral convictions are evident in his generosity and in his continuing prayers to God. His religious yearnings evoke a divine response in the form of a vision instructing him to invite Peter to visit him. The invitation is conveyed by servants and a "pious soldier" (10:7), whose religious stance, though he is a non-Israelite, is another indicator of the potential for the gospel among the nations of the world.

First, however, Peter must be persuaded of the appropriateness and the divine approbation of such associations with Gentiles, especially with an officer of the occupying Roman army (10:9–16). It requires a thrice-repeated vision and a six-times-repeated instruction to get through to Peter that God is urging him to enter into associations with those who, despised as "common" and "unclean," are to become the hearers of his message and the members of God's new people. Confirmation of the visions is provided by the arrival of the messengers from Cornelius, who ask for Peter by name and transmit the officer's invitation for Peter to visit him. Cornelius is described by them as a righteous God-fearer and as one whose favorable reputation has spread throughout "the whole Jewish nation."[26] Peter takes the first step in bridging the broad ethnic and ritual gap that has separated him from non-Jews by inviting the messengers to be his guests. He follows this by accompanying them to Caesarea—the center of Roman power in the land of the Jews—where he is welcomed by Cornelius, who has also invited his own kin and intimate friends.

Peter resists the initial efforts of his hosts to give him personal honors, calling attention instead to the Jewish tradition that would prohibit him from what he is doing: associating or visiting with those of other races (*allophylo*, 10:28). But God, through his recent vision, has set him straight: no human is to be classified as inherently clean or unclean. The new principle he has learned is then enunciated in Acts 10:34: God shows no national or ethnic preference, but is ready to accept those of whatever origin who fear him and do what is right. The truth of this claim is not merely an abstraction, Peter goes on to show, but rests on what God has performed through Jesus of Nazareth: his baptism, his divine anointing (*echrisen*) with the Spirit and power, and his works of healing and exorcism. The Jewish leaders' effort to be rid of him by execution as a rejected member of the covenant family[27] has been countered by God's raising him from the dead and enabling his followers to see and associate ("ate and drank") with him. The apostles chosen by Christ are now to bear witness that "he is the one ordained by God to be the judge of the living and the dead," no matter what their ethnic or cultic background may be. Consequently, "everyone who trusts in him receives forgiveness of sins through his name." The soundness of this understanding is seen as confirmed when the Holy Spirit descended on all who heard this message and they displayed the ability to speak in tongues. The evidence for God's approval of this open access to the life of his new people is persuasive even to the Jewish believers among them.

Acceptance in the community is demonstrated by baptism of the new converts "in the name of Jesus Christ." Peter continues his association with these new members of the covenant people.

The author of Acts makes his point even more emphatically by having Peter recount his experience in detail to the leaders of the community in Jerusalem (11:1–18). Those of Jewish origin and orientation have no rejoinder to Peter's rhetorical question, "Who was I that I could withstand God?" Finally, the apostles as a group give glory to God and establish the basic principle of inclusivity in the community: "Then to the Gentiles also God has granted repentance unto life." The policy in support of the universal inclusion of humanity in the people of God has now been officially formulated by the apostles. The next question for the community leaders will be, How should this ethnically and ritually inclusive expansion of the covenant community be carried out?

The Launching of the Worldwide Outreach

When those earlier associated with Stephen fled north and west to "Phoenicia, Cyprus and Antioch [in Syria]" after his martyrdom, some had begun evangelizing with great effectiveness among the "Greeks" (11:19–21). In order to provide responsible instruction for these new members of the community, who lacked life-long exposure to Jewish traditions, the Jerusalem leaders sent Barnabas to Antioch. The effectiveness of his work was such that he needed major assistance in offering instruction to the flood of new non-Jewish members, and he went to Tarsus to recruit Paul for this task. After coming to Antioch, Paul began to teach "a large company of people,"[28] who "were for the first time called Christians."[29] The church leaders in Antioch included Simeon, "who was called Niger,"[30] Lucius from Cyrene in North Africa, and Manaen, a member of the court of Herod Antipas. These three, with Barnabas, embody the sociocultural spread that was to characterize the movement from this point on. Similarly, the testimony of Paul and Barnabas over the whole length of the island of Cyprus is effective in convincing even the Roman official, proconsul Sergius Paulus, when he perceives the power of "the hand of the Lord" to strike blind a Jewish magician who opposed Paul (13:4–12) and hears the amazing contents of "the instruction about the Lord." Consequently, he joins those who "believe."

At Antioch of Pisidia, on the mainland of Asia Minor, Paul and his associates engage in what becomes for the author of Acts a customary pattern in spreading the good news. The initial proclamation of what God has done for his people and is now doing through Jesus declares that Jesus is descended from David and that, though he was rejected by the Jewish leaders in Jerusalem and killed by the Romans, God's raising him from the dead shows that through him forgiveness and freedom—which the law of Moses could not provide—have been made available for all who trust in him (13:26–41). Even the disbelief of many Jewish hearers is said to be a fulfillment of scripture (13:40; cf. Hab. 1:5). The favorable response of many Jews and proselytes is matched by eager interest in the message from "almost the whole city" (13:43–44), which infuriates the Jewish leaders. Paul responds by drawing from the prophecy of Isaiah to show that it is God's purpose to bring the light of salvation to the Gentiles, even to the ends of the earth (13:46–47; Isa. 49:6). Many respond in faith, but the chief Jews incite hostility among the leading men and women of the city, so that Paul and Barnabas must move on (13:48–51).

After similar activity and results in Iconium—a believing response from a great "multitude" of Jews and Greeks, together with violent hostility instigated by both Jewish and Greek leaders (14:1–6)—Paul and Barnabas experience a different kind of encounter with the Gentile crowds in Lystra (14:8–18). After seeing the healing of a cripple by Paul, the people leap to the conclusion that these two visitors are divine: Zeus, the chief of the gods in the Greek tradition, and Hermes, his chief interpreter. Acclaim by the crowds and an attempt to offer sacrifices to them are the response to Paul's declaration of how God works in the world. When Paul starts to describe God's creation and subsequent ordering of the universe and of human history, his hearers seem to understand this in terms of Stoic belief in the natural order and are thus the more eager to honor these two. The author of Acts is making the point of the compatibility of certain features of Christian affirmation with pagan philosophy, thereby demonstrating the potential for those who promote Christianity to establish rapport with their pagan hearers. Paul is prevented from clarifying the basic differences, however, by a riot and the cruel treatment to which he and Barnabas are subjected at the instigation of Jewish opponents who have come from nearby cities. By emphasizing these details of the story, the author of Acts is warning his readers of the mixed results their own testimony will evoke.

The opposition from Jewish leaders will find a counterpart in hostility from those in charge of the Greco-Roman cults and practices challenged by the apostles, and to these negative reactions from the people will be added the pressure of inquiries by Roman officials concerning this growing, spreading movement. Related to questions of official status is the matter of compatibility and conflict between the apostolic message and such important aspects of Greco-Roman culture as popular philosophy and popular religion, which are represented by everything from major religious institutions to professional prophets and exorcists. It is with such typical features of the Roman world that Paul and his associates are pictured as engaged in the final section of Acts (16–28). But first the standards for Gentile inclusion in the movement must be determined and explicitly enunciated. Precisely at the midpoint of this book (Acts 15) appears the account of the decision reached by the apostles in Jerusalem on the terms for admitting to the new community those of non-Jewish background.

The Formal Policy of the Apostles concerning Gentile Inclusion in the New Community

The issue of requirements from the Mosaic legal tradition for inclusion in the new community was raised by certain members who, having come to Antioch from Jerusalem, insisted that all males must be circumcised to become right with God and thus to share in the blessings of the new covenant ("be saved," 15:1). After local debate over the question, the decision was reached that Paul and Barnabas should pose the issue in Jerusalem in behalf of the church in Antioch and ask for a formal decision from "the apostles and elders" (15:2–5). After reporting en route to the communities in Phoenicia and Samaria on the success of the Gentile mission, Paul and Barnabas present the policy question of Gentile admission in Jerusalem, where the requirement of circumcision has its adherents among members from a Pharisaic background.

After recalling how God had chosen him to be the one to open the door of faith to the Gentiles and how divine confirmation had been provided through their response in faith and the outpouring of the Holy Spirit on them, Peter asserts that no such "yoke" is to be placed "on the neck of the disciples" and that all will find salvation solely "through the grace of the Lord Jesus." This viewpoint is given further support when Paul and Barnabas report the "signs and wonders God has done through them among the Gentiles" (15:12).

Finally, James recalls the passage from Amos 9:11 in which God promised to rebuild the structure of his people ("the dwelling of David"), with the result that "the rest of humanity will seek the Lord, and all the nations will invoke my name upon them" (15:16–17). Gentiles are to be welcomed into membership in the new covenant people, therefore, and only four obligations are to be placed on them. These four are of mixed intent: the first two concern religious and moral issues (abstinence from idolatry and immoral sexual behavior), but the others are matters of ritual restrictions (abstinence from eating meat that comes from animals killed by strangling or that still contains blood).[31] Details of forbidden sexual relations are offered in Lev. 18:1–23. Dietary rules against eating meat with blood in it appear in Gen. 9:4 and Lev. 3:17, 7:26–27, and 17:10–14. The rule against eating flesh of strangled animals is probably an inference from Deut. 12:16, where the blood of a slaughtered animal is to be drained out immediately. Although these requirements are completely incompatible with Paul's account of the agreement reached with the Jerusalem apostles (Gal. 2:6–10), they seem to be reported here in a spirit of modest compromise. The aim is to remove from Gentile Christian behavior the most obvious moral and ritual blemishes that might prevent cordial and easy relationships with Christians of Jewish origin. The importance of this compromise for the author of Acts is evident in his repetition of the policy decision. James is reported as communicating the decision in the form of an official letter (Acts 15:22–29). And it is articulated once again by James and the elders on the occasion of Paul's final visit to Jerusalem (25:17–25). As I shall note below, this stance of compromise on potentially divisive issues matches well with the account in Acts of Paul's participation in rites of purity for himself and others on the occasion of that visit.

New Territory and New Tactics for the Inclusive Mission

After Paul returns to Antioch, he sets out with a new companion, Timothy, to visit the flourishing churches of Asia Minor and to convey to them the policy decision reached by the Jerusalem apostles (16:1–5). But a vision of a man from Macedonia leads Paul to launch a new phase of his mission on the mainland of Europe.[32] His first encounter there is at Philippi, which was named for Philip of Macedon, father of Alexander the Great, described here as the chief city in the Macedonian district and a Roman colony. This designation meant that its local administration and basic laws were Roman rather than indigenous Greek. The symbolism is clear: the gospel is now to encounter those grounded in the traditions of both Hellenistic and Roman cultures.

When Paul goes looking for the local *proseuche*,[33] he finds there, not pious male Jews, but a gathering of women, including a prosperous Gentile woman who has come to honor the God of Israel (16:11–15). Made ready by the Lord to hear Paul's message, she and her whole household are baptized—which indicates once again that commitment to faith in Jesus and admission to the new community do not occur on a simply individual basis. This prosperous seller of a luxury item, purple dye,[34] now invites Paul as a guest to her home. He is pictured as continuing the encounter with the Jews and Gentile seekers at the "place of prayer" (16:16).

The kinds of engagement between the gospel and Greco-Roman culture are evident in the incident in Philippi (16:16–18), which results in a slave girl's loss of her ability—remunerative to her owners—to convey messages from the gods ("a spirit of divination"). This occurs when Paul expels the spirit, after the slave woman has acclaimed him and his companions as "servants of the Most High God," a designation of deity in wide use in the first century among people of various religious orientations. As a result, Paul and Silas are charged by her owners with being disturbers of the peace and advocates of practices in violation of Roman law. Beaten by the crowd and by the civil authorities, they are imprisoned and fettered, but an earthquake during the night releases them. The jailer, astounded by the seismic mode of their liberation and by the fact that they did not run away, listens to and is persuaded by their message about "the Lord Jesus." He asks how he might escape ("be saved") from his professional difficulty, but he hears from Paul how he and all his household might become right with God ("be saved")—an offer accepted by them all. The magistrates' grave problem of having beaten and jailed Roman citizens (for whom a full legal investigation and due process were mandatory) is eased by their agreement to depart from the city. But it also serves the author of Luke and Acts as another bit of evidence that the Roman authorities were uniformly unable to find Jesus, Paul, and their followers guilty of violating Roman law.

Similar developments are described in Thessalonica, which was the chief city of the Roman province of Macedonia and a major center for the worship of many gods and goddesses.[35] The participants in the synagogue there include birthright Jews as well as many Greek men and women who share in the worship of the God of Israel (17:1–4). Many of the latter group, however, join the new community that Paul and Silas are forming, to the great distress of the Jewish leaders, who then accuse the apostles before the city authorities[36] of being disturbers of the peace. Perhaps it is the apostles' proclamation of Jesus' resurrection (*anastasis*) that leads their Jewish opponents to declare that they seek to upset (*anastatosantes*) the whole inhabited world and are "acting against the decrees of Caesar" (17:6). It is precisely the maintenance of peace, order, and Roman sovereignty that is the responsibility of the local governing council. But no formal charge is brought, and after payment of a security bond by Jason, the host of the apostles, Paul and Silas are permitted to escape by night to Beroea. There the reception of their message in the Jewish synagogue is much more positive, including a considerable number of Greek women of high standing (17:12). The entrance into the new community of men and women of ethnic diversity and high social standing is clearly indicated in these details.

It is in Athens, traditional and symbolic center of Greek learning, that Paul has his first reported direct encounter with Greco-Roman intellectuals. His activity in this famed city includes not only debates with Jews and God-fearers in the synagogue, but also public debates with the wider public, including representatives of Epicurean and Stoic philosophy (17:16–18). Since he links a male named Jesus with a female word, *anastasis*, members of the Areopagus (the body responsible for law and order in the public area of Athens) assume that Paul is promoting a new religious cult honoring a pair of male and female divinities like Isis and Osiris, or Venus and Adonis. Hence, they call him to state his position about the deities in their formal assembly place. Near this spot was the towering Acropolis, with its temple of Athena (the Parthenon), the Erectheum (which combined features of worship of Athena and a shrine honoring Erectheus, the legendary king of Athens), and the theater of Dionysus. Also nearby were the splendid courts of the Stoa of Attalos, where crowds gathered and where Paul addressed all who would listen (17:17). Thus the symbolism of this encounter between the gospel and Greco-Roman culture is rich and powerful. The arbiters of public activities do not understand who the alien deities are that Paul is promoting and cannot comprehend "what this scrap-picker is trying to say."

Before this august body, Paul commends the fact that the people of Athens are devoted to the gods and open to new insights about them but deplores the multiplicity of the deities honored in the city as well as the opaqueness of their insights, since an inscription that reads "to an unknown [*agnosto*] god" implies that they do not know God (17:23). After affirming the creativity and omnipotence of the one true God and reciting phrases from Greek writers,[37] he asserts the sovereignty of God over all creation, his transcendence of spatial location, and his intention for all humanity to dwell in unity and harmony, seeking the deity who cannot be represented by human art or imagination. These times of failure to know God (*agnoias*, 17:30) will come to an end when God calls all humans to account and judges them through the one whom he has chosen for this task, as is evident in God's having already raised him from the dead (17:31). The compatibility of this expectation of divine judgment with that of Stoics in the Roman period is another indicator to the reader of Acts that there is a potential for Christians to engage and persuade those reared in a culture wholly alien to Jewish traditions. In spite of the one element in Paul's discourse that is incompatible with Stoic expectations—the resurrection of Jesus as a historical event—the expression of continued interest by some and the decision of some members of the Areopagus to join the new community are indications of the fruitfulness of this kind of engagement.

In Acts 18, the details of Paul's activities in Corinth reveal the ambiguities of relationships between the emergent new community and those committed to Jewish traditional life and practice (vv. 1–4). Among those whom he meets in Corinth are a pair, Priscilla and Aquila, who have been expelled from Rome by the emperor Claudius together with the other Jews there. Apparently the disturbance that led to their expulsion was the coming of the message about Christ, which led to a profound split within the Jewish community and the conversion of this pair. After a period of witness in the synagogue, Paul withdraws and carries on an operation in the house next door in a manner that closely resembles the study and fresh appropriation of scripture going on under Jewish auspices in another adjacent dwelling.[38] Most significant is the report that when the Jewish leaders accuse Paul of teaching contrary to Roman law, the proconsul Gallio expresses the official opinion that there is nothing subversive of Roman laws or authority in what Paul preaches.[39] Instead, the issues are said by Gallio to involve Jewish concepts and legal interpretations (18:15).

Paul's continuing commitment to and involvement in Jewish piety are evident when he has his hair cut—apparently in accord with Nazirite ascetic vows (Lev. 6)—before departing for the eastern Mediterranean (Asia Minor, Syria, and Palestine) to visit and "strengthen" members of the new community ("disciples") and also to debate with Jews in their synagogues (18:18–23). In Ephesus, Paul meets Apollos, who has been converted to "the way of the Lord" and is able to expound effectively "the things concerning Jesus," even though there are gaps in his knowledge that Priscilla and Aquila are able to supply, especially with regard to the presence and power of the Holy Spirit within the life of the community (18:24–28). Apollos symbolizes the diversity of the ways in which Jews throughout the Roman world responded to the news about Jesus, as well as their need for careful instruction to confirm continuities between the traditional Jewish understanding of covenant and the new features that Jesus is seen as adding.

The importance of the presence of the Holy Spirit in the lives of the members of the new community is underscored when Paul finds converts in Ephesus who have not received the Spirit. The formal laying on of hands conveys the Spirit, with evident results in their ability to speak in tongues and prophesy (as in 1 Cor. 14). When his debates in Jewish gatherings over a period of three months are met with fierce resistance, Paul moves to a public lecture hall,[40] taking the converts ("disciples") with him (19:1-9).

The author of Acts makes the astonishing claim that during the next two years all the residents of the province of Asia, both Jewish and Greek, hear "the word of the Lord" (19:10). Divine confirmation of Paul's message and his redefining of the covenant community in this inclusive way is provided by the miracles of healing and exorcism that he is reported as performing (19:10-12).[41] An attempt by Jewish exorcists to exploit the power of Jesus' name meets with divine punishment at the hands of one of the possessed and leads to the conversion of many of the magicians (19:13-19), thereby increasing the powerful effects of "the word of the Lord" (19:20).

Another kind of encounter with Greco-Roman culture is described as occurring in Ephesus in reaction to Paul's success in converting a "considerable company of people" from devotion to the fertility goddess Artemis, whose magnificent temple there was an architectural wonder that brought worshipers and wealth to this city. Devotion to the goddess and the income from producing sacred objects honoring her are seriously threatened by the effectiveness of Paul's preaching. Among those seeking to protect Paul from the wrath of the mob are "Asiarchs," wealthy aristocrats who constituted the regional council and whose duties included the maintenance and fostering of the local and imperial cults as well as the stability and welfare of the region. When the town clerk is finally able to quiet the crowd chanting the greatness of Artemis, someone named Alexander tells the mob that Paul and his companions are "neither sacrilegious nor blasphemers" and that it is the accusers who are the real disturbers of the peace.[42] The linking of Artemis with the meteor "which fell from the sky" may be an intentional analogy with the Christian claim that Jesus was sent from God. The pattern is set for the kinds of public opposition the new community will encounter, from both Jewish and Gentile instigators, and for the line of legal defense to which they should appeal.

As Paul brings to a conclusion his ministry in Greece and Asia Minor (20:1-37), his return visits to the cities where he has worked involve him in contacts with individuals whose names also occur in his letters, in the form of greetings or as co-workers.[43] Naming them serves a double purpose for the author of Acts: it shows that there is a large group of respected witnesses of the origins of these churches in predominantly Gentile settings, and it evidences the solid support that Paul and his mission had across the Mediterranean world. Mention of the Jewish holy days (20:6) and Paul's eagerness to be in Jerusalem on the day of Pentecost confirms the continuity between the new movement and the legally respected pattern of Jewish piety. When the community gathers to "break bread" (20:7), the term used is once again the verb (*synegmenon*) akin to the noun *synagoge*. The fluidity of the terms for church leaders is apparent when the elders (*presbyterous*) mentioned in Acts 20:17 are referred to in Acts 20:28 as overseers (*episkopous*). The latter term is used of the leaders as shepherds caring for (*poimainein*) the flock of God's people, an image used throughout both the Old and New Testament.[44] The flock (*poimniou*) has been "purchased" or "acquired" or "brought into being"[45] through the blood of God's Son, but it will be endangered by the "perverted things" that some will utter in order to draw away the disciples from God's true flock. In a concluding autobiographical sketch (20:32–35), Paul entrusts them "to God and the message of his grace," which can make them a holy people (*hegiasmenois*), and concludes with a reminder of his own selfless service (*hyperetes*) in their behalf.

Paul Confronts Charges of Violation of Religious and Civil Laws

Following reports of his tearful farewell to members of the community in Asia Minor (20:36–38) and then in Tyre, Ptolemais, and Caesarea (21:1–8), where he is warned that in Jerusalem he will be seized by the Jewish leaders and turned over to the custody of the Roman officials (21:9–16), Paul and his companions ("we") proceed to Jerusalem. Welcomed by the leaders of the community there, Paul reports to James that not only have Gentiles been brought to faith through his ministry (*diakonia*), but also the tens of thousands of Jews who have believed are "all zealous for the Law." This does not fit with the charges by the Jewish leaders that Paul is promulgating "apostasy from Moses" among Jews in the dispersion (21:21). To provide a public demonstration of his commitment to the legal traditions, Paul is urged to join and pay the expenses for a group of four who have taken a Nazirite vow in order to prove the purity of their devotion to God under the law (Num. 6:1–18). The terms for admission to the new covenant people agreed upon by the apostolic council in Jerusalem (Acts 15) are repeated (21:25–26), and Paul conforms to them. He gives public testimony in the Temple affirming his commitment to the recommended period of purification, but before it is complete, his enemies accuse him of teaching contrary to the law and of having brought an impure Gentile into the inner courts of the Temple (21:27–29).[46] The crowd seizes Paul and tries to kill him outside the Temple, but he is saved from death by a Roman officer, who takes him into the military barracks to protect him from his attackers and to assure that justice is done in spite of the popular demand that he be executed. Ironically, the Roman soldiers carry him to save him from the Jewish mob demanding his death (21:35).

At this point there begins a series of hearings before various civil religious authorities, all of them exploring the charge that Paul and his associates are violating Jewish and Roman law and therefore constitute a threat to the maintenance of law and order. The first of these encounters (21:31–40) leads to a hearing before the Roman military officer (*chilarch*) in charge of the troops stationed in the tower overlooking the Temple courts. The officer asks if Paul is the leader of the

Jewish nationalists (*sikarioi*),[47] to which he replies in Greek that he is from the renowned city of Tarsus in Cilicia[48] and then asks permission to address the crowd gathered below the tower. His speech is "in the Hebrew dialect" (probably Aramaic is intended), and he reports having studied in Jerusalem with Gamaliel.[49] He affirms the strict interpretation of the law to which he was committed and the zeal he had shown in his persecution of the men and women of "the Way," whose reinterpretation of the Jewish tradition he regarded as subversive (22:3–5). His efforts to destroy this movement had the sanction of "the high priest and the whole council of [Jewish] elders."[50] The heavenly vision and message granted to him (22:12–21) were interpreted for him by Ananias, whom he characterizes as "devout with respect to the Law." Paul describes how he was baptized and later instructed, in another vision that came to him as he was "praying in the temple," to go "far away to the Gentiles." Following his denunciation by the crowd, he learns that the Roman tribune is about to examine him by scourging, but he appeals to his status as a Roman citizen, which guarantees him a proper trial before any punishment can be administered (22:22–29).

The next hearing is before the regional council, consisting of local leaders in Jerusalem (*synedrion*). Paul's claim to have "lived before God in all good conscience"—a Stoic expression—draws a rebuke from the high priest, who regards this as a lie. Paul's defense builds on his claim to share with the Pharisees a belief in the resurrection, which evokes a dispute among the Jews and an affirmation of his innocence by the Pharisees. Again he is rescued from his Jewish antagonists by a Roman military officer. When the chiliarch learns of a plot to kill Paul, he decides to send him with a large military guard to Caesarea for a hearing before Felix, the incumbent governor (22:30–23:34). The high priest appears there, charging Paul with being "an agitator of Jews throughout the world" and with having "profaned the temple." Paul's defense asserts that, although he has taken his stand with the new community ("according to the Way"), he worships "the God of our fathers" and believes everything in "the law and the prophets." He had come to Jerusalem with "alms and offering" to undergo ritual purification (24:1–23). While explaining his faith to Felix and his Jewish wife, Paul makes his defense in terms that are Stoic in origin but compatible with Jewish tradition as well: justice (*dikaiosune*), self-control (*egkrateia*), and future judgment.

Paul is imprisoned for two years, but after the arrival of Festus, Felix's successor as governor, and the repetition of the charges of the Jewish leaders against him, another hearing takes place in Caesarea (25:1–12). Paul denies once again that he has violated either Roman or Jewish law, and then asks to have his case heard before the ultimate tribunal to which he as a Roman citizen has access: that of Caesar. Festus agrees to send him to Rome, but first arranges for another hearing in the presence of the puppet king, Herod Agrippa, and his wife, to whom he explains (25:13–22) that he has found no evidence to support the charges brought against Paul and has concluded that the issues are internal to the Jews' own religion (*deisidaimonia*).[51] He affirms the basic Roman legal principle that a trial must involve direct confrontation of the accused by his accusers and an opportunity for the accused to offer a defense (*apologia*) against the charges.

In a formal setting with all pomp and ceremony in the presence of the officials and prominent residents of the city, Paul offers yet another apology (25:23–26:23). Expressing gratitude that he can present his case before such a one as Agrippa, who knows well "all the customs and controversies of the Jews," Paul reaffirms his roots in Jewish beliefs and practices and then describes his encounter with the risen Jesus and his call by God to carry to Jews and Gentiles the light that has come from the crucified, risen Christ. Then Paul challenges the king to believe this message, the scriptural basis of which he knows so well, and affirms the complete truth and rationality of what he has asserted. Agrippa scoffs at the suggestion that he should identify with the Christian movement, but joins with the governor to declare the innocence of Paul with respect to the charges that have been brought: "This man is doing nothing to deserve death or imprisonment."

Paul's voyage in custody to Rome is portrayed in Acts with vivid details concerning route, winds, and escapes from imminent disaster (27:1–28:10). Greeted and hosted by members of the new community at the Italian port of Puteoli and along the Appian Way to Rome (28:11–16), the author is demonstrating the presence and activity of the new people of God in the commercial centers of Roman life, culminating in Paul's being welcomed by leaders of the Jewish community in Rome itself (28:17–22). Paul denies having acted against "the people or the customs of our fathers" (28:17) and when provided an opportunity, explains that his message of the kingdom of God is based on "the law of Moses and the prophets" (28:24). When some are convinced while others reject his message, Paul appeals to the prophet Isaiah (Isa. 6:9–10; Acts 28:26–27) to show that even the disbelief of the Jews is in fulfillment of the prophetic pronouncement about the future of God's people. He concludes with the declaration, "Let it be known to you that this salvation of God has been sent to the Gentiles, and they will hear." The narrative ends with a report of Paul continuing his life in custody in Rome, carrying out the twofold role of "preaching the kingdom of God and teaching about the Lord Jesus Christ" (28:31). The Roman authorities allow him complete freedom to carry on his work in the capital city, where he lives at his own expense.

The testimony that Jesus called the apostles to bear (Acts 1:8) has now moved from the central focus of Jewish tradition in Jerusalem to the center of Gentile power in Rome. Acts makes the case for its legitimacy in terms of both Jewish and Roman law, and its potential for bringing people from the entire range of religious, social, and cultural backgrounds into the new community of God's people. It has often been conjectured that the author of Acts intended to write a third volume in which he would describe the trial of Paul before the emperor, and possibly the further spread of the gospel to more remote parts of the Greco-Roman world. But he has made his point most effectively in this pair of books as we have them: from the outset of Jesus' career and in keeping with the message implicit and explicit in the Law and the Prophets, the divine intention was for men and women of all ethnic origins to be invited to participate in the life of the new covenant community. The strategies and the message, as well as the problems involved in this vast undertaking, are signaled in Luke and Acts, in which the author traces the divine purpose accomplished through Jesus and Paul for establishing the ethnically and culturally inclusive people of God.

The Community Models Develop   **7**
in the Post–New Testament Period

The continuing impact of the models of community that arose in postexilic Judaism and evolved in early Christianity is evident in the Jewish and Christian literature of the second and subsequent centuries, in spite of major developments in both movements toward institutionalization. Internal and external factors contributed to a process of reshaping for the early Christian communities as early as the end of the first and the opening years of the second century C.E. With respect to Judaism, these forces for change included such political events as the failure of the second Jewish revolt led by Bar Kochba (132–135), which brought to an end the option of a politically independent existence and identity for Israel.[1] Of direct importance for the Christians was the beginning under the Roman emperor Domitian (81–96 C.E.) of imperial efforts to hinder the spread of Christianity.[2] Even more significant was the formulation of imperial policy concerning the Christian movement, as evident in Trajan's correspondence with Pliny (*Letters* 96), which declared that Christians were not to be sought out, but when identified as such, they were to be punished if they refused to deny publicly the charge that they were Christians or to offer worship to the traditional Roman gods. These developments in the imperial assessment of Christianity drastically reduced the political option for Christians awaiting the coming of the kingdom of God, but they did not permanently eliminate the city model, as becomes evident in the post-Constantinian period.

Within the various branches of early Christianity, forces characteristic of religious movements in general were at work transforming the informal structures and spontaneous leadership of the movement into organized and defined patterns. These social developments are evident as processes that had already begun when the Gospels were written but are most apparent when one moves from the earlier stage of that tradition (Q and Mark) to Luke and Matthew, as I noted above in chapters 3 and 6. A similar evolution is even more obvious in the later Pauline tradition, which shifts from the informal, spontaneous, and ad hoc forms of leadership and group organization evident in the authentic letters of Paul to the explicit definition of roles and the resultant hierarchy of leadership in the deutero-Pauline letters.[3] The same trend can be discerned in the Johannine letters.[4] The writings subsequently produced in the early church from the second to the fourth century—the so-called Apostolic Fathers and the works of the Alexandrine fathers, as well as dozens of writers whose work is preserved only in fragmentary quotes by Eusebius in his *Ecclesiastical History* —show how dynamic were the trends toward authoritarian structures and explicit guidelines for moral life and church organization. These writings manifest not only the vitality of the movement, but also the diversity of the prescriptions that their authors had to offer for meeting various sociostructural needs. In what follows, I shall trace the ways in which the basic models for the community of faith survived or were altered in light of the subsequent historical developments. The roles perceived for Christ as well as for the leaders of the church varied widely in the period before the early fourth century, when the power of the empire became linked with the authority of the church through the establishment of the church under Constantine, and pressure mounted for ecclesiastical conformity and uniformity. The continuing influence of Hellenistic philosophy in the second and third centuries, especially the later Platonic and Stoic forms, led in some cases to conceptual conflicts within the church and in others to accommodation in a variety of patterns. I turn, then, to sketch some of the ways in which the models survived or were transformed in the second to fifth centuries.

The Community of the Wise

The continuing impact of the model of the community of the wise is apparent from the second century on in at least three different modes. The first of these is the community that claims to have been granted apocalyptic wisdom by God. The second is the synthesis of philosophical wisdom from the wider Hellenistic world articulated by pagan philosophers in connection with an older religious tradition. This approach is evident among those Christian thinkers who sought to show the compatibility of these philosophical insights with both Jewish and newer Christian scriptural traditions. The third mode is the rise of Gnosticism.

Apocalypse as Disclosure of Divine Wisdom to the Faithful

The failure of the Jewish revolts of 66–70 and 130–135 to establish an autonomous Jewish state did not bring expressions of apocalyptic hope to an end. Similarly, although the nonfulfillment of the early church's expectation of the *parousia* of Christ in triumph to establish God's rule in the world raised problems that were being dealt with in the later New Testament writings,[5] for many it did not stifle the apocalyptic hope. The continuing development of apocalyptic in relation to the traditions associated with Ezra (4 Ezra), Enoch (especially the Similitudes of Enoch), and the Sibyllines have been discussed in chapter 2. In the Vulgate's Christian additions to 4 Ezra (1:1–2:48 and 15:1–16:78), which probably date from the first quarter of the second century, Jews are denounced for failure to keep the covenant, and Gentiles take their place as the people of God. Predictions of the destruction of Babylon are probably references to the divine judgments that are to fall on Rome and its empire, including other peoples of the empire who oppose and harrass God's people (the church). The days of tribulation are near, and only the truly obedient will survive this time of severe testing.

Subtle transformations are discernible, however, in the apocalyptic mode of communication and in the corresponding understanding of the community as the recipient of divine information about the future of the world and of God's people. The more traditional apocalyptic outlook is evident in the Didache, an early-second-century Christian manual of church order, where there is a warning of the increase of lawlessness and of the surge of persecution of the faithful that will precede the "sound of the trumpet" announcing the resurrection of the dead and the coming of the Lord "on the clouds of heaven" (16.6). But in the mid-second-century Shepherd of Hermas, a shift has occurred. The Shepherd is composed of three major sections: visions, mandates, and parables. These revelations are followed by explanations, the major themes of which are the possibility of forgiveness for post-baptismal sins and the rule for life that the repentant faithful are to follow. Missing are the typical apocalyptic features of cosmic conflict and the future triumph of the power of God over the disobedient cosmos. Instead, apocalyptic features are in many cases treated as symbols and transmuted into promises of individual renewal and fulfillment. There is no disclosure of when the end of the age will occur, and no depiction of the age to come. Apocalyptic in the Shepherd seems to be in process of transformation into a didactic literary device rather than providing special information for the faithful in the face of cosmic conflict, like earlier apocalyptic.

The earlier style of apocalyptic understanding of the church and its destiny is set forth in a series of Christian apocalypses. The Ascension of Isaiah contains an account of the martyrdom of Isaiah (1–5) and a description of his heavenly journey and prophetic vision (6–11). The first part is probably of Jewish origin in the late first century C.E. and contains a tradition concerning the persecution of the faithful that may be echoed in Heb. 11:37. The visions that follow date from the second century but are reported in the extant version—edited by Christians—as predictions of the incarnation, death, and resurrection of Christ. In these visions, the heavenly journey of Isaiah is a precedent for the ultimate transport of the faithful into the presence of God. A cosmic conflict with Belial, and his evil angels will be followed by the destruction of the empire. But the major interest is the divine deliverance of God's people and the ultimate glorification of the exalted Christ. Similarly, the Apocalypse of Peter, which comes from the second half of the second century, is chiefly interested in life after death for the faithful as well as eternal punishment of the wicked.[6] But it also provides guidelines for leadership roles in the church (instructors, preachers, and leaders), and it includes the familiar apocalyptic features of the false Messiah, the day of universal judgment, the horrible punishment of the wicked (7–12), and the blessed state of the righteous (13–16). That such predictions were common among Christians in this period is apparent from the scornful comments of the philosopher Celsus concerning the Christian soothsayers and prophets who predicted salvation for believers and eternal punishment for those who rejected them and their message.[7]

The Apocalypse of Paul, in which mention of a Roman consul indicates a fourth-century date, manifests the further development of this trend of early Christian apocalyptic away from primary concern for the overcoming of the powers of evil to attention to the blessed future of the righteous and the doom of the wicked. References to the battle of the forces of good and evil are brief, but the blessed estate of the righteous is contrasted in detail with the punishment of the wicked. The entrance of the faithful into the city of God, with its river of milk and honey, is pictured over against the city of evil, filled with darkness and torture for the evil ones. There are depictions of successive heavens, of the renewal of the earth— for example, vines laden with ten thousand bunches of grapes—and of paradise, which is the final blessed state of the righteous. The concluding scene is of Christ commending Paul to the twelve apostles, with the message to renew the revelation given to Paul (2 Cor. 12). As in all the Christian apocalyptic documents (including adaptations of Jewish originals), wisdom concerning the future of the creation and of God's people is vouchsafed only to the elect community of the wise.

The continuing appeal of apocalyptic schemes in the early Christian world is evident in the rise and extended impact of the Montanist movement in Phrygia, which took its name from its founder, Montanus, whose claim to know the future was based on the word of prophetesses associated with him. Montanus urged his hearers to adopt a strict ascetic mode of life in preparation for the *parousia* of Christ and to abandon home and family in expectation of the end of the age. All who refused to adopt this discipline were to be excluded irrevocably from the people of God. Martyrdom was held to be the way to gain God's highest reward. Montanus's followers acclaimed him as the Paraclete incarnate and fostered expectation of the imminent coming of the end of the age. His critics, cited by Eusebius, accused him of exploiting this prophetic movement for personal gain.[8] The enduring effects of the movement were to discredit prophetic claims and millenarian expectations among the leaders of the church, but the broad appeal of the movement shows how effective this apocalyptic model for God's people was.

Several of the leading thinkers who enjoyed wide respect within the church, whose theological systems were oriented in other directions, also included in their writings predictions of the coming of the millennium, in which God's purpose for his people would triumph. For example, Justin Martyr (100–165 C.E.) affirms in his *Dialogue with Trypho the Jew* (80) that Jerusalem will be rebuilt at the end of the present age, and that God's new people will be gathered in the presence of the patriarchs and prophets during the millennium that will follow. Similarly, Irenaeus describes in his *Against Heresies* (5.31–33) how the faithful dead, like the disciples before them, will depart to an invisible place where they will await the resurrection, which will take place at the return of Christ. They will receive the promised kingdom when the creation is renewed and the final judgment takes place. Justin quotes with approval the description by Papias of the enormous fertility of vines and grain in the new age, which will result in the production by a single vine of what has been calculated as two and a half sextillion measures of wine![9] It is significant that Eusebius, patron of and adviser to Constantine when the establishment of the church was taking place, characterizes Papias as someone "of very little intelligence."[10] Tertullian pictures the kingdom of God on earth, after the return of Christ and the resurrection of the dead, lasting for a thousand years, based in the rebuilt city of Jerusalem (*Against Marcion* 3.24.3). This event has been foreseen by Ezekiel (48:30–35) and John (Rev. 21:2). The saints who have died will be raised in chronological sequence according to the degree of their merits, and will be refreshed with every spiritual good. This will be followed by the judgment of the wicked and the destruction of the evil world, and by the transport of the faithful to the heavenly kingdom.

As late as the fourth century, some Christian writers, such as Lactantius in his *Divine Institutions* (7:21–24), continue to describe the final judgment and the destruction of the world by fire, with the righteous surviving unharmed and the souls of the wicked confined until the final judgment. Cyril of Jerusalem (315–386) offers in his *Catechetical Lectures* (15.11–12) what might have been the politically dangerous prediction, in the epoch of Constantine, that before the true Christ comes, the adversary of God will seize power in the Roman empire, confirming his position by magical acts and declaring himself to be Christ. Many, including Jews, will be deceived by him. He will be cruel and murderous in his dealings, retaining power for three and one-half years, until the true Christ returns and destroys him by the breath of his mouth. Clearly, the hostile attitude toward an establishment of secular political power and idolatrous religion that pervades Jewish and early Christian apocalyptic did not disappear even with the union of church and empire under Constantine.

The Community's Synthesis of Philosophy and Scriptural Truth

Of a very different order from these apocalyptic writings and themes are the documents that, while purporting to display divine wisdom, give evidence of the impact of Hellenistic philosophy and the synthesis of Christian faith with Hellenistic philosophy in the second and third centuries. God has provided the faithful community with insight into the origin of the universe, his purpose, and the mode of life that should characterize his people. The precedent for this model, as I noted in chapter 2, was established by Jewish thinkers of the last two centuries B.C.E. and the first century C.E., of which obvious examples are the Wisdom of Solomon and the extensive writings of Philo of Alexandria.

The synthesis of concepts and insights derived from the Jewish biblical tradition with elements from Stoic philosophy is also apparent among Christians as early as the letters of Paul and James. Similarly, essential features of the Platonic concept of the realm of the ideal have been adapted to the Christian tradition in the Letter to the Hebrews. The direct apologetic writings of the mid-second century, however, set forth in more general terms the rationality and credibility of the Christian faith, employing the concepts, values, and assumptions of later Greco-Roman philosophy. The apology of Aristides of Athens addressed to the emperor Hadrian, for example, is content to infer the existence and activity of the God who is "unsearchable in his nature" behind and beyond the natural order of the visible world. Aristides contrasts the barbarians' deification of elements and forces in the cosmos and the Greeks' attribution of grossly immoral behavior to the gods (stealing, jealousy, oppression, incest, murder) with the Christian understanding of God as a being of unity, compassion, and lofty moral demands.

Justin Martyr, who was born in Flavia Neapolis (Nablus) in Palestine, was trained in philosophy and made his way to Rome, where he founded a school of Christian philosophy. In his apologetic writings he noted the failure of earlier peoples to use reason (*logos*) in understanding the universe and its origins. Socrates is commended by Justin for seeking to free humanity from obsession with and enslavement to the demonic powers, which have been treated as gods. The true God, Justin affirms, disclosed himself through the Word (*logos*) that took on human form: Jesus Christ. Understandably, Christians are called atheists by those devoted to the traditional gods of Greece and Rome, because they do not worship these deities fashioned by misguided humans. The coming of the true Logos was foretold by the prophets of Israel, and the people Jesus has called into being celebrate his life, death, and resurrection. At the end of the second century, the same theme is developed by Tertullian, a native of Carthage, in his *Apology*. By Roman standards, Christians are atheists, he declares, but the one invisible God that they worship brought forth the universe (*kosmos*) from nothing by the word of his command and by the power of reason. His plan encompasses the whole of human history, and in the present final cycle of the world,[11] God's faithful followers already include people from every country and place on the earth. So rapid has been the spread of this inclusive new community that Tertullian declares, "We are but of yesterday, and already we have filled your world: cities, islands, fortresses, towns, marketplaces, the camp itself, tribes, companies, the palace, the senate, the forum." Then he adds, with irony, "We have left you nothing but your temples only!"[12]

It was in the eastern intellectual center of Alexandria, however, that the most elaborate and effective efforts were made to show the basic correlations between

Greco-Roman philosophy and the truths derived from scripture. As I observed in chapter 2, the great Jewish thinker Philo developed the allegorical method of exegesis of Torah in order to show the basic compatibility between the insights derived from the Bible and those set forth in the then-dominant philosophical synthesis of Platonic and Stoic thought. Later, the leaders of the Christian school in Alexandria are described by Eusebius as "powerful in their learning and zeal for divine things" as they seek to foster the development of an intellectual community that will be respected by the pagan philosophical community, with which it shares many aspects of wisdom. In the year when Commodus assumed sovereignty as emperor (180), Pantaenus was made head of this school. He was described as "especially eminent" intellectually and "influenced by the philosophic system of those called Stoics." Until his death, he continued to "expound the treasures of the divine doctrine." On a mission to India, he is said to have found a copy of the Gospel of Matthew written in Hebrew. His prize pupil was Clement of Alexandria.[13]

For Clement, the gospel is the meeting point of Hellenistic and Jewish thinking, and philosophy is the gift of God through the Logos. Nothing is to be believed that is unworthy of God; hence reason is to be the judge of revelation. Any seeming conflicts between the Old Testament and the New are to be handled through the allegorical method of interpretation. All of scripture can be viewed at two levels: the literal, which is for the masses, and the mystical, which is for the enlightened. All knowledge rests on a set of axioms communicated to the wise by God. There were earlier insights by philosophers and teachers into the realm of the infinite, but that realm has now been fully disclosed through the Trinity. Knowledge is to be attained in stages: through baptism comes initiation into the little mysteries, and through self-control one can gain knowledge of the greater mysteries. Instruction from God accomplishes the proper orientation toward truth and leads to the ultimate experience of the faithful and wise: direct contemplation of God, which is called *epopteia*, a term borrowed from the Eleusinian mysteries. The Son of God is identified with wisdom, knowledge, and truth; through these divine instruments are communicated to the wise the nature and purpose of God.[14] Faith brings comprehensive knowledge of the essentials and enables one to become truly enlightened, with an accurate and noble conception of the universe. In his treatise known as *Stromateis*, Clement describes the process by which true knowledge is achieved: regarding the creation with wonder;[15] belief in what one hears about God and his providence; eagerness to learn by every means; partaking of the will of God; transition from moral laws to higher and more universal truths; steadfastness of soul in spite of bodily calamity; love for one's fellow creatures; freedom from control by the passions; engaging in praise of the divine and seeking what is noble; fixing one's eyes upon noble images; and despising pain and persecution. The result is that the beautiful soul becomes the temple of the Holy Spirit.[16]

It is in the writings of Origen, successor to Clement as head of the school in

Alexandria, that the synthesis of philosophy and scriptural exegesis reached its apex. Major influences shaping Origen's thought were the Philonic tradition of allegorical exegesis of scripture based on Platonic philosophical traditions and the rise of Neoplatonism in Alexandria during his lifetime under the influence of Ammonias Saccas and Plotinus. The result of these influences was that Origen's understanding of Christian faith and shared life fits more appropriately into the fourth of my categories, the community of mystical participation described at length in chapter 5, and is thus discussed below.

Wisdom as the Agent of Deliverance from the Material World: Gnosticism

Since the discovery of the Gnostic library at Nag Hammadi, scholars have debated when and in what cultural setting Gnosticism arose.[17] The Gnostic documents vary in subject matter and point of view, but the dominant theme in this collection—which matches well the long-known attacks on the Gnostics by Christian writers of the second and third centuries—is the divine gift of insight into the true nature of the human problem, involvement in the material world, from which Christ is able to provide escape for those with true knowledge into the eternal realm of the Spirit.

The scholarly theory of the nineteenth- and early-twentieth-century history-of-religions school about the existence of pre-Christian Gnosticism has come to be regarded with caution by most scholars, but use by Jewish and New Testament authors of such terms as "wisdom" and "knowledge" and of mythological imagery similar to that found in the Gnostic documents by writers before the Common Era still leads leads some contemporary historians of Christian origins to continue to assert the older theory. The appearance within the New Testament of terms that were later used by the Gnostics is obvious. Paul writes in his letters about *gnosis*, its imperfections and its transitory quality (1 Cor. 13:8–10). In the deutero-Pauline First Letter to Timothy, the writer calls for avoidance of "the profane chatter and contradictions of what is falsely called *gnosis*" (6:20). But there is no warrant for reading into these references to "knowledge" the elaborate ideas that can be documented in the Gnostic writings, which are not only later than the New Testament writings but also represent a fundamentally different worldview. The devastating critique by Carsten Colpe, which has been followed by other critiques of the scholarly theory of a pre-Christian gnostic redeemer, has led to a situation in which some scholars now acknowledge the lack of documentary evidence for pre-Christian Gnosticism but nevertheless proceed as though Gnosticism indeed existed before the rise of Christianity.[18]

The documents from Nag Hammadi show clearly how both Jewish and Christian traditions have been adapted and transformed by the Gnostics in order to set forth their views of the state of the created world, humanity, and the divine remedy for present difficulties. In the Apocalypse of Adam, for example, following a mythological depiction of the successive stages of world history (78–82), there is a report of the Gnostic equivalent of the New Testament accounts of the incarnation: in the one chosen by God "from all the aeons, he caused a knowledge of the undefiled one of truth to come to be," and thus "the great illuminator came forth," who enabled to shine "the generation of those men whom he had chosen for himself." They rejoice that God has given them a knowledge of the truth (83). The secret knowledge Adam conveyed to Seth is granted through holy baptism to those who possess eternal knowledge (85). Other items in this Gnostic literature refer specifically to material found in the New Testament Gospels, especially the teachings of Jesus, but they recast them in accord with the Gnostic worldview. For example, the various forms of the familiar saying of Jesus about becoming as a child to enter the kingdom[19] are transmuted in the Gospel of Thomas (37) into an instruction to divest oneself of all such basic human features as individual, sexual, and bodily identity. Creation of humans by God in his image, as set forth in the tradition of Genesis (1:26–27) and affirmed by Jesus (Matt. 19:4–6; Mark 10:6–8), is totally rejected in favor of a purely nonmaterial ontological image.

The theory that best accounts for and incorporates the documentary evidence concerning Gnosticism sees it as a movement among some Christians who were wrestling with the same issues as their Neoplatonist contemporaries and advancing their own analogous solutions. Both groups adopted a radically dualistic view of the cosmos and saw as the goal of human existence the transcending of the material world. In addition to the writings from the Egyptian Gnostic library (which date from the fourth century), there are numerous references to the Gnostics in Christian writers of the second through fourth centuries. What is evident from all these documents is that the Gnostic writers shared certain basic convictions with others in the ancient world. With the wisdom traditions of Judaism, they shared a belief in the divine origin of their understanding of the nature of God and the origin of the created world. With apocalypticism, they shared a dualistic theory of the origin and defeat of evil. In setting forth these views, they employed images and mythological motifs drawn from all over the Greco-Roman, Syrian, and Iranian worlds. But the Gnostics used this imagery, vocabulary, and formulation of issues in ways that presuppose an ontology (radically dualistic) fundamentally different from that of Jewish wisdom or the New Testament writings, in that the Gnostics (unlike the apocalypticists) had no expectation of the renewal of the creation. But ignoring such fundamental differences that lie behind the formal, external similarities between Gnosticism and both Jewish and Christian wisdom, some scholars continue to offer descriptions of pre-Christian Gnosticism.[20] Left wholly out of account is the fact that the dualism of apocalyptic is ethical, with conflict between the demonic, angelic, and human agents who are subject to evil and the agents of good: God, the obedient angels, and his faithful people. In the apocalyptic view, the material creation will be renewed, not transcended or destroyed as in the Gnostic schemes. Allegory enables the Gnostic interpreters of the tradition to recast it radically, so that the goal of the Gnostic community is not "May God's

The Post–New Testament Period

kingdom come on earth," as it is in Matthew's version of Jesus' prayer (6:10), but gaining total release from the realm of matter.

The most relevant antecedents and prototypes of Gnosticism are to be sought not in some scholarly construct of a redeemer myth, but in the rise of Neoplatonism concurrent with the emergence of Gnostic theories. It is important to perceive that the Gnostics are using the method of legitimation that appeals to ancient sources and claims the existence of basic precedents for what the group is now claiming. As I noted in chapter 3 above, examples of this tactic are to be found among the rabbis and in the community for which the Gospel of Matthew was produced. Hippolytus (d. ca. 235) shows in his *Refutation of All Heresies* how the Gnostics tried to confirm their point of view by taking over features of the ancient philosophers, and by claiming as one of their founders Simon Magus, a contemporary of Paul (Acts 8:8–13), whom they called "that power of God which is called Great" and in whose name they wrote books.[21] Yet Hippolytus himself is not hostile toward Greco-Roman learning, since his writings show that he supports synthesizing wisdom from the wider world with scriptural traditions. Book 1 of his antiheretical work draws on Greek philosophy, and book 6 is devoted to Persian and Egyptian astrology. But he sees the task of Christian thinkers as achieving syntheses with aspects of secular wisdom rather than allowing it to determine their basic outlook and presuppositions. The Gnostics, on the other hand, accommodated the entire structure and perspectives of their teachings to the dualistic view of the cosmos that had come into fashion among the Neoplatonists, with its denial of the divine origin of the creation, which led them to reject belief in the actual incarnation of Jesus and in the coming of God's rule on the earth. Gnosis was an escape from, not a remedy for, the world's evil state.

The Law-abiding Community

As I have noted, Jacob Neusner has traced in a deeply insightful manner the formation of the Mishnah and the Talmud in Judaism, the Mishnah from the destruction of the Temple and the failure of the Bar Kochba revolt, and the Talmud from the establishment of Christianity by Constantine. In an analysis of the first of these formative events, Neusner says that the destruction of Jerusalem and the Temple posed fundamental questions in the second century C.E.: "What, in the aftermath of the destruction of the holy place and the holy cult, remained of the sanctity of the holy caste, the priesthood, the holy land, and above all, the holy people and its holy way of life? The answer: the sanctity persists, indelibly, in Israel, the people, in its way of life, in its land, in its priesthood, in its food, in its mode of sustaining life, in its manner of procreating and so sustaining the nation." Two centuries later, the need for a consistent and authoritative basis for Jewish understanding and common life leads to the claim that "God's revelation of the Torah at Sinai encompassed the Mishnah as much as Scripture. Second, the Mishnah was handed on through oral formulation and transmission from Sinai to the framers of the document as we have it." Torah is defined by the Talmud as including "oral and memorized revelation, of the Mishnah, and by implication, of other rabbinical writings." It is "an encompassing symbol of Israel's salvation," and is embodied in a person: a rabbi." This holy way of life is now taught "by the sages at hand." Missing from the Mishnah are any "explicit and systematic theory of scriptural authority," any doctrine of the coming of the Messiah "as end and purpose of the system as a whole," and any indication that Mishnah is dependent on the scriptures. Accordingly, the definitive ritual consisted in studying the Torah as "the generative symbol, the total, exhaustive expression of the system as a whole." This process would make one holy, "like Moses, 'our rabbi,' and like God, in whose image humanity was made and whose Torah provided the plan and the model for what God wanted of a humanity created in his image."[22]

Thus, the model of the law-abiding community traced in chapter 3 above became paramount in Judaism, but it was also developing significantly in the church as well. The patriarchal positions that were introduced in the church in the third and fourth centuries gave individuals primary authority for guiding the lives of Christians over large geographical regions. Even when there were major divisions in Christianity based on the several ethnic and linguistic cultures where the gospel had taken root, the resulting institutional structures were headed by a patriarch for each group: Greek, Latin, Syriac, and Coptic. The "keys of the kingdom" and the wielding of ecclesiastical authority promised by Jesus according to Matt. 16:16–18 were assumed to be in use now among those exercising monarchic ecclesiastical rule, each over a particular segment of the church as a whole. The church councils that were called served to confirm and clarify the centralized authoritarian role of the bishops and patriarchs.

One might have assumed that the imperial establishment of the church under Constantine would have terminated all the models for community except the law-abiding one. But in fact, the unified structure of the post-Constantinian church neither encompassed the whole of Christianity nor eliminated other structures and strategies for the shared life of Christians—even within that segment under its direct control—as I shall note below when I consider the subsequent mutations of the models of the mystical and inclusive communities.

The Holy City

In chapter 1, I observed how widely the images of the city and the Temple were used as a way of representing the hopes of the people of Israel for the fulfillment of God's purpose for and through them. The most dramatic and detailed example is the Temple Scroll from Qumran, with its instructions for the rebuilding of the city and the Temple, including strict regulations to be enforced as a guarantee that only the worthy and pure share in the life of this renewed people of God in whose presence God dwells. Likewise among Christians, the image of the city of God as the locus of God's people, which is set forth most fully in the New

Testament in Revelation 21, continues to appear in the third and fourth centuries C.E. as the model for the consummation of God's purpose for the church. Other versions of the city model are to be found in this same period as well, but the emphasis in these occurrences is on sanctity and order within the common life of the community.

The *Shepherd of Hermas* builds on an image derived from Heb. 13:14, which warns that "here we [the community] have no lasting city," since "we are looking for the city that is to come." In the Similitudes of Enoch 1, the author calls on his readers to divest themselves of their tangible possessions and break their attachments to earthly things, which are "this city." Instead, they are to perform acts of charity, caring for the needs of afflicted souls and looking after widows and orphans, so that thereby they can be accruing true wealth, which will be theirs in the city of God. The city is the image for the context and the network of relationships in which Christians live.

Yet in the Apocalypse of Paul 22–29, the city of Christ is depicted concretely as located in the realm of the dead beside Lake Acherousia, where the penitent are baptized after their departure from the body and from which they then can enter the city.[23] They travel there in a golden boat, accompanied by the singing of three thousand angels. The city has twelve walls, twelve towers, and twelve gates. Four rivers encircle it, providing respectively milk, honey, oil, and wine for the inhabitants. (Those still plagued with pride are aided by the trees, which bow down and abase themselves as an act of penance in behalf of those in need of intercession with God.) Commendation is given to those who have performed acts of mercy, but the highest honor is reserved for those who have made themselves fools for Christ's sake. David is present in the dwellers' midst, helping to prepare them for the ultimate ascent of the saints to the seventh heaven, where they will enter the presence of Christ and of God the Father.

In other Christian writings from the pre-Constantinian period, temple imagery is also understood in ways that symbolize the ascent of the soul into the ever richer and more complete knowledge of God. In his *Commentary on the Gospel of John*, Origen gives an allegorical interpretation of Jesus' purging the Temple, employing imagery recalling the promise to Peter of the keys that give access to the kingdom (Matt. 16:18). Through the keys of higher knowledge, the hidden things of scripture are opened to the faithful. The new realm they enter is Jerusalem, the city of the great king (Matt. 5:35). The earthly Jerusalem is on a hill, but the true Jerusalem is not accessible on earth; instead, it is necessary for the faithful to develop the ability to perceive the things of the mind and thus to enter the eternal city. Care must be taken to avoid losing or dulling these capacities once they have been acquired. Jesus is now in the Temple, which is the house of God the Father where his word is declared. Those who try to exploit spiritual worship for material gain must be stopped. The Temple is the symbol of the soul skilled in reason and therefore transcending the concern for bodily needs. What is required is the discipline of Jesus' teaching, which will drive away false doctrine and insure that the service of God is performed in accord with heavenly, spiritual principles.[24]

In his *Commentary on the Revelation of John*, Victorinus (martyred in 304) also interprets the promise of the new city in Revelation 20–21 symbolically. The squareness of the city represents the solidity and enduring quality of the saints, just as the splendor of its streets is an expression of their holiness. The four groups of three gates are the paramount virtues: prudence, fortitude, justice, and temperance. The twelve gates, each of which is a single pearl, are the twelve apostles. The impossibility of closing the gates is an expression of the enduring quality of the doctrine the apostles proclaimed, which survives in the subsequent flood of heresy. The kingdom of Christ is already eternal in the community of the saints, but the full glory that is to be theirs will be manifest only in the final day of resurrection.

As a corollary of the development of temple imagery for describing the future of God's people, the leadership roles within the church are defined not only along instructional and administrative lines, but in terms of priestly roles as well. A major pointer in the direction of priestly office can be found in the Canons of the Council of Laodicea (mid-fourth century), which include specific instructions for the appointment of priests. The rich imagery of the sacrifice of Christ that one finds in the letters of Paul—for example, in his description of God's offering Christ as an atoning sacrifice for sin (Rom. 3:21–25)—has become a feature of the common life of the church in the ongoing priestly functions of its leaders. This trend will be strengthened in the design of churches, which are transformed from meetinghouses to sanctuaries where the central focus is an altar of sacrifice surrounded by a sacred area accessible only to qualified priests.

The most extensive and enduring use in the history of Christianity of the image of the city for the people of God is that of Augustine of Hippo (354–430) in his monumental work *The City of God*. There he contrasts the city of God and the city of this world. The city of God is the model according to which God wills the creation and intends to order the life of his people (18.1). God's city is already alive in this world, so that the two cities exist together in human experience. Through the prophets of Israel, the nature and goal of God's city become increasingly clear and explicit, culminating in the birth of God's son from the Virgin. Even before the incarnation, the cessation of prophecy and the destruction of the Temple showed that the true temple the prophets had announced was now in preparation (18.45). Participation in the new city was not to be limited to the people of Israel, since already in the Old Testament one can see that "those from other nations who lived by God's standards and were pleasing to God" were citizens of the spiritual Jerusalem. This is a clear indication of the ultimate inclusion of predestined Jews and Gentiles in the city of God, which is God's house and God's temple (18.47).

In the remaining time before the end of the age, Augustine seeks to encourage peace and order in human society in accord with law, in anticipation of the ultimate and total triumph of righteousness in the city of God. He refers to that part of the heavenly city that is on pilgrimage during the present era (19.17), and assures the faithful citizen that hope and peace can be experienced in the midst of the present strife and misery (19.20), even though perfect peace cannot be found (19.27). The last books of *The City of God* (20–22) expound details of the apocalyptic features of both the Old and the New Testament, including the final judgment with its rewards and punishments, the two resurrections, the binding of Satan, and the millennium. All these are necessary preparations for the eternal kingdom, which will be established in a new heaven and a new earth. All the redemptive work God has done and is still doing points to this world to come. Finally, Augustine describes the process of divine judgment and criteria for inclusion in or exclusion from the city of God.

There is an irony in the fact that the medieval church employed this model of the city to confirm its developing theocratic structures. As the institutional pattern became dominant, the eschatological dimensions of the earlier images of the heavenly city were only vestigial, or at most peripheral. Instead, the primary concern became ecclesiastical authority, reinforced by credal and ethical norms. In terms of the models of community I have employed, a basic shift occurred from city to come to law-abiding institution.

The Community of Mystical Participation

The Impact of the Mystery Cults on the Roman World

The wide impact of the mystery cults on Greco-Roman culture is best attested in literature and archaeological remains from the second and third centuries C.E. As early as the first century B.C.E., however, Diodorus Siculus states in his *Library* that Isis brings not only health, but also immortality. Her role in mystical ceremonies carried out among the Roman upper classes can be inferred from her appearance on frescoes from Pompei and Herculaneum, dating from the first century C.E. Isis was honored in Alexandria and at shrines near Athens and Delphi, and her worship in Rome is attested during the reign of Caligula (37–41). The Isis cult continued to flourish during the reign of Caracalla (198–217), and shrines in her honor dating to the Roman period have been found from Germany to York in the United Kingdom. The second-century evidence displays this goddess on reliefs in shrines, on coins, and in frescoes, but more significantly in major and enduring works of literature.

Chief among the latter are the early-second-century treatise of Plutarch on Isis and the early-third-century *Life of Apollonius of Tyana*, by Philostratus. For Plutarch in his *De Iside*, the search for truth is a sacred undertaking, not merely an intellectual quest, and by it the seeking one can come to know ultimate reality. By allegorical interpretation of features of the Isis myth, Plutarch is able to show how it conveys insights from Stoic and Pythagorean philosophy and enables one to discern the eternal principles behind the changing physical order. Reason (*logos*), which derives from philosophy, provides the norms and basic understanding of all human existence, but the profoundest insights come to those who are devotees of Isis, since she provides the revelatory vision (*epopteia*) of ultimate truth. Plutarch's intention is to foster devotion to Isis, whereby one can experience the revelation of ultimate truth, which can be attained only through participation in her mystical rites.[25]

The search for understanding of the physical universe and of the problem of evil that has pervaded human history is important for Philostratus in his reconstruction of the insights and methods of Apollonius. His *Life of Apollonius* is reputedly based on material from the first century C.E. provided by Julia Domna, who was a philosopher and the wife of Septimius Severus (reigned 192–211). Apollonius began as an ascetic in the Pythagorean tradition, but he later took up residence in the temple of Aesculapius, where the sick came to him in large numbers to be healed. He is said to have conversed with Vespasian and Titus and to have died during the reign of Nerva (96–98). Pictured as a man of wisdom, he constructed an addition to the temple of Aesculapius that embodied his mix of intellectual and mystical interests: a lyceum and an academy (*Life of Apollonius* 1.13). His philosophical orientation was a combination of Stoicism and Pythagoreanism (2.24, 5.36, 6.29, 7.14–15). He came to be greeted as divine because of his superior wisdom (3.28), which he saw as establishing and manifesting a special relationship between the gods and the true seeker, ultimately including participation in the divine substance (8.7). The goal of his life was not to establish a new religious cult, but rather to foster the insights and personal values of the neo-Pythagorean tradition, which affirmed the kinship of the wise and the divine.[26] Accordingly, the personal dimension of mystical participation in the divine life was the ultimate objective of Philostratus's work.

Another depiction of the power of Isis to transform the lives of her devotees is effectively presented in the *Metamorphoses* of Apuleius (123–180 C.E.).[27] There he describes in the first person the experiences of a man who in his search for meaning in life finds himself bewitched and harrassed until he finally undergoes a highly symbolic transformation into a braying ass. After running away from the humiliating and painful experiences to which he is subjected, he reaches a great shrine honoring Isis. While he is witnessing a grand procession in her honor, a priest offers him a garland of roses, which he devours, immediately regaining his true human form (9.15–16). He is granted a vision of Isis in all her glory, in which she tells him that she is the divine reality behind the many names of goddesses among the Greeks and Romans. Following elaborate ceremonies and a solemn cleansing, he is dedicated as a priest in her service (9.24), and in the course of the following year he passes through successive orders in the service of Isis and her consort, Osiris, who is identified as the greatest and most powerful of all the gods (9.30).

A work known as the *Ephesiaca*, by the third-century writer Xenophon,[28] describes the experiences of a pair devoted to Isis who travel around the eastern Mediterranean. The adventures of the hero, Habrokomes, include floating down the Nile, during which journey he undergoes threats to his life and trials similar to those experienced by the god Osiris. The images of the couple's love and their deliverance from harm through the intervention of the divine Osiris and Isis are the climax and center of these vivid stories. The intent of this narrative is not simply to engage the reader in a fascinating tale: the adventures also serve as models for the transforming mystical experience that is open to those who truly seek knowledge of and experience in the divine life.[29]

Mystical Philosophy

Philosophical mysticism came to fullest expression in the third century C.E. among Christian scholars and their intellectual critics. Both varieties of mysticism—Christian and pagan—build on the mystical dimensions of the ongoing tradition of Plato. A leading teacher of intellectual mysticism was Ammonius Saccas of Alexandria (175–243), whose pupils included the Christian Origen (185–254) and the pagan Plotinus (205–270?).

Plotinus represents the peak of the developing philosophical tradition, which, building on basic Platonic principles, differentiated the intelligible world—eternal and unchanging—from the realm of the senses, subject to the limitations of time and change. The Neoplatonists, as later historians of philosophy came to call them, posited a hierarchy of being and existence: at the top are the supreme principle, remote and transcendent, called the One, and the eternal ideas, which are located in the divine mind. The goal of true wisdom for humans is to fly upward from the body and ascend to the realm of the eternal. For Plotinus, the cosmic distance from human, material existence to the eternal realm can be bridged through two agents: the intellect or mind (*nous*), which encompasses the whole realm of eternal forms or ideas, and which has its counterpart in the human potential for grasping that level of reality; and the soul, which pervades and orders the material world but which also enables the human intellect to understand the cosmic order and to pass beyond it to direct contemplation of the One.

Porphyry (233–304) perhaps Plotinus's outstanding pupil, not only wrote a brief biography of his teacher but also arranged and edited his teachings in the *Enneads*. In his own philosophy, Porphyry emphasized asceticism as a method for transcending the material world. His system included a theory of *daimones*, which he saw as the powers that pervert the world and foster immorality. A major feature of Plotinus and his philosophical system, as W. R. Inge pointed out in his classic study of Plotinus, was the pilgrimage of the soul to the ultimate source from which it flowed. The method of mystical ascent "consists in removing everything extraneous to the reality which we seek to win and to be. First, the body is to be detached as not belonging to the true nature of the soul; then the soul which forms the body, then sense-perception. What remains is the image of the Spirit. When the soul becomes Spirit by contemplating Spirit as its own principle, the source of all being still remains unexplored." To accomplish this final objective requires "intense concentration of the mind and will on what are believed to be the essentials of the quest. But the method is based on the conviction that 'all truth is shadow except the last.' . . . So the ascent of the soul involves a continual rejection of outward shows and continual self-denial."[30] Plotinus asserts that "when the spirit perceives this divine light, it knows not whence it comes, from within or from without. . . . It is useless to ask whence it comes, for there is no question of place here. . . . We must not then seek it, but wait quietly for its appearance, and prepare ourselves to contemplate it, as the eye watches for the sun rising above the horizon or out of the sea."[31] There is in this mode of mysticism no dichotomy between the realm of the intellect and the spiritual sphere. Through the philosophical analytical process one can enter into direct contemplation of the divine.

Mystical Interpretation of Scripture

Features similar to those of the mystical philosophers are evident in both the intellectual scheme and the exegetical methods used by Origen. Eusebius describes how Origen, as a child prodigy, was encouraged by his father to engage in intensive study of the scripture before he began his formal studies of Greek literature and philosophy. From the outset, therefore, he sought to correlate scripture and philosophy, developing an exegetical method that used allegory and symbolism to uncover the fuller meaning of the biblical texts. He began teaching at the catechetical school in Alexandria at the age of seventeen, and took over as its head a year later (206 C.E.), succeeding Pantaenus and Clement.[32] After deciding to devote his energies solely to discerning the spiritual meaning of scripture, he sold off all the copies of ancient writings in his personal library. The rigidly ascetic life to which he devoted himself is most vividly exemplified in his self-castration in literal obedience to the teaching of Jesus in Matt. 19:12.

Origen's fame as scholar and teacher was so great that he was invited by leading Christians to visit the churches in various parts of the empire from Rome to Syria, especially in the cities of Greece. This provoked jealousy on the part of Demetrius, the bishop of Alexandria, who protested violently when in spite of his castration Origen was ordained by the bishops of Jerusalem and Caesarea, where he later continued his study and teaching. His enormous linguistic skills are evident in the *Hexapla* that he prepared, a parallel edition of six versions of the Hebrew text and the most widely used translations of the Bible. Origen attacked those whom he regarded as heretics, especially the Ebionites, who declared that Jesus' birth was fully human, and the Valentinian Gnostics.[33] Conversely, he was attacked by Porphyry on the ground that he used his allegorical method as a device to get rid of moral problems in the Hebrew Bible. Yet Porphyry had to acknowledge Origen's superb knowledge of the major philosophical traditions, Platonic,

Pythagorean, and Stoic. Modern scholarship has sought to press Origen into one of two categories, philosopher or mystic, as Henry Chadwick has noted,[34] but he actually combines these roles as he goes about the exposition of scripture and the formulation of theological perspectives for the church. Origen's concern, which is shared with mystic philosophers of other traditions, is to attain a direct vision of the divine and thereby to participate in the life that is divinely provided.

Among all his voluminous writings, this concern is set out with particular clarity in the *Commentary on the Gospel of John* and in the recently discovered *Dialogue with Heraclides*.[35] In the *Dialogue*, Origen declares that by the power of God, one can be transformed from an impure being into one who shares in true humanity (151–152). The old humanity is put off (Col. 3:9) and the new, enlightened humanity is put on (154–156). It is Jesus who unveils the eyes (Ps. 119:18) of the faithful seekers after truth so that the eyes of the mind can see. Changing the imagery, Origen asserts that this process of renewal enables the inner man to enjoy the "good smell of righteousness" and the fine "spiritual taste" (158). Combining details from Eccles. 2:14 ("the eyes in the head") and 1 Cor. 11:3 ("Christ is the head"), he concludes that the thinking faculty of the believer is Christ. Conversely, the "lost heart" in Isa. 46:12 is the failure of the individual to cultivate the true intellectual life.

As the youthful Origen demonstrated when he was prevented from offering himself to the authorities for martyrdom only by his mother having hidden all his clothes,[36] he had no fear of death but regarded it as a freeing from the body that brought one to be with Christ (165–167). Yet even in this life, he affirmed, the soul that is established in blessedness is no longer liable to death, since it already has eternal life and has begun to share in immortality. One must reach out in faith to accept God's offer of eternal life, which is Christ, who said, "I am the Life" (John 11:25, 14:6). The older biblical images of the cherubim and the chariot wheels likewise point upward to the ineffable mystery of this new life into which the faithful will enter. Like Paul, they "long to be absent from the body, and present with the Lord" (2 Cor. 5:6–8).

In his exposition of John's gospel, Origen pictures priests as those who devote themselves to the divine word, so that the study of the Gospels is indeed the first fruits offered by them. No one can grasp the meaning of the Gospels who has not leaned on Jesus' breast and received Mary as his own mother. The Gospel of John is the spiritual gospel, which presents clearly to those who have the will to understand all matters regarding the Son of God—both the mysteries presented in his discourses and the meaning of the enigmatic acts he performed. Jesus is the embodiment of the good things of which this gospel speaks. Origen shows that even simple words have multiple and profound meanings, such as "beginning" (*arche*): beginning in time and beginning in substance; type or copy; basic elements; design and execution. Wisdom contains all things as ideas before they come into tangible existence. Similarly, Christ's roles include light, resurrection, way, truth, life, door, shepherd, Messiah and king, teacher, master, Son, true vine, bread, and first and last. Since his mission is to enlighten the world whose light he is, he is called "Light of the world," and his modes of communication include knowledge, life, truth, and human renewal. In his capacity as Word [*logos*], he is active in the reason of every human being.[37]

Origen uses the image from John 6 of eating the flesh and drinking the blood of the Lamb of God to show that what is in view here is not consuming physical food, but taking and internalizing a range of spiritual insights. These include "eating at the head," which means devouring the essential doctrines about heavenly things, to "ending at the feet," which is inquiring about material things and the evil spirits. The whole of scripture must be approached and understood as "one body." Such activity is necessary only in this earthly life, since in the life to come, the vision of God and Christ will be direct and complete.[38] Although the authority of the church leaders is respected by Origen, who cooperates with them, the major goal of his work and of his injunctions to his pupils is that they share in the common life of the mystical community that Jesus called into being, for which he is preparing an ultimate mode of life in the very presence of God.

The Inclusive Community

As I have been noting in my analyses of the various models, the challenge was set out in the oldest layers of the gospel tradition and in the letters of Paul to include in the new community those who might have been excluded on ethnic, social, physical, or moral grounds. The effectiveness and expansion of this policy are particularly evident in Luke and Acts, but they are also implied in non–New Testament material from Christian and Roman writers that attests the rapid and effective spread of the movement across the Mediterranean world and the Middle East in the first century after the death of Jesus. The cultural engagement between Christians and the Roman world, in which Greco-Roman concepts and modes of communication were taken over and adapted by the Christians, is evident in the wisdom and mystical models sketched earlier in this chapter.

As the politically and culturally unifying forces of the Roman empire waned in the second and third centuries, and especially when the imperial rule was divided between the Byzantine and Roman centers of power, the church's culturally and linguistically diverse settings fostered differences. The centers of hierarchical power, the specifics of doctrinal standards, and the language of communication diverged. The growing power of the church in alliance with the claimants to imperial power resulted in the location of ecclesiastical authority in a hierarchy reinforced by political support. At the same time, much of the intellectual vitality of the church was based in the monastic centers, where careful study and preservation of earlier Christian documents continued. It was in such situations that intellectual engagement with the wider Roman world was carried forward as well, so that the wisdom model not only survived but flourished in the Constantinian period and later.

Conclusion

In the subsequent history of Christianity, the five community models of the church have continued to appear, often in forms that blend them with each other. In the late twentieth century, the resurgence and popularity of the models of apocalyptic wisdom and mystical participation are evident in the phenomenal growth of religious movements building on these traditions. The appeal of such movements to large numbers of people is reinforced by their insistence on conformity to the laws and by their earnest attention to the missionary role of potentially universal inclusion in the people of God. Combinations of these factors account for much of the vitality of newer Christian groups today throughout the world.

The roles perceived for Christ in the various communities through the history of Christianity correspond with the model that each community sees for itself in its own time. When the model is that of the Temple, Christ is seen as priest or sacrifice, and as agent for access into the divine presence. If the emphasis is on secret wisdom—especially concerning the end of the present world order and the vindication of the righteous—Jesus is perceived as the one through whom this apocalyptic information is being conveyed. If the wisdom claimed by the community is of a more abstract or timeless sort, then Jesus is understood to be the voice of divine truth. If the community is seeking to foster direct encounter with the divine in the experience of its members, then Jesus is represented (often using Johannine terminology) as the divine Word or Light. If the primary goal is to regulate the life of the community in strict accord with the divine will, then Jesus appears as a kind of second Moses, enunciating the law of God and working toward its fulfillment by the members. If the highest value of the community is outreach and inclusiveness, then the favorite image of Jesus is that of commissioner of his apostles to make disciples in all the nations (Matt. 28:19–20, Acts 1:8), to develop a community in which there are no sexual, ethnic, or social prerequisites for admission (Gal. 3:28), and to proclaim the gospel in such a way that all linguistic and cultural barriers are transcended (Acts 2:8).

Historically responsible study of the origins of Christianity, therefore, demands careful analysis of the diversity of sociocultural models for the people of God that can be documented in the older Jewish and Christian materials available to us. This analytical strategy enables one to understand the differences that are evident in the ancient sources, to interpret the texts responsibly, and to identify the roots of the great diversities that have continued to manifest themselves in the subsequent history of Judaism, but especially of Christianity. The diversities include not only the several models for the community of God's people and the differing roles assigned to Jesus as the agent of God for covenant renewal, but also the various individual and social norms for the behavior of the members of the community, as well as the range of responses to the political and cultural forces that surround them and contribute to the shaping of their destiny. For both historical and theological study of the beginnings of Christianity, as well as of the changing features of Judaism in the centuries just before and after the change of eras, an analytical strategy based on models of community is essential.

The Post–New Testament Period

Critical Note

Priority in the Gospel Tradition

In spite of earnest efforts by a few scholars to prove the priority of Matthew among the canonical Gospels,[1] the dominant assumption for the past seventy-five years has been that Mark was the earliest gospel and that a source of sayings (Q) was used by the authors of Matthew and Luke to supplement Mark, in addition to material that they added on their own.[2] During the past twenty-five years, building on the hypothesis of Q and Mark as the basic sources of the gospel tradition, interest has flourished in the points of view represented by the evangelists—and by the communities that each of them represents.[3] This assumption about sources and method of analysis of each gospel are followed in the present study.

Yet, in an article first published in 1968 and then reprinted in 1971,[4] Helmut Koester asserted that the Gospel of Thomas is more primitive than the canonical Gospels. His argument (largely from silence) builds on the claims that there is no evidence that Thomas was dependent on any of the New Testament gospels, that there is no mention of the death or resurrection of Jesus, that there are no Christological titles, that many of the sayings are found in more original form than in the canonical Gospels, and that Thomas is closest to an earlier version of Q.[5] Koester simply dismisses as later additions those features of Q that contrast this age and the age to come, or link present responsibility with future vindication or punishment. Emphasis in this supposedly earliest gospel tradition is declared to be exclusively on divine wisdom as conveyed through the sayings of Jesus. This thesis was also affirmed by James M. Robinson and has now been developed in detail by John S. Kloppenborg.[6] In a more recent essay on this subject, Robinson attempts to support the thesis that the original version of Q belongs to the genre of "wisdom gospel" and that thus the apocalyptic sayings and other eschatological features, as well as Christological utterances, are to be regarded as secondary.[7] After discussing the enduring impact of Albert Schweitzer, whose study of the historical Jesus led him to the conclusion that Jesus was apocalyptic in orientation, dying tragically when his expectation of the end of the age failed to take place, Robinson proposes the following stages in the development of the Q tradition: John the Baptist was apocalyptic in outlook, a point of view Jesus initially shared and then abandoned; thus the earlier layer of Q is sapiential, but the later edition (Q2) was apocalypticized. A third and final edition of Q introduced Torah observance, showing that the Q movement merged into the Matthean community, "bringing into Matthew and the Gentile church . . . the traditions of Jesus that Q had transmitted."[8] It is only in the later stages of the Q tradition that apocalyptic and Christological elements are added to the original wisdom material.

While one must reckon with the possibility that more authentic versions of the sayings of Jesus from the oral tradition have been preserved in the Gospel of Thomas, it is purely circular reasoning to decide antecedently that all apocalyptic features are late, and then trim the evidence to confirm the presupposed conclusion. What is proved by this strategy of identifying the earliest Jesus tradition with what is found in Thomas and proto-Q is merely that this artificial construct is more congenial to the scholars who have contrived it than is the canonical tradition. In the process of this critical surgery, revealing features are often overlooked. For example, in his discussion of the parable of the great supper, Koester correctly observes that Jesus' command to the disciples to seek banquet guests in "the highways and the hedges" (Luke 14:23) may be a Lukan addition to the original parable, but he ignores the force of the basic image of the eschatological banquet (which is attested at Qumran in the Messianic Rule [1QSa]) and the fact that the main point in the parable about the inclusion of outsiders derives from the late Jewish prophetic or apocalyptic tradition ("poor, blind, lame"; Isa. 35:6, 61:1). Similarly, while describing Jesus' sayings as "the turning point for the ages" and as providing "the rule of life for the community of the new age" and demonstrating the kingdom's presence, Koester dismisses from the original Q Luke 16:16, with its announcement that John ends the old age and Jesus proclaims the kingdom of God. He simply declares that Luke used a revised version of Q that "added to the timeless wisdom" of the original form the apocalyptic view.[9]

An analogous reconstruction of the stages of development of Q has been offered in an essay by Burton L. Mack, "The Kingdom That Didn't Come." Mack attempts to discern five different phases of the Q tradition. First, aphorisms and aphoristic imperatives call for egalitarian roles and public performance by those who follow Jesus but have no preaching mission. The aphorisms are then shifted to imperatives and linked with mission activities by groups that meet in houses but have not engaged in prophetic itinerancy. Next, sharp lines are drawn between those who follow Jesus and those who do not, and between those in the Jesus movement and those in the synagogues. Apocalyptic features are then incorporated into the Q source in order to threaten divine judgment on those who oppose

The Gospel Tradition

the movement. Finally, the apocalyptic mythmaking is expanded, with the result that Q sounds like Mark.[10] Mack thinks he can discern in the Gospel of Mark a similar, though much more elaborate, process of remaking Jesus on the model of apocalyptic myth. As he phrases it, "It was Mark's fiction of a fantastic infringement on human history that created Christianity's charter." He sees the development of this tradition as consisting of efforts to project back on Jesus the unconventional practices and problems (internal and external) that the movement experienced, and above all of attempts to explain why Jesus, the wise martyr and heir to a kingdom, was in conflict with Second Temple Judaism, and what was to happen when the promised kingdom did not come. "History must lie under violence until God comes again."[11]

What is assumed to be the original Q includes Luke's version of the Beatitudes and the parable of the supper, but ignored is the fact that these teachings are pervasively eschatological in perspective, speaking as they do of the coming of the kingdom of God and the Son of man. Mack arbitrarily extracts some aphorisms from the sayings of Jesus and seeks to link this material with an anachronistic construct of Cynic wisdom, dependable documentation for which comes only from the second century C.E.[12] Informed, responsible studies of Cynicism[13] offer a radically different picture of the Cynics than the one assumed by Mack and Kloppenborg. Central to the concern of the Cynics was the role of the king as *paidagogos* of the human race, manifesting the virtues of courage, helpfulness, and self-control. In the period about which we have dependable information, Cynic philosophers were engaged in advice to and debate with the Roman emperors. One of the best-known of the philosophers was Dio Chrysostom, who was exiled for his criticism of Domitian and then restored by Trajan, whom he served as adviser. One of Dio's main images for the proper role of the emperor was shepherd of the flock. Dio's solution to the problem of the poor was to force them to move to rural areas, which would ease the urban crisis and increase the food supply. Demonax (second century C.E.) declared the duty of the philosopher to be the fostering of law and order in the universe, especially manifest in the well-ordered state. These features have no kinship with the Q material, not even with the aphoristic core posited by Mack and Kloppenborg.

While Mack assigns a date after 70 C.E. to the later apocalyptic versions of Q and Mark, one must suppose that someone else had invented a similar apocalyptic myth about Jesus much earlier. Indeed, it arose so soon after his crucifixion that it was a central factor in the conversion of Paul. Mack says only that "Paul was converted to a Hellenized form of some Jesus movement that had already developed into a Christ cult."[14] But this ignores the central apocalyptic features of Paul's gospel and leaves unexplained how apocalyptic could have achieved such prominence within so short space of time.[15] A year or two after the crucifixion is an unlikely period in which a "myth" so radically different from the intention of Jesus would have developed, been transmuted into allegedly Hellenistic terms, and then transmitted to the major city of the Decapolis, Damascus, where it became so potent and visible that Saul went there with the intent of destroying a community of followers of Jesus. In contrast to Mack's thesis, careful analysis of Paul and the setting for his life and thought matches well with the extensive evidence of how pervasive apocalyptic was in Judaism of the first century B.C.E. and the first century C.E. Accordingly, it is self-evident that from the outset apocalyptic had a formative influence on early Christianity.[16] Mack's effort to dismiss apocalyptic features to the periphery of Paul's thought[17] is not only unconvincing, but (given Mack's eagerness to discern Hellenistic features in the teachings of the historical Jesus) ironically ignores the fact that the issues of the divinely determined cycle of the ages, moral accountability at the turn of the ages, and divine vindication of the morally responsible were important features in Stoic thinking of the first century B.C.E. and C.E. (see chapter 1 above), and not weird notions peculiar to some Jews and later Christians.

Before turning to an examination of the suitability and credibility of the sharp distinction made by Robinson and Kloppenborg between wisdom and apocalyptic material in the Q tradition, it is important to note a passing remark of Robinson, who describes Schweitzer's apocalyptic perception of Jesus as "a Procrustean bed in which the discipline squirms, ill at ease."[18] Schweitzer's analytical survey of scholarship that investigates the gospel tradition to discern how Christianity emerged from the activity and sayings of Jesus has stood up well over the nearly one hundred years since it was written.[19] Its conclusion—that Jesus' message and understanding of God and his purpose were profoundly influenced by contemporary Jewish eschatological expectations—has been confirmed by a scholarly consensus, but regrettably it has also led scholars who are disconcerted or intellectually embarrassed by these results to take flight to other conceptual systems. Schweitzer himself fled to medicine and central Africa. Bultmann fled to existentialism, justifying his retreat from eschatology by the demythologizing method. A contrived, historically inaccurate construct of Cynicism seems to be the new refuge for those fleeing what they regard as the embarrassment of apocalyptic.

There is no doubt that the expectation of divine intervention in human history, the defeat of the powers of evil, and the establishment of a new order in the world is intellectually difficult for those trained in the post-Enlightenment culture of the West. It seems to be particularly problematical for biblical scholars whose initiation into the field was in traditionalist ecclesiastical circles, evangelical or Catholic. The rejection of Schweitzer's "Procrustean" solution is motivated by a determination to transform the historical evidence into more comfortable intellectual modes rather than by an effort to come to terms in historically responsible fashion with evidence of a conceptual climate very different from our own. The remedy proposed by these historical revisionists is more appropriately termed "Procrustean" than is the intellectual problem that they are seeking to resolve.

A telling critique of Kloppenborg's sorting out of Q material into earlier purely sapiential levels and a later apocalyptic phrase has been gently but devastatingly offered by Richard Horsley.[20] (The critique applies by implication to Mack's five stages of Q as well.) Testing the nomenclature and classificatory system proposed by Kloppenborg, Horsley shows that the so-called sapiential material in what is identified as the older level of Q does not fit the category of "gnomological," which is a mode of wisdom communication that calls for obedience and assimilation, study and reflection. Rather, these pronouncements in Q demand an active response to a new social order, which will involve tense social interaction and conflict, as reflected in such familiar phrases as "love your enemies," "sheep among wolves," and "don't fear those who can only kill the body." Even advice about prayer and social conditions within the community is set in a framework of expectation of radical change, conflict, and renewal. The Son of Man is not a Christological title but a promised advocate in the divine court of justice (Luke 17:24, 26, 30). The primary concern of Q, Horsley states, is "with a new or restructured social order, which entails social conflict." Overshadowing the proverbs and sapiential sayings (fifteen to twenty of the logia) are prophetic pronouncements and warnings (about half of the 114 total logia). In contrast with Q, the Gospel of Thomas has no prophetic pronouncements against the Pharisees or rulers, or warnings of conflict with earthly authorities; instead, the sayings are individualized and gnosticized. Horsley sees Jesus in Q as a prophet, along with John the Baptist and his predecessors. This theme of Jesus' place within the prophetic tradition evidences a radical difference between Q and the Gospel of Thomas (pace Koester) and emphasizes firm continuities between Jesus and John the Baptist (pace Robinson).

As Horsley notes, most of the Q sayings that Kloppenborg classifies as sapiential are in fact strongly eschatological or even apocalyptic in their essence: the Beatitudes (Luke 6:20–36, 37–49), the insistence on a break with family for the sake of the kingdom (9:57–58), the call to proclaim the coming of God's rule (10:2–12, 13–20), the promise of God's sustaining of his people (11:2–4, 9–13), the promise of revelation of God's purpose (12:2–3, 4–20, 22–23), and the warning to Jerusalem about the rejection of God's messengers, to mention only some. The attempt by Kloppenborg and others to identify an early strand in Q that is free of eschatological features rests on presuppositions—especially antiapocalyptic prejudices—and has been arrived at by a purely circular process, which seeks to conform the evidence to what are regarded as more intellectually safe and respectable categories.

Another candidate that has been advanced for a precanonical gospel tradition is a document mentioned by Clement of Alexandria: the Secret Gospel of Mark. What has been claimed to be a fragment from this gospel was found in 1958 by Morton Smith at the West Bank monastery of Mar Saba in what was then Jordan. The fragment took the form of a quotation included in a copy of a letter purportedly from Clement inserted in the back of a seventeenth-century volume of letters by Ignatius of Antioch. Clement's letter, which is mainly a denunciation of a heretical sect, the Carpocratians, reports that Mark brought the original copy of his gospel to Alexandria from Rome and that he added certain secret material from notes of Peter. The result was "a more spiritual gospel" for the benefit of those who were making "progress toward *gnosis*," adding certain sayings that would lead the informed reader "into the innermost sanctary of the truth hidden by seven [veils]."[21] The major narrative addition describes Jesus spending the night with a youth he had raised from the dead, who came to him wearing only a linen cloth over his naked body, and then adds explicit reference to "naked [man] with naked [man]." Smith's inference from this document was that Jesus had founded a secret movement, into which members were inducted by nocturnal baptism in the nude, including sexual manipulation. After his death, the union was celebrated by eating Jesus' flesh and drinking his blood. These beliefs and practices were preserved in the oral tradition, of which traces may be found in John 11 and Mark 10:46a and 14:51–52. Smith's assumption was that this was historical: the Secret Gospel was the original, of which canonical Mark is an expurgated copy.

Others have variously assessed this fragmentary evidence. Ron Cameron welcomes the documentation of the diversity of the gospel tradition and proposes that canonical Mark is an abridgement of the more original Secret Gospel.[22] Helmut Koester thinks the "vocabulary and style of the additions are fully compatible with the Gospel of Mark." He maintains that the same process of redaction seen in the Secret Gospel was operative in the writing of the canonical Mark, which is not the original Mark (used by Matthew and Luke) but an abbreviated version of the Secret Gospel for public reading.[23] If these were to be the facts of the case, then the original Mark would be even more difficult to get at than the reconstructed Q source, and would—like Q—have to be inferred from Matthew and Luke. Koester offers no clues as to what parts of canonical Mark would be shown to be later, but one suspects that, as in his treatment of Q, the effective criterion would be his antecedent determination to liberate the Jesus tradition from apocalyptic. In fact, careful, detailed redactional analysis shows that canonical Mark—as it exists in the oldest manuscript copies, from 1:1 to 16:8—is the most plausible candidate for the basic narrative document used by Matthew and Luke, supplemented by Q and other traditions.

Notes

Introduction: Ancient History and Contemporary Historiography

1 This categorical distinction was offered by Ferdinand Christian Baur in his essay "Die Christuspartei in der korinthischen Gemeinde, der Gegensatz des paulinischen und petrinischen Christentums in der ältesten Kirche," in *Tübingen Zeitschrift für Theologie* 4 (1831):61ff.

2 A prime example of the long-standing anachronistic approach to Judaism at the beginning of the Common Era is the four-volume *Kommentar zum Neuen Testament aus Talmud und Midrasch*, by Hermann L. Strack and Paul Billerbeck (Munich: Beck, 1922–28). A once widely influential work, *Judaism in the First Centuries of the Christian Era: The Age of the Tannaim*, by George Foote Moore (Cambridge, Mass.: Harvard University Press, 1932), was effectively challenged by Erwin R. Goodenough, who showed how deeply Judaism in the first century was influenced by Hellenistic thought in his study *By Light, Light: The Mystic Gospel of Hellenistic Judaism* (New Haven: Yale University Press, 1935) and in his monumental ten-volume *Jewish Symbols in the Greco-Roman Period* (New York: Pantheon Books, 1953–64).

3 Jacob Neusner's numerous and substantive contributions to the study of Judaism in the period under examination in this work began with his studies in the rise of Pharisaism, *The Pharisees: Rabbinic Perspectives* (Leiden: Brill, 1971; repr. Hoboken, N.J.: KTAV, 1985). For the process of the rise of rabbinic Judaism, Neusner coined the phrase "formative Judaism" (in conscious contrast to that of G. F. Moore, "normative Judaism," in *Judaism in the First Centuries of the Christian Era*) and published an extended series of essays under that title. Among the hundreds of titles published by Neusner, most directly relevant to our interests is *Judaism in the Matrix of Christianity*, South Florida Studies in the History of Judaism, no. 8 (Atlanta: Scholars Press, 1991).

4 For the impact of the work of Wittgenstein on linguistics and more broadly on hermeneutics and the social sciences, see the analysis in my *Knowing the Truth: A Socio-*

logical Approach to New Testament Interpretation (Minneapolis: Fortress Press, 1989), 16–19. The hermeneutical implications of his work are spelled out effectively by Anthony Thiselton in The Two Horizons: New Testament Interpretation and Philosophical Description (Grand Rapids, Mich., Eerdmans, 1980).

5   Thomas S. Kuhn, The Structure of Scientific Revolutions, 2nd ed. (Chicago: University of Chicago Press, 1970).

6   Three basic studies in this field, which are discussed below, are Alfred Schutz, On Phenomenology and Social Relations: Selected Writings, ed. Helmut Wagner (Chicago: University of Chicago Press, 1970), Alfred Schutz and Thomas Luckmann, The Structures of the Life-World, trans. R. M. Zaner and H. T. Englehardt, Jr. (Evanston, Ill.: Northwestern University Press, 1973), and Peter Berger and Thomas Luckmann, The Social Construction of Reality: A Treatise in the Sociology of Knowledge (Garden City, N.Y.: Doubleday, 1967).

7   Ludwig Wittgenstein, Philosophical Investigations I, trans. G. E. M. Anscombe (Oxford: Blackwell, 1967).

8   Ludwig Wittgenstein, On Certainty, ed. G. E. M. Anscombe and G. H. von Wright (Oxford: Blackwell, 1969), sections 61–65, 86–90, 94–95, 103–111, 286–288, 415–434, and 559.

9   Thiselton, The Two Horizons, 378–384.

10 David Bloor, Wittgenstein: A Social Theory of Knowledge (New York: Columbia University Press, 1983), 25, 48.

11 Bloor, Wittgenstein, 71, 92, 181, 183.

12 Susanne Langer, Philosophy in a New Key: A Study in the Symbolism of Reason, Rite and Art (Cambridge, Mass.: Harvard University Press, 1976), 21–22, 44–45.

13 Grace De Laguna, Speech: Its Function and Development (New Haven, Conn.: Yale University Press, 1927), 345–346.

14 Langer, Philosophy in a New Key, 178–180, 200.

15 Clifford Geertz, The Interpretation of Culture (New York: Basic Books, 1973).

16 Kuhn, Structure of Scientific Revolutions, 126–135, 139.

17 Kuhn, 28–30, 46, 62, 67, 148–153.

18 Kuhn, Structure of Scientific Revolutions, 157, 198, 206–209. Kuhn wrote a foreword for a translation of a treatise by a Polish historian of medicine, Ludwig Fleck, Genesis and Development of a Scientific Fact, ed. T. J. Trenn and R. K. Merton (Chicago: University of Chicago Press, 1979). Written more than forty years earlier, Fleck's analysis of theories about syphilis shows that what were regarded as scientific facts based on laboratory investigation varied significantly with the social theories of the investigators. He concludes that "all empirical discovery can be construed as a supplement, development or transformation of thought style" and is shared by a "thought collective" characterized by common "problems of interest, judgments that seem evident, and methods used as means of cognition." Every "fact" must be in line with the interests of its thought collective, and irrespective of content or logical justification, it leads for

sociological reasons to the corroboration of the commonly agreed upon thought structure. Facts arise and are known only by virtue of the given thought style characteristic of a given thought collective.

19 Barry Barnes, *Scientific Knowledge and Sociological Theory* (London: Routledge and Kegan Paul, 1974), 47–68, 147–149.

20 Nelson Goodman, *Ways of World-making* (Indianapolis: Hackett Publishing, 1978), 15–18, 138.

21 Richard Bernstein, *Beyond Objectivism and Relativism: Science, Hermeneutics and Praxis* (Philadelphia: University of Pennsylvania Press, 1983), 69, 156–157.

22 Ian Barbour, *Myths, Models and Paradigms: The Nature of Scientific and Religious Language* (London: SCM Press, 1974), 66–67.

23 Barbour, *Myths, Models and Paradigms*, 142–145, 171–175.

24 Schutz, *On Phenomenology and Social Relations*, 72–73, 80–85.

25 Schutz and Luckmann, *Structures of the Life-World*, 284–285.

26 Peter L. Berger, *The Sacred Canopy: Elements of a Sociological Theory of Religion* (Garden City, N.Y.: Doubleday, 1969).

27 Berger and Luckmann, *Social Construction of Reality*, 92–94, 103–104.

28 Robert Wuthnow, James Davison Hunter, Albert Bergesen, and Edith Kurzweil, *Cultural Analysis: The Work of Peter L. Berger, Mary Douglas, Michel Foucault, and Jurgen Habermas* (Boston and London: Routledge and Kegan Paul, 1984), 260–262.

29 Geertz, *The Interpretation of Culture*, 89.

30 Clifford Geertz, "Common Sense as a Cultural System," in *Local Knowledge* (New York: Basic Books, 1983), 73–93.

31 Maurice Freedman, *Main Trends in Social and Cultural Anthropology* (New York: Holmes and Meier, 1979), esp. 99–100.

32 Dorothy Holland and Naomi Quinn, *Cultural Models in Language and Thought* (Cambridge: Cambridge University Press, 1988), 3.

33 Robert Wuthnow, *Meaning and Moral Order* (Berkeley: University of California Press, 1987), 48–50.

34 Robert Wuthnow, *Communities of Discourse* (Cambridge: Cambridge University Press, 1990), 542–558, 582.

35 The questions set out here were developed during the sessions of a seminar for college teachers funded by the National Endowment for the Humanities and held at Boston University in the summer of 1988 under the author's direction. This material was brought together by Prof. John E. Stanley as a summary of the presentations and discussion among the members of the seminar and visiting scholars.

36 A prime example of cognitive dissonance in Judaism and early Christianity would be that a prophetic promise (such as the end of the present age) failed to be fulfilled.

Chapter 1: Models of Community in the Literature of Postexilic Judaism

1   Jer. 21:6–10; 25:28–29; 38:3–12; 39:4–16.

2   Jer. 30:18; 31:6, 12; 51:10.

3   This theme of divine judgment on the city of Jerusalem and its rulers is sounded in Ezek. 22:1–31 as well.

4   This process is evident throughout the Pentateuch in its present form, but the priestly input is especially clear in Leviticus, where two strands of cultic tradition are evident: the priestly code, which emphasizes the purity of the officials who preside over the cult, and the holiness code, which calls for purity on the part of the people. Detailed evidence is offered by Jacob Milgrom in Leviticus, vol. 1, in the *Anchor Bible Commentary* (Garden City, N.Y.: Doubleday, 1989). On the development of the Pentateuchal tradition, including the priestly reworking of the narrative traditions, see Martin Noth, *A History of Pentateuchal Traditions*, trans. B. W. Anderson (Englewood Cliffs, N.J.: Prentice-Hall, 1972).

5   To which have been added the mix of narrative and legal precepts that constitute the books of Leviticus, Numbers, and Deuteronomy.

6   A prime example of this type of romance is *Ephesiaca*, by Xenophon, which is propaganda for the Isis cult, as is the *Metamorphoses* of L. Apuleius. A kindred literary type is what Gregory E. Sterling has designated "apologetic historiography" in his analysis of Gentile and Jewish historical writers of the Hellenistic period (Berossus, Manetho, Demetrios, Eupolemus, Artapanus), above all Josephus (in *Historiography and Self-definition: Josephos, Luke-Acts and Apologetic Historiography*, Supplements to *Novm Testamentum*, no. 54 [Leiden: Brill, 1992]). The strategy of these writers is to present "the story of a subgroup of people in an extended prose narrative written by a member of the group who follows the group's own traditions but hellenizes them in an effort to establish the identity of the group within the setting of the larger world." The chief aim of the group is self-definition of its community within the cultural context of the Greco-Roman world (16–19).

7   This recalls the familiar theme in Ps. 40:6–8, where priority is given to obeying the law before performance of sacrifices.

8   Jacob Neusner, *Ancient Judaism: Debates and Disputes*, Brown Judaic Studies, no. 64. (Chicò, Calif.: Scholars Press, 1984). Simplified versions of the ideas in Neusner's earlier, more technical volumes have been made available in a textbook, *The Rabbinic Traditions about The Pharisees before 70* (Englewood Cliffs, N.J.: Prentice-Hall, 1973), and in *The Pharisees*.

9   The term was used in the titles of two festschrifts in honor of H. C. Kee: *New Perspectives on Ancient Judaism: Religion, Literature, and Society in Ancient Israel, Formative Christianity and Judaism*, 2 vols. (Lanham, Md.: University Press of America, 1987) and *The Social World of Formative Judaism and Christianity* (Philadelphia: Fortress Press, 1988), both edited by J. Neusner, Peder Borgen, E. S. Frerichs, and Richard Horsley. The latter title has also been adopted as the name of a discussion section of the Society of Biblical Literature. Another volume analyzing critically the methods used in the study of

Judaism and early Christianity is Neusner's *Formative Judaism: Religious, Historical and Literary Studies*, Brown Judaic Studies, no. 37 (Chico, Calif.: Scholars Press, 1982).

10 Shaye J. D. Cohen, *From the Maccabees to the Mishnah* (Philadelphia: Westminster Press, 1987).

11 Morton Smith, "Palestinian Judaism in the First Century," in *Israel: Its Role in Civilization*, ed. Moshe Davis (New York: Harper & Row, 1956), 67–81.

12 Josephus *Antiquities of the Jews* 13.171–173, 18.11–17. (Loeb Classical Library, 1957).

13 For the evidence for this development, see H. C. Kee, "The Transformation of the Synagogue after 70 C.E.: Its Import for Early Christianity," New Testament Studies 36 (1990):1–24.

14 An illuminating analysis of the evidence for the lay options in Judaism around the turn of the eras can be found in Anthony J. Saldarini, *Pharisees, Scribes and Sadducees in Palestinian Society: A Sociological Approach* (Wilmington, Del.: Michael Glazier, 1988).

15 Geza Vermes, *The Dead Sea Scrolls in English*, 3rd ed. (London: Penguin Books, 1987), 1–18.

16 After mentioning "the chief priests, the Levites and the heads [of the tribes] . . . as well as the Levites," the War Scroll continues: "They shall rank the chief priests below the High Priest and his vicar. And the twelve chief priests shall minister at the daily sacrifice before God, whereas the twenty-six leaders of the priestly divisions shall minister in their divisions. Below them, in perpetual ministry, shall be the chiefs of the Levites to the number of twelve, one for each tribe. . . . Below them shall be the chiefs of the tribes together with the heads of the family of the congregation."

17 Or Sirach; this work is also known as Ecclesiasticus.

18 The influence of Stoic philosophy on Ben Sira, as well as some basic disagreements on ontological issues, has been detailed by Martin Hengel in *Judaism and Hellenism*, vol. 1 (Philadelphia: Fortress Press, 1974), 131–153.

19 A magisterial analysis and exposition of this work is that of David Winston in the *Anchor Bible, The Wisdom of Solomon* (Garden City, N.Y.: Doubleday, 1979).

20 Hengel, *Judaism and Helenism*, 1:176–180.

21 As in Ronald E. Clement's commentary *Isaiah 1–39* (Grand Rapids, Mich.: Eerdmans, 1980).

22 The first and last of these oracles are probably from the time of the exile (sixth century), but Isa. 24–27 likely dates from after the return from exile, in the fifth century B.C.E.

23 Michael Fishbane, *Biblical Interpretation in Ancient Israel* (Oxford: Clarendon Press, 1988).

24 Cf. Lev. 23:33–36, which describes a harvest festival that became historicized as a symbolic depiction of the transitory mode of existence of Israel during the Exodus from Egypt.

25 Although the Book of Daniel purports to have been written during the transition from

the reign of the neo-Babylonians Nebuchadnezzar and Belshazzar to that of "Darius the Mede" (Dan. 5:30), the details of the desecration of the Temple altar indicate that it was put in its present form after 167 B.C.E., in the reign of the Seleucid king of Syria, Antiochus IV Epiphanes.

26 There is a brief but perceptive discussion of the date of the Similitudes in John J. Collins, *The Apocalyptic Imagination: An Introduction to the Jewish Matrix of Christianity* (New York: Crossroad, 1987), 142–143. Collins dismisses the theory of J. T. Milik that the Similitudes were written by a Christian.

27 The text does not specify features of the Mosaic law, so the term may be used to refer to the law of nature, which was dominant in the Hellenistic culture and which influenced Jewish thinking, as noted below.

28 Enoch fragments from Qumran include a manuscript in which the order of material is altered from that in what used to be the basic source (Ethiopic Enoch) and follows the sequence here suggested.

29 In the introduction to his translation of Jubilees (in *The Old Testament Pseudepigrapha*, ed. J. H. Charlesworth, vol. 2 [Garden City, N.Y.: Doubleday 1985], 35–41), O. S. Wintermute seeks to differentiate Jubilees from what he regards as purer examples of apocalyptic (Daniel and Enoch), but if one takes into account the basic literary style, esoteric mode of communication, view of divinely determined history, and promise to the faithful remnant, Jubilees matches this model well.

30 These supplements are apparently Christian, since they include the assertion that God has abandoned Israel as his people.

31 Fragments of all parts of Enoch have been found, except for the Similitudes of Enoch. The proposal by J. T. Milik that the Similitudes were of Christian origin (he included them among writings of the Roman period attributed to Christians in *The Books of Enoch* [Oxford: Oxford University Press, 1976], 89–107) has not found wide scholarly acceptance.

32 J. A. Sanders, *The Dead Sea Psalms Scroll* (Ithaca, N.Y.: Cornell University Press, 1967), p. 105.

33 CD 2–3; adapted from Vermes, *Dead Sea Scrolls in English*, 84–85.

34 Quoted by Collins, *Apocalyptic Imagination*, 4.

35 David Hellholm, "The Problem of Apocalyptic Genre and the Apocalypse of John," in *SBL Seminar Papers 1982*, ed. Kent Richards (Chico, Calif.: Scholars Press, 1982), 168.

36 George Nickelsburg, in *Apocalypticism in the Mediterranean World and the Near East*, ed. David Hellholm (Tübingen: Mohr, 1983), 649.

37 David Aune, *Prophecy in Early Christianity and the Ancient Mediterranean World* (Grand Rapids, Mich.: Eerdmans, 1983), 49–78.

38 Plato *Timaeus* 71c–72b; Aune, *Prophecy in Early Christianity*, 38–39.

39 Walter Burkert, "Apokalyptik im frühen Griechentum: Impulse und Transformation," in *Apocalypticism in the Mediterranean World and the Near East*, 235–253.

40 J. Gwyn Griffiths, "Apocalyptic in the Hellenistic Era," in *Apocalypticism in the Mediterranean World and the Near East*, 273–299.

41 Jonathan Z. Smith, "Wisdom and Apocalyptic," in *Map is Not Territory* (Leiden: Brill, 1978), 102–103, 110–112.

42 Josephus *Contra Apionem* 1.129–153.

43 Noted by Diodorus Siculus 17.112.2ff.; see Frederic Cranmer, *Astrology in Roman Law and Politics* (Philadelphia: American Philosophical Society, 1954) 10.

44 Cranmer, *Astrology in Roman Law and Politics*, 19–24, 80.

45 J.H. Charlesworth, "Jewish Astrology in the Talmud, the Dead Sea Scrolls and *Pseudepigrapha*," *Harvard Theological Review* 70 (1977): 188.

46 Debatable is a fragment known as the Aramaic Horoscope of the Messiah, which Vermes (*Dead Sea Scrolls in English*, 305–307) thinks is a description of the birth of Noah.

47 An insightful analysis of the Sibylline Oracles is offered by H. W. Parke in *Sibyls and Sibylline Prophecy in Classical Antiquity* (London and New York: Routledge, 1988).

48 So John J. Collins, in his excellent analysis of these texts, *The Sibylline Oracles of Egyptian Judaism*, Society of Biblical Literature Dissertation Series, no. 13 (Missoula, Mont.: Scholars Press, 1974), 54.

49 Collins, *Sibylline Oracles*, 70.

50 Collins, *Sibylline Oracles*, 118.

51 Ragnar Hoistad, *Cynic Hero and Cynic King: Studies in the Cynic Conception of Man* (Lund: Carl Bloms Botrykeri, 1948).

52 The current attempt of some scholars to portray the historical Jesus as a Cynic on the antisocial model (discussed in the Critical Note below) builds on what Hoistad has shown to be a later (first century C.E.), critically distorted portrayal of the Cynics.

53 Hoistad, *Cynic Hero and Cynic King*, 126–128, 202, 221.

54 This theme recalls Heb. 12:6, which is a quote from Prov. 3:11.

55 The belief recalls Paul in 2 Cor. 5:8, "Absent from the body; present with the Lord."

56 Otto Eissfeldt, in *The Old Testament: An Introduction*, trans. P. R. Ackroyd (New York: Harper, 1965), 486–489, describes this book as a collection of disconnected, profane love songs, possibly mythological or cultic in background.

57 In his *Anchor Bible Commentary* on *Song of Songs* (Garden City, N.Y.: Doubleday, 1977). Roland Murphy, however, wants to see Song of Songs as a celebration of sex and marriage in a positive sense, as essential features of God's creation ("Towards a Commentary on the Song of Songs," *Catholic Biblical Quarterly* 39[1977]:482–496).

58 *Origène. Homélies sur le Cantique des Cantiques*, trans. O. Rousseau (Paris: Les Editions du Cerf, 1953), 10–13.

59 The references here are drawn from Rowan Greer's volume on Origen in the Classics

of Western Spirituality series (New York: Paulist Press, 1979), in his translation of the prologue to the *Commentary on the Song of Songs*, 217.

60 Origen, 231.

61 Origen, 237–239.

62 Origen, 234.

63 Henri Crouzel, *Origène et la "Connaissance Mystique"* (Toulouse: Desclee de Brouwer, 1961), 154, 525. Crouzel notes that Platonism is an essential ingredient in the development of his philosophical mode of hermeneutics (535).

64 Charles Bigg, *The Christian Platonists of Alexandria*, the 1886 Bampton Lectures (Oxford: Oxford University Press, 1913).

65 Pioneering analyses along these lines by Jewish scholars were those of Moses Hadas, *Hellenistic Culture: Fusion and Diffusion* (New York: Columbia University Press, 1959), and Victor Tcherikover, *Hellenistic Civilization and the Jews* (New York: Atheneum, 1959). More recent analyses of the impact of Hellenistic culture on the origins of Christianity include Hengel, *Judaism and Hellenism*, and John J. Collins, *Between Athens and Jerusalem: Jewish Identity in the Hellenistic Diaspora* (New York: Crossroad, 1983). Hengel has supplemented and updated his evidence in *The "Hellenization" of Judea in the First Century after Christ* (Philadelphia: Trinity Press International, 1989).

66 Philo *On the Cherubim* 101–105. Works of Philo are quoted from the Loeb Classical Library.

67 Philo *On the Migration of Abraham* 120–121.

68 Philo *On the Migration of Abraham* 9. Similar appeals are offered to overcome the attraction of earthly pleasures, 155–158.

69 Philo *On the Unchangeableness of God* 155–161.

70 Philo *On the Migration of Abraham* 35.

71 Philo *On the Migration of Abraham* 56.

72 Philo *On the Migration of Abraham* 216.

73 Philo *On the Contemplative Life* 10–11. The Therapeutae may be the same as the Essenes, or perhaps a movement similar to the Qumran community, which lived in monastic isolation from the mainstream of Jewish life.

74 Philo *On Flight and Finding* 108–110.

75 Philo *On Flight and Finding* 137–139.

76 Philo *On Flight and Finding* 176.

77 Philo *On Dreams* 157.

78 Goodenough, *By Light, Light*, 243–244. Although, for decades after its publication, Goodenough's analysis of the thorough hellenization of Philo seemed revolutionary, it

is now clear from archaeological and literary evidence that such hellenization permeated Judaism in this period, including the thinking of Palestinian Jews as well.

79 Philo's case is presented in *De Legatione ad Gaium.*

80 The Angelic Liturgy at Qumran was the name assigned to these writings by John Strugnell in his initial publication of the texts, in Supplements to *Vetus Testamentum* no. 7 (Leiden: Brill, 1960), 318–345. They have now been fully published by Carol Newsom (in the Harvard Semitic Museum Series), *Songs of the Sabbath Sacrifice* (Atlanta, Ga.: Scholars Press, 1985).

81 Vermes, *Dead Sea Scrolls in English*, 221–230.

82 Michael Stone, *Scriptures, Sects and Visions: A Profile of Judaism from Ezra to the Jewish Revolts* (Philadelphia: Fortress Press, 1980), 33–43.

83 *Sepher Ha-Razim: The Book of Mysteries*, trans. Michael A. Morgan (Chico, Calif.: Scholars Press, 1983).

84 David R. Blumenthal, *Understanding Jewish Mysticism: A Source Reader* (New York: KTAV, 1978), 7–8.

85 Gershom G. Scholem, *Major Trends in Jewish Mysticism*, 3rd ed. (New York: Schocken, 1954), 9, 20–21.

86 Ithamar Gruenwald, *Apocalyptic and Merkavah Mysticism*, Arbeiten zur Geschichte des antiken Judentums und des Urchristentums, vol. 14 (Leiden: Brill, 1980).

87 P. Alexander, in the introduction to this translation of the Hebrew Apocalypse of Enoch in *The Old Testament Pseudepigrapha*, ed. J. H. Charlesworth, vol. 1 (Garden City, N.Y.: Doubleday, 1983), 223–253.

88 Alexander, 3 Enoch, 241.

89 Alexander, 3 Enoch, 243–244.

90 Cohen, *From the Maccabees to the Mishnah*, 46–59.

91 Additions to Esther 8:17 in the Greek text, 16:15 in the Authorized Version.

92 The genre and intention of the Hellenistic romances are discussed in my *Miracle in the Early Christian World: A Study in Socio-historical Method* (New Haven: Yale University Press, 1983), 193–195, 252–254.

93 This is the date suggested by Hugh Anderson in his perceptive analysis and fine translation of 4 Maccabees in *The Old Testament Pseudepigrapha*, vol. 2, 531–564, in which he notes that the Temple cult is described in the present tense, implying a pre–70 C.E. date.

94 Among them are *sophrosune, philosophia, phronesis, logismos, andreai,* and *dikaiosune.*

95 Introduction and translation by P. W. Van der Horst in *The Old Testament Pseudepigrapha*, vol. 2, 564–582.

96 Josephus *Contra Apionem* (Loeb Classical Library, 1936). Not the original title, and inappropriate for this broadly aimed apologetic.

Chapter 2: The Community of the Wise

1   Paul D. Hanson has made a major contribution to the study of apocalyptic, not only in his illuminating detailed analyses, but in his insistence that apocalyptic must be interpreted "within the context of the community struggle discernible within the material studied" (*The Dawn of Apocalyptic* [Philadelphia: Fortress Press, 1975], 29). This insight is further refined and developed in his masterful analysis of the changing images of covenant community in *The People Called: The Growth of Community in the Bible* (San Francisco: Harper & Row, 1986).

2   Clearly, the models employed in this study are not classificatory categories. Rather, certain qualities of the models overlap with others. They are assigned here on the basis of what seems to be the most distinctive emphasis of each document on the issue of how the community is perceived. In Richard A. Edwards's ground-breaking study *Theology of Q: Eschatology, Prophecy and Wisdom* (Philadelphia: Fortress Press, 1976), he draws attention to what he calls "the interaction of themes," which he develops in contrast to the efforts of scholars to assign the Q material to fixed, airtight categories.

3   All references to Q in this analysis are designated by where they appear in Luke, which is widely recognized as having preserved the more original version of Q material. My own reconstruction of Q is offered in *Jesus in History*, 3rd ed. (Fort Worth: Harcourt Brace, 1996).

4   "Son of man" is discussed below under the second motif, Jesus as revealer and agent of God.

5   The verb in the conditional clause is in the indicative, which could be rendered "since you are," rather than in the subjunctive, which would imply contrariness to fact. The title Son of God is presumably linked with passages like Ps. 2 where the royal agent of God is described.

6   The repeated verb in 22:29, *diatithemi*, is a cognate of the term for covenant, *diatheke*.

7   The symbol of the eschatological meal is found in both the Markan (Mark 14:25) and Pauline traditions (1 Cor. 15:23–26), and is implied in the Messianic Rule from Qumran (1QSa).

8   In contrast to Matthew's version, which minimizes the contrast between present plight and deprivation and future reward, emphasizing instead the present blessedness of the obedient.

9   The allegorical details are elaborated extensively in the Matthean version of this parable (Matt. 24:14–30).

10   Eusebius *Ecclesiastical History* 2.15.

11   Rudolf Bultmann, *The History of the Synoptic Tradition*, trans. John Marsh (New York: Harper & Row, 1963), 347.

12   Martin Dibelius, *From Tradition to Gospel*, trans. B. L. Woolf (New York: Scribners, n.d.), 230.

13   Helmut Koester, *Ancient Christian Gospels: Their History and Development* (Philadelphia: Trinity Press International, 1990), 285. It is ironical, however, that Koester then

asserts that canonical Mark is not the same as the abbreviated version of Secret Mark used by Matthew and Luke in writing their gospels (302).

14 Burton Mack, *A Myth of Innocence: Mark and Christian Origins* (Philadelphia: Fortress Press, 1988).

15 Mack, *Myth of Innocence*, 3.

16 Mack, *Myth of Innocence*, 12.

17 Mack, *Myth of Innocence*, 20–24.

18 Mack, *Myth of Innocence*, 27–52, 73–74, and 78–88.

19 Mack, *Myth of Innocence*, 124–131.

20 Mack, *Myth of Innocence*, 230–245, 319–331.

21 I have laid out this familiar evidence in a form intended for lay readership in *What Can We Know about Jesus?* (Cambridge: Cambridge University Press, 1990).

22 Martin Hengel, *Studies in the Gospel of Mark* (Philadelphia: Fortress Press, 1985), 29, 52.

23 Herman C. Waetjen, *A Reordering of Power: A Socio-Political Reading of Mark's Gospel* (Minneapolis: Fortress Press, 1989), 1–26.

24 *Kurios*, which occurs in Mark thirteen times, in five cases refers to Jesus (2:28; 7:28; 11:3; 12:36, 37), in an equal number of instances refers to God (12:11, 29, 30, 36; 13:20), and in three passages could be understood as either Jesus or God (1:3; 11:9; 12:9). Significantly, most of the references to God are in those sections of Mark where Jesus is reinterpreting Torah.

25 I have treated this factor at length in two books: *Miracle in the Early Christian World*, 146–173, and *Medicine, Miracle and Magic in New Testament Times*, 2nd ed. (Cambridge: Cambridge University Press, 1988), 72, 78–80.

26 The term for Jesus' spoken control of the stormy wind is the same word, *epitimao*, that is used for control of the demons. See H. C. Kee, "The Terminology of Mark's Exorcism Stories," *New Testament Studies* 14 (1968): 307–314.

27 This phenomenon is linked with Merkavah mysticism, as is shown by Gruenwald in *Apocalyptic and Merkavah Mysticism*. The experience in the Jewish tradition is akin to that of Paul, reported in 2 Cor. 12:1–4.

28 Richard Horsley has quite properly drawn attention to the importance of these dimensions of the gospel tradition in his *Sociology and the Jesus Movement* (New York: Crossroad, 1989), where details are offered of the social conflicts and tensions in Palestine in this period.

29 This contrasts with Matthew's version (3:13–17), where the voice addresses others: "*This* is my beloved Son."

30 The motif of God overcoming the powers of evil symbolized by the sea monster occurs in Job (3:8; 26:12–13; 41:1–34) and elsewhere in the Psalms (104:26) and the prophets (Isa. 26:20–27:1).

31 The suffering and deprivation of the faithful community at the hands of hostile rulers are depicted in the opening stories of Dan. 1–7. Although the absence of manuscripts of the Similitudes section of 1 Enoch from the finds at Qumran has led some scholars to assign it a late date and to attribute it to Christians (so Milik, *Books of Enoch*, 89–98), more careful and reasoned scholarly opinion points to the early first century C.E. (prior to 70) as a more likely date. See John J. Collins, *The Apocalyptic Imagination*, 142–154. E. Isaac, in *The Old Testament Pseudepigrapha*, vol. 1, 7, assigns the Similitudes to the first century B.C.E.

32 For Neusner's earlier studies of the rise of Pharisaism, see the introduction, n. 3, and chap. 1, n. 8.

33 Cohen, *From the Maccabees to the Mishnah*, and Saldarini, *Pharisees, Scribes and Sadducees*.

34 In Phil. 3:5–6, where a concise autobiographical summary affirms his impeccable genealogical and ritual credentials (from the tribe of Benjamin, of unbroken Hebrew ancestry, circumcised in infancy), he reports that his mode of interpreting the Torah was that of the Pharisees.

35 Documented by him in Gal. 1:13–14.

36 For an insightful analysis of Paul from a Jewish scholarly perspective, see Alan F. Segal, *Paul the Convert: The Apostolate and Apostasy of Saul the Pharisee* (New Haven: Yale University Press, 1990).

37 Acts 9:30, 11:25, and 22:3.

38 Strabo, in his *Geography* (14.673–674), notes that most of those studying philosophy in Tarsus were from the city and nearby, rather than coming from great distances.

39 Wisdom as preexisting the creation is affirmed in the Jewish wisdom tradition (Wisd. of Sol. 9:1–4; 10:1–2), and as the product of God's initial act of creation (Ben Sira 1:1–10). Analogous to this concept, but not simply identical with it, is Paul's understanding that Jesus had an existence prior to his physical birth.

40 Hanson, *Dawn of Apocalyptic*, 369–380.

41 "For I made the world for [Israel's] sake, and when Adam transgressed my statutes, what had been made was condemned. And so the ways of this world were made narrow and difficult; they are few and evil, full of dangers and involved in great hardships. But the ways of the future world are broad and safe, and truly yield the fruit of immortality."

42 "And with regard to the righteous ones, those whom you said the world has come on their account, yes, also that which is coming is on their account. For this world is to them a struggle and an effort with much trouble. And that accordingly which will come, a crown with great glory."

43 The argument here seems to be based on the principle, implicit in Jewish law and presumably in Roman law, that marital obligations are lifelong. Torah allows for divorce and remarriage (Deut. 24:1–4), while deploring infidelity on the part of the wife (Num. 5:20–29; Prov. 6:24–29; Hos. 3:3).

44 A useful range of viewpoints on the issues concerning the place of historic Israel in

the purpose of God is provided in the collection of essays edited by Karl P. Donfried, *The Romans Debate* rev. ed. (Peabody, Mass.: Hendrickson, 1991). A more radical approach to the subject is set forth by Heikki Raisanen, *Paul and the Law* (Philadelphia: Fortress Press, 1986).

45 This source was proposed by Origen in his *Commentary on Matthew,* in exposition of Matt. 27:9.

46 With 2 Pet. 1:5, cf. Jude 3; with 1:2, cf. Jude 5; with 3:2, cf. Jude 17–18; with 3:14, cf. Jude 14; with 3:18, cf. Jude 25. The descriptions of the false teachers match closely: with 2:1–2, cf. Jude 4; with 2:10–11, cf. Jude 8–9; with 2:18, cf. Jude 16; with 2:13, cf. Jude 12; with 2:17, cf. Jude 12–13. The evil style of life is the same in detail: with 2:10, 12–13, 18, cf. Jude 7, 10, 12. The same examples of divine judgment listed in Jude 5 ff. are rearranged in 2 Peter 2:4–7. Clearly, 2 Peter is heavily dependent on Jude, and not vice versa.

47 For example, Lev. 19:18 in James 2:8; Exod. 20:13 and Deut. 5:17 in 2:11; Gen. 15:6 in 2:23; Josh. 2:1–15 in 2:25; and Prov. 3:34 in 4:5. Possible allusions to or parallels with noncanonical texts include Enoch 98:4 in James 1:14; Enoch 48:7 in 3:6; and Test. Napht. 8:4 in 4:7. At one point, a text of unknown origin is quoted (4:5).

48 The crucial term here is *anastrophe,* which implies a recurrent or typical way of life. Significantly, the term occurs only once in the Pauline letters (Gal. 1:13), where Paul refers to his former mode of living in Judaism.

49 In the introduction to her commentary on James (*A Commentary on the Epistle of James,* Harper New Testament Commentaries (San Francisco: Harper & Row, 1980), Sophie Laws demonstrates James's use of the language and literary styles of Hellenistic philosophy, while noting that he is scarcely master of the field. Rather, he adopts and adapts it to serve his own purpose.

50 A summary of such occurrences appears in K. L. Schmidt's article on *threskeia* in *Theological Dictionary of the New Testament* 3:156. The term is used in Col. 2:18, where the object of the worship is the angels. In Acts 26:5, it appears in Paul's reference to his Pharisaic position within Judaism ("the strictest party of our religion").

Chapter 3: The Law-abiding Community

1 Archelaus in Judea, Herod Antipas in Galilee and Peraea, and Philip in the northern and eastern territories beyond the Sea of Galilee.

2 Or, more accurately, the One whose Teaching is Right.

3 The relation of the Dead Sea group to the Essenes, described in the writings of Philo of Alexandria (*Quod Omn.* 75–91; *Hypothetica* 11.1–15) and Josephus (*Jewish Wars* 2.8.2–13), is still debated. Since these writers picture the Essenes as living in the towns and cities of Israel, it it possible that the Dead Sea group was either a more radical version of the Essene movement or its headquarters, to which only the fully committed members withdrew to live the pure life in isolation from what they regarded as the perverted and polluted situation in the land of Judah under the priestly incumbents. For a fuller discussion, see the article on the Essenes by John J. Collins in the *Anchor Bible Dictionary,* vol. 2 (New York: Doubleday, 1992) 619–626.

4   Described in the appendix to the Scroll of the Rule, which provides detailed instructions for the ongoing common life of the community.

5   The best introduction to and translation of these writings in English is Vermes, *Dead Sea Scrolls in English.*

6   See references to Neusner's basic work on the Pharisees in introduction, n. 3, and chap. 1, n. 8.

7   A useful set of essays on the origins and development of the synagogue is *The Synagogues: Studies in Origins, Archaeology and Architecture*, ed. J. Gutman (New York: KTAV 1975). The origins are also discussed in *The Synagogue in Late Antiquity*, ed. Lee I. Levine (Philadelphia: American Schools of Oriental Research, 1987) and in Cohen, *From the Maccabees to the Mishnah.* For a thorough and perceptive review of ancient sources and modern scholarly studies of the synagogue, see L. Michael White, *Building God's House in the Roman World: Architectural Adaptation among Pagans, Jews, and Christians* (Baltimore: Johns Hopkins University Press, 1990). A spectrum of views about the synagogue and other aspects of Jewish life in the diaspora in the Roman period can be found in *Diaspora Jews and Judaism: Essays in Honor of, and in Dialogue With A. Thomas Kraabel*, ed. J. A. Overman and R. S. MacLennan, South Florida Studies in the History of Judaism 41 (Atlanta: Scholars Press, 1992).

8   "Defining the First Century Synagogue: Problems and Progress," *New Testament Studies* 41, 1995.

9   Jacob Neusner, *Messiah in Context* (Philadelphia: Fortress Press, 1984), 18–21.

10 Erwin R. Goodenough, *Jewish Symbols in the Greco-Roman Period*, vol. 8, *Pagan Symbols in Judaism* (New York: Pantheon Books, 1958), 167–218. Symbols in the Dura synagogue are discussed in vols. 9–10 (1964). There is a brief survey of this phenomenon by Michael Avi-Yonah in *The Dura-Europos Synagogue: A Re-evaluation (1932–1972)*, ed. J. Gutman (Missoula, Mont.: American Academy of Religion, 1973), 117–136.

11 See the discussion of the kinship of Judaism with Stoicism in chap. 2 above.

12 See H. C. Kee, "Ethical Dimensions of the Testaments of the Twelve as a Clue to Provenance," *New Testament Studies* 24 (1978): 259–170. Also H. C. Kee, "Testaments of the Twelve Patriarchs," in *The Old Testament Pseudepigrapha*, vol. 1, 775–838.

13 See the discussion in chap. 1 above.

14 Adolf Deissmann, *Light from the Ancient East* (New York: Harper, n.d.), 451–452.

15 For differing points of view on the "God-fearers," see R. S. MacLennan and A. T. Kraabel, "The God-Fearers: A Literary and Theological Invention," in *Diaspora Jews and Judaism*, 131–144. For interpretation of the evidence that affirms their existence and their importance in the synagogues, see the essay in that volume by J. A. Overman, "The God-Fearers: Some Neglected Features"; also White, *Building God's House in the Roman World*, 88–90.

16 See the archaeological evidence from excavations in Galilee that demonstrates abundantly the extensive use of Greek among Jews resident there in the first and second centuries C.E., presented in a series of essays in *The Synagogue in Late Antiquity.*

17 The most plausible time and setting for the Gospel of Matthew is in the late first century C.E., prior to the second Jewish revolt under Bar Kochba (130–135). Jews and Christians were alike claiming to be the true heirs of the traditions of Israel. Important works tracing this development include those by J. Andrew Overman, *Matthew's Gospel and Formative Judaism: The Social World of the Matthean Community* (Minneapolis: Fortress Press, 1990); Amy-Jill Levine, *The Social and Ethnic Dimensions of Matthean Salvation History* (Lewiston, N.Y., Edwin Mellen, 1988); and the masterful scholarly survey and creative reconstruction of Matthew's Gospel by Anthony J. Saldarini, *Matthew's Christian-Jewish Community* (Chicago: University of Chicago Press, 1994). Saldarini sees the Matthean group as Jews seeking to persuade other Jews that Jesus is the Messiah and that his reinterpretation of the Law of Moses is the divinely intended guideline for the covenant people.

18 It is significant that the argument in support of the divine agency in the virgin birth of Jesus rests on the Greek translation, *parthenos*, rather than on the Hebrew original, *almah*, which means simply "young woman." The cultural setting of Matthew's gospel, profoundly Jewish though it is, communicates itself in the language of Hellenism.

19 The intended linguistic link between Nazareth and the Hebrew text is probably *ntsr*, "branch" in Isa. 11:1, although closer in sound to Nazareth is the root *nzr*, transliterated as Nazirite, the ascetic especially devoted to Yahweh.

20 Traces of Isa. 8:23 and Ps. 107:10 are also discernible in this passage from Matthew.

21 The passages are 1:22, 2:5, 2:15, 2:17, 2:23, 4:14, 8:17, 12:17, 13:35, 21:4, and 27:9–10.

22 In Acts 10:47, this term is part of a formula for determining the appropriate candidates for baptism.

23 In Luke 4:19, the location is simply "Jerusalem."

24 The terms "Father in heaven" and "kingdom of heaven" [lit., "of the heavens"] are distinctively Matthean. The former and the alternative "heavenly Father" are frequent in the Sermon on the Mount: 5:16, 45, 48; 6:1, 9; and 7:11, 21. The latter phrase occurs throughout Matthew and is found only in this gospel: 3:2; 4:17; 5:3, 10, 19, 20; 7:21; 8:11; 10:7; 11:1, 12; and 13:11, 24, 31, 33, 44, 45, 47, 52. The "kingdom of the Father" is a special case, discussed below with the parables in Matthew.

25 This term, which occurs only once outside Matthew's gospel (Luke 12:28), also appears in 8:26, 14:31, 16:8, and 17:20.

26 Healing a leper (8:1–4; cf. Mark 1:40–45); healing Peter's mother-in-law (8:14–15; cf. Mark 1:29–31); calming a storm (8:23–27; cf. Mark 4:35–41); driving demons into a herd of swine (8:28–34; cf. Mark 5:1–20); healing a paralytic (9:2–8; cf. Mark 2:1–12); and curing Jairus's daughter and a woman with a bloody flow (9:18–26).

27 This passage is added from another Q pericope, Luke 13:28–30, where the emphasis falls on the inclusiveness of the new community of the covenant.

28 This is a Q tradition; cf. Luke 10:23–24.

29 The weeping and grinding of teeth by the failed members of the covenant community is a favorite theme of Matthew, who includes it six times in his gospel: 8:12; 13:42; 50; 22:13; 24:51; 25:30. Elsewhere in the New Testament, this image of judgment appears only in Luke 13:28.

30 Matt. 4:23; 9:35; 10:17; 12:9; 13:54; 23:24.

31 These themes run throughout the Sermon on the Mount, but appear even more forcefully in Matt. 23.

32 *Ekklesia*, which means a convened gathering, is of course a synonym of *synagoge*. To differentiate their respective ways of understanding themselves as God's people, the Christians chose the former designation, and the Jews in the emergent rabbinic tradition, the latter.

33 Instead of using an analogy to indicate how the kingdom is to be freely accepted, just as children take what is offered to them (Mark 9:32–37), the disciples are here called to "become like children," accepting lowly rank.

34 The Greek term here, *Gehenna*, derives from the Valley of Hinnom, the area southeast of Jerusalem that served as drainage and dump for the city and seems to have been characterized by smouldering rubbish fires.

35 I shall return to the theme of the little ones in the analysis of the parable of the last judgment (25:31–46).

36 These pejorative terms are used here in the traditional exclusivist sense, even though it is clear from the rest of Matthew that Gentiles and tax collectors were welcomed into the new community (8:5–13; 9:9–13).

37 This term appears only here and in Tit. 3:5 in the New Testament. Clearly, it is taken over from the wider Hellenistic world. The concept of new birth, though not this specific term, appears in John 3. But since the crucial term *anothen*, usually translated "again" (John 3:3, 5), can also mean "from above," the intended significance in John may be that, just as Jesus is the Word of God come to dwell in human form ("made flesh," John 1:14), so those who will enter God's kingdom must have a new birth from God ("from above"). In Matt. 19:28, the image is of a world reborn.

38 The incident referred to here is actually a combination of details from 2 Chron. 24:20–21 and Zech. 1:1.

39 Mark 13:9b–12 has already been quoted by Matthew in his version of the sending of the twelve (10:17–21), however.

40 The Q parallels are found in Luke 12:35–40; 17:23–27, 34–35; and 12:42–46.

41 The Lukan version of this parable (19:12–17) has also been shaped allegorically, but in a different direction. A wellborn (*eugenes*) son has gone to another land to receive a kingdom. In his absence, certain citizens reject his rulership, while those assigned responsibilities vary in the effectiveness with which they fulfill their duties. On his return, the latter receive appropriate rewards, while the "enemies" are slaughtered in his presence.

42 For the origin and frequency of this image of punishment, see notes 29 and 34 above.

43 The theme of blood vengeance recurs in the historical and prophetic traditions of Israel: 2 Sam. 1:16; 14:9; Jer. 51:35.

Chapter 4: The Community Where God Dwells among His People

1 "City" carries many of the connotations of "kingdom" in the gospel tradition. It emphasizes the primary locus of God's activity, while "kingdom" emphasizes the exercise of authority and the accomplishment thereby of the divine purpose.

2 Although the analysis of Paul's letters in the previous chapter employs the model of the "community of the wise" in its apocalyptic mode, it is clear that Paul used other models as well in his depictions of both Jesus and the new community. We shall see below that other documents that build on one primary model also rely in certain ways on other models of the covenant community and the correlative agent of God for the renewal of his people.

3 The passage has phrases from Lev. 26:11, Ezek. 37:27, Isa. 52:11, Ezek. 20:34, 41, and 2 Sam. 7:8–14.

4 Antecedents for this concept of the community as growing are to be found in 2 Cor. 9:10 and 10:15, where the members are instructed to see that their "righteousness" and "faith" continue to grow. But in Colossians, the notion is considerably amplified: after an initial description of the gospel as "growing and bearing fruit" (1:6), the community is exhorted to continue "growing in the knowledge [*epignosis*] of God" (1:10), and the promise is uttered that the "whole body will grow with growth from God" (2:19). In 2 Pet. 3:18, the community is instructed to "grow in grace and in knowledge."

5 The themes—expressed in metaphors—of the structuring of the church and its organic growth, which are of central importance for the Ephesian letter, are treated in chap. 7 below, where formalization and institutionalization of the community are examined.

6 "Sonship" is a variant of three other communal terms found in Paul's letters and other New Testament writings: nation (*ethnos*), race (*genos*), and people (*laos*), all of which are used in 1 Peter. See below.

7 The terms used by Paul, *leitourgia* and *heirourgeo*, are used by Josephus to refer to priestly services (*War*, 1.26; *Antiquities*, 3.107, 6.102, 7.333).

8 As R. Meyer notes in *Theological Dictionary of the New Testament* 4:215–225, *leitourgeo* is philologically akin to *laos*, and was used in earlier nonbiblical Greek sources with reference to civic responsibilities discharged primarily by wealthy individuals for the benefit of the larger society. Later it occurs for any form of obligation, such as paying taxes, to the larger body politic. In the Septuagint and in some Greek literature and inscriptions from the second century B.C.E. and later, however, it refers to cultic service. Most of the occurrences of the term in the Septuagint are in sections of Torah dealing with cultic regulations: Exod. 28–29 (thirteen occurrences); Num. (twenty-five times); and Ezek. 40–46, where the renewal of the Temple is described (sixteen times).

9 The antagonism is reflected in the familiar controversy between Paul and Peter over

whether Gentile believers were obligated to observe the ritual and dietary laws of the Jewish tradition (Gal. 2:11–14).

10 An excellent analysis of 1 Peter is John H. Elliott, *A Home for the Homeless: A Sociological Exegesis of 1 Peter, Its Situation and Strategy* (Philadelphia: Fortress Press, 1981).

11 The nature of the "priesthood" in 1 Peter 2 is analyzed by Elliott in *The Elect and the Holy: An Exegetical Examination of 1 Peter 2:4–10.* (Leiden: Brill, 1966). His conclusion about *hierateuma* is that it "depicts the community of the faithful as a corporate and active body of priests, as the continuation and yet also the consummation of the Chosen People of God" (197). Elliott sees this term not as referring to the Eucharist or even to the suffering of the people of God but as pointing to a life of holiness under the power of the Spirit (225), but in fact the suffering of Christ is the model for what the community must expect to experience.

12 In the Septuagint.

13 The Hebrew text reads *leberith 'am*, (for a covenant of the people) and the Septuagint reads *eis diatheke genous*. In both cases, the literal translation would be "covenant of *a* nation."

14 See the analysis of this and other redemptive-history passages in chap. 1 above, where the history of Israel is presented in terms of divine purpose and the destiny of God's people.

15 Representative texts include Judg. 2:20; 1 Kings 14:19–24; 2 Kings 21:2; 2 Chron. 28:3, 33:32, and 36:14; and Ezra 7:13.

16 The reference recalls Deut. 21:22, where the violator of the law who is "hanged on a tree" is to be buried on the same day as his death, in order to avoid defiling the land.

17 This passage is translated from the Septuagint; the crucial latter part does not correspond to the briefer version in the Hebrew text.

18 As in Paul's Letter to the Romans (13:1–7), the community members are to obey human institutions, including the emperor and imperial governors, since these earthly rules are the instruments for maintenance of civil law and order (1 Pet. 5:13–17).

19 1 Pet. 2:22 alludes to Isa. 53:9; 1 Pet. 2:24 alludes to Isa. 53:4, 12, and 53:5, 6.

20 *Basileus* (twenty-one times); *basileia* (eight times); *basileuo* (six times).

21 *Parembole* carries the meaning of an established military structure in its appearances in Acts (21:34, 37; 22:24; 23:10, 16, 32), as it does in two of the occurrences in Hebrews (13:11, 13).

22 Conjectures about the identity of this "beast" and gematria calculations based on the numerical equivalents of letters have variously interpreted its number, 666, ranging from Nero Caesar (if spelled in Hebrew) to Domitian (if his name and titles are abbreviated) to the initials of all the Caesars from Julius Caesar to Vespasian (if Otho and Vitellius are omitted). An interesting parallel is the sibylline oracles (1.328–29), where the number of Jesus is given as 888.

23 Exod. 26:35, 30:27, 31:8, 35:14, 37:17, 40:4, 40:24; Lev. 1–4; Num. 3:31, 4:9, 8:2–4.

24 1 Kings 7:49; 1 Chron. 28:15; 2 Chron. 4:7, 13:11.

25 Similarly, 1 Macc. 1:21 reports the plunder of the sacred lamp stand by Antiochus IV, and its replacement by the priests when the Temple is renewed and rededicated (4:42–51).

26 These "anointed ones" are probably in the same tradition as the later Qumran document, 1 QSa, where the Messiah of Aaron has precedence over the Messiah of Israel at the eschatological meal.

27 Kee, *Miracle in the Early Christian World*, 78–104.

28 This is pictured in Ps. 74:13–14, where God breaks the heads of the dragons and crushes the head of Leviathan. In Isa. 41:9, the prophet recalls how Rahab was "cut in pieces" and the dragon was "pierced."

29 An illuminating critical survey of the portrayal of Jesus as "the Lamb" is Raymond E. Brown's commentary on the Gospel of John in the *Anchor Bible* (Garden City, N.Y.: Doubleday, 1966), vol. 1, 60 ff. John the Baptist sees Jesus as the apocalyptic Lamb who will overcome evil in the world. Elsewhere in the New Testament, the sacrificial death of Jesus is linked with Isa. 53, as in Acts 8:32, Matt. 8:17, and Heb. 9:28. In John 12:38, the tie with Isa. 53:1 is explicit. In the Septuagint version of Isa. 53, a different verb is used in the description of the vicarious suffering of God's Lamb (*pherein*) than is found in John (*airein*), just as different terms are used in the Septuagint for the sacrificial animal: *probaton* instead of John's *amnos*, while in Jer. 11:19 the word is *arnion*. In Exod. 39:38–46, the daily offering is an *amnos*, while in Lev. 4:32 the *probaton* is the sin offering, just as it is what Abraham offers to God in Gen. 22:8. Thus Brown concludes that in the Hebrew scriptures and especially the Greek version of them there is a mixture of features and terms in relation to the sacrificial lamb, as there is in Isa. 53:7 (*probaton* and *amnos*), so that the relationships of the images in the Jewish scriptures and the New Testament are conceptual rather than linguistic.

30 Both the rhetorical style of this letter and its sophisticated terminology are unique among the New Testament writings. The traditional designation, "To the Hebrews," is useless, since the issue of the obligation of Christians to observe the law of Moses is absent, having been replaced by the intellectual issue of the relationship of the system of sacrifice and divine access set forth in the Jewish scriptures to the sacrifice and resulting access to God provided through Jesus. The instrument by which the author builds his brilliant case is philosophy, combining features of middle Platonism and late Stoicism. A fine analysis of these features is offered by James W. Thompson in *The Beginnings of Christian Philosophy*, Catholic Biblical Quarterly Monograph no. 13 (Washington, D.C., 1982). The attempt to discount the Platonic features of Hebrews by Lincoln D. Hurst, in "Eschatology and 'Platonism' in the Epistle to the Hebrews" (*SBL Seminar Papers 1984*, [Chico, Calif.: Scholars Press, 1984], 41–74), is unconvincing.

31 Homer *Iliad* 6.88, 20.52.

32 Homer *Iliad* 14.230; *Odyssey* 6.177.

33 Homer *Iliad* 17.144; *Odyssey* 11.14.

34 Aristotle *Politics* 1280b40.

35 Aristotle *Politics* 1278b11, 1279b26, 1283b31, 1289a15, 1292b34, 1293a37; Herodotus *Persian Wars* 9.34; Xenophon *Memorabilia* 3.9.15.

36 Aristotle *Politics* 1302b16, 1332b31.

37 Works of Plutarch are quoted from Loeb Classical Library editions published in 1936 and 1976.

38 Goodenough, *By Light, Light,* passim.

39 Philo *On Flight and Finding* 103ff.

40 Philo *On the Cherubim* 31.

41 Philo *On Creation* 140–144.

42 Philo *Life of Moses* 2.133–135.

43 Philo *On Special Laws* 1.116.

44 Phrases in the christological hymns of Heb. 1:5–13 are taken from Ps. 2:7, 44:7, 96:7, 101:26–28, 103:4, and 109:1, as well as from scenes of the empowerment of Moses (Deut. 32:43) and David (2 Sam. 7:14).

45 The term is used by Plato to indicate originating power (*Cratylus* 401d) and by Aristotle as the agent of origin (*Metaphysics* 983b20).

46 Especially Ps. 21:23, Is. 8:17–18.

47 Cf. Eph. 1:20, 2:6; Philo *Giants* 62; Ignatius *Trallians* 5:1–2; Polycarp 2:1.

48 So Epictetus 1.29, 49.

49 W. H. C. Frend, *The Early Church: From Beginnings to 461* (London: SCM Press, 1982), 124–125.

50 The details of Augustine's *City of God* are more fully discussed in chap. 7.

Chapter 5: The Community of Mystical Participation

1 Richard Reitzenstein, *Hellenistic Mystery-Religions: Their Basic Ideas and Significance,* trans. John E. Steely, Pittsburgh Theological Monograph Series, ed. D. Y. Hadidian (Pittsburgh: Pickwick Press, 1978).

2 Alfred Loisy, *Les mystères païens et le mystère chrétien* (Paris: Emile Nourry, 1914).

3 A scholarly analysis of the phenomenon of mysticism written two generations ago from within the community of classical scholars—Charles A. Bennett, *A Philosophical Study of Mysticism* (New Haven: Yale University Press, 1931)—offers generalizations about mysticism that are analogous to those of Reitzenstein. Comparing Plato and Paul, Bennett asserts that for both of them, discipline and law are succeeded by freedom in mystical experience: "The mystic, as it were, forestalls the process of history by anticipating in his own life the enjoyment of the last age" (31). Or again, "Mysticism is a perpetual return to the vision of God, to the original datum, a return therefore to the old; but to the old not as exhausted but as an inexhaustible datum from which may be drawn out new suggestions, new dogma." Bennett is correct in observ-

ing that Paul regards the life of faith as a present sharing in the life of the age to come, but he fails to take adequate account of Paul's critique of the present age as dominated by the powers of evil or his insistence that the goal is the reconciliation of the world to God (2 Cor. 5:19), not an escape into some generalized "freedom" (176).

4   Lewis R. Farnell, *Greek Hero Cults and Ideas of Immortality* (Oxford: Clarendon Press, 1921).

5   George Mylonas, *Eleusis and the Eleusinian Mysteries* (Princeton: Princeton University Press, 1961).

6   The role of Asklepios as healer is summarized in my study *Medicine, Miracle and Magic*, 60–70, 91–92.

7   Adapted from the translation in Farnell, *Greek Hero Cults*, 277.

8   This and other examples of such linkage are cited by Farnell, *Greek Hero Cults*, 370.

9   H. J. Rose, *Religion in Greece and Rome* (New York: Harper, 1959), 94.

10 Described in Livy *History of Rome* 39.8–19.

11 Philo *On Flight and Finding* 137–139.

12 John Dillon, *The Middle Platonists: A Study of Platonism*, 80 B.C. to A.D. 220 (London: Duckworth, 1977), 220–224.

13 The text used here is that of J. Gwyn Griffiths, in *Plutarch's De Iside et Osiride* (University of Wales Press, 1970).

14 Scholem, *Major Trends in Jewish Mysticism*, 9, 20.

15 Blumenthal, *Understanding Jewish Mysticism*, 6–8.

16 The assembling of magical texts from a variety of times and sources, a project that began in 1963 under Mordecai Margalioth, led to the publication of *Sepher Ha-Razim*.

17 Gruenwald, *Apocalyptic and Merkavah Mysticism*, 12.

18 Gruenwald, *Apocalyptic and Merkavah Mysticism*, 99, 128.

19 The throne of God in the heavenly sanctuary is depicted as a chariot in the Qumran *Songs of the Sabbath Sacrifice* (4Q 405:20).

20 Gruenwald, *Apocalyptic and Merkavah Mysticism*, 130–132.

21 Stone, *Scriptures, Sects and Visions*, 33–43.

22 Brown (*Anchor Bible, Gospel according to John I–XII*) perhaps overstates the case when he observes (529) that *logos* in John is closer to biblical and Jewish strains than to anything purely Hellenistic. The profound and pervasive influence of Hellenistic thinkers on Judaism is broadly evident, although the Jewish writers have adapted and exploited these insights in their new interpretations of biblical traditions.

23 The Greek text *theos en ho logos* does not assert that God and Word are interchangeable terms, as would have been implied if the definite article, *ho*, preceded *theos*. But it does

indicate that the Logos shares in the essential, eternal divine nature, and is neither an additive nor a belated attempt to remedy a miscarried plan for the creation.

24 The quotation in 7:38, "Out of his heart shall flow rivers of living water," does not come directly from the Jewish scriptures. As Raymond Brown has suggested (*Anchor Bible, Gospel according to John*), if the point is that God can make humans become fountains of wisdom, possible links of this passage are with Prov. 18:4, Isa. 58:11, and Ben Sira 24:30–34. But if the aim of the saying is to recall God's provision for the basic needs of his people in times of difficulty, then the link would be with the Exodus experience of Israel as reflected in Ps. 105:40–41, Isa. 43:20, 44:3, and 48:21, and Deut. 8:15. Another possibility is the eschatological figure of divine supply for God's people expressed in Ezek. 47:1–11. In any case, there is evidence here of John's use of scriptural imagery concerning God's care for his people, rather than direct quotation of scripture.

25 See the discussion in chap. 2 above and the comprehensive analysis of this biblical theme in Bernhard W. Anderson, *Creation versus Chaos: The Reinterpretation of Mythical Symbolism in the Bible* (New York: Association Press, 1967).

26 Peder Borgen, *Bread from Heaven: An Exegetical Study of the Concept of Manna in the Gospel of John and the Writings of Philo*, Supplements to *Novum Testamentum*, no. 10 (Leiden: Brill, 1965).

27 The healing of the official's son in John 4:46–54 has a parallel in the only Q miracle account (Luke 7:1–10; Matt. 8:5–13).

28 A much more detailed comparison of these stories is offered by Brown, *Anchor Bible, Gospel according to John I–XII*, 240–243.

29 1 Cor. 11:23–25; Mark 14:22–25; Matt. 26:26–29; Luke 22:15–20.

30 Wayne A. Meeks, *The Prophet-King: Moses Traditions and the Johannine Christology*, Supplements to *Novum Testamentum*, no. 14 (Leiden: Brill, 1967). Meeks cites at length (147–148) a passage from the second-century-B.C.E. *Drama of the Exodus* by one Ezekiel, quoted by both Eusebius and Clement of Alexandria from a first-century-B.C.E. source, Alexander Polyhistor, in which the royal upbringing and kingly role of Moses are described.

31 Even the details of the story are filled with symbolic meaning: the application of spittle would have been a defiling act in terms of the law of Moses (Lev. 15:8; Num 12:14; Deut. 25:9), but here it effects the restoration of vision; the remedy for the man's blindness is an anointing, the verb for which, *echrisen*, is cognate to Christos; the washing in the pool signifies cleansing, and the name of the pool, Siloam (= "sent" [*apestalmenos*] implies God's purpose at work in the event; the climax comes in the transformation of the man so that now he "sees."

32 Brown, *Anchor Bible, Gospel according to John XIII–XXI*, 669–672, notes that in Ben Sira 24:1–23, Wisdom is compared with various trees, plants, and "a vine" (24:16). The people are invited to come and share in the fruits which these produce. All this is identified with "the book of the covenant of the Most High" (24:23). Other passages cited by Brown where the vineyard imagery portrays positively or negatively the relation of God to his people include Hos. 10:1 (the surge of idolatrous worship), 14:7

(the abundance of God's forgiveness to Israel); and Ezek. 15:1–6 (Israel as a useless vine), 19:10–14 (Israel destroyed as a worthless vine).

33 Cf. Brown, *Gospel According to John XIII–XXI* (675), who suggests that *ampelos alethine*, quoted in John 15:1 from Jer. 2:21 (Septuagint) be translated as "real vine" rather than the more literal "true vine."

34 *Koimao* is used as a euphemism for death ("lie down, fall asleep") from Homer on and in the Septuagint. In the New Testament, it takes on the distinctive connotation of a temporary state, to be overcome when the resurrection occurs.

35 This term is found in a wide range of New Testament writings, including 1 Thess 4:13, 15; 1 Cor. 11:30, 15:18, 20, 51; Matt. 27:52; and Acts 13:36.

36 This term, which is not found in the Septuagint, is best understood as "helper" or "advocate" (in the sense of a counselor or informant rather than an intercessor). It is anachronistic to credit it to the Mandaean literature (so Behm In *Theological Dictionary of the New Testament* 5:806–809), which is probably later in origin than the New Testament, or to the Odes of Solomon, which appears to be Christian in origin and roughly contemporary with the Gospel of John (so Charlesworth, *Old Testament Pseudepigrapha*, vol. 2, 726–727).

37 It is in keeping with the group-centered outlook of the fourth evangelist that Jesus' command to love is modified: in the synoptics, the injunction is to love one's neighbors (Matt. 5:43; Mark 12:31; Luke 10:27) and even one's enemies (Matt. 5:44; Luke 6:27), but in John 13:34–35, the command is to "love one another."

38 *Homologein* is here a technical term for formal confession of faith, in this case, proper Christology. Here is further evidence of the shift in meaning of faith (*pistis*) from "trust" to "correct belief."

39 Ignatius *To the Trallians* 9, 10.

40 Ignatius *To the Smyrnaeans* 1–4.

41 An enormous literature has been produced since these discoveries became known and the documents were published. Translations of the basic writings with an account of their discovery are most readily available in *The Nag Hammadi Library in English* ed. J. M. Robinson (New York: Harper, 1977). Attempts to prove that the gospels found in this library antedate those of the New Testament include Elaine Pagels, *The Gnostic Gospels* (New York: Random House, 1979), J. D. Crossan, *Four Other Gospels: Shadows on the Contour of the Canon* (Minneapolis: Winston, 1985), Helmut Koester, *Introduction to the New Testament* (Philadelphia: Fortress Press, 1982), 2:154, and Koester, *Ancient Christian Gospels*: 75–128.

42 Fully documented by Dillon, *Middle Platonists*, and discussed earlier in this chapter in connection with the mysticism of Plutarch and Philo of Alexandria. The intellectual history of the theory of pre-Christian Gnosticism and a demonstration that it is no more than an unwarranted, prejudicial construct have been set forth persuasively by Edwin M. Yamauchi, *Pre-Christian Gnosticism: A Survey of the Proposed Evidences* (Grand Rapids, Mich.: Eerdmans, 1973).

43 Tertullian *On a Prescription against Heretics* 7.

44 Tertullian *Against the Valentinians* 1.

45 Tertullian *Against Valentinus* 17.

46 Tertullian *Against Marcion* 3.8, 18–19.

47 This dating is proposed by Chr. Maurer, *New Testament Apocrypha*, vol. 1, ed. W. Schneemelcher and trans. R. McL. Wilson (Philadelphia: Westminster, 1963), 180. The proposal of J. D. Crossan *(Four Other Gospels)* that the of Gospel of Peter represents the oldest source for the passion narrative, which he defends on the basis that Mark has "omitted" details found in the Gospel of Peter, represents perverted logic, based on an argument from silence and ignores the unmistakable tendency of this document toward esoteric, Gnostic reworking of the tradition, and must therefore be described as preposterous.

48 Whether or not one considers this cry of dereliction as authentic, it is undeniably a reference to scripture and fits well with the overall aim of the gospel tradition to show that the death of Jesus was in accord with divine purpose as evident in the fulfillment of scripture.

49 Even as he shows the uniqueness in Jewish literature of Philo's hypostatization of power, W. Grundmann notes that "the powers take up a middle role between God and man" rather than *dynamis* serving as an encompassing designation for God *(Theological Dictionary of the New Testament* vol. 2, 2:298).

50 Koester, *Introduction to the New Testament* 2:154.

51 A concise summary and evaluation of this extra–New Testament evidence is offered in my *What Can We Know About Jesus?* 6–15.

52 This is the translation of H. Koester and T. Lambdin in *The Nag Hammadi Library in English*, 118. Others translate the second phrase as "without you"; the meaning seems to be that the kingdom is a state that surrounds and penetrates the individual. Significantly, the second phrase is omitted in Oxyrynchus Papyrus 654.

53 This term, which is used by all the translators of this logion, fits well with the notice that, so secret is the information, the "left hand" of the recipient is not to disclose it to his own "right hand"—a radical adaptation of the counsel about avoiding publicity for one's acts of generosity (Matt. 6:1–4).

54 Gen. 1:27; the principle is affirmed in the synoptic tradition: Mark 10:6–9, Matt. 19:4–6. The unity described in the Markan passage is achieved through marriage, and is affirmed there as essential to the divine intention for human life. I have treated this issue in an essay, "Becoming a Child in the Gospel of Thomas," *Journal of Biblical Literature* 82 (1963):307–314.

55 A characteristic example of this esoteric meaning is the passage in his commentary on John where Origen identifies the ass and the colt mentioned in connection with Jesus' final entry in to Jerusalem as respectively the Old and the New Testaments. The city that Jesus is about to enter in this story is, not surprisingly, the heavenly Jerusalem *(Commentary on John* 10.18).

56 Attributed to Heracleon, whom Origen links with Valentinus and his heretical views.

Chapter 6: The Ethically and Culturally Inclusive Community

1 Similar themes are sounded in Ps. 117:1, 126:2, 138:4–5, 145:12, 18–21, and 148:11.

2 The terms relate to the order of the cosmos—astronomical and calendrical—as well as to the natural order of humans, animals, and plants (7:17–20). After a long string of abstract adjectives describing the transcendent nature of Wisdom (7:22–23), her role is depicted in the perspectives and technical terminology of Platonic tradition as "penetrating and pervading all things by reason of her purity" (7:24), as "a pure effusion of the glory of the Almighty" (*aporroia tes tou pantokratoros doxes eilikrines*), and as the "refulgence [*apaugasma*] of eternal light" and "the image [*eikon*] of God's goodness" (7:26).

3 A similar conviction is expressed in 21:11, 23:27, 24:22, 28:7, 32:23–24, and 42:1–2.

4 The definitive introduction to and translation and annotations of these writings are by John J. Collins, in *The Old Testament Pseudepigrapha*, vol. 1, 317–472. This edition builds on Collins's earlier study, *The Sibylline Oracles of Egyptian Judaism.*

5 Reported by Dionysus of Halicarnassus (late first century B.C.E.) in his *Roman Antiquities* (4.62).

6 The most likely candidate for this role as benefactor of the Jews is Ptolemy Philometor, who reigned 180–145, with Ptolemy Physcon as co-ruler 170–164. A discussion of options is offered by Collins in *The Old Testament Pseudepigrapha*, vol. 1, 355. The cordial and supportive attitude of the Ptolemies toward the Jews in this period is confirmed by Josephus in *Contra Apionem* 2.149.

7 Excerpts have been preserved in Eusebius, Clement of Alexandria, and Pseudo-Eustathias. Translation and discussion by R. B. Robertson, in *Old Testament Pseudepigrapha*, vol. 2, 803–814.

8 As implied by Richard Pervo in *Profit with Delight: The Literary Genre of the Acts of the Apostles* (Philadelphia: Fortress Press, 1987). Although he is mildly critical of the theories of B. E. Perry and Erwin Rohde that entertainment was its single purpose, he regards the romance as showing the spirit and taste of the Hellenistic age and the goals of the individual writer. Pervo regards the author of Acts as intending to both edify and entertain (137).

9 Douglas R. Edwards, *Religion and Power: Pagans, Jews and Christians in the Greek East* (New York: Oxford University Press, 1993).

10 For the rationale of proposing the Hellenistic romance as literary model for these Jewish writings, see C. Burchard, "Joseph and Asenath," in *The Old Testament Pseudepigrapha*, vol. 2, 183–187, which includes a basic bibliography of this literary genre.

11 On the appeal of the direct encounter with God in Joseph and Asenath, see H. C. Kee. "The Socio-Cultural Setting of Joseph and Asenath," *New Testament Studies* 29(1983):394–413.

12 Eusebius *Ecclestiastical History* 7.32.16–18.

13 Eusebius *Praeparatio* 8.9.38–8.10.17, 13.13.3–8; 13.12.9–16, and 13.12.1f.

14 Eusebius *Praeparatio* 9.18.1. This material is analyzed by Collins, *The Old Testament Pseudepigrapha*, vol. 2, 889–903, who sees it as part of Jewish apologetic literature rather than as a source of otherwise unavailable historical information (891).

15 Eusebius *Praeparatio* 13.12.1f.

16 Test. Reuben 6:4, 4:1; Test. Benjamin 6:6; Test. Issachar 5:1; Test. Benjamin 6:6; Test. Asher 6:1, 7:5; Test. Reuben 4:4. For a discussion of the Stoic background of this Jewish ethical system, see my article "Ethical Dimensions of the Testaments of the Twelve as a Clue to Provenance."

17 Hengel has indicated the presence of this feature in Greek literature of both the classical and Hellenistic periods (*Judaism and Hellenism*, vol. 1, 182, 233). Hesiod's periodization of history is also noted by Collins, *The Sibylline Oracles of Egyptian Judaism* 101 and n. 22.

18 Luke 1:47 = Hab. 3:18; 1:48 = 1 Sam. 1:11; 1:48b = Gen. 30:13; 1:49b = Ps. 111:9; 1:50 = Ps. 103:17; 1:51 = Ps. 89:10; 1:52 = Eccles. 10:14, Ezek. 21:31; 1:53 = Ps. 107:4; 1:54 = Isa. 41:8, Ps. 98:3; 1:55 = Mic. 7:20, 2 Sam. 22:51.

19 Luke 1:68–79 contains in sequence allusions to or reflections of Ps. 41:13, 11:9, 18:2, 132:27, 106:10 and 18:7; Mic. 7:20; Ps. 105:8 and 106:45; Jer. 11:5; Ps. 107:10; and Isa. 59:8.

20 Mark locates the story a third of the way through his gospel (6:1–6) and gives no details of Jesus' message there.

21 Cf. the seventy or seventy-two translators of the Septuagint, the aim of which was to make the Jewish scriptures available to Gentiles.

22 As noted in chap. 2, the span of time here indicated reaches from the first murder reported in the first book of the Hebrew scriptures (Abel in Gen. 4:1–16) to the last murder in the last book in the canon (2 Chron. 23:12–21).

23 The important place of women in the new community is sketched in my essay "The Changing Role of Women in Early Christianity," *Theology Today* 49/2 (1992):225–238.

24 Eunuch (*sarif*) in the Hebrew scriptures is a term for a certain kind of governmental official assigned to oversee the women (wives and concubines) in the royal household. His castrated condition precluded his becoming sexually involved with those in his charge. This eunuch, however, was an officer under the Ethiopian queen whose title was Candace, the queen mother and the real head of the government.

25 Curiously, there is no hint in Acts or in the letters of Paul as to how the Christian community was established in Damascus. There is no mention in Acts of evangelism being carried on outside Judea, Samaria, and the highway from Jerusalem to Gaza in the south. Historically, the establishment of a Christian group in Damascus may have been the consequence of the activity of Jesus and the disciples in the cities of the Decapolis (Mark 5:20), in the districts of Tyre and Sidon (7:24, 31), and in such Hellenistic centers to the north as Caesarea-Philippi (8:27). Luke, however, omits these references to Jesus' activity in Hellenistic districts and accounts for the lack of response of the Samaritan villagers by asserting that the top priority in God's plan is the confrontation between Jesus and the Jewish authorities in Jerusalem (9:51–53).

26 Cornelius is described in Acts 10:2 as devout (*eusebes*) and as one who feared God (*phoboumenos ton theon*). Throughout the present century, debate has continued as to whether the "God-fearers" mentioned repeatedly in Acts (*phoboumenos ton theon*, *seobomenos, sebomenos ton theon*) were Gentile proselytes who became full members of the Jewish community, Judaizing pagans, benevolent and high-minded pagans, pious Jews, or half-paganized Jews. Kirsopp Lake (in *Beginnings of Christianity*, vol. 5, [New York: Macmillan, 1932; repr. Grand Rapids, Mich.: Baker, 1965], 74–95, came to the conclusion that God-fearer had no definite meaning. A. Thomas Kraabel ("The Disappearance of the God-Fearers," *Numen* 28 [1981]:113–126) declared that the God-fearers were the invention of the author of Acts. This position has been reaffirmed in the joint essay by Kraabel and MacLennan, "The God-Fearers: A Literary and Theological Invention." Overman has effectively challenged the argument of these essays, however. A full and persuasive case, based on an inscription from a synagogue in Aphrodisias in Asia Minor where God-fearers (*theoseboi*) are listed, not only proves their existence but indicates their role as supporters of the synagogue and participants in its study and worship. Joyce Reynolds and Robert Tannenbaum, *Jews and God-Fearers at Aphrodisias* (Cambridge: Cambridge Philological Society, 1987), 48–66, basing their argument on the evidence from inscriptions, Acts, and the Talmud, define a God-fearer as "someone who is attracted enough to what he has heard of Judaism to want to come to the synagogue to learn more; who is, after a time, willing . . . to imitate the Jewish way of life in whatever way and to whatever degree he wishes (up to and including membership in community associations, where the activity includes legal study and prayer); who may have held out to him short codes of moral behaviour to follow; . . . who may follow the exclusive monotheism of the Jews and give up his ancestral gods, but need not do so; who can if he wishes, take the ultimate step and convert, but need not do so" (65).

27 Once again, the image of "hanging on a tree" means not only death by execution but formal rejection by God and the covenant community (Deut. 21:22–23).

28 The author of Acts uses several curious terms with reference to the emergent Christian community. The one that occurs here, *ochlos*, while meaning literally "crowd," refers to the large numbers joining the movement. This term is also used for the original "crowd" of 120 in Jerusalem (1:15) before the outpouring of the Spirit on the day of Pentecost, the "crowd" of priests who became "obedient to the faith" (6:7), the group met by Barnabas in Antioch, and the "crowd" in Ephesus and throughout Asia that his opponents accuse Paul of turning from devotion to Artemis. Even more frequently used is another quantitative term, "multitude" (*plethos*), to refer to the emergent Christian community. The potential size of the movement is indicated in Acts 2:6 and 5:16, but direct reference to the large group of devotees is found in Acts 4:32, 5:14, 6:2, 5, 14:12, 15:12, 30, 17:4, and 19:8, 9. One of the most curious contexts where this term is used is the passage (15:6–21) where the gathering (the verb is *synago*) of the apostles and elders to reach a decision about the terms of Gentile admission to the community is described as a "multitude."

29 This term is derived from a latinized adjective (*christianos*) based on the Greek term for anointed one, *christos*. The designation *christos* would have been meaningless to Greek speakers as either a personal name or as a descriptive term, but a similar-sounding term, *chrestos* (good, kind, benign), was familiar as an adjective and as a name. The

Roman historian Suetonius, in his *Life of Claudius* (25), apparently confused the two names when he told of the conflict that arose among Jews in Rome at the instigation of "one Chrestos," which is almost certainly a mistaken reference to the arrival of the message about Jesus as the "Christos" (Kee, *What Can We Know about Jesus?* 9–10). In the other New Testament texts where *Christianos* appears, it seems to have derogatory implications in 1 Pet. 4:16, when it is mentioned as the designation of the persecuted members of the new community, and in Acts 26:28, where Agrippa chides Paul for trying so quickly to convert him to the Christian movement.

30 Niger, which means "black" in Latin, may have been used because Simeon was of African origin.

31 Certain manuscripts of Acts (the so-called Western text, as found in the Greek ms. D, some manuscripts of the Vulgate, and several of the church fathers, from Irenaeus to Jerome and Augustine) omit the phrase "and from what is strangled." The remaining three items in the text could be understood to imply only prohibitions of certain personal acts: idol worship, sexual immorality, and [the shedding of] blood = murder. In the overall context of Acts, however, it seems clear that the list of four items is original, and that the issues are a mix of moral and ritual requirements, representing a compromise between Christians of Jewish and Gentile origins.

32 The prohibition against going into the northern territory of Bithynia (16:7) may serve the author of Acts as proof that the gospel is now to go into new, unevangelized lands, especially since 1 Pet. 1:1 links Peter with Bithynia, presumably as the founding apostolic figure there.

33 *Proseuche* was the designation for the place where Jews gathered, rather than *synagoge* (which referred to the group assembled). Found throughout the Jewish dispersion, such places could be homes or public halls, where meetings took place for prayer, study of scripture, and worship. These were the antecedents of the synagogue as institution in the second and subsequent centuries. Cf. Martin Hengel, "Proseuche und Synagoge: Jüdische Gemeinde, Gotteshaus und Gottesdienst in der Diaspora und in Palaestina," in *The Synagogue: Studies in Origins, Archaeology and Architecture;* White, *Building God's House in the Roman World,* 87.

34 Made from murex shellfish, this costly dye was used for stripes on the scarves worn by the highest officials in Roman government as a kind of badge of their exalted status.

35 The deities worshipped in Thessalonica in this period included the Cabiri (fertility deities, whose worship was probably imported from Phrygia and who came to be linked with the Dioscuri, Castor and Pollux), Isis, Serapis, Zeus, Asklepios, Aphrodite, Dionysos, and Demeter. Also evident today in the remains of the ancient city are shrines to deified Roma and the cult of the emperors, including both Julius Caesar and Augustus.

36 Their title, politarch, is attested in inscriptions from various parts of this region as the title of the five or six persons who constituted the council in Macedonian cities.

37 The origin of the first of these quotations is not certain: it may derive from Epimenides, or it may be only a commonplace Stoic phrase. The second is from Aratus's *Phaenomena* V.

38 A fragmentary inscription found in Corinth that seems to have read "Synagogue of the Jews" is of undetermined but almost certainly much later date than the time of Paul. It evidences how "synagogue" evolved from informal house-based gatherings to special structures with public identity. Cf. my article "Early Christianity in the Galilee: Reassessing the Evidence from the Gospels," in *Galilee in Late Antiquity*, ed. Lee Levine (New York: Jewish Theological Seminary of America, 1992), 3–22.

39 Gallio is mentioned as proconsul of Achaia (in which Corinth was located) by the Roman historian Tacitus (*Annals* 15.73) and also is named on an inscription found at Delphi as serving in this office during the reign of the emperor Claudius (41–54 C.E.). This provides a clear indication of the date for Gallio's term of office (51–52) and thereby offers a fixed point for the chronology of the career of Paul.

40 The Greek term for lecture hall, *schole*, does not mean "school" in our modern sense. In the rabbinic tradition, such public halls were utilized as gathering places for instruction and worship.

41 The claim that healing powers were present in objects that had touched Paul indicates a shift from miracle (God's restorative action) to magic (powers inherent in sacred objects), which is discussed in my book *Medicine, Miracle and Magic in New Testament Times*, 119–120.

42 Acts does not indicate whether Alexander is a Jew, a Christian, or a devotee of Artemis, although he is "prompted by the crowd" and "put forward by the Jews." What he offers is said to be an *apologia*, or defense, but his point of view is not clear, even though the result is to save the lives of Paul and his companions. His main argument seems to be that accused Christians must be dealt with fairly by civil authorities following due legal process.

43 For example, Aristarchus in Philem. 24 and Col. 4:10; Gaius in Rom. 16:23; possibly Sopater in Rom. 16:21 (Sosipater); Tychicus in Eph. 6:21 and Col. 4:7; and, above all, Timothy in 2 Cor. 1:19, Rom. 16:21, 1 Thess. 3:2 and 6, 1 Cor 4:17 and 16:10, and Phil. 2:19, in addition to frequent mention in the Pastoral Epistles.

44 In the Psalms, 23:1, 29:9, 74:1, 77:20 (where the reference is to the Exodus), 80:1, 95:7, 100:3 and 122:3–8. In the Prophets, Isa. 40:11; Jer. 23:1–4, 31:10, and 50:19; Ezek. 14:11; Mic. 7:14; and Zech. 10:3 and 11:16. In the Gospels, Matt. 10:6 and 25:32–33, and Luke 10:1–29; in the Letters, Heb. 13:20 and 1 Pet 2:25 and 5:5.

45 Cf. Isa. 43:21, Jer. 13:17, Zech. 10:3, 1 Pet 5:3, and 1 Clem. 44:3.

46 An inscription recovered from the Temple built by Herod makes explicit that for a non-Israelite to enter the area surrounding the inner courts of the Temple is a capital offense: "Let no foreigner enter within the screen and enclosure surrounding the sanctuary. Whoever is apprehended in so doing will be responsible for his own death, which shall take place immediately." This inscription was on the wall that separated the outer Court of the Gentiles from the Court of Israel (quoted from Adolf Deissmann, *Light from the Ancient East: The New Testament Illustrated by Recently Discovered Texts of the Graeco-Roman World*, trans. L. R. M. Strachan [New York: Harper, 1927], 79–81).

47 The Sicarii are mentioned by Josephus (*Wars* 2.54–57) and Eusebius *Ecclesiastical History* (2.21) as fanatical nationalists who launched the Jewish revolt in 66 C.E. It would

be anachronistic to have this charge made against Paul some ten years earlier, but the author of Acts wants to make the point that the new community is not engaged in political revolution.

48 Tarsus, capital of the Roman province of Cilicia, was important as a port city near the mouth of the Cydnus on the main travel route eastward to Syria. Cicero was governor there in 50 B.C.E., and Mark Anthony met Cleopatra there in 41 B.C.E. Under Augustus, the city flourished as an intellectual center, surpassing both Athens and Alexandria, and was famed chiefly for its Stoic philosophers. Curiously, in his surviving letters Paul makes no mention of the city, nor does he report having studied in Jerusalem under Gamaliel.

49 The author of Acts probably combines traditions about the two Gamaliels known in the rabbinic tradition. The first, who is listed under Hillel in the rabbinic document *Pirke Aboth,* was active in the middle of the first century C.E. The second was the leader of the rabbinic assembly and a primary agent in the adjustment of Judaism to its existence without the priesthood and the Temple following the failure of the revolt of 66–70 C.E. The latter Gamaliel would likely have been a contemporary of the author of Acts.

50 This council is referred to as *presbyterion,* rather than as the standard Hellenistic-Roman *synedrion,* a semi-autonomous regional council. The latter term was later taken up by Jewish tradition and transliterated into Hebrew as Sanhedrin. The selection and use of this title in the rabbinic sources represent an intention by the emergent religious authorities to legitimate their claim that there was from an early period an authoritative Jewish body making decisions and pronouncements on religious issues.

51 This term might carry negative connotations, implying that the religion of the Jews is a "superstition."

Chapter 7: The Community Models in the Post–New Testament Period

1 This option continued to be closed for Judaism until the effective rise of the Zionist movement in the current century, which culminated in the United Nations' approval of the establishment of the State of Israel in 1948.

2 This policy seems to have been launched by Domitian, although decades earlier Nero, as is well known, put the blame on the Christians for the burning of Rome, as attested by Tacitus (*Annals* 15.44). Domitian's punishment of his niece, Domitilla, is reported by Cassius Dio (lived 150–235) to have been a reaction against her having adopted "Jewish customs" and "atheism," but the antiquity of a Christian catacomb named for her suggests that the real reason for the imperial reaction against her was her conversion to Christianity.

3 I have sketched these developments in two recent essays: "Changing Modes of Leadership in the New Testament Period," *Social Compass: International Review of Sociology of Religion,* 39/2 (1992):241–254; and "From Jesus Movement toward Institutional Church," in *Conversion to Christianity: Historical and Anthropological Perspectives on a Great Transformation,* ed. Robert W. Hefner (Berkeley: University of California Press, 1993), 47–63. The fuller picture of institutional development in early Christianity is traced

in my book *Understanding the New Testament,* 5th ed. (Englewood Cliffs, N.J.: Prentice-Hall, 1993).

4   Raymond E. Brown, *The Community of the Beloved Disciple* (New York: Paulist Press, 1979).

5   The delay of the *parousia* seems to have been a problem as early as the time of Paul, who discusses the participation in the day of triumph of those Christians who have already died (1 Thess. 4:14). If 2 Thess. is authentic, Paul later had to describe events that must occur before the *parousia* could take place (2:1–11) and to deal with the charge of some that it had already happened (2:2). In Col. 1:12–18, the triumph earlier linked with the return of Christ is described in the past tense, implying that it has already occurred. In the Gospel of Matthew, parables are attributed to Jesus (or adapted from other synoptic sources) in which he advises his followers of the delay in the *parousia:* it will not occur until the evangelism of the world is complete (24:14), and the time of its occurrence cannot be predicted (24:42, 45–51; 25:1–13).

6   Eusebius (*Ecclesiastical History* 6.14.1) notes the reference by Clement of Alexandria in his *Hypotyposeis* to "the apocalypse known as Peter's."

7   Origen *Contra Celsum* 7.9.

8   Eusebius *Ecclesiastical History* 5.3.4, 5.16–18.

9   W. A. Jurgens, *Faith of the Early Fathers* (Collegeville, Minn.: Liturgical Press, 1970), 102.

10 Eusebius *Ecclesiastical History* 3.39.13.

11 The Stoic concept of the cosmic cycles is evident here.

12 Tertullian *Apology* 37.4.

13 Eusebius *Ecclesiastical History* 5.9–10.

14 Details of this scheme of mystical knowledge are set forth in the enduringly useful analysis by Bigg, *Christian Platonists of Alexandria,* 80–93.

15 As in Plato *Theaetetus* 155.

16 Clement of Alexandria, *Stromateis* 6.15.124, 7.16.96, 7.10–11. *Stromateis,* which is usually translated as *Miscellanies,* had as its original title (according to Eusebius) "Titus Flavius Clement's miscellaneous collection of gnostic notes bearing upon the true philosophy."

17 A typical and still useful discussion of the origins of Gnosticism is R. McL. Wilson, *The Gnostic Problem* (London: Mowbray, 1958). A more recent assembling of theories can be found in a collection of scholarly essays, *Nag Hammadi, Gnosticism, and Early Christianity,* ed. Charles W. Hedrick and Robert Hodgson, Jr. (Peabody, Mass.: Hendrickson, 1986).

18 Carsten Colpe, *Die religionsgeschichtliche Schule: Darstellung und Kritik ihres Bildes vom gnostischen Erlösermythus,* (Göttingen: Vandenhoeck und Ruprecht, 1961). A prime example of a later critique is Yamauchi, *Pre-Christian Gnosticism.* Helmut Koester, in his two-volume *Introduction to the New Testament,* acknowledges the lack of documentary evidence for Gnosticism before the second and third centuries C.E. and pronounces the futility of

asking whether Gnosticism derives from Platonism, Judaism, or Christianity. Ironically, he is himself what might be called agnostic on the question of whether Gnosticism can be accounted for on the basis of historical dependencies or developments (1:384–385). He can say only that by the second century Christians were attributing these views to Jesus, and he downplays the possibility of input from Greek philosophy in this period. Nevertheless, he describes the Wisdom of Solomon as a Gnostic document, since those who recognize the voice of wisdom come to understand their true origin, and he sees kinship between Gnosticism and Philo's exegetical methods. He perceives Gnosticism as the catalyst that amalgamated the mythical concepts of wisdom, cosmogony and astrology, dualism and the Genesis teaching about creation, law and apocalypticism, and God, demons, and angels. Curiously, he describes some of the Gnostic documents, such as the Apocryphon of John, as lacking Christian elements, even though the whole structure of the writing presupposes Jesus' special relationship with his disciples and critique of his Jewish contemporaries.

19 Matt. 18:3, "become like children"; Mark 10:15, "receive the kingdom of God like a child"; Luke 18:17, "receive the kingdom of God like a child." See my essay, "Becoming a Child in the Gospel of Thomas," *Journal of Biblical Literature* 82 (1963): 307–314.

20 For example, Kurt Rudolph, in the article on Gnosticism in the *Anchor Bible Dictionary* 2:1036.

21 Hippolytus notes the following dependencies, or "thefts" as he calls them: Valentinus on Plato and the Pythagoreans (6.16, 24, 32); Basilides on Aristotle (7.2); the Naasenes on both Homer (5.3) and James, the Lord's brother (5.2).

22 Neusner *Judaism in the Matrix of Christianity*, liii, lvi, xlviii–xlix, liv, and lv.

23 Text and a discussion of origins of the Apocalypse of Paul by W. Schneemelcher can be found in *New Testament Apocrypha*, vol. 2, trans. R. McL. Wilson et al., (Philadelphia: Westminster, 1964), 755–759. The name "Acherousia" derives from the River Acheron, which flows through the realm of the dead in Greek mythology.

24 Origen *Commentary on the Gospel of John* 10.131, 132.

25 Plutarch *De Iside* 363D, 365B, 367D, 367E, 371B, 375C, 382B. For a more extensive sketch of Plutarch's Isis mysticism, see my book *Miracle in the Early Christian World* 141–145.

26 A fuller account of Apollonius's views is also offered in *Miracle in the Early Christian World*, 255–265.

27 The *Metamorphoses* is popularly known as *The Golden Ass.*

28 Not to be confused with the fourth-century-B.C.E. soldier and historian Xenophon, author of the *Anabasis*, which chronicles the experiences of the Greeks who fought in Asia as mercenaries in the army of Cyrus of Persia.

29 A full and insightful analysis of the Hellenistic romances in their cultural setting is offered in Edwards, *Religion and Power.*

30 W. R. Inge, *The Philosophy of Plotinus*, Bampton Lectures for 1917–18 (1929; repr. New York: Greenwood Press, 1968), 2:146–147.

31 Plotinus *Enneads* 5.5.8.

32 Eusebius *Ecclesiastical History* 6.2, 3.9.

33 Eusebius *Ecclesiastical History* 6.18–19.

34 *Origen: Contra Celsum*, ed. Henry Chadwick (Cambridge: Cambridge University Press, 1953), xiii.

35 In a small library found by British soldiers in a heap of rubbish near Cairo in 1941 was a sixth-century copy of Origen's *Dialogue with Heraclides*, a report of a discussion at a synod of bishops about the orthodoxy of a bishop named Heraclides. An introduction and translation are offered in *Alexandrian Christianity*, ed. Henry Chadwick (Philadelphia: Westminster Press, 1954), 430–455.

36 Eusebius *Ecclesiastical History* 6.1.

37 Origen *Commentary on the Gospel of John* 1.3–4, 1.9–11, 1.16–22, 1.22–42, 2.3.

38 Origen *Commentary on the Gospel of John* 10.13.

Critical Note: Priority in the Gospel Tradition

1 W. R. Farmer has been a leading figure over a period of decades in the attempt to discredit the two-source (Mark and Q) theory of the origin of the synoptic Gospels (*The Synoptic Problem: A Critical Analysis* [New York: Macmillan, 1964]). Supporting his position has been David L. Dungan, ("Mark—the Abridgement of Matthew and Luke," in Jesus and Man's Hope, vol. 1, ed. D. G. Miller and D. Y. Hadidian (Pittsburgh: Pittsburgh Theological Seminary, 1970) 51–97. The fatal admission of the untenability of the hypothesis that Mark derives from the other gospels was offered by Farmer himself when he tried to demonstrate Mark's dependence on Matthew by an analysis of Mark 16:9–20—which on the basis of manuscript evidence is overwhelmingly regarded as a later addition to Mark. Farmer's approach leaves totally unexplained the fact that Matthew and Luke are completely independent of each other up to the point at which they converge with Mark and after the abrupt ending of Mark at 16:8. The longer ending of Mark shows a clear dependence on Matthew, while Mark as a whole is most plausibly understood as one of the basic sources for both Matthew and Luke.

2 The classical statement of this view is B. H. Streeter, *The Four Gospels: A Study of Origins* (New York: Macmillan 1924), although Streeter's four-source hypothesis (which posited special literary sources used by Matthew and Luke, called respectively M and L has been displaced by the scholarly assumption that community expansion and modification of the gospel tradition is reflected in the different structures and content of Matthew and Luke. A concise critical review of synoptic studies, including the plausibility of the two-source hypothesis, is offered in my essay "Synoptic Studies," in *The New Testament and Its Modern Interpreters*, ed. E. J. Epp and G. W. MacRae (Atlanta: Scholars Press, 1989), 245–269.

3 Studies of the theological and tactical features of the gospel writers have become an important part of New Testament research, of which the following are typical examples: Joachim Rohde, *Rediscovering the Teaching of the Evangelists* (Philadelphia: Westminster, 1968); J. D. Kingsbury, *Matthew: Structure, Christology, Kingdom* (Philadelphia:

Fortress Press, 1975); J. A. Fitzmyer, *Luke the Theologian: Aspects of His Teaching* (New York: Paulist Press, 1989). Explicit analyses of the social setting have appeared in Overman, *Matthew's Gospel and Formative Judaism,* H. C. Kee, *The Community of the New Age: Studies in Mark's Gospel* (Macon, Ga.: Mercer University Press, 1983). Richard A. Edwards, in addition to his detailed literary analysis of Q, the results of which were published in *A Concordance to Q,* Sources for Biblical Study, no. 7 (Missoula, Mont.: Scholars Press, 1975), has written *A Theology of Q.*

4   Helmut Koester, "One Jesus and Four Primitive Gospels," *Harvard Theological Review* 61 (1968):203–247, reprinted in *Trajectories through Early Christianity,* ed. James M. Robinson and Helmut Koester (Philadelphia: Fortress Press, 1991).

5   Koester, *Ancient Christian Gospels,* 85–87.

6   James M. Robinson, "*Logoi Sophon:* On the *Gattung* of Q," in *Trajectories through Early Christianity,* 71–113; John S. Kloppenborg, *The Formation of Q: Trajectories in Ancient Wisdom Collections,* Studies in Antiquity and Christianity (Philadelphia: Fortress Press, 1987).

7   James M. Robinson, "The Q Trajectory," in *The Future of Early Christianity, Festschrift for Helmut Koester,* ed. Birger A. Pearson (Minneapolis: Augsburg/Fortress, 1991), 173–194.

8   Robinson, "The Q Trajectory," 193. Similarly, Hans Dieter Betz, *The Sermon on the Mount* (Philadelphia: Fortress Press, 1985), and R. A. Piper, *Wisdom in the Q-Tradition* (Cambridge: Cambridge University Press, 1989), see sapiential collections lying behind Q in the subsequent form used by Matthew and Luke.

9   Koester, *Ancient Christian Gospels,* 159–162, 166.

10 Burton L. Mack, "The Kingdom That Didn't Come," in *SBL Seminar Papers, 1988,* 608–635.

11 Mack, *Myth of Innocence,* 356–357. Mack has set out his theory more fully in *The Lost Gospel: The Book of Q and Christian Origins* (San Francisco: Harper, 1993).

12 A prime example of the inaccessibility of the older Cynic tradition is the fact that what is known about Diogenes is anecdotal and no certain writings of his have survived. The letters supposedly written by his pupil Crates are recognized by scholars to be spurious. The content of the writings of Menippus can only be inferred from the titles of works he is reported to have written. Extensive evidence about the Cynics is available only from the time when Arrian produced what were reportedly verbatim notes of lectures by his teacher, Epictetus. This, however, is a century too late to serve as the major conceptual background for the teachings of Jesus.

13 Donald R. Dudley, *A History of Cynicism: From Diogenes to the Sixth Century A.D.* (1937; rpr. Hildesheim: Georg Olms, 1967); Hoistad, *Cynic Hero and Cynic King.*

14 Mack, *Myth of Innocence,* 315, 98.

15 The centrality of apocalyptic in the thought of Paul has been effectively demonstrated by J. Paul Beker, *Paul the Apostle: The Triumph of God in Life and Thought* (Philadelphia: Fortress Press, 1980). The most careful analyses of the evidence for the chronology of Paul's career point to his conversion as early as the year 34, about a

year after the death of Jesus. See Robert Jewett, *A Chronology of Paul's Life* (Philadelphia: Fortress Press, 1979). That chronology is utterly in conflict with Mack's notion that Mark invented the apocalytic understanding of Jesus around the year 70.

16 An important study that demonstrates this is Christopher Rowland, *The Open Heaven: A Study of Apocalyptic in Judaism and Early Christianity* (New York: Crossroad, 1982).

17 Mack, *Myth of Innocence*, 99.

18 Robinson, "Q Trajectory," 190.

19 The title of the English translation of Schweitzer's epochal work preserves the full German title, which indicates the basic intent of the work: *The Quest of the Historical Jesus: A Critical Study of the Program from Reimarus to Wrede* (London: A. & C. Clark, 1954). The original German edition was published in 1906.

20 Richard Horsley, *"Logoi Propheton,"* in *Future of Early Christianity*, 195–203.

21 Morton Smith published the text and a translation of the letter, including the excerpts from the Secret Gospel, in *Clement of Alexandria and a Secret Gospel of Mark* (Cambridge, Mass.: Harvard University Press, 1973), as well as a more popular account in *The Secret Gospel: The Discovery and Interpretation of the Secret Gospel according to Mark* (New York: Harper & Row, 1973). The quotations here are from *The Secret Gospel*, 14–15.

22 Ron Cameron, *The Other Gospels: Non-canonical Gospel Texts* (Philadelphia: Westminster Press, 1982), 68.

23 Koester, *Ancient Christian Gospels*, 302.

Index

Aaron, 30, 41, 91

Abba, 143

Abraham: and astrology, 41; as an example of faith, 78; founder of a covenant community, 56, 61, 75, 79, 97

Acherusian Lake, 147

Acropolis, 201, 202

Acts of the Apostles: apostolic council, 204; conversion of Paul, 194–195, 231; Cornelius, 195–196, 261n; inclusive community and world mission, 179–180, 187, 192, 193, 196, 197, 199, 206–207, 226; Jesus' resurrection, 202; laying on of hands, 203; outpouring of the Holy Spirit, 192, 196, 199; Paul and Apollos, 202; Paul and Barnabas, 197–199; Paul and Silas, 200, 201; Paul and Timothy, 200; Paul baptizes a Gentile woman and her household, 202; Paul concludes ministry in Greece and Asia Minor, 203–204; Paul and opponents in Jerusalem and Caesarea, 204–206; Paul in Rome, 206; Paul's "to an unknown god" sermon, 201–202; Peter's sermon, 192–193; terms for church leaders in, 204. See also Spirit

Adam, 138–139, 246n

Aelia Capitolina, 90. See also Jerusalem

Aescupalius, 222. See also Asklepios

Alaric, 143

Alexander the Great, 18, 33, 138, 200

Alexandria, 40, 184, 214. See also Gnostic library; Nag Hammadi Library; Philo of Alexandria

Allegory, 42, 45, 214, 216–217. See also Philo of Alexandria

Ammonites, 22

Ananias, 195, 205

Anastrophe, 247n

Anaxagoras, 53

Angelic liturgy, 48

Anna (the prophetess), 123, 187–188

Anthropologists, 1, 5, 11

Anthropology, 12

Antichrist, 135, 171

Antioch, 24

Antiochus IV Epiphanies, 21, 31, 32, 34, 52, 88, 93, 253n

Antipater, 26, 89

Aparche, 136

Apocalypse, 39, 210–212

Apocalypse of Abraham, 49, 156

Apocalypse of Adam, 215–216

Apocalypse of Baruch. See Baruch, Second

Apocalypse of Elijah, 81

Apocalypse of Enoch, 82

Apocalypse of Paul, 219

Apocalypse of Peter, 210–211

Apocalypse of Weeks, 35

Apocalypticism: ethical dualism of, 77, 216; Jewish and Christian, 40, 43, 44, 83, 96, 186, 209–210, 212; literary style, 32, 36; major documents before 70 C.E., 156; purpose of, 55; questions concerning, 66; worldview of, 31

Apocrypha, 1

Apokalypsis, 74, 78
Apollonius, 222
Apostasy, 37, 82, 83, 86
Apostolic Fathers, 54, 143, 209
Apuleius, 155, 185, 222
Aquila, 202
Aramaic, 94, 118
Archelaus, 89, 247n
Archive of Hor, 40
Aristeas, Letter of, 184
Aristides, Aelius, 133, 149, 184, 213
Aristobulus, 185–186
Aristotelianism, 45
Aristotle, 7, 43, 138, 154
Artapanus, 186
Artaxerxes I, 17
Artaxerxes II, 17
Artemis, 203
Ascension of Isaiah, 49, 210
Ascension of Moses, 82
Asceticism, 223. See also John the Baptist
Asklepios, 133, 148, 149
Assyria, 32, 33
Assyrians, 24–25
Astrology, 41, 98, 186. See also Matthew, Gospel
    of; Abraham
Astronomical Book, 35, 41. See also Enoch,
    First
Astronomy, 98
Attalus I, 133
Augustine of Hippo, 143–144, 220–221
Augustus Caesar, 44, 89
Aune, David, 40
Aurelius, Marcus, 149

Babylon, 33, 132
Babylonian exile, 16, 17, 19, 20, 23, 25, 29, 32,
    38, 90, 98, 121, 132
Bacchic worship, 150. See also Euripides
Balbus, 43
Baptism, 62, 66, 79, 84, 99, 129, 175, 192–194,
    196, 214
Bar Kochba revolt, 42, 146, 208, 217, 249n
Barbour, Ian, 7, 8, 9
Barnes, Barry, 6, 7
Baruch, 23–24
Baruch, First, 23
Baruch, Second, 37
Baur, Ferdinand Christian, 1
Beelzebul, 103, 104, 105. See also Satan
Bel and the Dragon, 25
Belial, 210
Bellah, Robert, 9
Ben Sira: embodied as a woman, 31, 132;

national restoration and God's presence,
    127; source of, 158; Wisdom in created
    order, 30, 256–257n; Wisdom in the law,
    29, 182–183
Bennett, Charles A., 254–255n
Berger, Peter L., 10–11
Bernstein, Richard, 7, 8, 9
Berossus, 40, 41
Biblical interpretation, 30
Bigg, Charles, 45
Bishop (episkopos), 172
blasphemy, 105, 166
Bloor, David, 3, 4
Book of the Covenant. See Covenant, Book of
Book of Daniel. See Daniel, Book of
Book of Dreams. See Dreams, Book of
Book of Enoch. See, Enoch, First
Book of Ezra. See Ezra, Book of
Book of Jubilees. See Jubilees, Book of
Book of Ruth. See Ruth, Book of
Book of the Watchers. See Watchers, Book of
    the
Borgen, Peder, 161
Bread of the Presence, 132
Brown, Raymond E., 158, 166, 253n, 256
Bultmann, Rudolf, 2, 63, 232
Burkert, Walter, 40

Cabiri, 262n
Caesar, 131
Caesarea, 196. See also Acts of the Apostles
Caesarea Maritima, 49
Caiaphas, 117
Cain, 143
Caligula, 47, 221
Cameron, Ron, 234
Canaanite deities. See "Dawn"; "Day Star"
Canaanite mythology, 44
Candace, 260n
Capernaum, 69
Caracalla, 221. See also Isis
Carpocratians, 234
Cassius Dio, 264n
Celibacy, 111
Celsus, 211
Chadwick, Henry, 225
Chariot, 94, 96, 156. See also Ezekiel
Chresmodoi, 40
Christianity: apocalyptic formation, 232; church
    as spiritual Israel, 178; cognitive dissonance
    with apocalypticism, 14–15, 237n; commu-
    nity models, 227–228; conquest of Mediter-
    ranean world, 148–149; and cynicism, 42;
    inclusion of Gentiles, 98, 220; ecclesiastical

conformity and uniformity, 208–209; origins and development of, 1, 2, 13, 25, 63–65, 264–265n

Christos, 261–262n

Cicero, 43, 96, 149

Circumcision, 36, 78, 88. *See also* Acts of the Apostles

City: as a "new Jerusalem," 135–137; in Greek tradition, 138–139; in the gospel tradition, 251n; in Judaism, 138; in Revelation to John, 129–131; model of covenant renewal, 17, 18, 121; role of human agent, 19. *See also* Jerusalem; Judaism; Letter to the Hebrews; Revelation to John; Zion

Claudius, 202

Clement of Alexandria, 45, 63, 214, 224, 259n

Clement, First Letter of, 143, 233–234

Cleopatra, 42, 264n

Cohen, Shaye J. D., 26, 50, 73

Colossians, Letter to the, 77

Colpe, Carsten, 215

Commodos, 214

Common sense, 12

Community, 16

Community Rule, 28. *See also* Dead Sea Scrolls

Constantine, 143, 209, 212, 218, 226–227

Constantinople, 143

Copper Scroll, 92. *See also* Dead Sea Scrolls

Corinthians, First Letter to the, 78, 81, 82

Cornelius, 195–196

Cotta, 43

Council (*synedrion*), 69, 89

Council of Laodicea, 220

Covenant, Book of, 29

Cranmer, Frederic, 41

Crassus, 41

Crates, 42, 268n

Crossan, J. D., 258n

Crouzel, Henri, 45, 242n

Culture, 11, 12, 13

Cumae, 43, 44

Cynicism, 42–43, 64, 231, 232, 268n

Cyril of Jerusalem, 212

Cyrus, 17, 18, 19, 22, 34

Damascus, 232, 260n.

Damascus Document, 28, 36, 38

Daniel, Book of, 40; additions to, 25; apocalyptic genre, 31, 93, 156, 186; and cynics, 42; disobedience to the law, 25; resurrection of the dead, 34; transformation of, 69; visions in Revelation to John, 130

Darius, 17, 34

David, 21, 28, 51, 98, 99

"Dawn," 32

Day of Atonement, 50, 76–77

"Day Star," 32

Dead Sea, 20, 28, 89

Dead Sea community, 20, 27, 28, 29, 48, 91–92, 247n

Dead Sea Scrolls, 1, 20, 27, 28–29, 36, 38, 48, 49, 91, 92, 156

Decapolis, 68, 232. *See also* Acts of the Apostles

Deir Alla, 40

Delphi, 43

Demeter, 148, 149

Demetrius (Bishop of Alexandria), 171, 224

Demonax, 231

Demotic Chronicle, 40

Dewey, John, 9

Diaspora, 94, 97. *See also* Philo of Alexandria; Septuagint

Dibelius, Martin, 63

Didache, 81, 171, 210

Dillon, John, 153

Dio Chrysostom, 231

Dioceses, 171

Diogenes, 42, 268n

Dionysos (Bacchus), 149, 150, 154, 201

Dioskuroi, 148

Diotrophes, 171

Divorce, 71. *See also* Luke, Gospel of; Matthew, Gospel of

Domitian, 37, 131, 133, 208, 231

Domna, Julia, 222

Douglas, Mary, 11

Dreams, Book of, 35. *See also* Enoch, First

Dualism, 174, 176

Ebionites, 224

Ecclesiastes, 45

Ecclesiasticus. *See* Ben Sira

Ecstatic speech, 81, 196. *See also* Corinthians, First Letter to the

Edomites, 183

Edwards, Douglas, 185

Edwards, Richard A., 224n

Einstein, Albert, 6

Ekklesia and *synagoge*, 250n. *See also* Christianity; Judaism

Ekpyrosis, 41

Elders, 84

Eleazar, 52

Eleusian mysteries, 145, 174, 214. *See also* Demeter

Eleusis, 148

Elijah: and Jesus, 65, 69; and John the Baptist, 66, 105; widow from Sidon, 189

Elisha, 189

Empedocles, 154

Enoch, First: apocalyptic genre, 31, 156; astrology, 41; date of, 34–35; son of man, 36; successive epochs in, 38. *See also* Enoch, Similitudes of

Enoch, Second, 36–37, 49

Enoch, Similitudes of, 35–36, 72, 156, 219, 246n

Enoch, Third, 48–50

Ephesians, Letter to the, 121

Epictetus, 162

Epicureanism, 173, 201

Episteme, 7. *See also* Knowledge

Epistemology, 4

Eschatological meal, 58, 244n

Esdras, First, 21–22

Essenes, 247n. *See also* Dead Sea community

Esther, 51

Eucharist, 62, 67, 84, 163, 252n

Euclid, 6

Eumenes II, 133

Eunuch, 194, 260n. *See also* Acts of the Apostles; celibacy

Euripides, 150

Eusebius: adviser to Constantine, 212; Christian leaders in Alexandria, 214; *Ecclesiastical History*, 209; Gospel of Mark, 63; on Montanus, 211; on Origen, 224; *Praeparatio Evangelica*, 185

Eustathius, 97

Evil, 15, 36

Exagoge, 185

Exodus, 108, 116, 132, 166

Exogamy. *See* Judaism, intermarriage with indigenous peoples; Solomon

Exorcist, 203

Ezekiel: chariot image, 47–48; and Exodus, 185; and foreigners, 50; oracles of, 181; priestly tribe, 91; visions of, 20, 92, 156

Ezra: after the exile, 25, 29, 50; chief priest and reader, 22; magistrates and judges, 23; prayer of, 127

Ezra, Book of, 17, 22, 23, 29

Ezra, Fourth Book of, 37

Faith, 9, 82

Farmer, W. R., 267n

Farnell, Lewis R., 148

Feast of Tabernacles, 160

Felix, 90, 205

Festival of booths, 34, 181

Festus, 205

First Letter of Clement. *See* Clement, First Letter of

First Letter of John. *See* John, First Letter of

First Letter to Timothy. *See* Timothy, First Letter to

First Maccabees. *See* Maccabees, First

First Peter. *See* Peter, First

Fishbane, Michael, 32

Flavian emperors. *See* Domitian; Titus; Vespasian

Fleck, Ludwig, 236–237n

Florus, 90

Fourth Eclogue of Vergil, 41

Fourth Ezra. *See* Ezra, Fourth Book of

Fourth Maccabees. *See* Maccabees, Fourth

Freedman, Maurice, 12

Frend, W. H. C., 143

Gabriel, 34

Galatians, Letter to the, 77, 79, 83

Galba, 65

Galilee: disciples gather after resurrection, 109; Greek spoken, 248n; Jesus' place of origin, 160; Jesus is rejected in, 105; socioeconomic condition of, 65

Galilee, Sea of, 89

Galileo, 5

Gallio, 202, 263n

Gamaliel, 194, 205, 264n

Geertz, Clifford, 5, 12

Gehenna, 250n

Genesis: Abraham and Isaac, 122–123; creation story, 77, 157–158, 216; promise to Abraham, 128

Gnostic library, 1. *See also* Nag Hammadi Library

Gnosticism, 145, 146, 172–173, 175, 215, 216, 217, 266n

Goodenough, Erwin R., 47, 138

Goodman, Nelson, 7

Gospel of John. *See* John, Gospel of

Gospel of Luke. *See* Luke, Gospel of

Gospel of Mark. *See* Mark, Gospel of

Gospel of Matthew. *See* Matthew, Gospel of

Gospel of Peter. *See* Peter, Gospel of

Gospel of Thomas. *See* Thomas, Gospel of

Greco-Roman world: cults of, 198; dispersion of Israel, 128, 157, 186; human situation, 145; Jewish and Hellenistic culture, 95–96, 97, 179; learning, 150, 201, 206; mystical question, 146; Pharisees and Hellenistic philosophy, 26; Tertullian on, 173

Greer, Rowan, 45, 241–242n

Griffith, J. Gwyn, 40

Gruenwald, Ithamar, 49, 156

Habakkuk, 180

Habrokomes, 223. *See also* Isis

Hadrian, 90, 149, 213

Haggai, 23, 127. *See also* Temple

Hanson, Paul D., 77, 244n

Heracleon, 258n. *See also* Origen

Herodotus, 40

Hesiod, 40, 186

Hillel, 102

Hippolytus, 217

Historiography, 1, 2, 3

Hoistad, Ragnar, 42

Holiness Code, 20–21

Holland, Dorothy, 12

Holofernes, 25

Holy Spirit, 202–203. *See also* Acts of the Apostles; Spirit

Homer, 138, 148

Homologien, 257n

Horsley, Richard, 233, 245n

Horus, 40, 154. *See also* Isis

Hosea, 44, 128

Human sexuality, 146

Husserl, Edmond, 9

Hyrcanus, John II, 21, 89

Idumea, 89

Ignatius, 172

Ignatius of Antioch, 234

Inge, W. R., 223

Interpreter, 3, 4, 6, 15, 16

Irenaeus, 173, 174, 212

Isaiah: agents of covenant renewal, 19; and aliens, 50–51, 181–182, 188; an anointed one, 71; apocalyptic sections, 100, 105; ascension of, 156; Exodus, 134; Jerusalem, 18, 32–33; Paul appeals to, 206; prophecies of, 57; servant songs, 126, 128, 194

Isis: cult of, 148, 149, 150, 154–155, 223, 262n; woman imagery, 221–222; son of, 40; symbolism of robes, 155

Israel: archaeological finds, 1; apocalyptic worldview, 31; exile by Assyrians, 32; history of, 36; international relations, 18; royal messiah, 91; uniqueness of, 29; vineyard imagery, 70. *See also* Jacob

Jacob: at Bethel, 47, 153; and wisdom, 161, 183

Jacob, Star of, 28

James (brother of Jesus), 199, 204

James, Letter of: aim of, 83–85; moral accountability, 86–87

James, William, 9

Jannaeus, Alexander, 26, 89

Jeremiah: and *genos*, 126; prophecies of, 18–19, 127; role of, 180–181

Jerusalem: fall of, 20, 23; Israelites who remained during exile, 17; restoration of, 17, 18, 19, 24; role of sentinels, 19; symbolic center, 36, 57. *See also* City; Zion

Jesus of Nazareth: career of, 64–65, 99; cleansing of the Temple, 70; cynic comparison, 42, 241n; cry of dereliction, 174, 258n; death and resurrection, 68–69, 143, 160, 164; prototype of a new people, 158; role as God's agent, 66, 68, 70, 71, 72, 97, 100, 108–109, 244n. *See also* Origen

John the Baptist, 56, 57, 58, 61, 62, 66, 99, 100, 104, 108, 109, 161, 175, 189, 230, 233, 253n

John, First Letter of, 170–171

John, Gospel of: human relations to the divine, 145; Jesus as good shepherd, 123, 165; Jesus as light of the world, 164–165; Jesus' triumph over death, 167–168, 169, 170; Jesus as "true vine," 167; miracle stories, 162; Pharisees' challenge, 163–164, 165, 166; Samaritan woman, 161; word and logos, 157, 158–160, 161

John, Second Letter of, 171

John, Third Letter of, 171–172

Jonah, 51, 56, 105, 108

Jonathan, 21

Joseph of Arimathea, 68, 118

Josephus: astrology, 41; *Contra Apionem*, 52, 53; Dead Sea community and Essenes, 247n; historian, 162; Jewish knowledge of astrolgy, 41; and Pharisees, 26; and Sadducees, 27

Joshua, 91, 124

Josiah, 21

Jubilees, Book of, 35, 36, 50. *See also* Pseudepigrapha

Judah (the king), 36

Judah (the Patriarch), 95

Judaism: apocalyptic traditions, 55, 232; cognitive dissonance, 14, 15, 237n; cultic aspects, 17; dietary rules, 199; distinctiveness of God's people, 73; festival of booths, 34; formative, 25–26; Hellenistic culture, 1, 45, 95; historical reconstruction of, 1; intermarriage with indigenous peoples, 17, 22, 50; mystical features, 146; nationalistic revolts, 18, 209; rabbinic, 27, 88, 92–93, 94–95, 97, 100, 101, 102, 107, 110, 111, 113, 114, 120, 187, 264n; Palestinian, 1, 95; piety of, 57, 61, 80, 84, 97, 101, 105, 168, 185, 189, 202, 203; pre-70 institutions and officials,

Judaism (*continued*)
    101; postbiblical period, 96–97, 114; post-
    exilic, 15, 22, 25; proselytes and god fearers,
    33, 34, 96–97, 114, 261n; role of the law,
    24, 27, 34, 35; sabbath, 71, 185; syna-
    gogues, 26, 69, 93–94, 169, 263n; worship
    of Yahweh, 18, 21. *See also* Babylonian
    exile; Ferdinand Christian Baur; Merkavah
    Mysticism; Jacob Neusner
Judas Maccabeus, 35, 88, 89
Jude, Letter of, 55, 82, 83, 86
Judean desert, 20
Judges, 19, 24
Julius Caesar, 41
Justin Martyr, 212, 213

Kaseman, Ernst, 77
Kloppenborg, John S., 229, 231, 232–233
Knowledge, 7–8, 10. *See also* Sociology of
    Knowledge
Koester, Helmut, 63, 229, 230, 234, 244–245n
Kuhn, Thomas S., 2, 5, 6, 7, 9

Lactantius, 212
Laguna, Grace de, 5
Langer, Suzanne, 4, 5, 12
Language: development of, 4–5; elements of, 2;
    games, 3, 4; and religious experience, 3
Last Supper, 117, 162, 175
Law, 24. *See also* Judaism; Moses
Laws, Sophie, 247n
Lazarus: Gospel of John, 168, 169; Gospel of
    Luke, 190
Lenski, Gerhard E., 65
Letter of Aristeas. *See* Aristeas, Letter of
Letter of James. *See* James, Letter of
Letter to the Ephesians. *See* Ephesians, Letter to
    the
Letter to the Colossians. *See* Colossians, Letter
    to the
Letter to the Galatians. *See* Galatians, Letter to
    the
Letter to the Romans. *See* Romans, Letter to the
Letters of Paul. *See* Paul, letters of
Levi, 28, 36
Leviathan, 71–72
Levine, Amy-Jill, 97, 249n
Levites, 20, 21, 22, 23, 28, 38, 132, 143
Leviticus, 20–21. *See also* Holiness Code
Logiken latreian, 122, 124
Logos, 139, 146, 152, 155, 162, 255n. *See also*
    John, Gospel of; Word
Love, 151–152
Luckmann, Thomas, 10–11

Luke, Gospel of: Anna the prophetess, 123,
    187–188; Beatitudes, 58, 59–60, 189, 231,
    233; centurion, 189; cost of discipleship, 60;
    Good Samaritan, 189; Great Supper, 61–62,
    189–190; inclusive community, 179–180,
    187, 191, 192, 226; Jesus denounces Phar-
    isees, 191; Jesus as "son of man," 59, 60, 191;
    Jesus and traditional piety, 188–189; Lord's
    prayer, 101; Markan tradition in, 191; para-
    ble of loving father, 190; parable on present
    and ultimate outcome, 59; parable of the
    supper, 231; postresurrection stories, 192;
    role of Jesus and Jewish expectations,
    187–188; Zacchaeus, 190–191; Zechariah,
    123. *See also* Q source

Maccabean revolt, 52, 88, 96, 183
Maccabees, 21, 89, 93, 145–146. *See also*
    Judaism; Judas Maccabeus
Maccabees, First, 20, 21
Maccabees, Fourth, 52, 96
Maccabees, Second, 20, 21
Mack, Burton, 63–65; 230, 231, 232
Magi, 98. *See also* Astrology; Matthew, Gospel of
Mantinikes, Diotima, 146
Marcion, 174
Mark, Gospel of: apocalyptic community model,
    55; death and resurrection, 64; earliest
    gospel, 229; inclusive community, 66–69;
    interpretation of law and purity, 69, 70;
    Jesus calms the storm, 71–72, 245n; Jesus
    cleanses the Temple, 123; Jesus as commu-
    nity model, 70–71, 72; miracle stories, 64,
    67–68, 72; opponents to Jesus, 69–70; ori-
    gins and intent of, 62–65; Parable of Sower,
    71; temptation of Jesus, 69; transfiguration,
    63, 68–69; wisdom in, 85–86. *See also* Judas
    Maccabeus; Temple
Mark, Secret Gospel of, 233–234
Marriage, 79, 246n
Martyrdom, 167, 211
Martyrs, 131, 136
Mary (Mother of Jesus), 75, 98, 225
Masada, 48, 90
Matthew, Gospel of: apocalyptic discourse,
    115–116; baptism of Jesus, 99; career of
    Jesus, 98, 99; commissioning of apostles,
    103–104; date of, 249n; death and resurrec-
    tion, 118; disputes in community, 110;
    dreams in, 98; features of, 97, 98–120;
    genealogy of Jesus, 98; Hebrew version,
    214; Jesus' cleansing of Temple, 112; Jesus'
    continual presence, 119–120; Jesus and
    ecclesiastical authority, 102, 218; Jesus' heal-

ings, 103, 105; Jesus' rejection of dietary laws, 108; Judas's betrayal and repentance, 117, 118; leadership in new community, 109–110; Lord's prayer, 101, 217; Markan tradition, 103; Marriage and divorce, 111; opponents to movement, 104; Parable of the fisher's net, 107; Parable of God's grace, 111–112; Parable of the Sower, 106; Parable of the two sons, 112; Parable of the unforgiving servant, 110–111; Parable of the weeds, 106–107; Parable of the wicked tenants, 112–113; participation in new community, 101, 102, 106; Peter's confession, 109; place within the gospel tradition, 229; Sermon on the Mount, 100, 103, 250n; temptation of Jesus, 99–100; transfiguration, 109; women at the tomb, 118–119

Meeks, Wayne A., 162, 256n

Melchizedek, 37, 141

Merkavah mysticism, 47–48, 155–157, 244n

Messiah, 37, 95

Messianic Rule, 28, 230. See also Dead Sea community; Jesus of Nazareth

Metatron, 49

Methusaleh, 37

Meyer, R., 251n

Micaiah, 67

Middle Platonism, 73, 123, 124, 153, 173, 253n

Miletus, 52

Mishnah, 1, 2, 25, 27, 92, 94, 95, 217–218

Moabites, 22

monastic centers, 226–227

Montanus, 211

Moses: canonical form of legal tradition, 23; covenant with, 128; and Jesus' crucifixion, 164; in Jubilees, 36; law of, 26, 27, 30, 52, 69, 91, 100, 141, 162, 163, 185; Logos speaks to, 47; seer of end time, 37; song of, 135, 140, 166; story of, 99, 126, 193; wisdom's role, 31; Yahweh's name disclosed, 161. See also Judaism

Mount of Olives, 177

Mount Vesuvius, 184

Mylonas, George, 148

Mystery cults, 145, 148–150, 221–223

Mysticism, 44, 47, 145, 146, 147–148, 152, 172, 223, 254–255n. See also Merkavah mysticism

Mystics, 48–49

Myths, 5, 9–10, 231–232

Nag Hammadi Library, 215, 216. See also Gnostic library

Nazirite vow, 202, 204

Nebuchadnezzar, 19, 38, 76

Nehemiah, 17, 25, 50

Nehemiah, Book of, 22, 23

Neoplatonists, 216, 217

Neo-pythagoreanism, 222

Nero, 65, 264n

Nerva, 222

Neusner, Jacob, 2, 25–26, 73, 93, 94, 217

New Testament: apocalyptic view, 175; historical literary criticism, 63–65; models of community, 39; Sadducees in, 27; themes in, 86;

Newsom, Carol, 48, 243n

Newton, Isaac, 5

Nicanor, 21

Nickelsburg, George, 39

Ninevites, 61

Noah, 129

Octavian, 131

Old Testament Apocrypha, 51

Oracle of the Potter, 40, 41

Oracles, 43

Origen: castration of, 224; Commentary on the Gospel of John, 157, 158–159, 178, 219, 225–226, 258n; De Principiis, 177–178; Dialogue with Heraclides, 225; pupil of Saccas, 223; Song of Songs, 45; successor to Clement in Alexandria, 214–215

Orpheus, 149

Orphic lifestyle, 150

Osiris, 154, 155, 222, 223. See also Horus; Isis

Overman, J. Andrew, 97, 249n

Palingenesia (rebirth), 41. See also Stoicism

Pantaenus, 214, 224

Papias, 63, 212

Paraclete, 167, 169–170, 211

Paradigm, 5, 6, 8–9. See also Language; Sociology of Knowledge

Parousia, 85, 86, 265n

Parthenos, 249n

Passover, 50, 68, 117, 185, 188. See also Judaism

Paul (Apostle): charismatic gifts, 122; chronology of career, 263n, 268–269n; cultic imagery of Christ's death, 122, 220; cultic imagery of Paul's role, 123; Jesus and divine wisdom, 75, 76; law of nature, 73–74; Pharisaic background, 73, 264n; philosophical influences on, 73–74. See also Acts of the Apostles; Stoicism

Paul, letters of: antagonism with Peter, 251–252; apocalyptic community, 55; new covenant people, 121; wisdom in, 86

Pausanias, 40

Pentateuch, 23, 31, 45, 238n
Pentecost, 192, 203, 261n. *See also* Acts of the
  Apostles
Pergamum Museum of Berlin, 133
Persephone, 148, 149. *See also* Demeter
Perushim, 27
Pervo, Richard, 259n
Peter, 62
Peter, First: apocalyptic and Greco-Roman syn-
  thesis, 123; author of, 124; Jesus as "chief
  shepherd," 129; new community of,
  124–125, 127–129; role of suffering, 125;
  Temple imagery, 125
Peter, Gospel of, 174–175
Peter, Second, 2, 55, 82–83, 86
Pharisees: belief in resurrection, 205; boundaries
  of covenant people, 60; development and
  goals of, 93, 94; features of, 26; interpreta-
  tion of scripture, 27; and Jesus, 59, 69, 103,
  105, 113; reliance on scripture, 73. *See also*
  Judaism, rabbinic; Stoicism
Philip (Apostle), 193–194
Philip of Macedon, 200
Philistines, 183
Philo of Alexandria: Alexandrian tradition of,
  157, 177; allegorical method, 50, 96, 186,
  214; charioteer imagery, 47; Dead Sea com-
  munity and Essenes, 247n; Logos in, 158;
  On Change of Names, 161–162; *On the Cheru-
  bim*, 150, 151; *On Creation*, 138–139; *On
  Dreams*, 152, 153; *On Drunkenness*, 166; *On
  Flight and Finding*, 152; *On Noah's Work as
  Planter*, 166–167; *On Virtues*, 139
Philometor, Ptolemy, 259n
Philosophers, 1, 2
Philostratus, 221, 222
Phronesis, 7, 8
Physcon, Ptolemy, 259n
Pilate, Pontius, 89, 90, 118, 191
Pistis Sophia, 177
Plato: concerns of, 145; philosophy of, 185;
  Phaedo, 147; *Phaedrus*, 147; *Symposium*, 146;
  teachings of, 43, 53, 186; *Timaeus*, 154
Platonism, 31, 45, 141, 153, 214, 215, 223,
  242n;
Plotinus, 215, 223–224;
Plutarch, 40 ,138, 150, 153–154, 155, 221–222;
Pluto, 148
Pompey, 41, 89
Pope, Martin, 44
Porphyry, 223, 224–225
Posidonius of Apamea, 41
Prayers, 84
Preexistence, 75

Priscilla, 202
Proverbs, 44, 45
Psalms, 18, 75, 166, 180, 181
Pseudepigrapha, 1
Pseudo-Eustathias, 259n
Pseudo-Phoclides, 52–53
Pythagoras, 53, 185, 186
Pythagoreanism, 153, 154, 222
Pythian oracles, 40

Q source: apocalyptic addition, 231; community
  model in, 55; five motifs of, 56–62; inclusiveness of community in, 60–62; Jesus as
  "son of man," 58, 59; Luke's gospel use of,
  103, 110, 189, 191, 229, 244n; Matthew's
  gospel use of, 104, 105, 113, 229; role of
  wisdom, 85; stages of, 64, 230–231, 234
Queen of the South, 61
Quinn, Naomi, 12
Qumran, 28, 34, 35, 38, 230. *See also* Dead Sea
  community; Dead Sea Scrolls
Qumran community, 28, 41, 43, 60, 156

Rabbis, 27, 45, 94, 95, 114. *See also* Judaism, rab-
  binic; Pharisees
Raphael, 24
Reason, 147, 222
Reitzenstein, Richard, 145, 146
Revelation, 49
Revelation to John, 123; an apocalypse, 55–56,
  129–130; city of God, 218–219; closing
  visions, 135; consummation of God's purpose, 136–137; destruction of Rome, 131;
  letters to the churches, 132–133, 136; sac-
  erdotal theme in, 134–135
Reynolds, Joyce, 261n
Ritual, 5
Robinson, James M., 229, 230, 232
Romans, Letter to the: Abraham and Adam,
  78–79; dietary rules, 80; grace, 79; human
  evil, 74; inclusiveness of community, 74–75,
  79–80; justification, 76;
Rome: augurs in, 43; control of eastern Mediter-
  ranean, 18, 31; imperial cult, 89, 133, 262n;
  Jewish alliances with, 21; laws codified, 95;
  support of priestly elite, 90
Romulus, 43
Rorty, Richard, 8
Rose, H. J., 149
Rousseau, O., 44
Ruth, Book of, 51

Sabbatical Year, 21
Saccas, Ammonius, 215, 223

Sadducees, 27, 91, 113

Saldarini, Anthony, 73

Salome, Alexandra, 26

Samaritans, 160, 162, 183

Sanhedrin, 264n

Satan, 35, 69, 133, 221. *See also* Beelzebul

Scholem, Gershom, 49, 155–156

Schutz, Alfred, 9, 10

Schweitzer, Albert, 230, 232

Science, 5, 6, 7, 8

Scribes, 40–41, 69

Scroll of the Rule, 28, 48, 92, 248n. *See also* Dead Sea Scrolls

Second Baruch. *See* Baruch, Second

Second Enoch. *See* Enoch, Second

Second Letter of John. *See* John, Second Letter of

Second Maccabees. *See* Maccabees, Second

Second Peter. *See* Peter, Second

Segal, Alan, 97

Seleucids, 18, 21, 23, 24, 133

Seneca, 43, 44, 72, 96, 162

Sepher Ha-razim, 49

Septimus Severus, 222

Septuagint, 76, 126, 158, 161, 185–186, 251n, 253n, 257n

Sergius Paulus, 197

Shepherd of Hermas 210, 219

Sibylline Oracles, 40, 42, 43, 183–184, 185, 186, 252n

Sicarii, 263–264n

Siculus, Diodorus, 221

Simeon, 188

Similitudes of Enoch. *See* Enoch, Similitudes of

Simon Magus, 217

Smith, Jonathan Z., 40

Smith, Morton, 26–27, 233–234

Sociologists, 1, 2, 6

Sociology of Knowledge, 1, 2, 3, 4, 9, 10, 11, 12

Socrates, 43, 213

Sodom, 59

Solomon, 21, 28, 30, 31, 45, 48, 50, 56, 59, 166

Solomon, Testament of, 41

Solomon, Wisdom of, 30, 31, 44, 96, 126, 137, 139, 182, 213, 266n

Song of Songs, 44, 45

Song of the Three Children, 25

Songs of the Sabbath Sacrifice, 48

Soul, 146, 147, 150, 155

Spartans, 21

Spirit, 71, 81, 105, 202, 203. *See also* Acts of the Apostles

Stanley, John E., 237n

Star of Jacob. *See* Jacob, Star of

Stephen, 193, 197

Stoicism, 27, 41, 43, 45, 52, 73, 82, 84, 85, 86, 87, 96, 140, 153, 185, 186, 198, 201, 205, 213, 222

Stoics, 31, 40, 53, 158, 162, 182, 214

Stone, Michael, 48

Suetonius, 262n

Symbols, 4–5, 10–11, 12, 18

Talmud, 1, 2, 25, 27, 49, 92, 94, 95, 217, 218. *See also* Judaism; Mishnah; Neusner, Jacob

Tannaim, 49

Tannenbaum, Robert, 261n

Tarsus, 264n

Tartarus, 147

Teacher of righteousness, 49, 91, 156

Temple: access of a prince, 20; cleansed by Judas Maccabeus and Jesus of Nazareth, 88, 70; cult of, 20, 21, 25, 27, 28, 90, 91, 93; destruction of, 37, 42, 49–50, 68, 69, 70, 90, 94, 95, 113, 120, 123, 156, 184, 217; in heaven, 25; limitations of, 141; rebuilding of, 17, 22, 33, 166; return of secred vessels to, 22, 23, 24; Revelation of John, 131–134; sanctuary, 18, 20, 21, 36, 90; symbolism of, 121, 139, 219; universal worship, 183–184; weights and measures, 20

Temple Scroll, 27, 28, 48, 92, 218. *See also* Dead Sea Scrolls

Tertullian, 173–174; 212, 213

Testament of Solomon. *See* Solomon, Testament of

Testament of the Twelve patriarchs, 96

Theomanteis, 40

Therapeutae, 46, 151

Theseus, 149

Third Enoch. *See* Enoch, Third

Third Letter of John. *See* John, Third Letter of

Thiselton, Anthony, 3

Thomas, 168

Thomas, Gospel of, 175–177, 216, 229, 230, 233

Timothy, 200

Timothy, First Letter to, 215

Titus, 37, 65, 90, 222

Tobit, 24

Torah, 19, 26, 49, 69, 71, 91, 94, 156, 214, 217, 218

Trajan, 133, 172, 208, 231

Treatise of Shem, 41

Trinity, 214

Tyconius, 143

Ur-Markus, 63

Valentinus, 173, 174, 178, 258n
Vergil, 44
Vergil, Fourth Eclogue of, 41
Vermes, Geza, 27, 48
Vespasian, 37, 90, 222
Victorinus, 220
Volkmar, Gustav, 63
Vulgate, 210, 262n

Waetjen, Herman C., 65
War Scroll, 28, 48. *See also* Dead Sea Scrolls
Watchers, Book of the, 35, 48, 157
Weber, Max, 9
Wisdom: agent of God, 24, 158, 225; divine disclosure of, 37; in Isis literature, 31; and Love, 146; Mosaic origins of, 27; in obedience to the law, 29–30, 183; in Philo, 46; preexisting creation, 246n; transcendent nature of, 259n; virtues produced by, 182. *See also* John, Gospel of; Isis; Philo of Alexandria
Wisdom of Solomon. *See* Solomon, Wisdom of

Wittgenstein, Ludwig, 2, 3–4
Word (Logos), 213, 226, 250n, 255–256n
Wuthnow, Robert, 12, 13

Xenophon of Ephesus, 185, 223

Year of Jubilee, 21

Zadok, 27; sons of, 28, 38
Zagreus, 149
Zebedee, sons of, 112
Zechariah, 19, 22, 23, 33–34, 123, 127, 181, 187
Zeno, 138
Zerubbabel, 22
Zeus, 88, 90, 133, 147, 148, 149, 198
Zion: proclaiming good news, 19; redemption of, 18; renewed covenant community, 17, 30; tabernacle in, 29, 33, 121, 142. *See also* City; Jerusalem; Temple
zodiac, 41, 94, 96 *See also* astrology